WAGES OF VIOLENCE

WAGES OF VIOLENCE

NAMING AND IDENTITY IN POSTCOLONIAL BOMBAY

Thomas Blom Hansen

PRINCETON UNIVERSITY PRESS   PRINCETON AND OXFORD

Hansen, Thomas Blom
Wages of violence : Naming and Identity in Postcolonial Bombay

Library of Congress Control Number : 2001095813
ISBN 0-691-08839-X (cloth : alk. paper)
ISBN 0-691-08840-3 (pbk. : alk. paper)

This book has been composed in Galliard

Printed on acid-free paper. ∞

www.pup.princeton.edu

Printed in the United States of America

1   3   5   7   9   10   8   6   4   2

1   3   5   7   9   10   8   6   4   2
(Pbk.)

Contents

Acronyms   vii

Introduction The Proper Name   1

Chapter 1. Deccan Pastoral: The Making of an Ethnohistorical
Imagination in Western India   20

Chapter 2. Bombay and the Politics of Urban Desire   37

Chapter 3. "Say with Pride That We Are Hindus": Shiv Sena
and Communal Populism   70

Chapter 4. Thane City: The Making of Political Dadaism   101

Chapter 5. Riots, Policing, and Truth Telling in Bombay   121

Chapter 6. In the Muslim Mohalla   160

Chapter 7. Living the Dream: Governance, Graft, and Goons   194

Conclusion. Politics as Permanent Performance   227

Notes   235

Glossary   251

Bibliography   255

Index   267

ABVP	Akhil Bharatiya Vidyarthi Parishad (student wing of the Hindu nationalist movement)
BJP	Bharatiya Janata Party (political wing of the Hindu nationalist movement)
BKS	Bharatiya Kamgar Sena (Indian Worker's Army). Shiv Sena's trade union wing
BMC	Brihanmumbai Municipal Corporation (previously Bombay Municipal Corporation)
BVS	Bharatiya Vidyarthi Sena (student wing of the Shiv Sena)
CPI	Communist Party of India
CPI (M)	Communist Party of India (Marxist). (Breakaway party from CPI, has been in power in the state of West Bengal for more than twenty years)
EBC	Educationally Backward Classes (category devised by the Government of Maharashtra in 1967)
ISI	Inter Services Intelligence (secret service in Pakistan)
MLA	Member of Legislative Assembly (lower house)
MLC	Member of Legislative Council (upper house)
MP	Member of Parliament
OBC	Other Backward Classes (administrative category created in 1950. Became an important political identity in North India in the 1980s)
PSP	Praja Socialist Party (socialist party with roots in North India)
RSS	Rashtriya Swayamsevak Sangh (parent organization of the larger Hindu nationalist movement)
SIMI	Student Islamic Movement of India (radical Islamic organization)
SLS	Sthanik Lokhadikar Samiti (Local People's Rights Organization)
SMS	Samyukta Maharashtra Samiti (movement for the creation of the state of Maharashtra)
SP	Samajwadi Party (North Indian socialist party)
SRA	Slum Rehabilitation Authority (in Mumbai)
TADA	Terrorist and Disruptive Activities Act
TMC	Thane Municipal Corporation

WAGES OF VIOLENCE

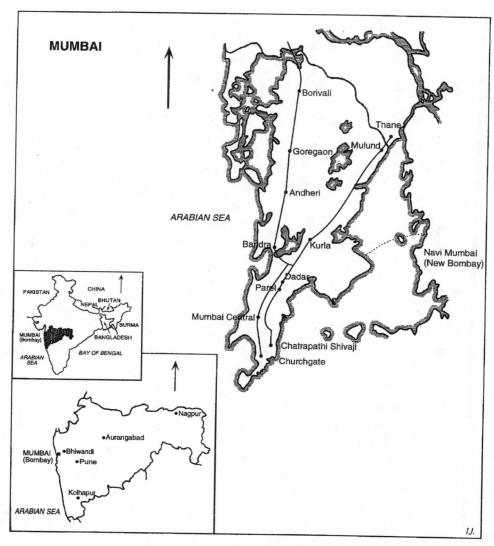

Mumbai and its environs. By Ingrid Jensen, Rockilde University, Denmark.

The Proper Name

IN NOVEMBER 1995 the city of Bombay was officially renamed Mumbai. The government of India finally gave in to the request by the state government of Maharashtra to change the name of the city on all letterheads, official stamps, tags, and so on. Newspapers tried to estimate the cost of this operation, and the renaming caused a brief if intense debate in the city and state. The state government, headed by the regional party Shiv Sena (Shivaji's Army), and the Hindu nationalist Bharatiya Janata Party (BJP) argued that the renaming was meant to highlight the local origins of the city's name derived from Mumbadevi, a local goddess of Koli fishermen who originally lived on the islands and marshland that became the city of Bombay.

The renaming aimed at undoing the Portuguese and later British perversions of this name. Vernacular newspapers in the city and the rest of the state supported the "vernacularization" of the city's name and argued that the city really was not renamed. The only novelty was, it was argued, that the vernacular pronunciation of Bombay in Marathi, one of the city's two main languages, was now properly spelled in English. According to this view, the renaming was a minor, entirely justifiable, and long overdue act of redress on behalf of the vernacular world. Parts of the English-language press, some quarters in the Congress Party, and some intellectuals and spokespersons from significant minorities in the city, such as the Urdu-speaking Muslims, opposed the renaming on the ground that Bombay's cosmopolitan character should be reflected in its name. In many of the city's newspapers one could find a stream of letters to the editor bemoaning the loss of the old name, and with it the older experience of Bombay, the dreams of Bombay as a metaphor of India's diversity, the imaginings of modernity, and the hopes associated with that name.

I recall a conversation I had with an elderly, retired civil servant a few weeks before the final decision was made. I sat in one of the suburban trains one evening, reading through an issue of *Times of India* that carried an article about the renaming issue. The elderly gentleman leaned over and said: "First these people created havoc in our city, and now they also want to take away the proper name of this city. It is a disgrace." I asked him why he felt so strongly about it. Was the issue not just one of how to spell the name? "Look," he replied, "people have known this place as Bombay for two hundred years, all over it is written as Bombay, on every second house and statue in the city. Why should it be changed? . . . All over the country people know this place as Bombay, they know it from films and all. . . . I grew up here; yes, I do occasionally say Mumbai when I speak my mother tongue, but its proper name is Bombay."

The man got off at Marine Lines. He lived in a pleasant neighborhood only a five-minute walk from Marine Drive, in the heart of what one may call classical Bombay, with its apartment blocks and elegant houses from the 1930s and 1940s, that stretches from Churchgate Station to the elite areas of Malabar Hill. As I reached for my notebook and wrote down his words, the expression "its proper name is Bombay" kept coming back to me. I realized how precisely the different connotations carried by Bombay and Mumbai, respectively, actually condensed many of the social transformations and political conflicts in this part of India in the past century.

What does a proper name imply? Just as a proper noun refers to the individuality or inherent properties of an object or person, a name cannot be "proper" unless it marks, or symbolizes, the individuality and properties ascribed to its object. To be recognized by a proper name signifies respect for the choice and meaning of this name, just as proper names accord a measure of uniqueness and subjectivity to persons or groups. The right to name, and the entitlement to hold a name for oneself, shapes the style and ways that objects or persons are known and how their assumed properties are described. Following Kripke, we can say that for a name to become proper it must become a "rigid designator," a signifier that creates meanings but cannot be substituted by a set of descriptions. A rigid designator defines a context and "holds" sets of connotations as designated objects, none of which can fully describe the designator (Kripke 1980, 48). Or, to go a step further, we can argue that proper names do not describe objects or places. They create and fix those objects. As Žižek argues, "[the identity of an object] is *the retroactive effect of naming itself*: it is the name itself, the signifier, which supports the identity of an object." (Žižek 1989, 95) (Žižek's emphasis). Mundane processes of using names, affixing them, enunciating them, and so on, have exactly this quality of constant reiteration that builds up and stabilizes the imputed properties of a place, a group, a nation.

This notion of reiterative practices of naming as a creation and fixation of identities, and of the use of names as claims to certain identities, properties, or entitlements, is a central thread in this book. The underlying argument throughout the following chapters is that politics of identity generally is driven by the paradox that no identity, no sense of community, and no imputed property of a place ever can be self-evident or stable. There are always multiple meanings, many narratives, and inherent instabilities within such entities. One can say that the rigidity of the designator ultimately is impossible or that the name never can become completely "proper." The reply to this is, however, always more reiteration of a particular meaning of a name, new inflections or supplements that can support and extend particular meanings of a name or a designator, or maybe to invent a new name altogether. The efficacy of a name, and thus an identity, in terms of the fixing or accruing of meaning and connotations, depends, therefore, on its constant performance—in authoritative writing, in public speech, images, songs, rumors, and so on.

For a name of a huge entity like a city to be "proper," it must, in other words, be able to mark the space of the city, its historicity, and the identity of its people in a clear and unequivocal manner. In the era of modern nationalism there cannot be two cities with identical names within the same state, at least not if they are of a certain size. The name of each city must be marked and fixed in time and space, in order for its people, its communities, and its social worlds also to be fixed in space (by a post fix "am Main," "upon Tyne," etc.) and historicized by being prefixed as new or old, for example.

The question of naming revolves, therefore, around the question of which space, and whose, should the name fix and territorialize as its object; which, and whose, history should it refer to and demarcate; and in which language should the name properly be enunciated. In this perspective, the question of Bombay/Mumbai appears as something slightly more complicated than merely a change of the English spelling of the vernacular pronunciation.

At a first glance, the change of the name was a rather straightforward assertion of the nativist agenda of claiming Bombay and all its symbols of modernity and power to be the natural property of local Marathi speakers, which Shiv Sena had been pursuing since its inception in 1966. Within this agenda, built on the discourse of the linguistic movement of the 1940s and 1950s, the Samyukta Maharashtra Samiti (SMS), the name Mumbai would amount to a fixation of the city in the regional space of Maharashtra, as well as in the history, culture, and language of the Marathi—speakers of western India. As I will show in detail in the following chapters, this nativist discourse tried to efface the fact that most Marathi speakers were as alien in the city as everybody else by defining itself against "outsiders" constructed as enemies of Marathi speakers—Gujaratis, south Indians, Muslims, the central government, the established and "cosmopolitan" elite in the city, and so on.

However, the renaming also resonated with broader and nationalist concerns with decolonization of the mind, the discomfort shared by conservatives as well as leftist forces with the continuing dominance of English as a medium for education, cultural products, and the business world. The advocacy of vernacularization of public culture[1] as such has been

prominent in western India since the nineteenth century. To these powerful sensibilities, the renaming of Mumbai appeared as a much needed mark
of distinction vis-à-vis a colonial past as well as a globalizing present. Bearing the official and authorized name of Mumbai, the city could be reinscribed in a national territory as a "proper" Indian city, within a national
history and an emerging national modernity that recognized its indigenous cultural and linguistic roots, and its name could be properly enunciated in the vernacular. These sentiments were shared across the political
spectrum in a variety of ways, from conservative Hindu nationalist forces
to intellectuals, writers, educators, artists, and many others of leftist political persuasions. To be sure, the name Mumbai has occasionally been used
in official documents of the state as well as the municipality over several
decades. Prominent socialists campaigned for the change of name in the
1960s, and the initial moves to finally change the name were made by a
Congress chief minister in 1992.[2]

Others, like the gentleman in the train, bemoaned the change of the
name Bombay. In this name, it was argued, was contained a unique experience of colonial and postcolonial modernity—dynamic, intensely
commercial, heterogeneous, chaotic, and yet spontaneously tolerant and
open-minded. This was the Bombay of ethnic and religious mixing, of
opportunities, of rags-to-riches success stories, of class solidarity, of artistic
modernism and hybridized energies that so many writers have celebrated
in novels and poetry. Obviously there were many different ideas of Bombay. There were the visions of the city's elite, always concerned with the
unruliness of the endless crowds overflowing what was supposed to be the
city's neat and elegant urban spaces. There were the nationalist dreams of
India's new secular modernity arising from factories, offices, and institutions to override the older sectarian divisions of caste, language, and religion that abounded in the city. And there were the humble dreams of a
better life, a good job, a bit of money entertained by the millions of people
migrating to the city in search of a livelihood. This side of Bombay—the
poverty, the little rays of hope, spontaneous solidarities and yet insur-
mountable difficulties facing the poor in the city—has recently been viv-
idly represented by Rohinton Mistry in *A Fine Balance* and, earlier, in
Such a Long Journey.

But these dreams had already been shattered and the celebration of the
city's mythical cosmopolitanism had already been questioned years before
the renaming actually took place. The critical events were, of course, the
devastating riots that rocked Bombay in December 1992 and January
1993—the most protracted and serious urban conflagration in post-Independence India. In his essay, *This Is Not Bombay*, Dilip Padgaonkar, then
the editor of *Times of India*, reflected in 1993 on the causes and consequences of the riots. Like many other citizens of Bombay he felt immensely

frustrated as he watched the demise of one type of dream, or imagination, of the city and the emergence of another much uglier, far more violent side of the city, "its flip side," as he put it:

> Few Bombay'ites now claimed that the city drew its pride, as in the past, from its cosmopolitan character . . . just beneath the surface you discovered the anguish of the city. Bombay had experienced a swift and sharp polarisation between religious communities and ethnic groups on a hitherto unprecedented scale. Conversations you heard in April (1993)—conversations that followed the initial, self-deluding remarks about the return of normality—sounded more or less alike. They betrayed the same hatred and prejudices, the same fears, the same despair. (Padgaonkar 1993, 3–4)

Something had changed in Bombay. The city had seen riots and communal enmity before but never on that scale. Most people in the city will agree today that it is no longer the same city as it used to be, that Mumbai is not like Bombay. As a friend of mine, born and brought up in the central parts of the city, said some years ago:

> We have lost the optimism we used to have, you know, that life is hard but it is getting better next year when I find myself a new job, finish my school or whatever . . . now we have the same sense of chaos and corruption as in other parts of the country. Maybe we were just naïve, but there was this feeling of Bombay being ahead of the country, you know, that we had more scope, that we were more advanced, and all that.

Is this sense of loss, however widespread it may be, just a sentimental delusion, one may ask, a local appellation of the narrative of loss of order, morality, authenticity and community that seems intrinsic to most experiences of urban modernity? Is it not more true that this narrative of an ideal Bombay is a historical fantasy that conceals the fact that Bombay always was fundamentally divided by class, caste and religion? Is it not so that urban violence, state repression, and corruption were always a part of the city's life, as Chandavarkar has shown in his recent round of studies of colonial Bombay (Chandavarkar 1998)? Is not Bombay's Janus face that emerges from Salman Rushdie's *The Moor's Last Sigh* (1995) the truth of the city—the intimate dependence of the elite and middle-class life of the city on the underworld, on sectarian violence, and on brutal exploitation; in brief, all that official nationalism for so long sought to repress and efface?

We must answer yes to all these questions. The history of Bombay does not at all fit into the standard depictions of the city as full of pragmatic business-minded go-getters and spontaneously peaceful and secular citizens. But this insight prompts a series of new questions regarding how these dominant discourses of the city were made possible, who produced them, and why they began to crumble in the 1980s? Does the renaming of Bombay signify a new set of ideas of how urban modernity is going to be inhabited and governed, how space is going to be used, appropriated, and symbolically marked? Is it, as many older residents in the city believe, the parochial forces from the hinterland, the older notions of a "Marathi Mumbai" that now finally have conquered and defeated an "alien British Bombay," such as Meera Kosambi depicts the conflicting images of Bombay of the nineteenth century (Kosambi 1995)? Has Bombay in the same move been domesticated as Mumbai and reinscribed within a Hindu nationalist discourse of vernacular modernity in India, a Mumbai that may be Hindu in symbolic complexion and rhetoric but essentially retains most of the institutions and structures of the political economy developed by the postcolonial state?

Answering these questions presupposes that one begin to unlearn some of the well-established "rural bias" in much South Asian anthropology and come to terms with how ordinary social life is configured in urban India, how localities and identities are produced there.[3] As it will become clear in the following, the contending discourses on community, on modernity, and on political authority that I trace in the following chapters feed into a protracted and complex negotiation of the proper place of the urban experience, with all its ambivalences and condensed desires and impurities, within the dominant political imaginaries of western India.

INTERPRETING MUMBAI DREAMS

Unruliness, ambiguity, intensity, and anxiety are defining characteristics of the urban experience in most parts of the world. As Appadurai and Holston observe: "Like nothing else, the modern urban public signifies both the defamiliarizing enormity of national citizenship and the exhilaration of its liberties." Cities, the authors point out, have always been privileged sites for negotiations and enlargement of the meaning of citizenships, the definition of rights, the claims to certain entitlements from the state, as well as the rise of both reactionary and radical social movements (Appadurai and Holston 1996, 188–89). They observe further that the proliferation and intensification of global flows of capital, goods, and people in the last decade "tend to drive a wedge between national space and its urban centers" (189), turning vast cityscapes into zones of indeterminacy with multiple economic logics, multiple forms of law, and multiple forms of community and solidarity. These dynamics challenge several of the ideals of the nation-state—uniformity of the law and the capacity of national citizenship to encompass and override other loyalties—and have contributed to the growth of xenophobic and exclusivist movements and agendas in many large cities across the globe.

Such a wedge between Bombay and its hinterland has existed for more than a century but has been compounded and intensified over the past decades. In that light, the most striking feature of the renaming, and of what was staged as a conquest of the city by triumphant nativist and Hindu nationalist forces, was exactly the emptiness of their gestures and the absence of any broader vision of social or political transformation. The essential message was that of an ethnic marking of the city, its domestication within national as well as regional space: now Mumbai is "our city," now it is a symbol of "our modernity." The "we" for which Shiv Sena and BJP claimed to speak and to represent was the ordinary Marathi speaker, the elusive *Marathi manus*, and an even more elusive community of Hindus. The power of this representation did, undoubtedly, lie in its lack of precision and its reliance on an older notion of Bombay controlled by all that made average Hindus of the hinterland feel insecure: a sophisticated elite, an immoral and excessively Westernized intelligentsia, the working classes, the slum dwellers, the Muslims, and a future Mumbai that was marked by the familiar and nonthreatening, a Bombay with all its money, glitz, and power tamed and familiarized with all its threatening cultural and social difference effaced and thus transformed into "our Mumbai," into "our place" in the world.

My contention is, in other words, that if we are to understand the transformation of Bombay into Mumbai, and the nature of the Mumbai dreams growing out of a violent movement like Shiv Sena, we need to see the importance of social imaginaries, of desires of recognition, and the attraction of the public spectacles of violence and assertion that Shiv Sena has employed so successfully over the years. My proposition, which will be preposterous to some, is that categories and logics derived from Lacanian psychoanalysis and elaborated by the work of Slavoj Žižek may be helpful in this endeavor. Many anthropologists reject psychoanalysis altogether because of its often ethnocentric and universalizing claims. Lacanian thought, however appreciated in literary criticism and film studies, has rarely been invoked by anthropologists or social scientists, partly because of its highly abstract and general nature.[4] To my mind, however, the possibilities of Lacanian categories lie exactly in their highly abstract outline of logics of identification that make them easier to "think with" and redeploy in other cultural contexts than, say, more conventional Freudian categories derived from clinical practice.

The basic Lacanian proposition I think with in this book is closely related to the logic of naming outlined above and what I have called the "impossibility of identities" (Hansen 1999, 60–65). The formation of subjects takes place in a constant interplay between three orders, or registers: the Imaginary (more immediate and sensory experiences, desires, and imaginings), the Symbolic (the conventions of society and culture—Lacan often calls this *nom de pere*, name of the father, the Oedipal moment of the prohibitive command), and the Real (the central dimensions of experience that cannot be fathomed and symbolized fully—for example, death, contingency, violence, pain). The subject is split between these inherently conflictual registers and is always formed around a "lack" in being, an incompleteness because the symbolic order always is blocked and perforated by the injunctions of desire and fascination of the apparitions of the Real. This play between the "Law" and the forbidden is what Lacan called *jouissance*, or (perverse) enjoyment, and is at the heart of the impossibility of identity as well as the drive toward overcoming this "lack." Especially Slavoj Žižek has, with admirable creativity, shown the potentials of this type of thinking in areas as diverse as film studies, nationalism, the fascination of totalitarianism, consumption, and much more.[5]

I do not deploy these categories in the following because I believe that they can form the ultimate template on which questions of identity and subjectivity in Mumbai, or in India, can be plotted. But I believe that some of this abstract Lacanian logic makes rather good sense in interpreting questions of leadership, identification, the anatomy of resentment between Hindus and Muslims in contemporary Mumbai, and anxieties and desires generated by the urban landscape. I do not pretend to exhaust these questions, and even less to find the truth. But I invite readers to judge whether they, too, find that the mode of thinking and conceptualizing that informs the subsequent analysis—and occasionally is drawn out in more explicit form—is able to produce interesting, or maybe even provoking, conclusions. If so, this theoretical proposition will be wholly justified.

THE ARGUMENT

This book analyzes the historical formation of the political discourses, the identities, and the conflicts that changed Bombay from being the preeminent symbol of India's secular, industrial modernity to become a powerful symbol of the very crisis of this vision.

Many editorials in newspapers and commentary in the public debates have argued that the success of Shiv Sena and the proliferation of xenophobic discourses in Bombay is an anomaly, a symptom that something had gone wrong in its urban modernity. The rise of ethnic xenophobia and the souring of intercommunity relations in the city that engulfed the entire state in the 1980s have often been attributed to mismanagement by the Congress Party, excessive corruption, and the complacency and irresponsibility of the elites in the city and the state.

Another version of the search for anomaly was that Bombay's peculiar, fragmented, and disorganized structure of capitalist production in the 1970s and 1980s created a "predatory capitalism" of speculation and unproductive capital that dissolved the organized working class and prepared the ground for subsequent political and cultural changes in the city (Lele 1995). Older studies argued that the pattern of migration to Bombay created an imbalanced configuration of ethnicity, class, and status that prompted the growth of regional nativism and ethnic chauvinism (Katzenstein 1981; Gupta 1982).

My explorations of postcolonial Bombay tries to make three arguments that all, one way or another, are informed by my basic theoretical propositions regarding the instability of naming and the impossibility of identities. I argue, first, that Hindu nationalism and the politics of xenophobia should not be understood as anomalies inflicted by dark forces or structures of peripheral capitalism, but rather as possibilities always folded into India's unique experience of modernity and democracy. I try to show that the ostensibly clear distinction drawn today between "secular forces" and "communal forces" is more spurious than many would like to believe. I also try to show how relatively unexceptional much of Shiv Sena's discourse and practices are in the context of the historical formation of narratives and identities of caste and religious community in western India. But I argue that unlike most other parties or organizations in Mumbai, Shiv Sena has enthusiastically embraced modern city life and technological progress, and has provided young men especially with an ideal of an assertive, often violent, mode of being urban. Herein lies a key to much of its success.

Second, I argue that the rise of Shiv Sena and the transformations of Bombay were made possible by the decline of an older political culture that espoused paternalist social and cultural incorporation of the large majority of the population into a highly unequal system of political clientelism. This culture had been undermined over the years by a democratic revolution, and a rhetoric of entitlements and political aspiration which democracy in postcolonial India had promoted over four decades (for a fuller argument along these lines, see Hansen 1999). This extension of the languages of democracy allowed the assertion of new and plebeian identities, but it also intensified struggles over material and symbolic resources and produced more anxiety, more violence. The Shiv Sena addressed these anxieties quite effectively by offering the rhetoric of ethnoreligious unity and solidarity that repackaged older anti-Muslim myths with registers of regional cultural pride and an effective strategy of staging a series of violent public spectacles. I argue that Shiv Sena developed the longstanding traditions of plebeian insubordination and assertion in public spaces in Mumbai into a highly violent strategy of political performances that openly defied and challenged the idea of legality and changed popular perceptions of governance and the state.

Finally, I take issue with the interpretation of a phenomenon like Shiv Sena as growing out of caste groups, class segments, or communities—as if these constituencies, equipped with certain collective interests and cosmologies, always existed. Most of the time these distinctions operate in dispersed practices and as a historically produced phenomenology of difference, distinction, and appropriateness, as well as fantasies of the imputed attributes of other groups. But these identities are always fragmented, imprecise, and contested, and thus ultimately unattainable. My argument is, however, that it is this very lack of precision and correspondence that makes naming and its attributed distinctions (as well as the rumors thereof) between respectable and not respectable, clean and dirty, and so on, so effective and flexible.

I argue that some of the most effective (and imprecise) caste and community identities in contemporary Mumbai and Maharashtra, such as the notion of the Maratha, have been shaped through protracted formation of particular forms of naming and organization as ideological poles and "designators" throughout the twentieth century. Caste groups or religious communities, I contend, are not "out there" as groups *an sich* but only exist as collective identities when they are named in public rituals, organized, and reproduced through performative practices as groups and categories for themselves. I try to show how boundaries of caste and community have been both dislocated and hardened in the last decades in Mumbai. This process produced anger and anxieties, reconfigured social imaginaries, and made it imperative for many people to carve out a new sense of "our place in the world."

STRUCTURE OF THE BOOK

This is not an exhaustive account of the history of Bombay and Maharashtra in the postcolonial era but rather a string of explorations of the political-ideological-cultural formations in the area in this period, particularly in the last few decades. The explorations that follow do not attempt to write any comprehensive history of the culture of politics in the state but seek to shed light on that larger history through ethnographies of changing politico-cultural practices in Mumbai. Some of my arguments and the material I present do, I hope, have wider relevance beyond the city and South Asia circuits.

Chapter 1 outlines the formation of a widely popular and effective ethno-historical imagination centered around the history of the eighteenth-century Maratha Empire. I argue that this register of historical

THE PROPER NAME 11

myths, symbols, and narratives were shaped, from the late nineteenth century on, around the idea of a continuous antagonism between the Brahman elite and the large Maratha caste. The "naming" and fixation of these communities in historical narratives and in the political dynamics of the postcolonial democracy have made them into effective markers of cultural and political identities in contemporary Mumbai.

Chapter 2 explores the formation of a distinct regional identity in Maharashtra from the 1940s on and how the distinctions between a cosmopolitan Bombay and a Marathi Deccan were crucial to the formation of the movement for Maharashtra as a mono-lingual state. I also explore how Shiv Sena in the 1960s and 1970s reworked the discourse of regionalism and redeployed it as xenophobic populism in the face of the ambivalences and anxieties that the urban experience of Bombay produced among many Marathi speakers. I analyze how Shiv Sena in the first decades of its existence developed both a regular organization and the essential features of an aggressive and highly visible politics of the public spectacle.

In chapter 3 I explore what has been called the rebirth of Shiv Sena in the 1980s. I try to put Shiv Sena's new radical anti-Muslim strategies in the context of broader political transformations in the state. More important, however, I explore the changing strategies and local forms of organization of Shiv Sena in this period, how the organization increasingly is pervaded by localized networks of builders and operators of questionable legality in the gray sectors of the economy, and how Sena's entanglement in the world of competitive politics created new challenges and a crisis of authority in the organization.

In chapter 4 I tell a more detailed story of Shiv Sena's emergence and development in one of its oldest strongholds in Thane, a large industrial suburb north of Mumbai. I explore in detail how the wider changes, but also continuities, in the Shiv Sena's organization, production of authority, use of violence, and political strategies were played out on the ground.

Chapter 5 starts from the riots and the bomb blasts that shook the city in 1992–93. I explore the events and the subsequent official inquiry and strategies of the Bombay police in the light of a longer history of communal violence, policing, reconciliation, and spatial practices in the city. I analyze the production of truth as it took place in the official inquiry into the riots conducted by the Shrikrishna Commission between 1993 and 1997. I try, subsequently, to shed light on practices of the police in the city, and the relations between the police and ordinary residents in parts of central Mumbai.

In chapter 6 I move the perspective to how Muslim identities in Mumbai and Maharashtra have been shaped and altered over the past decades. Mainly concentrating on central Mumbai, I try to demonstrate how curtains of social stigma and stereotypes have separated Muslims from the surrounding society ever more effectively. I explore strategies of employment and livelihoods in central Mumbai, the shaping of identities between religious authority and immoral strongmen (dadas) in the popular neighborhoods, and how Muslims have responded to the emergence of a new aggressive Hindu politics by rethinking widely held notions of community and political identity. I also look at public discourses of gangsterism and mythologies of the predominantly Muslim gangster dons.

In chapter 7 I look at the trajectory and performance of the Hindu nationalist coalition ruling Mumbai and Maharashtra between 1995 and 1999. I analyze some of the larger plans launched by the cabinet in this period, particularly in terms of housing and infrastructural development in Mumbai, and how these plans fared. I discuss the controversies regarding corruption in the state, and I try to make sense of the rather systematic contempt for the judiciary and democratic procedure displayed by Shiv Sena in particular. I analyze some of the cultural policies of Shiv Sena and its allies, and how the access to power and resources has reconfigured its position in the city and the state. I reflect on what these may tell us about the shape and content of the idea of Mumbai that has driven Shiv Sena leaders and enticed their supporters.

In the conclusion I reflect on what broader lessons the fragmentation of governance and public authority and the logics of majoritarian democratic politics in Mumbai may teach us about the relationship between state, community, and politics in contemporary India.

ABOUT THIS BOOK

This book has grown out of almost a decade of engagement with politics and culture in Maharashtra. The material for this book has been gathered in the course of annual stints of fieldwork and visits to Mumbai or elsewhere in the state since 1990. It was several longer stays, first in 1992–93 in Pune and Bombay, and later the winter of 1996–97 in Mumbai, that gave me vital insights into how people wore their shifting identities both in urban and rural Maharashtra. It was my own experiences during the riots in Bombay in 1992–93 and the subsequent changes in the city that made it important to me to study and conceptualize more carefully the links between xenophobic ideology and the experiences of modern urban life in India. My experiences in January 1993 taught me how lethal the militant Hindu identities and the casual, everyday anti-Muslim common sense I had listened to and recorded for a long time actually could be. These experiences also revealed to me what the atmosphere of a riot situation is like—the fear, the suspension of normal parameters of judgment, the uncanny silence, but also the dispersion and disorganization that characterizes most riots, the heavily mythologized images of what may or may not happen next, and so on.

Let me reflect a bit on methodology—a subject so important in our training of students and yet relatively absent in most analyses of ethnographic material. As will be evident in the following chapters, the materials that went into this book have come from multiple sources: archives, newspapers, official publications, pamphlets, books, and programs published by parties and organizations. I have also over the years conducted a wide range of interviews with political leaders, local councilors, panchayat members, activists, social workers, policemen, bureaucrats, religious leaders, business people, local traders, and so on. However, the most valuable source of knowledge has been the hundreds of conversations and interviews I have had over many years with a wide range of so-called ordinary people in each of the areas I worked.

My preferred method when doing urban ethnography has been to select a neighborhood, a locality bounded physically by roads or other markers, comprising a couple of municipal wards and therefore constituting a political as well as an administrative unit. Such areas are objectified units of governance, but they also constitute spaces where people live, experience, and seek to produce their own worlds. As Appadurai has pointed out, the neighborhood as a physical and lived-in space is not necessarily in itself a locality. A locality is produced when quotidian spatial practices are made intelligible through a larger grid that gives them a context and a meaning as being different from its others and its neighbors, or as a smaller part of a larger whole (Appadurai 1996, 178–88).

The very notion of boundaries, the contestation of what a locality really is or means to whom, where it starts and ends, assume critical importance if one, like I did, intended to study and map the variations in local configurations of identity and political organization. As we all know, interactions in urban space are not bounded by, or defined by, physical localities in the same way as in rural areas. Most larger and supra-local urban structures manifest themselves in every neighborhood, albeit in differing forms: the labor market, networks of trade and associations, urban governance and services, political networks. All these structures transcend the locality, much of their dynamism derive from the fact that they are supra-local phenomena, and yet their effects can only be studied in localities. Instead of despairing in the face of the elusive and often unfixable nature of social boundaries in urban space, I decided to make the localized notions of what the locality was, where it began and ended, what characterized it, and so on—in brief, the local phenomenology of locality and space—into an object of scrutiny.

In the localities I zoomed in on over the years—in Thane north of Mumbai, in the old city of Pune, and in central Mumbai—I tried to map them in various ways. I met as many of the local "somebodies" as possible—councilors, local representatives of larger or smaller organizations and associations, politicians, prominent activists, some of the prominent business people, police officers, and so forth.

In some areas I also managed to do more systematic surveys of the socio-demographic composition of the locality, according to the standard sociological technologies. These results were interesting in that they represented a different form of knowledge against which I could compare other forms of local knowledge of the area—how many various categories of people there were, where they lived, how they lived their lives, and so on. The third and most vital component in my work was long conversations with a range of ordinary people in the locality—often families or groups of people. I tried to meet and get to know a fairly representative cross-section of people within the given time limits—something I could never quite live up to but that nonetheless enabled me to get to know a dozen rather different families in each locality I worked in.

However, as anyone who has carried out extensive fieldwork will know, the more structured parts of one's work is constantly interrupted by, and mixed with, scores of casual unplanned conversations with all sorts of people. Some of these turn out to be the most interesting part of the research. Some open new perspectives, and others remain a single succinct statement, as in the case of my fellow passenger at the suburban train in Mumbai. In the chapters that follow, both voices appear: those emanating from my structured work and those from the more unstructured parts of my research. Throughout the text, I try to bring the voices into context, as well as the statements I employ to support a given argument. This is not just to give a certain ethnographic flavor to the text; the location, timing, and context of a given narrative is obviously crucial to the interpretations to which it can lend itself. I do not pretend, however, that what I represent in the following, and use in my analysis, is completely true to the authentic meaning or intention of the narratives I recorded on location. Indeed, the very idea that such authentic selves, speech, or intentions exist and can be made available to scientific knowledge is, to my mind, the ultimate illusion. A quick glance at our own unclear, multifaceted, and often undecidable motives for using certain words and gestures rather than others should bring the point home. This does not mean that the voices and narratives that emerged from hundreds of conversations are inauthentic; rather, it means that they cannot be regarded as testimonies to any "truth" or final meaning. Social sciences are not truth-producing disciplines, and this book does not pretend to represent any truth of postcolonial Bombay and Maharashtra. It is an "account of accounts," my interpretation of the primary and secondary material at my disposal, material which in the case of interviews is produced through my agendas and my questions and made possible by the hospitality and kindness of so many ordinary people. In other cases, I talked to people with clear agendas, people who wanted me to see the world in a particular way and who represented their world in that light.

Every bit of the material I present is a tiny fragment of a larger corpus of text—thousands of pages of transcripts, archival material, newspapers— and is the result of a heavy process of selection and editing. To claim anything else would be dishonest. The acknowledgment of the weighty presence of the social scientist in every bit of the production of ethnographic material does, however, not preclude critique of the quality of the interpretation, the grasp of categories or vernacular meanings, of voids and shortcomings in the material presented. On the contrary. Social science is ultimately about producing interpretations that seek to be convincing by virtue of the cohesion of their argument, the quality of the material they present, and the subtlety of the analysis of this material. To my mind, reflections on the way material has been collected and generated is part of this procedure that can convince readers. But putting the cards on the table also renders one more vulnerable and open to critique of what one did not do, the questions one did not ask, and so on. In his recent book, Akhil Gupta writes that he has tried to avoid the standard procedure of creating an "analytical closure" around the ethnographic material. Instead of knitting all the loose ends together, he has tried to render the material more open to reinterpretation and rethinking (Gupta 1998, 30). Although I find this a laudable strategy, the present book is more conventional in its attempt to interpret a range of evidence of events, processes, and discourses spread over several decades and various localities. The methods I adopted in generating this material were, no doubt, ethnographic, but the aim of this book is to generate a more general argument on the logics of democracy, identity, community, and locality at play in the political culture of Bombay/Mumbai and Maharashtra in the postcolonial era. Although I tend to wrap my material in theoretical reflection, I hope that this analytical closure does not prevent readers from getting a feel of the polyvalent character of statements and processes under scrutiny.

Mumbai and the entire state of Maharashtra has, throughout the 1990s, been marked by high levels of political tension, violent rhetoric, and physical violence between Hindus and Muslims as well as between caste communities. Violence, antagonism, anxiety and fear did not only constitute phenomena I wanted to study, they also suffused the localities I worked in, the narratives I recorded, the problematics of everyday life, and so on. This constantly raised the issue of my own position in the localities. What was I up to? Whose side was I on in the ongoing battles over symbols and space? Why did I talk to some persons rather than others? A lot of my work was carried out during periods when the Ramjanmabhoomi/Babri Masjid issue was on everybody's lips, and later when the riots and bomb blasts in Mumbai were at the center of many conversations and stories. The general sense of upheaval and conflict felt during these periods and the topicality of the issues into which I probed made it quite unproblematic to establish and justify my presence and interests. For once I felt that my status as a foreigner appeared as somewhat advantageous because so many people assumed me to be somehow outside, and maybe even fairly neutral. Besides, many informants were keen on explaining to me why all these upheavals took place, what the real stories were, and so forth.

But I could not cross boundaries freely. Needless to say, I could not mix freely with both Hindu activists and Muslims or supporters of leftist parties in the same locality. The deep communal divides between Hindus and Muslims and the web of suspicions, anxieties, and politicization of everyday life that enveloped most of the places I worked forced me to concentrate on only one community in each locality. That choice enabled me to mix more freely, to develop friendships and relations with people and organizations there, but it also raised the issue of loyalties and empathy vis-à-vis many of my informants.

One cannot remain neutral when working with violent nationalist organizations such as Shiv Sena, or the Hindu nationalist movement, their local activists, followers, and sympathizers. Their discourse, style, and aims were, and remain, the antithesis to everything I ever believed in, politically and ethically. I tried to understand how these milieus were structured and I was able to develop meaningful relations with a large number of individuals, but true empathy could never develop. In fact, the deeper I probed into these milieus, the more difficult it became for me to continue my "act"—pretending I was a friend of the cause and sympathetic to at least some of the convictions and worldviews of my informants.

Later, I found it more congenial to work among Muslims in Mumbai. This was partly because I felt the need to highlight the social world of a community that has been demonized and battered by Hindu chauvinism in the last decade, and partly because I no longer needed to put up an act. This was not because I necessarily shared the worldviews of my informants there or that I prefer the social world of Muslims to that of Hindus per se, but rather linked to the instinctive sympathy I developed for the victims of violent Hindu majoritarianism.

This book tells a story about Mumbai and Maharashtra centered around material generated in localities marked by high levels of Hindu-Muslim conflicts and often a strong presence of the Hindu nationalist and majoritarian forces. I fully realize that this merely is one among several possible narratives that could have been told about contemporary Mumbai, but I felt this was the most urgent and compelling. It is also marked, probably in more ways than I realize, by my own strong aversion to the virulent anti-Muslim rhetoric that dominates the Hindu Right. I do not apologize for this, because I could not do it any other way.

Violent ethno-religious and political conflicts between the self-professed representatives of communities are strangely totalizing phenomena. They leave no privileged and neutral "voyeuristic" space for the social scientists or others. Violence, fear, and communal hatred are not mere cultural performances whose features and effects can be studied dispassionately at a distance. Researching identities, community, and violence means one gets involved, one hears, records, and writes about these topics in certain ways, and one invariably takes a stand; indeed, one must take a stand, not as the waving of certain flags but as a reflection on where one's allegiances and emotions are, what sympathies and empathies drive one to interpret events in certain ways rather than others. I began to study the rise of Hindu majoritarianism in Maharashtra because I thought it was an important process with far-reaching implications for the entire region. But I also had to realize how strenuous and ethically complex a venture that proved to be, both personally and politically. One conclusion I drew is that as much as one needs to understand the perpetrators of hate-speech and violence, one also needs to "de-exoticize" ethno-religious identities and alert oneself to their profoundly political nature and to their sometimes lethal consequences.

We need to understand that as academics we are producers and codifiers of knowledge of xenophobias and violence, and our statements are never innocent. They may well become part of the rewriting, justification, or consolidation of such identities. As I have discussed elsewhere, the Hindu nationalist movement in India, aware of the authority of science and "foreign experts," is a keen consumer and reinterpreter of a whole range of social science literature (Hansen 1999, 80–88). My own view is that the task of the social scientist is to produce knowledge and writing that defies ethnic closures by documenting and exploring the richness, diversity, and multivocality of the social world of even the smallest of localities. Good scholarship is usually unsettling to established or widely held ideas, and scholars, to my mind, should strive to make their work as useless as possible for those who promote ethnic closures.

The research for this book over the years has been made possible by grants from the Danish Council for Development Research; the ENRECA program, a research collaboration between International Development Studies, Roskilde University, Centre for the Study in Social Sciences in Calcutta, and Center for Basic Research in Kampala; as well as the research program "Livelihood, Identity, and Organization in Situations of Instability"—an interdisciplinary group of researchers in Copenhagen with whom I had the privilege to work between 1996 and 2000.

Many years of association with this part of India means that I have incurred innumerable debts to colleagues and friends in India, as well as in my own part of the world. My research in its early phases was assisted in crucial ways by Dr. Ramesh Babu, then head of the Department of Civics and Politics at Bombay University, and Dr. R. K. Hebsur of the Tata Institute of Social Science in Mumbai. I am grateful to the people with whom I worked closely over the years: Urmila Budhkar, Prasad Srinivasan, Rajeshwari Krishnamurty, and, not least, Mahesh Gavaskar, who also became a good friend whose deep insights into the society and culture in Maharashtra benefited me immensely. I am also grateful to friends in Mumbai, Pune, and Delhi whose wit, help, and encouragement always made my stays there enjoyable: Asif and Sherifa Khan, Sadjid Rashid, Indra Munshi, Thomas Matthew, Bela Malik, Pradeep Rawat, Satish Kamat, and Surendra Jhondale. I thank colleagues from Bombay University, SNDT Women's University in Mumbai, Pune University, and Babasaheb Ambedkar University in Aurangabad, who generously shared their insights into society, politics, and culture in this part of India.

I am also grateful to the librarians and staff at the Gokhale Institute of Politics and Economics in Pune, the School of Oriental and African Studies in London, the Centre of South Asian Studies in Cambridge, the Nordic Institute of Asian Studies in Copenhagen, the Royal Library in Copenhagen, and the Center for Research, Information, and Documentation in Mumbai.

Parts of the chapters and the material that went into this book have been presented at seminars in Copenhagen, Stockholm, Paris, Toulouse, London, Oxford, Cambridge, Edinburgh, Oslo, Delhi, Mumbai, Pune, Kampala, and Durban.

I am grateful to comments, questions, and criticism from participants in these seminars, as well as to other scholars who over the years have given me valuable suggestions that forced me to rethink arguments: Raj Chandavarkar, Dipankar Gupta, Sudipta Kaviraj, Peter van der Veer, Christophe Jaffrelot, Gérard Heuzé, Partha Chatterjee, Zoya Hasan, Nandini Gooptu, Terence Ranger, Roger Jeffery, Patricia Jeffery, Akhil Gupta, Emma Tarlo, Veronique Bénéï, Denis Vidal, Johnny Parry, Jens Lerche, Raminder Kaur, Preben Kaarsholm, Bodil Folke Frederiksen, Ninna Nyberg Soerensen, Fiona Wilson, Finn Stepputat, Henrik Ronsbo, Arild Ruud, Olle Törnquist, Mangesh Kulkarni, Carol Upadhya, Ashgar Ali Engineer, and many others.

A special thanks to Chris Fuller, Arjun Appadurai, Gyan Prakash, and Jonathan Spencer for valuable comments and criticism that helped me turn earlier drafts of this manuscript into what I hope has become a more coherent book. Thanks to Mary Murrell, Fred Appel, Karen Ancharski, Tim Sullivan, and Rita Bernhard of Princeton University Press whose unfailing professionalism and support made the process of producing this book a most gratifying experience. Finally, a warm thanks to Mrs. Inge Jensen, probably the best secretary in the world, at Roskilde University for many years, for never losing her patience with me.

Needless to say, the responsibility for shortcomings, errors, and other deficiencies in the text remain solely mine.

Deccan Pastoral: The Making of an Ethnohistorical Imagination in Western India

EMBLEMS OF HISTORY

The sense of living as a historical being, to be the rightful inheritor of the deeds of the past, is crucial to the making of national identity. Knowledge of historical events and chronologies are, of course, transmitted through historical textbooks that always were primary concerns of nationalists and nation states worldwide. In everyday life, however, history is most frequently represented in emblematic forms—names, images, places or significant dates that over time have acquired a status of master signifiers, that is, condensations of meanings, myths, and tales that provide nodal points in otherwise hazy chronologies and events.

The importance of historical emblems was brought home to me by a brief incident in the beginning of my work in Mumbai, then Bombay, in 1991. I was walking around in a slum area in one of the city's suburbs with a local schoolteacher. We saw a group of boys sitting around a carefully constructed castle-like structure made of sand and earth. The top and sides of the castle were lined with palisades made of matches, and from the sides were tiny figures hanging from thin threads. The boys explained that this was a model of an eighteenth-century Mughal fort being taken by Chatrapati Shivaji and his Maratha warriors in a daring operation. The week before, their teacher had told them of this particular episode, and they became so excited that they decided to construct a model of the fort so that it would be ready for the annual public celebrations of Shivaji the following week, the Shivaji Jayanti—a festival commemorating the anniversary of Shivaji's death and sponsored by the state government and most political parties in the state. The boys told us that they still needed to add some grass as vegetation in the landscape and, most important, small pieces of cloth as flags and standards for the two armies, "green for the mussulman, saffron-colored for Shivaji's soldiers—they were all Marathas and staunch Hindus," one boy explained to me.

This is the master signifier of regional history that overshadows the rest: Chhatrapati Shivaji, the seventeenth-century warrior king whose armies created the Maratha confederacy, which, from the Peshwa Palace in Pune, played a dominant role in subcontinental politics throughout the eighteenth century. There is no town in the state without streets, schools, or parks named after Shivaji. His deeds and daredevilish military exploits form the stuff that children's tales and stories are made of, and he holds a prominent place in history books and in the political imaginaries in the entire region. Shivaji is literally depicted as the father of the state, the originary source of power that was reborn with the formation of the state of Maharashtra, predominantly comprising speakers of the Marathi language, in 1960. The Chhatrapati (he who has a right to a palanquin, or chariot) rose from the dusty plains of the Deccan Plateau to organize the mightiest military force the subcontinent had seen for centuries, and to form a state that, according to the dominant historical renditions, derived its ethics, rituals, and organization from an autochthonous Hindu tradition.

Shivaji is to be found all over—as statues, little figures, calendar art, posters—always represented in hypermasculine poses, his face turned to the side to accentuate his manly profile, his straight nose and the sharply cut beard at his chin. He is often mounted on a virile and muscular horse, with his mythical sword, given to him, according to legend, by the powerful goddess Bhawani, lifted in a rather unmistakable representation of the act of foundational violence from where the Maratha state, and, by implication, modern Maharashtra, originates. The powers attributed to Shivaji, his status as a mythical and omnipresent emblem of the origin and power of the state, runs parallel with Taussig's reflections on the flow of magic, fables, and myths of "the Liberator" and the fetishization of his sword as the origins of state in Latin America. Though "covenants without the sword are but words," fables and myths are essential to state formation. The Hobbesian idea of the covenant as the basis of the state is such a necessary fable.

> No matter how historically inaccurate this fable obviously is, it is nevertheless a telling account of the mythological principles inevitably and necessarily involved in modern state formation which no history can articulate, but which all histories require. . . . [T]hese stories of the coming into being of the state are not only fantastic history . . . precisely as fantasy is essential to what they purport to explain such that any engagement with the thing called the state will perforce be an engagement with this heart of fiction. (Taussig 1997, 124–25)

The Shivaji mythology is a nodal point, the historical fiction at the heart of state practices, political rhetoric, and historical imagination in this part of India. Shivaji is also the favorite icon of the Shiv Sena. Shiv Sena leader Bal Thackeray likes to think of himself as a modern Shivaji. The local branches of Shiv Sena are located in buildings decorated like eighteenth-century stone forts with saffron flags on top, and in most of them one finds massive busts or statues of Shivaji. As the Shiv Sena came to power in the state in 1995 the government renamed both the international airport and the main station, Victoria Terminus, a landmark in the city, after Chhatrapati Shivaji. Shiv Sena's rather effective appropriation of this preeminent emblem of the ethnohistory in the region means that invocations of Shivaji now reverberate with xenophobic connotations associated with Shiv Sena. This conceals, however, how widespread, hegemonic, and effective the historical mythology of Shivaji has been in molding the historical and political imaginaries in the region, across class, community, the left-right dichotomy, and across the gulf between city and countryside. The following example may throw light on Shivaji's status in contemporary Maharashtra.

In April 1993, a few months after riots had shaken Mumbai and only a month after bomb blasts widely believed to have been executed by Muslim gangsters as revenge after the riots, the fortnightly magazine *The Illustrated Weekly* carried an article wherein a young academic analyzed how the political mythology of Shivaji and other icons of nationalist historiography were built on a questionable factual basis. The author suggested, among other things, that Shivaji in no way was opposed to Muslims as such (as is claimed by right-wing historians) and that Mughal forms of administration heavily influenced his rule. The article created a major outcry in the vernacular press. The journalist and the editor were accused of contempt for Maharashtrian culture. *Saamna*, Shiv Sena's mouthpiece, recommended that the editor be publicly flogged. Moderate Congress Party members were also outraged, demanding immediate and swift legal action against the writer and editor. The pressure forced the state government to take legal action against the weekly under the Indian Penal Code, Section 153 A, which touches on promotion of enmity between religious and cultural communities. The High Court did not find, however, that the weekly had overstepped the limits of its freedom of expression. This did not impress Marathi newspapers, which accused the writer of "imperialist prejudice" and likened the editor to a journalistic version of gangsters like Dawood Ibrahim and Arun Gawli.

As noted by Kulkarni in his excellent account of the controversy, it was significant that newspapers and public figures known for their resistance to the Hindu Right joined the chorus condemning the article. They saw it as yet another effect of the polluting impact of English-language education (Kulkarni 1997, 125–34). The controversy testified to the massive consensus in most quarters of Maharashtrian society regarding Shivaji's unassailable status as a regional and national hero.

A historical genealogy of the Shivaji myth and its performative forms in contemporary India in everyday rituals, educational practices, and other kinds of "banal nationalism" (Billig 1995) still awaits its author.[1] My intention in this chapter is more modest and more concerned with the histo-

riographical debates. I am focusing on the political struggles over historical signifiers and community boundaries that made Shivaji into "the father
of the state," and the notion of the Maratha as the quintessential Maharashtrian into a hegemonic ethnohistorical register in the region. I claim
no firsthand knowledge of the history of the Deccan but try instead to
trace some of the central dynamics in the nineteenth- and twentieth-cen-
tury history of Maharashtra that shaped its contemporary forms of historical consciousness.

The high caste intelligentsia in Pune, in the nineteenth century, originally advanced the notion of a single Marathi linguistic identity rooted in
a relatively homogeneous culture of the Deccan Plateau. These ideas of a
distinct regional culture that informed the movement for a linguistic state
in the 1950s eventually led to the formation of Maharashtra as a political
unit in 1960. The continued and often violent assertion of this identity
seems, however, to indicate that a shared Maharashtrian identity remains
haunted by its own incomplete character.

Shared linguistic codes provide a reservoir of meanings and references
that allow for the resonance of subtle inflections, twists of phrases, and
other practices central to the experience of language community, as well
as its double, linguistic closure, that is, the drawing of boundaries and
exclusion of others from exchange. Larger linguistic communities within
regions or states always had to be manufactured out of a mass of dialects
and social groups whose style and vocabulary often referred to widely differing social worlds. Nationalism based on language always needed to con-
ceal, even suppress, such differences in order to create at least a semblance
of a language community and of a closure. But language communities are
inherently unstable and without final closures. As Balibar has reminded
us, "the language community is not sufficient to produce ethnicity" (Balibar 1991, 98) because, by definition, it is open. Languages can be acquired
and mastered, even turned into mother tongues over a generation. But
"the language community is a community in the present which produces
the feeling that it has always existed . . . it 'assimilates' anyone, but holds
no one." Because of this lack of history, the language community needs a
supplement, an extra mark of closure (99).

This resonates well with how the notion of a Marathi linguistic and
cultural community over the past century or more has been challenged
and modified by lower-caste insubordination, by the deep gulf between
the social worlds of urban centers and rural life, by the differences between
regions in the state, and by the presence of large groups falling outside the
imputed Marathi community—Muslims, south Indians, Gujaratis, north
Indians—in the urban centers of the state.

One of the central propositions in this book is that the history of Maharashtra is marked by a series of often violent attempts to overcome this

incompleteness in the heart of the Marathi identity by linking it to another supplementary mark of distinction of greater clarity and stability, such as blood and the body. Maharashtrian identity has throughout been stabilized by references to *savarna jati*, the caste communities of pure blood, or the *Hindu samaj*, the larger Hindu community as opposed to Muslims. It is in this history of the supplement, premised on the exclusion of Muslims and lower-caste communities, that one finds the keys to the often violent negotiation of identity spaces and historical symbols in modern Maharashtra.

SPEAKING OF MAHARASHTRIAN PASTS

The modern political and cultural history of Maharashtra is marked by the evolution of two distinct and antagonistic political and social identities, Brahmans and Marathas, which over time have produced their own objectified reality as fairly well-bounded communities in the social world. Historical constructions created by the local intelligentsia of Deccan in the nineteenth century gave rise to the narratives of Brahmans and Marathas as transcendental social categories engaged in perennial competition and conflict through the centuries. The material available for this construction was found in the social structure of the villages of the Marathi-speaking areas in the Deccan Plateau, and in the political history of the Maratha Empire.

Most accounts seem to agree that the Deccan culture of the eleventh to sixteenth centuries was characterized by tensions between the landowning Maratha elites and Brahman communities. Whereas the latter group represented a Sanskritized version of Hinduism, some of the former group patronized early literary works in Marathi in the thirteenth and fourteenth centuries. The Muslim conquest meant a weakening of the cultural hegemony of the Brahmans. Gradually the lifestyle and language of parts of the elite Marathas were Persianized and the religious bhakti movements seem to have introduced more egalitarian notions of the relation between deities and worshipper, as religious discourses now were rendered in the local language and less mediated by religious virtuosi.[2] In the Deccan area, an important articulation of bhakti was the Varkari cult, a devotional movement founded by an excommunicated Brahman, Dnanadev, whose primary work, Dnaneshwari, is a long comment on the Bhagavad Gita in Marathi, celebrating the pre-Sanskritic deity Vithoba (Omvedt 1976, 53–55). The Varkari cult grew very strong within the peasantry and in lower castes in the following centuries and seems to have presented a constant challenge to Brahmanical orthodoxy. A parallel tradition of worship, resembling that practiced by the Kshatriya communities and focusing on tribal gods representing strength and martial values, such as Bhavani and Khandoba (supreme god of the Dhangar shepherd community), also enjoyed widespread popularity among the numerous Kunbi peasant communities and other lower-caste groups.

The militant traditions in the Deccan area refer overwhelmingly, however, to the glory of the Maratha Empire and its founder, Shivaji. The legendary Maratha king, Shivaji Maharaj (1627–1680), came from a *patil* (headman) lineage that had obtained *jagirdar* (major landholder) status and ruled an area near Pune. Shivaji organized a small but highly efficient army of peasants and managed in his lifetime to defeat his jagirdar rivals and take on the powerful Mughal Empire in a series of daring raids. The Maratha Kingdom thus created in the Deccan region expanded during the reign of Shivaji's successors, constantly engaged in warfare against the Mughal emperors, particularly Aurangzeb, who, in vain and at huge costs, tried to subdue the vigorous Maratha armies. The governance of the Maratha Empire was gradually taken over by a group of Chitpavan Brahmans (see below), who were initially able ministers and administrators, but in 1713 the first Chitpavan *Peshwa* (chief minister or ruler) was appointed. The Peshwa rulers expanded their powers and influence throughout the subcontinent in the following century, until they met their defeat at the hands of the British in 1818.

The Maratha Confederacy was a loose network of alliances between various princes paying tribute to the Peshwa in Pune, sustained by the dynamic Maratha armies—led by, and loyal to, a number of Maratha *sardars* (military commanders)—who had control over large areas (Gordon 1994, 82–99; Kadam 1993, 13–30). The administration of the empire was relatively weak, nor did the empire produce long-term political or economic cohesion. The result of the Peshwa rule was, however, that the Brahmans—especially the Chitpavans—acquired unprecedented power and came to exercise a social and political domination which, despite their small numbers, rivaled that of the much larger and well-entrenched Maratha elite.

The kingdom and reign of Shivaji, his struggle against Mughal power, and the might of the Maratha Confederacy serves today as an important mythical reservoir for virtually all political forces seeking justification in the region's history. As in most cases of contested historical interpretation, the richness of the sources and evidence makes them susceptible to several interpretations, depending on the political agenda and ideological front at a given time.. Here, I wish to cite the three most influential interpretations of the Maratha past and examine the context and social environments in which they arose.

Undoubtedly the most influential interpretation of the Maratha Confederacy and the region's history is the one first advanced by the liberal reformer of western India, M. G. Ranade, in his *Rise of Maratha Power* (Ranade 1961). According to this rendition, which in many ways was further developed by G. S. Sardesai's massive *New History of the Marathas* written in the 1930s (Sardesai 1986), the region was unified for centuries by a shared language (Maharashtri), which subsequently was developed into modern Marathi, and a relatively incorporative social structure with a shared cultural ethos. Shivaji tried to unite all the various Marathi speakers in his kingdom, and his attempts to instill a sense of cohesion and community was made possible by the relaxation of caste divisions in the wake of the bhakti movements which, in Ranade's view, made a more egalitarian and integrative religious community possible. Ranade's account emphasized the emergence of an incorporative regional spirit, the *Maharashtra dharma*, defined by language and specific religious practices.

With the formation of the state of Maharashtra in 1960, this regionalist emphasis of the existence of an integrative Maharashtra dharma informing the culture and institutions of the area became the basis of subsequent official history books. This official discourse has promoted the idea that the autochthonous registers of patriotic attachments to land, locality, and culture enabled Marathas to resist what a liberal political scientist called the "fury of the Muslim onslaught" (Sirsikar 1995, 33). This allegedly independent spirit made Maharashtrians pioneers in the formation of nationalism, in social reform, industrialization, the development of an independent press, modern art forms, and so on, as argued by B. R. Sunthankar in his account of modern Maharashtrian history, a work sponsored by the chief minister of Maharashtra (Sunthankar 1993, 170–97). Sunthankar's work is indicative of this broader trend of inclusivist historical writing that uses the terms *Maharashtrian* and *Maratha* more or less interchangeably. With provincial zeal, every Maharashtrian hero and eminent personality, from conservative nationalists like Chiplunkar and Tilak to reformers sharply opposed to Brahmanical Hinduism like Jotirao Phule and Ambedkar, are listed as testimonies to the evolution of the same great spirit. Sunthankar reluctantly includes a few Muslims like M. A. Jinnah in his list of eminent personalities, but otherwise the notion of Maharashtra dharma is quite evidently based on the exclusion of Muslims. In a section on conflicts between Hindus and Muslims, Sunthankar argues that because "Islam does not recognize the world outside the territory of its own," it was inevitable that "Muslims, by and large, kept aloof from the mainstream of Indian politics" (322).

Another interpretation of Shivaji emphasized the non-Brahmanical character and legitimacy of his rule. The non-Brahman reformer Jotirao Phule characterized Shivaji as a "Shudra King"—an heir to what Phule claimed was the pre-Aryan Kshatriyas of the Deccan (O'Hanlon 1985, 264–65). The local Brahmans had denied the Marathas or Kunbi peasantry any Kshatriya status, Phule argued, and Shivaji therefore relied more on the Prabhus, a Kayastha literate community of scribes, for his administration. According to this interpretation, Shivaji opposed the local power of Brahmans in the villages and tried to establish a more direct link between king and subjects. This manifested itself, for instance, in his making privileges and landholdings accessible to the lower-caste Kunbis, who in various ways had distinguished themselves in combat or services to the king. Here, as this interpretation suggests, Shivaji was inspired by the bhakti movement and by pre-Aryan gods like the goddess Bhavani, who, according to the myth, gave Shivaji his invincible sword. Phule and the subsequent non-Brahman movement elaborated a Shivaji mythology in which the takeover of the Maratha Confederacy by the Chitpavan Brahmans was a symbol of treason and oppression, a historical wrong that had to be rectified.

A more recent example of historical scholarship in this vein is V. S. Kadam's *Maratha Confederacy*, which argues that centralization of the empire was weak and has generally been overestimated by Brahman historians merely to serve Brahman self-aggrandizement (Kadam 1993, 49–51). In Kadam's account, the unquestionable center of sovereignty created by Shivaji disintegrated as the Peshwas took over the rule from the descendants of the Chhatrapati. The real power slid back to the dispersed Maratha commanders, who defined power in the subcontinent throughout the eighteenth century (113–33).

The third important interpretation emerged from orthodox Brahman scholars such as Tilak in the late nineteenth century and culminated in the work of V. K. Rajwade in the early twentieth century. According to this interpretation, Shivaji was a Hindu rebel against Muslim domination and an unparalleled military hero whose legitimacy and popularity among his own people arose from his defense of the Hindu religion. Ramdas, the Brahman saint-scholar affiliated with Shivaji, was identified as his supreme spiritual guide. Shivaji's protracted struggle to be recognized as Kshatriya, his lavish coronation, and his use of the symbols of Brahmanical Hinduism were taken as evidence of his deep commitment to Brahmanical Hinduism and his desire to Sanskritize his own caste. Like the other interpretations, this one also served a purpose in the emerging antagonism between Brahmans and Marathas: to claim the Peshwas as legitimate heirs to Shivaji's empire and thus portray themselves, the Chitpavan Brahmans, as legitimate and authoritative spokesmen and interpreters of Hindu culture, Maharashtra dharma, and the national spirit. This portrait of Maharashtra dharma was developed by the conservative Brahman intelligentsia in Pune and other cities in the region, and still today remains the preferred historical narrative among militant and right-wing Hindus.[3]

Chris Bayly has recently argued that modern nationalism in India was shaped and conditioned by older registers of local and regional patriotism that "created conceptual frames, clusters of institutions and popular sentiments which facilitated the rooting of later nationalism. . . . What modernity did was to transform and redirect these emergent identities rather than to invent them ex nihilo" (Bayly 1998, 4–5). The Marathas are, for Bayly, the "paradigmatic example of pre-colonial Indian patriotism" (21) in that the empire was based on a strong inclusivity, with less emphasis on caste boundaries, a reinvigoration of "the traditional Hindu state" and the virtues of Kshatriyas (24), and a popular legitimacy based on the local panchayat institutions.

Bayly's more general point about continuities in what he terms "ideologies of good government" is indeed important. But Bayly downplays, if not ignores, the importance of the new epistemologies and narrative frames that made it possible to imagine and claim "ownership" to a collective past in a radically new way. Bayly is well aware of the longstanding debates among historians of this period, but he is strangely inattentive to the fact that the particular framing of Maharashtrian history to which he subscribes is but one of several fiercely contested historical narratives. Those contested histories are still at the heart of political imaginings in the state.

Let us turn to the historical production of what arguably remains a central discursive axis in Maharashtrian public culture: the antagonism between Brahmans and Marathas and the construction of these caste signifiers as complex ideological poles with broad and deep connotations in history and social practices, and their subsequent crystallization as effective social realities as communities and political identities.

BRAHMANS AND MARATHAS: THE PRODUCTION OF COMMUNITIES AND IDENTITIES

As elsewhere in India, the colonial encounter in western India from the 1830s on produced resistance, reform, and strategic use of the new opportunities opened by Western education and incipient commercialization of agriculture in the Deccan Plateau (Kumar 1968, 151–88). In Pune, Bombay, and smaller cities, a range of new public arenas, newspapers, learned societies, and native associations evolved into a vernacular public sphere. Here, social reformists clashed with the defenders of Hindu orthodoxy reacting to the open challenge to Hindu religion and social customs posed by missionaries.[4] Bombay was the main center for liberal and reformist forces, among whom M. G. Ranade—scholar, civil servant, and later judge at the Bombay High Court—was the mentor and leading inspiration (Tucker 1972)

Another form of reform movement also arose, however. Satyashodhak Samaj (Truth-Seeking Society) was founded in Pune in 1873 by Jotirao Phule, who, inspired by utilitarian philosophy and Christianity, constructed a historical narrative of Deccan society as having evolved from a community of Shudra peasant cultivators. According to Phule, this community was imbued with robust, earthy, and egalitarian values of a harmonious pre–Aryan Golden Age destroyed by the conquest and subsequent domination of northern Aryan Brahmanical groups, who distorted and perverted the social order (O'Hanlon 1985, 251). The Satyashodhak Samaj created a network of educational institutions, magazines, newspapers, publishing houses, and charity trusts independent of the Brahman establishment in the provincial cities in Deccan. In line with other reformers at the time, the early non-Brahman leaders regarded the imposition of British rule as a historical opportunity for reform and revitalization of an ancient civilization suffering under centuries of rigid, hierarchical, and overly ritualized Brahman dominance. The non-Brahman movement regarded Brahmanical hegemony as a "colonialism within colonialism" (Gavaskar 1995) and its removal a precondition for any endeavors toward self-rule.

Both the reformists and the non-Brahman movement were in constant conflict with the Hindu orthodoxy and revivalist forces that found their leading and most eloquent spokesmen among the Chitpavan Brahmans in the old Peshwa capital of Pune. Chitpavan Brahmans, originally from the coastal belt in Konkan, had, through the rule of the Peshwa dynasty, established themselves in western India, both as landowners, administrators, officers, and intellectuals. This small community (a few percent of the population) only acquired this position after protracted conflicts with the native Brahmans in Deccan (*Deshastas*), who, for centuries, refused to recognize the purity of the Chitpavans. Over time, however, the extraordinary energy and willingness of the Chitpavans to enter the military and other services earned them both high status and power in Deccan, and especially in Pune[5] (Johnson 1973, 55–68).

The Chitpavan writer and orator Bal Gangadhar Tilak combined orthodoxy with nationalism in innovative ways. Tilak's most successful achievement was to make the worship of the god *Ganesh* into a ritual of nationalism. The Peshwas had occasionally celebrated Ganpatiutsav lavishly over several days of public festivals, but in the nineteenth century the *Ganpatiutsav* had become a family-based festival among the higher castes, concluded by the immersion of a small Ganesh idol in the nearby river.[6]

Riots in August 1893 between Hindus and Muslims in Bombay provided the immediate cause for the reshaping of the festival. Tilak alleged that the riots were instigated through a secret pact between the Muslims and the British, and six weeks later he and his followers turned the annual Ganpatiutsav into a public manifestation of Hindu culture and the Hindu community (Krishnaswamy 1966, 214).

Large Ganesh idols were constructed; dancing parties and *melas* (singing parties) were organized. The organization of this collective endeavor was carried out by local Ganpati *mandals* (committees), which quickly evolved into centers of intense political activity. The festival culminated on the last evening when the idols were carried in large processions from the many neighborhoods to be immersed in the river. Tilak and his followers encouraged the mela songs to be militantly anti-Muslim in tone and meaning (Krishnaswamy 1966, 357–58). The popular response was considerable, and the festival in this public form spread to towns all over Maharashtra. In the following years riots began to occur in connection with the festival, and the authorities forced the organizers to downplay the communal themes during the festival. Though successful in staging public political manifestations of a hitherto unseen magnitude, the anticolonial but also communal implications of the Ganpatiutsav had remained limited to mandals in higher-caste neighborhoods in Pune and provincial cities. Most of the mandals set up in poorer areas populated by Marathas and lower-caste communities initially emphasized religious themes, and their melas rarely took up nationalist issues (Cashman 1970, 360–73).

From 1922 the non-Brahman movement introduced the so-called *Chatrapati melas* that celebrated Shivaji within the Ganpatiutsav. The songs and plays enacted at these melas ridiculed Brahmans, their abuse of power and privilege in Pune, and praised the Marathas as the true people of Deccan and of the nation. These melas offered platforms for a certain carnivalesque and plebeian ridiculing of authority, and for the display of popular forms of Hindu worship. This annoyed the Brahman establishment in Pune. Tilak's newspaper, *Kesari*, which had been instrumental in the initial introduction of the Ganpatiutsav twenty years earlier, recommended that the colonial authorities censor the "indecent language" of the mela songs and control the "mischief of the mobs" celebrating the festivals (Omvedt 1976, 236–37).

The somewhat limited mass appeal of the Ganpatiutsav in its early years prompted Tilak to promote Shivaji as a potentially powerful symbol of regional identity, resistance to foreign domination, and a corporate Hindu identity. Tilak envisaged a systematic popularization of the myth of Shivaji as a national and anti-Muslim hero through an annual festival. He approached the Maratha nobility in the princely states of the Deccan in order to obtain legitimacy and funding of the festival and renovation of the neglected and dilapidated Raigad Fort where Shivaji had been crowned.

The response from the old aristocratic Maratha elite was hesitant and lukewarm, and the first three Shivaji festivals, which took place in the years 1895–97, were only modestly attended. The liberal Brahmans found Tilak's interpretation of Shivaji too violent and aggressive, and the Maharaja of Kolhapur, a direct descendant of Shivaji, strongly opposed Tilak and the Pune Brahmans. Instead, the Maharaja lent his support to the celebrations of Shivaji initiated by the non-Brahman Satyashodhak Samaj from 1895 on (Cashman 1975, 98–121). Through these competing representations, the cult of Shivaji was gradually invented, and it spread to Bombay and elsewhere in the Bombay Presidency. Most of the myths and tales of Shivaji were given their modern form at around the turn of the century. In 1900 a major reenactment of Shivaji's coronation ceremony at Raigad was organized, and it was decided to celebrate Shivaji Jyanti every year in April to commemorate the death of the Chhatrapati.

Historically the term *Maratha* emerged in the seventeenth century from being an imprecise designation for speakers of Marathi to become a title of martial honor and entitlements earned by Deccan peasants serving as cavalry men in the armies of Muslim rulers and later in Shivaji's armies. Like the term *Rajput*, the term *Maratha* traveled from being a relational term designating a particular military service to become a marker of an endogamous caste.[7]

The exact empirical boundaries of the Maratha caste cannot be established without looking at the past in terms of the present. Nineteenth-century sources allow several interpretations. In the *District Gazetteer of Thane* from 1882, for instance, Kunbis, Agris and Kolis were all described as discrete castes, and yet, within each, elite layers were called "Maratha-Agris," "Maratha-Kolis" (115–29), and so on, which indicated the use of the Maratha label as a symbol of superiority even within caste groups not connected to Marathas in endogamous terms. In the *District Gazetteer of Pune* from 1882, Kunbis were described as falling into two classes, Kunbis and Marathas, that could not be clearly discerned (p. 284). In the 1931 census Marathas and Kunbis were lumped together in one category.

The Marathas' political dominance and traditional control of land and military power made them a central category in the Deccan, the designator that held all the other elements in their place. In spite of an elaborate kinship system organized around the *ghar* (family), *kula* (clan—ninety-six in all), *devak* (totem), and *bhaubund* (patrilinear local group), the openness and flexibility of these categories meant that Marathas never constituted a jati in any conventional sense. Although rules of endogamy were adhered to at some levels, the community was, if at all, united at the level of what has been called "fictitious kinship"—local alliances, loyalties, and affinities that bound groups of Marathas internally and established links with other caste communities (Lomova-Oppokova 1999).

The leadership of the Satyashodhak Samaj was drawn mainly from the educated urban strata of Phule's own *Mali* (gardener) community but also from Maratha-Kunbis and other lower castes. In the 1880s these leaders began an extensive touring of the rural districts, where they held mass rallies, set up schools, and extended the organization throughout the countryside. The movement also promoted what it called "Kshatriya dharma," the performance of religious rites without the assistance of Brahmans. Phule preferred designating the cultivating castes as Shudra and found the Maratha designation exclusive and narrow, a term carrying too many of the hierarchical connotations of the Brahmanical ideology of *varna* (literally color, referring to the four main caste categories as defined in Sanskrit texts) he had criticized all his life.

From 1900 the non-Brahman movement came under the leadership of Shahu Maharaj—a descendant of Shivaji and a representative of the Maratha aristocracy. In this period the discourse of the Satyashodhak movement increasingly began to refer to and define Marathas as a broader social category. There was also a gradual merger at the local level with the incipient Maratha caste organizations that concerned themselves mainly with education. When Shahu left the organization in 1920 the Satyashodhak Samaj ceased to exist, but the effects of the broad non-Brahman mobilization seemed both remarkable and largely irreversible: Brahmans and Marathas had turned into collective identities of a rather different character than they had in the nineteenth century. Through conflict, confrontation, and organization, they had, like other groups such as the Malis, Dhangars, Prabhus, and Mahars, turned into castes "for themselves," that is, they had assumed political and social identities that made them into more well-bounded social groups.

In 1920 leaders of the Maratha League and the Deccan Ryots Association formed the Non-Brahman Party. Both organizations had been created to campaign for separate non-Brahman electorates according to the provisions made possible by the Montagu-Chelmsford electoral reforms of 1919. The government had granted seven reserved seats in Deccan to non-Brahmans, which, under the name "Marathas and allied castes," comprised virtually all peasant castes. The British administration interpreted the lack of support for the Congress movement in Deccan as an indication of the Marathas' loyalty toward the Raj. Indeed, for decades, Marathas, as well as the untouchable Mahar community, had been preferred as recruits for the colonial army, as well as police in the Bombay Presidency, and this practice continued during World War II. As Epstein notes, specific developmental programs were planned in the 1940s for these districts as recognition of the Marathas' contribution to the empire (Epstein 1988, 84–85).

Largely ignoring nationalist politics of the Congress Party in the 1920s, the Non-Brahman Party saw the Brahman elite in Pune as its main opponent. Despite intense criticism from the nationalist press, the constant confrontations with Brahman orthodoxy enabled the activists of the Non-Brahman Party to mobilize broadly among the Maratha and non-Brahman groups in Pune and other cities and gain a high degree of visibility during festivals and political campaigns.

In this conflict women and women's bodies became central metaphors for the purity and strength of communities. Orthodox Brahmans feared the "desecration" of Brahman women if touched, or raped, by the stereotypical rustic, strong, but primitive Maratha men. The assault of a Brahman girl by a young Maratha man in Pune in 1926, and the resulting court case where the young man was defended by B. R. Ambedkar, the untouchable leader, whipped up sentiments in the Brahman community. Counterattacks were launched against non-Brahmans, and petitions were sent to the colonial government requesting that it protect the respectable Brahman community against the non-Brahman "mobs" and "hoodlums." At the Ganpatiutsavs in the 1920s non-Brahman melas openly, and sarcastically, played on how non-Brahman men desired the fair-skinned Brahman women, and constantly hinted at the allegedly immoral abuse of widowed woman (who were not allowed to remarry) within Brahman families (Omvedt 1976, 236–41).

The allegedly close and rather friendly relationship between the colonial power and the non-Brahman movement remains a sore point in Maharashtrian history. As Véronique Bénéï (1999) has shown recently, the publication of the first *District Gazetteer* in Marathi in 1989, one of the many moves made by Chief Minister Sharad Pawar's administration to bolster regional identity, generated considerable controversy in Kolhapur in western Maharashtra. As Bénéï argues, the actual fact of the friendly relation between Shahu Maharaj and the British, depicted by the *Gazetteer*, did not seem to be the contentious issue per se; rather, it was the style in which these were recorded and inscribed into an official government publication, thus giving the period the stamp of official truth. This controversy, which stirred the wrath of political parties and organizations from the Congress Party to Shiv Sena, amply demonstrated that the location of the non-Brahman movement and the mythology of the proud Maratha as the quintessential Maharashtrian remains unstable and fraught with ambivalence.

THE "MARATHA'IZATION" OF MAHARASHTRA

From 1930 on, many younger leaders from the Non-Brahman Party joined Congress in its civil disobedience campaigns. Brahmans of Gandhian persuasion and younger non-Brahmans made their first joint efforts in the famous Mahad Satyagrahas, organized by Bhimrao Ambedkar, as a protest against the refusal to allow untouchables to enter temples. This was far from unproblematic as several non-Brahmans refused to work with Brahmans and demanded that Ambedkar should rid his movement of its substantial number of activists of Brahman birth. Marathas often found it difficult to show due respect to the Mahar activists in the movement, and they strongly opposed Ambedkar's controversial public burning in 1927 of the *Manusmriti*, the ancient Hindu law book (Gokhale 1993, 99–107).

The mass support built over decades among peasants in the Deccan and elsewhere in the Bombay Presidency around the non-Brahman ideology—increasingly condensed in a single signifier, the Maratha—was now gradually incorporated into the nationalist movement. This inclusion introduced a subtle change of profile and leadership as the antagonism between Brahmans and Marathas gradually was reenacted within the Congress as a symbol of difference and contradiction.

Maratha was becoming the most potent symbol in the political imaginary in Maharashtra, capable of binding together extensive metonymic chains: Maratha denoted martiality, the legacy of Shivaji, true Hindus, rural virtues, cooperative strength, regional identity, non-Brahmanism, and bhakti tradition; whereas Brahman stood for effeminacy, legacy of the Peshwas, urban culture, learning (and arrogance), pan-Indian solidarity, and so on. The gradual "Maratha-ization" of a Congress Party that was ever more firmly rooted in the countryside further alienated the orthodox Brahmans from the wider nationalist movement.

Two events after independence further entrenched the link between Congress and the Maratha identity. First, the extension of universal franchise gave the non-Brahman and Maratha leaders a large potential mass base given the widespread resentment of Brahmans in many rural areas in Deccan. Second, the murder of Gandhi by a Chitpavan Brahman in 1948 boosted anti-Brahman feelings throughout western India. Brahman homes and estates were burned, and families and individuals attacked several places in western Maharashtra, Pune, and the Nagpur region (Patterson 1988). Although part of this rage was spontaneous, it was also subtly encouraged by non-Brahman Congress leaders who sought to establish their credentials in the party.

After independence, political power in Maharashtra became not only "Maratha'ized" but also inextricably tied to the structures of power and patronage in the rural districts of Deccan, where the cooperative movement became pivotal in the evolution of commercial agriculture (Attwood 1993, 74–121). Sugarcane growing and the cooperative structure also became the single largest source of patronage in rural politics in Maharashtra. If the sugar growers united behind a political party—as they had for decades behind the Congress—their influence on the party at all levels and their ability to mobilize massive electoral support in rural areas made it very difficult to rule the state without their support.

The consolidation of the Congress Party in Maharashtra into one of the most effective and smooth "political machines" in modern India was directly linked to its being embedded in the heart of the rural economy. The Congress machine derived its strength from a large network of institutions, such as educational societies that ran private colleges and secondary schools, affiliated hostels, the granting of scholarships to students from disadvantaged backgrounds, and so on (Rosenthal 1977, 159–90).

Another crucial arena of politics was the Panchayati Raj institutions. Party politics was supposed to be kept out of these institutions in order to let local democracy blossom and produce new leadership at the district level, as the Naik Commission recommended in 1961.[8] However, many political careers were launched within these institutions, and the presidents of the Zilla Parishads at the district level became powerful local figures whose influence soon rivaled that of the members of the Legislative Assembly (MLAs). An official study in 1974 deplored the fact that Panchayati Raj had encouraged politics rather than promoting development: "politics has been entering village life very rapidly thereby dividing the once peaceful and united villages into factions and groups not necessarily wedded to any political ideology but on the basis of loyalty to individuals" (Narain 1974, 117).

The resilience of the Congress Party's power and the size and ostensible might of the Maratha-Kunbi caste cluster thus gave rise to the most solid construction in the contemporary political imaginaries in Maharashtra: that the party is but an expression of the dominance of the Maratha caste. The solidity of this myth testifies to how successfully political leaders in the Congress Party have constructed the Maratha designation as a powerful symbol, one to which, over time, they have added considerable empirical strength as a political and social identity. I contend that the construction of a Maratha-Brahman antagonism as an ideological and political structure made it possible to generalize and simplify a large number of dispersed cultural differences and localized practices into opposed cultural systems and cosmologies. This in turn produced and gave substance to the Maratha-Kunbi caste cluster as a meaningful identity with very real effects in the social world.

I propose, in other words, that caste is an idiom of kinship that coexists and intersects with a variety of other social idioms that offer loci of identification. Discourses of kinship—of jati, kula, devak, and so on—may be employed to create a network of patronage that generates political careers and clout within a party and government. They may also be deployed to construct common interests among commercial farmers, and to carve out a moral ground for demands and rights by espousing the pure, rural, and rustic virtues of the *bahujan samaj* as opposed to the depraved and degenerate urban elite.

Maratha has been turned into a grand symbol out of multiple resources gathered by rich and middle peasants, by political entrepreneurs, by non-Brahman ideologues constructing "Maratha-ness" out of a Kshatriya as well as a Varkari tradition, by rural and urban educators, by cooperative innovators, some of whom belonged to Kunbi or Maratha-*Kulas* and who, in the contested arenas of local politics or the cooperative movement, used their caste as a constituency and claim to legitimacy. In other words, *Maratha* does not denote a continuity of caste understood as an empirical collectivity of individuals held together by a hegemonic elite, as Lele (1990) suggests. Rather, it signifies a continuity of an idiom of kinship— of "Maratha-ness" as an ideological position reinvoked and reinterpreted again and again by older and new ascending elites, over time acquiring its own materiality in social practice as those encompassed by the caste community begin to practice this new homogenized Maratha-ness.[9]

In this perspective, the linking of the term *Maratha* to sugarcane and the Congress Party is only the latest addition to the list of complex signifiers around which the ethnohistorical and political imagination are constructed in modern Maharashtra. I have mentioned the cult of Shivaji, the notion of the Brahman *"bhatji"* with rich historical connotations associated with the rule of the Peshwas, and the notion of Maharashtra dharma as other central and complex signifiers. As I will try to demonstrate in the following chapters, these signifiers have become what Reinhard Koselleck calls *Begriffe*, that is, concepts that stand apart from ordinary words or notions because they cannot be precisely defined by a referent but possess a substantial claim of generality and always have many different meanings. Such historically evolved concepts of high density and complexity are, like Kripke's, "rigid designators" marked by resilience over time and an ability actually to define a context, a range of connotations, and a whole semantic field, rather than be easily defined by a new context and new discourses (Koselleck 1985).

The ethnohistorical imagination in Maharashtra is structured around the central concepts I have discussed, all endowed with rich and deep connotations. It is these concepts that make it meaningful and significant for boys in Mumbai slums to build replicas of the Raigad Fort of Shivaji's time, and it is also why the invocation of Maratha bravery, or Brahman cowardice, as we shall see, makes such eminent sense in political speeches in Mumbai in the 1990s.

CHAPTER 2

Bombay and the Politics of Urban Desire

AMBIGUITIES OF THE URBAN

Bombay, from its inception, was regarded by Marathi-speaking intellectuals as an alien substance in the land, a bridgehead of imperial culture and modernity that was fascinating, yet parasitical on the population of the inland territories (Kosambi 1995, 16–22). The desire to domesticate Bombay within a Marathi social and linguistic world was strongly expressed in the 1950s and continued to fuel the political imagination in the state in the 1990s. Historically Bombay has always been described in deeply ambiguous terms, both as a site of innovation, creativity, and power but also of amorality, congestion, and social evils. Bombay was the ultimate modern Indian city, the imaginary space amply represented in the Bombay cinema, within which the dangers, virtues, intensity, loss, and loneliness of modernity and urban culture were negotiated. Bombay was the metropolis of western India, but the film industry made it into a national city—an epitome of the incipient Indian modern. In an essay on the cultural effects of representative democracy, Kaviraj discusses the images of Bombay invoked by the cinema and film songs of the 1950s as lonely, stressful, but also full of promise: "Still, the city was, in a Baudelairean way, beautiful—degrading, freeing, mysterious, corrupting rustics by its freedom. The city was both joyous and fearsome precisely because of the logic of democracy—of a mixing, of a leveling of a certain kind" (Kaviraj 1998, 152–53).

As we shall see in the following chapters, these notions of Bombay as both national and modern, but also the home of amoral, excessive, and corrupted elites and lifestyles, were all pivotal in the linguistic movement in the 1950s and has remained central to the agrarian populism of the Congress Party. In the next three chapters I will try to show, furthermore, that the history of Shiv Sena's aggressively populist discourses over the last three decades also amounts to an ongoing negotiation of "the urban" and the experience of urban culture. Shiv Sena has clearly emerged as the foremost promoter of the urban and the modern in Maharashtra: in its street-smart jargon and its use of popular slang and other symbols of popular assertiveness; in its mobilization and reliance on young, mobile, and plebeian men as activists and audience, celebrating their independence, masculinity, and self-reliance through the Shiv Sena; and in its unapologetic enjoyment and celebration of the pleasures and possibilities of modern urban life—technology, consumption, good jobs, sumptuous living, and the music, dance, and aesthetics of the Hindi film.

BOMBAY "CLASSIQUE" AND ITS DEMISE

Bombay grew into the leading commercial center of British India in the nineteenth century on the basis of textile mills and overseas trade. The city was, first and foremost, built and developed by an indigenous industrial and commercial bourgeoisie comprising Parsis, Gujarati Hindus, and Muslim communities earning their wealth on the extensive Arabian trade, along with Jews, Armenians, and others (Chandavarkar 1994, 21–70).[1] The textile industry, as well as a host of others, continued to grow throughout the 1940s, making Bombay the industrial and financial capital of India. The expanding labor force in Bombay was initially drawn from the coastal belt of Konkan, south of the city. After the famine in the Deccan area in the 1870s, large numbers of Maratha-Kunbis and other peasant castes of the Deccan and Gujarat arrived in the city. Until the 1940s Marathi speakers from these areas accounted for about half the city's population, and held mostly manual and unskilled jobs. The business community was, from the outset, dominated by Parsi, Marwari, Muslim, and Gujarati merchants and industrialists, who owned most of the capital and in vital ways dominated the public and political life of Bombay in the nineteenth and first half of the twentieth centuries. Among these elite groups that eagerly promoted the cosmopolitan, modern, and non-Maharashtrian character of Bombay, the Parsi community was the most powerful and the most loyal supporters of colonial rule. As Tanya Luhrmann has pointed out in a study of the trajectory of Parsi identity, the period between the mid-nineteenth century and the 1930s saw a remarkable metamorphosis of the Parsi community from a trading community of the Gujarat coast to the most Westernized and well-organized colonial elite in India. Many Parsis saw the establishment of British rule as a decisive and fortuitous event that permitted the release of what was seen as "dormant qualities that lay concealed in the Parsi bosom" during centuries of existence at the fringe of a predominantly Hindu society (Luhrmann 1996, 97–125).

In this period Bombay also became home to some of the most successful Gujarati entrepreneurs, a large concentration of Gujarati speakers, and a leading center in the formation of modern Gujarati culture and intellectual life; in brief, it became "the cradle of modern Gujarat" (Mallison 1995, 76–87).

It was in the first half of the twentieth century when "classical" Bombay took shape as a bustling industrial city, marked by imposing imperial designs and architecture, by elegant elite areas, and large and expanding working-class neighborhoods in the mill districts. More than any other city in the subcontinent, Bombay attracted large groups of people from many corners of India and emerged as the quintessential modern Indian city and the hub of organized capitalism, working-class culture, trade unions, and modern institutions of all kinds.[2]

In the spheres of cultural production, leisure, and consumption, this classical Bombay blossomed in the 1950s and 1960s. Celebrations of Bombay's diversity, no-nonsensical atmosphere, and creativity abound in the many travelogues and city guides one can pick up at any book vendor around the central Fountain Square in the Fort area and are often reproduced in academic work on the subject.[3] The city was marked by an intrinsic restlessness and modernity, a place where older affiliations and loyalties were swamped and subsumed by the all-pervasive logic of money and business. If class emerged as the foremost metaphor of Bombay's social worlds in much academic work, the key markers in popular discourses were, as Appadurai notes, those of "business" and money in its most fluid but pregnant form: cash. In this "cosmopolis of commerce . . . people met in and through 'business' (a word which is taken over from English and used to indicate professions, transactions, deals and a whole ethos of commerce) and through 'business' forged and reproduced links across neighborhoods, ethnicities and regional origins" (Appadurai 2000).

The medium of exchange in Bombay, more than anywhere else, was cash, and Bombay was, Appadurai suggests, a "city of cash," full of sensual appeal, moral ambiguity, and a vehicle of a fluid and highly evanescent status and power (Appadurai 2000).

Bombay's "Bollywood" film industry grew rapidly as it received intense political attention and new sources of governmental funding after 1947. This enabled the industry to embark on technological innovations and to establish rather effective systems for nationwide distribution that soon established the Bombay cinema as the dominant national film industry and as a crucial site for negotiating changes in ideological representations of the nation, family, romance, class, and community (Prasad 1998, 29–51, 52–113). Many films were set in and around Bombay, and the enormous growth in spectatorship and cinema halls throughout the country meant that millions of Indians saw the city in terms of the glamorous life of film stars, the home of intense desires for individual success, fame, and riches. The films provided shared symbols and star icons, and their often hugely popular songs were heard across the country. Bombay was known and celebrated as the "city of gold," but the film industry added new and important layers to this mythical place. As Gangar puts it, "Bombay is simply a *swapaneer nagari*—a city of dreams. It is a generic city that exists everywhere in India in various forms" (Gangar 1995, 210).

The decades following independence also witnessed rapid growth. Around the turn of the century the city had approximately one million inhabitants and twice that number in 1941, but from 1951 to 1971 the population more than doubled to around six million, making the greater Bombay area the largest urban agglomeration in the subcontinent. The industrial license system designed in the 1950s led to a remarkable diversification and growth in the industrial base in Maharashtra and Bombay. The previous dependence on the textile and consumer goods sectors gave way to a sustained growth in machine manufacturing, chemical industry, shipbuilding, electrical engineering, and many other heavy and technically advanced industries.

Apart from putting heavy strains on the civic facilities of Bombay and initiating a fast expansion of the city northward, the continued centralization of capital and production in Bombay, even on a national scale, presented a difficult political problem. After the formation of Maharashtra as a unilingual state in 1960, strong political forces based in towns and villages in the Deccan demanded that the wealth generated in the city and the dynamism of its entrepreneurial spirit should be spread out in order to benefit the development of the entire state.

Various government commissions from the 1950s on had drafted policies to decongest Bombay and to spread industrial investments to the rural hinterland. Industrial restructuring arrived, however, in a less-regulated form. From the late 1970s a spectacular industrial growth began to take place in small flexible industries in Bombay and Thane (Harris 1995, 52). Here, industries could escape trade unions avoid labor regulations, and evade tax requirements, and soon this sector emerged as an indispensable network of subcontractors and auxiliary industries to many of the larger companies.[4] The large textile strike in Bombay in 1982–83, which paralyzed the large mills in central Bombay for more than eighteen months, intensified this development (see van Wersch 1992). During and after this strike, small, labor-intensive power loom industries employing short-term hired labor on insecure contractual terms at very low wage levels were mushrooming in the greater Bombay area. Besides price competitiveness based on a savage exploitation of labor in places like Bhiwandi, the power loom industries offered a flexibility and rapid delivery that for some years enabled the large, and trimmed, textile mills to maintain acceptable profit margins.

In the entire Bombay-Pune area, construction of houses, apartments, and infrastructure, as well as real estate brokerage, turned into the most profitable economic sector, enabling the lucky and politically well-connected entrepreneur to grow very rich in only a few years. As will become evident in the following chapters, the political economy of construction and real estate has considerably affected political stakes and dramatically transformed the character of urban politics in the 1980s.

These transformations of Bombay's political economy over the last three to four decades laid the framework for the growth of new movements and new cultural phenomena—in particular, the ever stronger quest for incorporating and domesticating the city within the parameters of a vernacular political imaginary. The demise of the configuration of social, political, and cultural forces that dominated classical Bombay, first in its economic organization and later in politics and culture, meant that hitherto widespread languages of contention in the city also began to change. The discourses of caste and community entitlements that had developed and matured in provincial cities and rural districts in Maharashtra began, from the 1950s, to merge and combine in new ways with the multiple distinctions of class, education, community, and social respectability that historically had operated in Bombay. The first most decisive and far-reaching process of reorganization of political discourse and institutions in this direction was undoubtedly the emergence of the movement for a unilingual state of Maharashtra.

THE EMERGENCE OF REGIONAL IDENTITIES: *SAMYUKTA MAHARASHTRA SAMITI*

In the 1920s the Congress Party was reorganized along linguistic lines, making the regions important loci of political identity and mobilization. As still more activists from the non-Brahman movement in Maharashtra drifted toward the Congress in the 1930s, it became imperative to develop some consensus regarding the contested meanings of Maharashtra dharma. The issue continued to ferment in literary and intellectual circles in Maharashtra and gradually a new "syndicated" version of Maharashtra dharma and ethnohistory emerged. Shivaji was no longer merely signifying Marathas but the ethos of all Marathi speakers, and the Hindu culture of the region was eulogized as more authentic and more firmly rooted in the common people than elsewhere in the subcontinent because of the historical strength of the popular *bhakti* (devotional) traditions in the region.

In 1939 an organization called Samyukta Maharashtra Sabha was formed by a group of writers and intellectuals, among them K. S. Thackeray, father of the later Shiv Sena chief, Bal Thackeray. The Sabha, who comprised both right-wing intellectuals and prominent Communists, began to propagate the idea of a unified Marathi-speaking state by pointing to the plight of the Marathi speakers, who constituted the majority of the Bombay Presidency but, according to the Sabha, were exploited by alien *Shethjis* and *Banias*, that is, moneylenders and urban capitalists belonging to the Parsi, Gujarati, and Marwari communities. The Samyukta movement wanted the city of Bombay, in which Marathi was the most widely spoken language, to belong to a Marathi-speaking state, but the city's economic and political elite feared that Bombay would decline under a government committed to developing the rural hinterland.

With the formation of Samyukta Maharashtra Samiti (SMS) in 1946, a remarkable ideological convergence took place. Radical non-Brahman leaders saw the demand for a monolingual state as a way to ensure non-Brahman social mobility and public assertion. The "alien" Gujarati Shethjis thus took the place of the Bhatjis (priests/Brahmans) as the primary enemy of the ordinary Marathi speaker. The Marathi language became the privileged symbol of community and history that united Brahmans with non-Brahmans. The non-Brahman leaders also seemed to realize that the notion of the Maratha as a signifier of the ordinary people could only become effective within a monolingual state. To the socialists and Communists in the movement, the portrayal of the Gujarati, Parsi, or Marwari communities as alien parasites appeared as anti-capitalism in new guises that depicted the Bombay industrialists as antagonistic to the interests of the common people.

Under heavy and concerted pressure from business interests in Bombay, it was decided to grant Bombay the status of Union Territory in order to prevent it from slipping into the hands of the movement for a monolingual state, which conservative forces regarded as a Trojan horse of the Left. However, the Congress leadership in Bombay had clearly underestimated the force of popular emotions that had erupted over the issue. On January 16, 1956, Nehru announced the decision to declare Bombay a Union Territory, and large demonstrations immediately ensued. The Bombay police dissolved the mass meetings and arrested several of the movement's leaders. Later the same day, police fired at demonstrators protesting the arrests, which set off a series of riots over the following six days. More than eighty persons were killed by police gunfire during this period (Phadke 1979, 155).

These events became known as the "Battle for Bombay," and those killed by the police were praised as martyrs (*hutatmas*) for the Maharashtrian cause by the Samyukta Maharashtra Samiti. Some of the anger was allegedly directed against Gujaratis, and a considerable number of Gujarati families left the city after the riots.

Shortly after these events the SMS formed a united political front, consisting of almost all non-Congress parties, and over the following three years launched a protracted campaign for a unilingual state. This successful campaign portrayed Maharashtrians—now all Marathi speakers, Marathas as well as Brahmans—with their purer and uncontaminated Hindu culture as pitted against Bombay's urbanized, Westernized, decadent urban elite and politicians.

Beneath this high-pitched cultural populism, which left many traces in the ethnohistorical imaginary, the movement, although united in its goal of achieving statehood, was a rather fragile coalition of disparate forces that never became organized into a permanent structure. The cohesion of the movement, therefore, vitally depended on the determined resistance it faced from the political establishment. The confrontation with the Bombay police and the martyrdom of the *hutatmas* in 1956 gave the movement an almost irresistible momentum throughout the following months and reinforced the split within the Congress Party over the issue.

In the following years the linguistic movement won significant electoral victories in general elections and even managed to win a majority in the Bombay Municipal Corporation in 1957.[5] When the state of Maharashtra finally was formed in 1960, the Samyukta Maharashtra Samiti had already more or less disintegrated. Ironically Y. B. Chavan, who for years had opposed the formation of the state, emerged as the de facto creator of a unilingual Maharashtra through an adroit merging of disparate regions into a single administrative unit.

The broad popular support for the SMS undoubtedly had been an outlet for a range of local disgruntlements. As a chronicler of the movement concluded, with some disappointment, the popular reception of a Marathi identity had probably been rather feeble:

> By the hindsight of history it is easy to conclude that the voters were neither fascinated by the programme of the Samiti nor were they perturbed, as Dange [Communist leaders—T.B.H.] fondly believed, by the corruption in the administration or the failure of Congress to solve the problems of the toiling poor. In fact the moment the CHC [Congress High Command] decided to split the bilingual state, the toiling masses in Maharashtra promptly turned towards the Congress and continued to support it despite its miserable record and poor performance as the party in power. (Phadke 1979, 247)

The most important effect of the SMS was that with the vigorous campaigns of the 1950s, the vernacular press and Marathi-speaking intellectuals had rallied around a single narrative of the emergence of a Marathi-speaking people, unique in their courage and independence, not to be subdued by Muslim invaders, and, indeed, the first real Indian nationalists. The importance of this religious supplement—Hindu and anti-Muslim— to the regional/linguistic construction of a Maharashtra dharma was brought out succinctly in a recent biography of former chief minister and Congress strongman Sharad Pawar. Speaking of the uniqueness of the Marathas, the author writes:

One must remember that after the decline of Moghul supremacy it was Maratha who established Indian self-rule . . . The Maratha power sought to establish a central *Hindu Padshahi* or empire in Delhi controlling all other rulers
. . . and to retrieve as much land as possible from the Muslims. (Ravindranath
1992, 23–24)

Congress tried in the following years to capture this legacy in practices of
naming, in the writing of history books, in celebrations of Shivaji, and so
on. The Flora Fountain Square in Bombay's Fort area was renamed Hutatma Chowk (Martyr Square), commemorating the victims of the battle
of Bombay. But the main emphasis was on consolidating the hold over the
vast rural hinterland and to depict Marathas not only as the core constituency of the party but as the heart of the new state.

In May 1960 leading academics in the state were called on by the chief
minister, Y. B. Chavan, to analyze the obstacles confronting the new state.
In his opening address Chavan reminded the audience of "the special responsibility of the intellectual class in drafting plans and visions for the
future of the state of Maharashtra" (Ganghadhar 1960, 3). A judge of the
Bombay High Court urged the academics to "make a concentrated effort
to sustain the cosmopolitan character of Bombay . . . just as Bombay must
take an interest in the life of Maharashtra—its culture and traditions" (9).
The deep historical rifts between disparate narratives of the regional history and the antagonistic relationship between the concept of Maratha
and that of the Brahman persisted, however, and could not easily be pa-
pered over by exhortations of the new Maharashtrian spirit.

In a paper entitled "Social Problems in Maharashtra," Prof. T. K. Tope
deplored the attacks on Brahmans in 1948 after the assassination of Gandhi. In a slightly condescending tone, Tope ascribed the attacks to the fact
that "followers of Phule did not understand his philosophy and turned it
into a revolt against the Brahman class as such" (Tope 1960, 117). He
suggested that "Bhakti saints and Shivaji are promoted into leading symbols of the new state as that will bridge caste differences" (119) and fore-
saw that Marathas would dominate the new state. "In the new Maharashtra, Marathas will conduct the affairs of state. They will not be the critics
of the state, but its administrators. . . . [T]he Brahmans should accept self-
imposed restrictions in the public sphere and not aspire for political leadership but help in education and industry" (122). But Tope did not believe
that all was lost for the Brahmans. On the contrary he quoted Nehru,
stating that "socialism is not unlike the old Brahman idea of service, but
it means Brahmanisation of all classes and groups and the abolition of class
distinctions" (123).

On a more high-pitched note, poet and author P. Y. Deshpande asked
how "the emotional integration" produced by the "the triumph of the

popular will [the linguistic movement—T.B.H.] against the steel frame
of modern power politics" could be retained (Deshpande 1960, 125).
Deshpande warned artists and creative intellectuals against getting too
closely involved in "power politics" and called, instead, for "a cultural
platform that can ensure the ethical standards of public life . . . and to
enrich the creativity, spontaneity and culture that tend to dry out in the
face of modern mechanisation" (130).

Underneath these and other statements from this landmark seminar
lurked not only the fear of "modern mechanisation" but the fear of what
the elevation of predominantly Maratha politicians from the rural hinterland would do to the management of political affairs in the state and in
the city of Bombay. Here, among higher-caste intellectuals, as well as in
innumerable other discussions of public ethos and civic sense from the
period, it was clear that notions of "power politics," "electoral politics,"
and so on, all referred to a sphere of unruliness and contamination that
increasingly slipped out of control as peasants and lower-caste politicians
invaded this part of the public culture. As we shall see, neither Brahman
intellectuals nor artists were able to revitalize and capitalize on the legacy
of the linguistic movement. Instead, Shiv Sena reframed the cultural populism of the linguistic movement into an aggressive and xenophobic style
of politics.

THE GROWTH OF BOMBAY AND THE BIRTH OF SHIV SENA

The creation of Maharashtra in 1960 generated enthusiasm and high expectations among many Marathi speakers, who were now promised the
city of Bombay—the new capital of Maharashtra—as their place in the
world, as a Marathi cultural space, and as a site of economic prosperity
and social mobility. Yet, uneasiness with urban life among first-generation
migrants to Bombay from the rural hinterland was widespread. When
large numbers of Marathi speakers arrived in Bombay, in the 1950s and
1960s, they found themselves at the lower rungs of the labor market and
in competition with skilled or specialized communities from other parts
of India, for example, Muslim weavers from North India or literate South
Indians whose skills in English gave them easier access to clerical jobs.[6]

The Marathi-speaking middle class in Bombay, who had been the most
consistent supporters of the Samyukta Maharashtra Samiti, experienced
similar discrepancies. Because this group had not been subject to any substantial changes in their career prospects or job opportunities, and given
the discourse of the Samyukta movement that had drawn distinctions between pure Maharashtrians and aliens in Bombay, the blame for all hardships could rather effortlessly be projected onto non-Maharashtrians. This

was the line taken by cartoonist and journalist Bal Thackeray in his weekly *Marmik* (Satire) launched in 1963 and soon one of the most popular magazines among Marathi speakers in Bombay. In its first years the magazine, under the heading *Vacha ani Thanda Basa* (Read and sit silent) began to publish lists of names of leading executives in well-known firms and public undertakings to show that few Maharashtrian names figured among them. Soon Thackeray changed the name to *Vacha ani Utha* (Read and rise) and began urging his readers, the ordinary *Marathi Mumbaikar* (Bombay'ite), to protest against what seemed to be open discrimination.

Backed by his father and a circle of friends, Bal Thackeray formed the organization Shiv Sena in 1966. In the jubilee edition of *Marmik* in 1997, Thackeray recalled the founding of the Sena as inconspicuous and modest: "Very few of us were there. . . . At around 9.30 in the morning, one of our family friends, Naik, brought a coconut from the grocery store and broke it. Intoning *Chhatrapati Shivaji Maharaj Ki Jai* [Hail Chhatrapati Shivaji Maharaj], we started the Shiv Sena."[7]

Some months later, *Marmik* announced a mass meeting to be held in Shivaji Park in the predominantly Maharashtrian middle-class neighborhood of Dadar in Bombay. It was an exhortation to all "proud sons of Maharashtra . . . to bring about a Maharashtrian resurgence." Thackeray and his associates had worked hard to mobilize young men connected with youth clubs (*mitra mandals*) and gymnasiums (*akhadas* or *vyayamshalas*) in the Marathi-dominated parts of the city. The response was overwhelming and marked the actual birth of Shiv Sena as a significant force in Bombay. More than 200,000 people responded enthusiastically to the call. At the meeting, Prabodhankar Thackeray, the SMS veteran, told the crowd: "Maharashtra is not the land of the weak and the timid. It is the land of tigers." Bal Thackeray thundered against the *Madrasis*, the South Indians who stole jobs from Maharashtrians, and announced with one of the word plays that has since become a Thackeray signature: "It has been decided to keep the Sena away from politics (*rajkaaran*). Because *rajkaaran* is like *gajkaaran* (ringworm)."[8] Sena was born as a movement that insisted on being nonpolitical, on doing "social work," a youthful, restless organization that refused to see itself as a responsible or even accountable political party. The central idea of the Sena (meaning *army*) was strength, courage, and defiance of public authority, and the image of a roaring tiger, along with the saffron flag, became part of the movement's signature in Bombay's cityscape.

A pamphlet Shiv Sena published in this period read:

> The Maharashtrians have a genuine feeling that over the past 25–30 years, they have been sliding fast to the position of hewers of wood and drawers of water. . . . More than 40 leading Industrial houses in the City of Bombay and

some Government departments were surveyed from this point of view [ethnic composition of employees—T.B.H.]. There was definitely something radically wrong, something rotten in the State of Maharashtra. This survey showed that out of 1,500 executives on the rolls of those establishments, only 75 were Maharashtrians, while an overwhelming majority (about 70%) were South Indians. (*Shiv Sena Speaks*, Bombay, 1967)

Contrary to the perceptions propagated by Shiv Sena and many others at this juncture of rapid urban growth in Bombay, the proportion of Maharashtrians in Bombay was actually not going down, nor was the proportion of South Indian migrants rising dramatically. The ethnic composition of Bombay remained rather stable from 1951 to 1971.[9] The specter of South Indians taking over the Maharashtrian capital referred less to numbers than to the relative position of various communities in Bombay's economic and political structure. There is little doubt that the most vital condition for Shiv Sena to emerge as a radical sons-of-the-soil movement ostracizing the numerous South Indian migrants in the city was the sharpened competition over middle-class, white-collar jobs. Major studies of both the initial and early phases of Shiv Sena's existence thus conclude almost unanimously that Shiv Sena was a vehicle for the social interests of the Marathi-speaking middle classes in the city (Katzenstein 1981; Gupta 1982).

One may ask, however, to what extent ex post accounts of the social composition of the popular constituencies of a movement or party effectively can account for its objectives, strategies, and operational principles. One obvious problem in such reverse projections of the intentions and nature of Shiv Sena from its electoral constituency is that the evidence presented by the two studies suggests that both the social profile and attitudes typical of Shiv Sena supporters were almost identical to those found among supporters of the Congress Party (Katzenstein 1981, 71–91).

In contemporary Mumbai, Shiv Sena's record of aggression, hate-speech, and violence is often attributed to its alleged "lumpen" character and its dependence on marginalized and brutal males from the lower classes. It is worth remembering, however, that Shiv Sena emerged from middle-class environments and that its ideology depended on the most revered tenets and emblems of the official Maharashtrian historical imagination. From Shiv Sena's early phase, rather disparate elements of proletarian street culture, entrepreneurial aspirations, as well as Marathi speakers' middle-class desires of respectability and recognition have coexisted within the organization. Its members and activists were drawn from dissimilar social groups, and its mobilizing strategies were directed more toward attracting a Marathi-speaking Hindu constituency around powerful regional and religious symbols than toward any particular social group.

Shiv Sena's general ostracizing of alien others believed to dominate Bombay, its appeals to an aggressive masculinity, and the security and sense of self-esteem it provided to young, frustrated males in the metropolis, was, and remains, undoubtedly more central to its success than its articulation of any specific class interests of certain upwardly mobile Marathi speakers.

The wider social and economic processes in Bombay generated the desire for respectability, security, and upward mobility among many groups; they also sustained powerful discourses of solidarity among workers and within popular neighborhoods; and they produced despair, exclusion, and an insecure existence at the fringes of the formal economy and formal institutions. These social and economic processes merely provided the possibility of a whole range of social phenomena and political identities. Shiv Sena was only one, though admittedly the most successful, product of these circumstances.

Therefore, to understand the emergence and trajectory of a movement like Shiv Sena, one needs to examine the movement's rather spectacular ability to sustain a high-profile presence in the public culture of the city since 1966. This capacity has at least four dimensions. The first is Shiv Sena's successful use of the ethnohistorical imaginary and at times xenophobic discourse of regional pride—inherited from the SMS and later authorized by the state government and Congress Party in the 1960s. Shiv Sena's aggressive, intolerant, and popular-satirical discursive style twisted and renewed this register into a street-smart, no-nonsense mode of being Maharashtrian that in just a few years made Shiv Sena widely popular among Marathi speakers in Bombay.

The second factor accounting for Shiv Sena's ability to maintain a high profile is its organizational and spatial grid of local units assisting local citizens. These networks of self-help organizations were established by the movement in the 1960s in most parts of Bombay and were extended elsewhere in Maharashtra in the 1980s. Often regarded as the movement's backbone, the efficiency and vibrancy of these local networks are often overestimated by sainiks and observers alike. Their real significance seems to lie in the rumors they inspire and the spectacular coordinated actions and campaigns they occasionally make possible when replying to a call from Thackeray, the *Senapati* (army commander). This interaction of Sena's self-help network with families, male peer groups, business undertakings, and other informal associations has made it an integral part of what Appadurai calls the city's "nervous system" (Appadurai 2000).

The third dimension central to Shiv Sena is violence, both as a rhetorical style and a promise of strength, as well as in actual practice at both the local, everyday level and in public confrontations since the 1960s. The movement's determination to use violence in most situations, its celebration of youth, masculinity, and the "ordinary," and the cynicism of its leadership have, since the 1960s, created enormous de facto legal impunity for the public actions of sainiks and their leaders and a concomitant fear of the movement among its adversaries and victims.

Finally, Shiv Sena has a complex and ambiguous relationship with the world of electoral politics and political institutions. The movement has been aligned with a number of political formations but for years developed within the protective shadow of the Congress Party. Since 1988 Shiv Sena has established a close affiliation with the Bharatiya Janata Party (BJP), the major right-wing formation in Indian politics. It has also extended and consolidated its own web of alliances, and institutions of ruthless manipulation and corruption, during its time in power in the Bombay Municipal Corporation and later, in the 1990s, in the state government. Thus a key feature of Shiv Sena's political profile is the simultaneous presence of formal, institutionalized politics, violent street-level agitation, informal networking, and local brokerage.

SHIV SENA SPEAKS

Initially Shiv Sena's articulation of the lack of suitable white-collar jobs appealed directly to the large middle-class groups in Dadar and the adjacent area, the heart of Bombay's Marathi-speaking community. The movement soon acquired a large supportive audience in the densely populated working-class neighborhoods in the nearby mill districts. Here, Thackeray's hard-hitting rhetorical style, his praise of the Marathi speaker (*Marathi manus*) and the virtues of the common man and ordinary life, was reminiscent of the ideology of the *Samyukta Maharashtra Samiti* imparted to the Bombay working class for more than a decade by the powerful socialist and Communist movements.[10] The rhetorical stings against Bombay's economic elite, the "alien" cosmopolitanism, and the extolling of the virtues of the working man were themes that the SMS's charismatic speaker, Acharya Atre, the legendary communist leader "Comrade Dange," and the union leader George Fernandes had made a stable in the discursive registers of Bombay's popular culture since the 1950s.[11]

Yet, something in Bal Thackeray's twisted word plays, his humor, his personal style in the satirical weekly, *Marmik*, was new and appealing. *Marmik*, until publication of the daily newspaper *Saamna* (Confrontation) in 1987, remained the main organ of Shiv Sena. Framed in a simple, populist, and entertaining style, *Marmik* became a public platform of criticism against the political establishment in Bombay, reaching a large readership in the greater Bombay region. Still, the sustained success of Shiv Sena was, and remains, the attractiveness of its violent, masculine postures and its use of ordinary street language (*Bombaya boli*) at public events and rallies to thousands of young men in Bombay and other places in Maharashtra.[12]

To become a Shiv sainik literally means to become a soldier in Shivaji's army. To represent the organization's aura of assertive and violent masculinity and the respect and fear it commanded in the low-income neighborhoods of the city remains a major attraction of Shiv Sena. The discussion of ideology cannot, therefore, be confined to my brief discussion of public discourses below and in the following chapters. The ideology of Shiv Sena is crystallized in its organizational forms and mundane social practices, where lack of intellectual sophistication is a matter of pride. As one of Thackeray's famous one-liners goes: Shiv Sena is not an ideology or a program, it is a state of mind. The construction of a sainik as an assertive male was succinctly put to me by Satish Pradhan, a longstanding member of Shiv Sena: "A Shiv sainik is not a man that if someone comes up to him and slaps him, then he will not simply show the other cheek. We are not that type. My hands work out and he will get the slap, not me. I will not be slapped and allow him to slap . . . if someone enters my house and runs away with my *roti* (Indian bread) then what should I do? I have to slap him and take the *roti* away because that is my *roti* and not his."[13]

In the construction of identity and a programmatic profile of Shiv Sena, Bal Thackeray has, throughout the history of the movement, tried to gauge popular moods and has devised an often changing range of effective others and enemies. In his rhetoric and writings, he has rather ingeniously interconnected the various anxieties of the ordinary Marathi speaker toward strangers. As Eckert notes, the Shiv Sena always reproduces a constitutive, if imprecise, "they." "What is common to the depictions of all of its enemy images is that they are made out to be existential threats to the lives and livelihoods of every 'good Indian' " (Eckert 2000, 85).

The South Indians posed the initial threat, then Communists, the city elite, and later the Muslims in India became the more effective other. Some of the early representations of South Indians as barbaric, bloodthirsty Communists, aligned with larger interests of the Gujarati city elite in a secret parallel government defied all logic. But they appealed to the fears and anxieties of lower-middle-class families, who felt squeezed between the city's powerful economic and political elite and large, self-conscious working-class communities. In one of the few programmatic statements from Shiv Sena's early period, Thackeray deployed the widespread style of rumors of communal atrocities when he alleged that "bloodthirsty slum dwellers," encouraged by their Communist leaders, had plundered victims of a railway accident: "These South Indian vultures from nearby huts swooped over the injured and dying women lying in agony, cut their limbs with sickles to snatch their ornaments" (*Shiv Sena Speaks* 1967, 24).

Despite changes over the years, the Shiv Sena discourse has been inter-woven rather consistently with a reiterative celebration of Maharashtrian culture, its martial values, manliness, cultural authenticity, and individual character, which currently are perverted and de-purified:

> Economic deterioration and even its total downfall can be repaired; but a *Nation's Character* once destroyed, can never be supplied. . . . *Character* is a coat of triple steel giving security to its wearer. Apart from the economical situation, the ruthless banditry that is playing havoc in Bombay and elsewhere throughout Maharashtra, has deprived its people of their national character and culture. . . . The dense black cloud of intruders from outside has deprived the blooming generation of Maharashtra of its ancestral zeal and enthusiasm to fight out the battles of life with determination and chivalry—the hallmark of Character. . . . The question of rejuvenating the Character of Maharashtra must be solved at all costs." [Italics in original] (*Shiv Sena Speaks* 1967, 25)

This passage is strongly reminiscent of the wider Hindu nationalist dis-course of an organic national culture, as well as of the SMS notion of the contamination of Bombay. "Outsiders," a recurrent metaphor for per-ceived excesses of modernity, had a devastating impact on the original, pure values of Maharashtrian culture, Thackeray claimed. The only way to manage Bombay, and thus cope with its modernity, was to assert the superiority of this original, essential cultural matrix. The essence of Ma-harashtra was the Marathas, and the entire Hindu nation should be cau-tious not to alienate them: "A disgruntled Maratha is a risk which the Nation can ill afford to bear" (15) because "the Marathas as a race are renowned as the best of the Warrior classes of India since long [ago]" (47). In this early document, Thackeray merely rearticulated an already authorized discourse of Marathas as the martial guardians of the Hindu nation, and recommended that the government should make military training compulsory for all able-bodied Maharashtrians.

Finally, Thackeray portrayed Shiv Sena as a young, vibrant antiestablish-ment. To this day the aura of youthful exuberance, lack of respect for authority, virility, and physical courage have been carefully cultivated by Thackeray in speeches and in his appearance, for example, his consistent attempt to look young and vital, his use of hair dye, his fondness of female beauty, and so on. The rather consistent rejection of *rajkaaran* (politics) as dirty, useless, and compromising still plays a central role in the celebra-tion of the youthfulness and maverick character of the Sena, even into the 1990s when Shiv Sena became the second largest party in the state.[14]

> Let us declare bluntly once and for all that Shiv Sena refuses to have any link with "politics" or so-called Political Parties. As a Volunteer Organization it claims to have the privilege to support honest, non-corrupt and patriotic per-

sons. It will stake everything to oppose parties or persons who have mortgaged their wits and will to agencies outside India. That is the policy of Shiv
Sena to be followed during the recent election. (*Shiv Sena Speaks* 1967, 34)

In spite of such populist antiestablishment rhetoric, Shiv Sena has never
espoused the antipolitical stances represented by Gandhian communitari-
ans or the Hindu nationalist movement (Hansen 1999, 50–57). For years
Shiv Sena has advocated authoritarian governance, and on many occasions
Thackeray has advocated *thokshahi* (dictatorship) as a form of rule. He was
one of the few political leaders outside the Congress Party who lauded
Indira Gandhi's imposition of emergency rule between 1975 and 1977.
Most of Shiv Sena's demands over the years indicate a strong belief in the
state as an agency capable of imposing order on society. Shiv Sena demanded that 80 percent of all jobs in the organized sector and 80 percent
of all housing facilities be reserved for Marathi speakers; that compulsory
military training be required of Maharashtrian males; and that there be
slum-clearance drives against illegal settlements, expulsion of illegal immigrants from the state, higher salaries for police constables, the scrapping
of prohibition, and stringent measures against the *matka* (gambling, allegedly operated by South Indians). Shiv Sena also demanded stringent
measures against "owners of hotels and restaurants which engage servants
only of the owner's caste or clan and refuse to engage servants from the
native stock" (*Shiv Sena Speaks* 1967, 35). One of the more prominent
demands was to make English compulsory as a medium of instruction at
all stages of education in order to enable Maharashtrians to compete with
people from other parts of India (47–49).

Clearly the Sena discourse was addressed to audiences who could recognize themselves in the eulogy of the virtues of the common man, and
particularly in the celebration of young Marathi-speaking males as defenders of the community and the natural inheritors of Shivaji's virtues. Their
desire to affirm their manliness, their fantasies of power, money, consumption, and status, along with their need for a group identity amid turbulent
city life made them receptive to Thackeray's speeches, but naturally re-
sponsive as well to other, competing discourses also promising self-respect
and social order.

Shiv Sena reconstructed the bewildering experiences of cultural diversity and the anxieties of ethnic difference into a series of clear-cut, well-
organized others harboring secret and malign designs aimed at keeping
the *Marathi manus* down. But Sena also encouraged action, not carefully
planned campaigns according to rules of civic conduct but action that
allowed men to show their justified anger, to protest, to demand their
due—in brief, to take charge of the situation. This "actionism," the claim
that sainiks as ordinary men "get things done" instead of waiting passively,

was, as Eckert rightly points out, one of the crucial innovations that Sena brought into Bombay's neighborhoods (Eckert 2000, 16–39). One should add that Thackeray's exhortations to young Maharashtrians to start businesses of their own, such as food stalls selling *vada pav* (bread and vegetable sauce)—the quintessential Bombay street dish—also fed into the Sena's actionist ideology.

The attraction of these ideological constructions lay in the fact that the perceived mediocrity of the Maharashtrians, their lowly status in education, wealth, and power, their lack of eloquence, enterprise, and political influence, was made into their most precious virtue. Thus the physical qualities of Maharashtrian males were valued as being indispensable to the nation, equivalent to the high cultural achievements of other communities. As we shall see in the following chapter, Thackeray employed similar, well-tested discursive techniques in the 1980s, when he depicted the good natured, naïve Hindu as being exploited and endangered by the designs of cunning, secretive Muslims.

THE *SHAKHA* GRID

After Shiv Sena's initial success in 1966, Thackeray and his closest friends began to create a regular organization. Borrowing the RSS (Rashtriya Swayamsevak Sangh) notion of the local *shakha*, a wide network of such shakhas was quickly established in both middle-class and low-income areas in Bombay and Thane. These shakhas were small buildings with one or two fairly simple rooms containing chairs and often a picture or statue of Shivaji. There was always a saffron flag, *bhagwa dwaj*, outside the shakha, which provided a daily meeting place for the activists and their friends in the locality. The shakha was led by a *shakha pramukh* and a lieutenant, the *gata pramukh*, whose responsibilities were to enforce discipline among the young activists and to arrange local religious festivals and celebrations, especially the important Ganapatiutsav and, of course, the Shivaji Jyanti, which remains a major occasion in the organization's annual cycle of activities.

Actually these conspicuous public celebrations are not confined to Shiv Sena but have had a long history in Bombay and other cities in western India from the 1890s on. They are organized by local *mandals* (committees) that meet the expense by collecting money from local traders, and are often patronized by local politicians and business people. These public festivals, with their increasing pomp, expense, and grandeur, are closely tied to the locality's wider politics of representation, to the production of the neighborhood, as Eckert puts it (Eckert 2000, 39). To produce a neighborhood is, in some ways, an extension of the identifying effects of

naming, that is, to claim a certain identity, a belonging, and thus, by implication, a set of entitlements for a particular area and for the people living
there. The festivals provide a stage where local organizations, upcoming
politicians, parvenu businessmen, local brokers, and strongmen can flaunt
their power and status in an effort to acquire respectability through visibility and patronage. The strong competition among *mandals* to produce
these festivals is in many ways symbolic of the precarious nature of the
neighborhoods and the instability of their local configurations of power
and prestige. Indeed, to be someone, to enjoy respect and authority, is not
a given, but needs to be nourished through reiterative performances of
various kinds. Festivals provide one such screen onto which parties, organizations, and individuals may project their prestige and visibility, as well
as an occasion to confirm the neighborhood's identity.[15]

Shiv Sena's unquestionable performative skills and ruthless fund-raising
tactics, together with the determination of local sainiks to remain the primary representatives of the neighborhood, have made these festivals larger
and more central sites of representation over the years. Shiv Sena has also
transformed the symbolic importance and style of these festivals in many
areas of Bombay into more aggressive celebrations of Maharashtrian community. In the 1980s the Sena incorporated other festivals, such as the
Dassera and the Navrati festival originating in Gujarat, in an effort to
appeal to the wider Hindu community.

The shakhas have also been effective in projecting themselves as a representation, if not the heart, of the neighborhood, and, by implication, the
Sena as a representative of ordinary, local people. The shakhas are seen as
the place to go for assistance and various forms of patronage. They receive
local complaints over the lack of civic amenities, corrupt officials, landlords' harassment of tenants, complaints about employers, neighborhood
and family quarrels, and so on. The pramukh and activists are expected to
resolve these problems, either directly or by going to local officials, trade
unions, or local members of the Municipal Corporation and other elected
representatives of the area. They are also expected to be brokers (*dalal*)
and "social workers" in their areas, to pressure the administration and
politicians to improve roads, sewage, housing, water, and so on. The support and sympathy Shiv Sena has enjoyed in many neighborhoods and its
spectacular political successes—particularly its ability to survive almost ten
years in a political wilderness between 1975 and 1984—was in many ways
owing to this network of local welfare strategies. However, as with the
festivals, the sainiks are far from alone in these endeavors to project themselves through these types of services, which have a long history in Bombay
and elsewhere in India.

The popularity of sainiks as brokers and protectors owes much to their
image of being violent, ruthless, aggressive defenders of the common man

by means of employing the common man's only strength—his strength in numbers—and his language—fists and muscles—in order to assert his rights vis-à-vis the establishment. "Being a Shiv sainik means half the job is done" is a popular expression in the organization, emphasizing the Shiv sainik's commitment to action and affirming the resolution and effectiveness of Shiv Sena. The Shiv sainik's aggressiveness as a way to achieve self-respect is integral to the sainik's identity, which is nurtured by the leadership and repeated in numerous parables. Modhav Joshi, member of the Legislative Assembly from Thane City, highlighted a crucial element in the ethos of Shiv Sena—the need to gain respect through power and, if necessary, violence—when he expressed the following:

> Thackeray has told us that you should be polite and talk to the person, but if he does not talk and shows you the law, there is also nature' s law and I can use it—that is, to hammer the person. I do not want *goondaism* [criminal methods—T.B.H.] in the Shiv Sena and I want hundred percent gentlemen. But if you do not allow me to speak, then how am I to express myself? . . . I am not a beggar, no doubt I am needy and I too have some respect. If you simply throw me out I will not tolerate that![16]

The themes of respect, revenge, and natural law were repeated by another veteran Shiv Sena leader, Satish Pradhan, who asserted: "The principle of natural justice is also accepted by us, and this is the principle of natural justice—that whatever is mine is mine, and what is yours is yours. . . . It is just like playing with fire. If you sit beside it, it will give you warmth, but if you play mischief with it, it burns your house. Shiv Sena is that way."[17]

Observers of Shiv Sena—from Katzenstein to V. S. Naipaul's admiring portrait of Shiv sainiks in his *India: A Million Mutinies Now* as well as standard journalism—generally assume that the shakha grid is the heart of the Sena, namely, that it explains the movement's staying power. Even Julia Eckert's incisive account of the Shiv Sena tends to accept the sainiks' own claims of their proficiency in "getting work done," or its mythical ability to communicate informally and effortlessly (Eckert 2000, 64). Many left-wing activists view this grid, and the famous communication network via small blackboards outside the shakhas, as the Sena's innermost secret, its means of achieving the kind of identification, loyalty, and communication that the leftist parties never attained.

My contention is, however, that the efficacy of the shakhas in terms of actually providing services is rather exaggerated. First, most localities in Bombay have always harbored a number of competing centers of brokerage and influence, and the Sena's superiority in this regard has been far from either self-evident or stable.

Second, my own experiences with how Shiv Sena functions in Thane (see chapter 4), in central Bombay, as well as in Pune, Aurangabad, and rural districts in Maharashtra (see, e.g., Hansen 1996c), tell me that shakhas are by no means active throughout the year; rather, they are often closed, working daily only before and during the festival season from August to October. Further, quarrels and envy between sainiks over leadership and authority often impede local shakhas in their ability to function. Often these altercations are overcome only by a strong command from Thackeray or the local district chief, compelling the sainiks to embark on certain campaigns or to protest various actions. The Shiv Sena is an open, informal organization at the local level, without formal membership or any effective social control. It mainly exists as a movement when engaged in high-profile, often violent actions. The "actionist" ideology of Shiv Sena is also reflected in its organization, which, in daily practice, is often far removed from the daily displays of devotion Sena leaders like to claim.

Third, the dysfunction of the shakha does not necessarily mean that Shiv Sena is absent from an area. Known sainiks of varying ranks or people known to be associated with Shiv Sena can represent the organization, and ordinary people will come to these individuals' homes or offices to ask for help or favors. Or Shiv Sena can exist simply as a "public mood," as a memory of past actions in the locality, as reputations of people associated with the Sena, or as rumors of violent deeds that took place far from the locality. I have met many people who declare themselves sainiks but who would not vote for the local Shiv Sena candidate or who would approach a Congress politician for help because of his superior local reputation. I have met people who would ask a local Sena man for help, who would even vote for him because of his good local reputation, but who would oppose Shiv Sena at the general elections.

Similar observations, of course, could be made about other political movements in India. I am merely suggesting that the idea of relatively stable "support bases" and "constituencies" of parties or movements is highly evanescent and largely depends on strategic performances, as well as local configurations of power, in different localities. Even a fairly well-organized movement like Shiv Sena is vitally dependent on its continual public representation by means of signs, signatures, discourse, and rumors. My argument, to which I shall return below, is that the true "secret" of the Sena's success lies more in its incessant repetition of statements, one-liners, and rumors, and in its capacity and will to stage violent high-profile actions, than in its physical presence in every city neighborhood.

Nevertheless, Shiv Sena does have a relatively formal structure that is maintained by a highly centralized and dictatorial style of leadership within the movement and that centers around Bal Thackeray and his family. Above the shakha level is the *zilla pramukh*, the district chief, who commands all activities in the district and is the direct head of all the shakhas in the area. Depending on the energy and ingenuity of the zilla pramukh, this post in the Shiv Sena can be very influential, and enterprising pramukhs can exercise a relatively free hand and have access to considerable resources through client networks. In many cases, being the zilla pramukh has been a springboard to a more advanced career in the party such as a legislator or higher-level leader.

Above this level is the *vibhag pramukh*, the area commander. This post was designed in the 1960s, and the individual in this role acted as a liaison between the Shiv Sena leadership—Bal Thackeray—and the rank-and-file workers. But with the growth of Shiv Sena in the 1980s, the function changed to acting as a liaison between the leadership and the district chiefs, and thus became primarily an intra-party position under the name of *zilla samparka pramukh*. This leadership level was later expanded to include a range of leaders: heads of trade unions; leaders in the women's wing, *Mahila Aghadi*; chiefs of other specialized organizations; and so-called *upa-netas* (deputy leaders) who assisted the top leadership in carrying out decisions and generally enforcing discipline in the movement. The apex of the organizational structure is the *karya karani* a group of senior leaders or councilors (eight in 1969, twelve in 1991, fourteen in 1998), also known as the *netas*, who assist the *senapati pramukh* (the commander-in-chief), Bal Thackeray, in making decisions and supervising the organization.

As Shiv Sena achieved astounding electoral successes in the 1990s, an expanding group of legislators and members of Municipal Corporations also had to be incorporated in the structure. It is, however, indicative of Shiv Sena's view of the relative unimportant role of legislative and democratic procedures that the influence of elected sainiks never matched that of the men in charge of the organization. These men were handpicked by Thackeray on the basis of personal loyalty (*nishta*) to the Thackeray family. As we shall see, the ministers serving in the cabinet between 1995 and 1999 were generally men also handpicked from the organization rather than MLAs with experience and insight into formal political procedures, political negotiations, and bureaucratic functioning.

From the outset the organizational structure was a highly centralized and authoritarian reflection of Thackeray's professed ideal of *thokshahi* (dictatorship). Elections or even competing candidates for various posts have rarely occurred, and have never been accepted by Thackeray. All officials are appointed by the top leadership, mostly Thackeray himself, though appointments to lower-level posts are made by the zilla pramukhs in consultation with the supervising member of the karya karani, and finally approved by Thackeray. The central concept in the Shiv Sena is loyalty (*nishta*) to the leadership, and decisive factors in achieving careers within the organization is one's proximity and personal standing with Thackeray.

Thackeray takes any challenge to his authority very seriously. City corporators, middle-level leaders, or shakha pramukhs who do not obey unconditionally or neglect to perform their assigned jobs are openly supervised by emissaries from the central leadership, who report directly to Thackeray. If Thackeray is dissatisfied, he reduces their rank or ridicules them publicly. This climate of fear, combined with unmediated sycophancy vis-à-vis superiors, has certainly made the Shiv Sena an inhospitable place for talented and ambitious men. For many years the consolidation and expansion of Shiv Sena beyond Bombay was constrained for this reason.

In the early years of the organization, the appointment of shakha pramukhs and contestants for civic bodies relied primarily on the individuals' activities regarding Shiv Sena and their loyalty to the organization and to Thackeray. A majority of these leaders came from lower-middle-class backgrounds, and a few were college graduates or owned small businesses. Their common feature was an earlier political involvement in either the RSS or the SMS (Gupta 1982, 100–2) As Shiv Sena entered elections for the Legislative Assembly in the 1970s and consolidated its share of seats in the Bombay Municipal Corporation, two new considerations came into play in the selection of candidates, namely, their ability to win the seat on their own reputation and to generate money and patronage for the organization. This attracted a large number of local businessmen, who were able both to finance their own campaign and attract funds from the business community. In this respect Shiv Sena was moving closer to the Congress style of electioneering, while at the same time retaining a fairly dense grass-roots network of activists. Though notoriously unverifiable, another feature of the "Congress culture," namely, the open purchase and trade in party tickets for the elections, began in the 1970s and soon became a major source of finance for the party. Contributing to the party's financial status was the direct extortion of protection money from South Indian and Muslim shopkeepers and from industrialists, who paid off the Shiv Sena unions to avoid industrial unrest. Add to this the spoils routinely extracted by members of the Municipal Corporation from builders and contractors.[18]

Although considerable powers and competence have been devolved to the second-rung leadership and elected representatives, Thackeray's style of leadership—especially his demand for unconditional loyalty and his ongoing ability to maintain a direct rapport with the rank and file—has ensured his continued, uncontested leadership. Thackeray's authority seems to be generated and sustained by what Alberoni has identified as the pivotal characteristic of charismatic leadership, namely, the "nonreciprocal love relation" between the leader and his followers (Alberoni 1984, 144–50).

Thackeray rules by alternately extending and withdrawing his attention and affection and making sure that no one feels entirely comfortable with their position. As the leader, he does not rely on the affection of any particular individual—only that of the aggregate masses of rank and file—whereas the followers owe all their loyalty and love only to Thackeray. This creates a permanent atmosphere of uneasy suspense, where followers at various levels strive for Thackeray's attention and where the interpersonal relationships and ranking among leaders derive from their real or perceived proximity to Thackeray. His unrivaled position as crowd pleaser and charismatic orator, and the inordinate affection extended to him by the rank and file, their belief in his wisdom, shrewdness, and concern, all contribute to making this unusually autocratic and "whimsical" style of leadership possible.

Shiv Sena's most attractive feature undoubtedly remains Thackeray's public assertion of masculine/martial values, his straightforward language implying a subversion of existing hierarchies of class, caste, and power, and his substitution of these ascribed authorities with the Sena's loud, energetic, and often permissive community and subculture. During fieldwork I conducted in 1992–93, I interviewed some one hundred sainiks and asked them all, at some point, what had attracted them to Shiv Sena. In virtually all cases the answers ranged from "its aggressiveness" to "its straightforward language" to "Shiv Sena is more attacking."

Thackeray's inordinate popularity initially, and still today, has everything to do with his use of street language, the *Bombaya boli*, and public, derogatory nicknames for opponents; his promotion of himself as the brave, fearless leader who is honest, straightforward, genuine, and so on. Several young people told me that they liked the fact that Thackeray simply admits he loves beer and drinks it often. Given the discrepancy between the view that drinking and smoking in public is amoral and decadent, and yet is prevalent in most social strata—including among politicians and others of the nouveau riche—Thackeray is admired for simply exposing the obvious hypocrisy on this issue.

Thackeray transmits an image of himself as a common man who speaks and acts with common sense according to a simple moral code and sense of justice. He presents himself as a man who fears no one, who has no lack of self-respect and self-confidence—not because of his manners, education, or money but because of his strength and will to use force to make himself seen and heard. Shiv Sena is taken seriously because of Thackeray's command over thousands of young men, all loyal to him; and each young man is taken seriously because of his association with Thackeray—a logical conclusion among the rank-and-file sainiks. For the rank and file, self-respect and strength are crucial and desirable effects of their affiliation with the Sena. In the shakha, or with friends and peers at Sena rallies, they laugh and ridicule others, feel stronger, more self-assured, more manly and capable. When Thackeray derides the authorities, Muslims, public morality, or the complacency of the average Indian of these young men's parents' generation, he speaks on these young men's behalf—against being compliant with parents, bureaucrats, and the hierarchy—and he uses a language and style they wish to command themselves yet dare not use against authorities. In Alberoni's terms (1984, 142–48), Thackeray absolves them from their feelings of guilt for failing to support their families or for their attraction to the hedonistic pursuits of life (alcohol, prostitutes, crime, and so on). He embodies their desire to speak their minds, to be violent, fearless, self-made men.

Thackeray's unique position allows him to transgress the normal rules of conduct and speech, and elevates him, in the eyes of his followers, above the social yardstick applied to ordinary individuals. This dynamic of centralized charismatic authority within the Shiv Sena is therefore crucial to any broader understanding of the logic and trajectory of the organization.

However, the organization must continue to expand and to maintain the illusion of action and movement if it is to survive the incessant rivalry and infighting among the *Netas* and lower-rank leaders, as well as the high-profile defections and denouncing of Thackeray by a number of leading men in the past decade. It is exactly this need for suspense, action, and anger that adds the element of compulsion to Shiv Sena's style of functioning. If the organization falls into a mode of "business-as-usual" and complacently relies on the shakha grid, entropy and disorganization sets in.

A similar need for action governs the organizational wings of the Shiv Sena. The *Bharatiya Kamgar Sena* (BKS)—literally, the Indian Workers Army—expanded over the years into the largest and most powerful subsidiary of the Shiv Sena. In many large companies it displaced the once powerful Communist and socialist unions, often by violent methods, as we shall see below. Several factors enabled the BKS to gain considerable strength in the early 1970s: the sainiks' aggressiveness, the tacit support of several large industrial houses enamored by the prospect of ousting Communist unions, the dominance of Marathi speakers in blue-collar jobs, and the pro–Shiv Sena atmosphere in the entire city. Occasionally the BKS was as militant in its language and methods as the Left-leaning unions, but at the same time it was able to secure employment and extend political patronage. This has ensured the BKS considerable success in Bombay's working-class environments, which are accustomed to direct action and straightforward language.[19] With the spread of industry into Maharashtra's interior in the 1980s, the BKS was able to establish additional units in Pune, Nasik, and Aurangabad, each led by a strong leader who governed through bonds of personal loyalty. In some cases these units became personal "fiefdoms," forming a basis for dissent and defection from Shiv Sena, as occurred in 1998 with Moreshva Save in Aurangabad and Ganesh Naik in Navi Mumbai.

The *Sthanik Lokhadikar Samiti* (SLS) (Local People's Rights Organization) was formed in 1972 as a parallel organization to the BKS. The SLS organized Marathi speakers, already employed largely in white-collar jobs, in intra-company groups where they would press for and monitor more local employment in their respective companies. All the local groups were organized into a statewide association named Sthanik Lokhadikar Mahasangha, coordinated since 1977 by Sudhir Joshi.[20] Over the years the SLS has encouraged young Maharashtrians to seek high-status employment and has conducted classes preparing young people for competitive exams, for interviews, in the designing of applications, and so on. The organization occasionally staged demonstrations and launched agitation inside and outside such large, prestigions employers as the Reserve Bank of India, Air India, and a number of well-known five-star hotels pressing for them to hire more Maharashtrians.

The SLS has undoubtedly been Shiv Sena's most effective creation. Its activities have forced the state government to adopt a set of "Directive Principles" recommending employment of Marathi speakers. Furthermore, a large number of employees in leading positions in both the private and public sectors owe their position and power to the intervention of Shiv Sena. These networks of patronage have been crucial to Shiv Sena's staying power and continued influence on the Bombay scene for more than thirty years. SLS leader Sudhir Joshi told me that after Shiv Sena had become a large and influential organization in the 1980s, "the work of SLS has become much easier as the Shiv Sena is held commonly in respect now . . . the actions of the SLS are simply not so necessary anymore." All that remained to be done now, Joshi said, was to stop migration to Bombay, tear down all illegal slum settlements, oust all the street vendors and hawkers from the city, and let Bombay return to its previous glory and beauty.

THE WAGES OF VIOLENCE

There was a thing that Raman Fielding knew,
which was his power's secret source: that it is not
the civil social norm for which men yearn, but
the outrageous, the outsize, the out-of-bounds—
for that by which our wild potency may be unleashed. We crave permission openly to become
our secret selves.
—Salman Rushdie, *The Moor's Last Sigh*

Shiv Sena's double strategy—one benevolent and ostensibly committed to social improvements, the other violent and aggressive—has been one of the most striking features of the movement's public presence since its inception. The Sena became famous and feared on the basis of often violent street politics. But since its leadership also wanted to be recognized as respectable and powerful by the established elite in the metropolis, the arenas of electoral politics were, from the outset, contested on issues such as civic discipline, employment, and nativism. Shiv Sena's public image reflects this discrepancy between its populist strongman bravado, asserting a "plebeian" quest for equality, and its conservative, socially conformist cultural values of bravery, chivalry, and defense of family and nation. Shiv Sena needed, and still needs, populist and violent street politics to attract its human capital—young, aggressive, frustrated men—but at the same time is careful not to antagonize or alienate its middle-class constituency so crucial to its self-image and the desire for respectability and social ambition within the party's leading ranks.

Shiv Sena made violence an integral part of politics and public culture in Bombay. The publicity and fear generated by spectacular retaliatory actions against critics of Shiv Sena; the heroic postures and aura gained through violent campaigns against price hikes, against certain companies refusing to give preference to Maharashtrians; the destruction of South Indian restaurants; the attacks on, even murders of, political opponents, critical journalists, newspapers, and so on—all these elements from the outset were key to Shiv Sena's profile. The party carefully nurtured this image, these practices, for two reasons: to "keep the boys happy" within the organization and to promote its image among the electorate as a party of action, admitting no compromise.

I will return to Shiv Sena's politics of violence during the 1980s and 1990s in subsequent chapters. Here, I wish to draw attention briefly to two episodes in the Sena's early years that became paradigmatic for its politics of violence: the protracted war against the Communist trade unions in central Bombay in the late 1960s and the violent campaign for the inclusion of the Marathi-speaking enclave Belgaum into Maharashtra that led to Thackeray's arrest and paralyzed Bombay for almost a week in 1969.

As Shiv Sena consolidated itself in every sector of Bombay, its primary opponent at the grass-roots level soon became the Communists, especially in working-class districts like Parel and other parts of the city's old industrial heartland. Bal Thackeray was opposed to the Left-dominated trade union movement, and his activists were more than willing to take on the Communists in what often became violent street battles. The party's clear anti-Communist stance attracted support from big industrial houses and from leaders in the Congress Party. Soon Thackeray was able to negotiate arrangements whereby members of the new Shiv Sena union were to keep other unions out of the factories in return for the employment of a number of Marathi-speaking Shiv Sena loyalists. These extra employees, described as *goondas* (musclemen, rogues), rarely had any specified tasks in the mills other than securing the workers' support and loyalty to Shiv Sena. The explicit aims of the BKS, outlined in *Marmik* on 11 August 1968, were to "protect the worker from being exploited by the Communist Party . . . the workers will be asked to produce more, and then to ask for more . . . the worker has been kept in poverty because he has held up production by resorting to constant strikes." Another professed aim was to promote the interests of Maharashtrian workers over those of the other workers.

A former confidante of Thackeray, who participated in meetings between Shiv Sena and large industrial houses such as Ambanis, Nirlons, and Bajaj, related the following:

> The entire cooperation happened because Shiv Sena was needed and useful for the industrialists in fighting the Communist unions. . . . Once Sena's dominance was established in a mill, it was easy to sustain because of the considerable "nuisance value" of Shiv Sena. Its reputation was such that the *lalbhais* [red brothers] simply did not dare come back; they were afraid of being beaten up. . . . The problem was that these extras, the Shiv Sena employees, had nothing to do. They began playing mischief and behaved sometimes like the rulers of the company.[21]

This battle continued with increasing ferocity, violence, and killings in the late sixties. Shiv Sena attacked Communist rallies and offices, and broke up a number of strikes called by trade unions controlled by the Communist Party of India (CPI). In Purandare's hagiography of Shiv Sena, a former leftist labor organizer gives a rather chilling account of the demoralizing effects of Shiv Sena's relentless brutality:

> Our struggle went on for a long time and Sena finally resorted to murder. . . . A man named Joshi, not even a member of our union, was accosted by Sena men near the Kurla railway station and stabbed to death. The Sena just wanted to spread terror. . . . A company in Goregaon, too, was under the *Lal Bavta* (red flag). To crush us there, the Shiv Sena badly beat up one of our local union leaders. He was morally aghast. He said, what am I going to do? . . . The other workers got the message and got out of our movement.[22]

The campaign against the Communists culminated in the murder of the popular veteran CPI activist and legislator Krishna Desai in 1970 in the Communist stronghold in Parel. After this incident Shiv Sena seemed the victor in the conflict and managed to curb Communist influence in the industrial sector as well as in electoral politics. It was the sainik's capacity for brutality that, in the years to come, consolidated its dominance in street politics in Bombay.[23]

The campaign against the Communists had been supported by the Congress Party and even by the Praja Socialist Party, which had an electoral alliance with Shiv Sena in 1968. But the Sena campaign for the inclusion of Belgaum into Maharashtra in 1969 developed into a direct confrontation between the Sena and the state government. The question of Belgaum's status was an unresolved issue left over from the formation of Maharashtra, and Thackeray had taken it up several times in *Marmik*. Occasioned by high-level negotiations that were to be held in Bombay in late January 1969, Shiv Sena prepared for violent protests against what it saw as the intransigence of the Union government on the issue. The slogan was "105 Hutatmas for Mumbai. How many for Belgaum?" To demonstrate their will to sacrifice and, if necessary, become *hutatmas*, sainiks blocked the cars of ministers by lying down on the road while others engaged the police in street fighting. In the following days the situation spiraled out of control. State Reserve Police forces were called, and on February 2 Thackeray told thousands of sainiks assembled in Shivaji Park: "We care about neither *lathis* [sticks] nor bullets. . . . We don't wish to take the law into our hands, but if just demands are killed unjustly, we'll retaliate strongly. Shiv Sena leaders may be put into prison. But if that happens, Shiv sainiks will be furious, and the police force will prove inadequate."[24]

In the following days the situation escalated: Hundreds of people were arrested, many were injured, and police *chowkis* (police posts), buses, and shops were destroyed. On February 9 Thackeray and other Sena leaders were arrested. As talk of their arrests spread, sainiks and their sympathizers rioted throughout Bombay, and the following day the state government asked the Indian Army to restore order in the city where almost sixty people had died in police firings in less than two days. The government also took the somewhat unusual step of distributing an appeal from Thackeray in jail urging his followers to stop the violence. Apparently the appeal worked; the violence subsided, and Bombay returned to normalcy. In Purandare's account, this was a victory for Shiv Sena as well as the party's baptism in blood and violence:

> Bal Thackeray's Shiv Sena had realized its potential. It had completely disrupted normal life in Mumbai for close to five days, and it had paralysed the entire state machinery. Mumbai slipped over the edge, but till the Shiv Sena chief issued his diktat, the authorities could do nothing. . . . The tiger had become a man-eater. (Purandare 1999, 121)

Whether this was indeed a victory and Thackeray's role so heroic is debatable. Critics of the Sena alleged that Thackeray had given in to the government's demands for fear of remaining in prison and that "the tiger had become a pussycat" when faced with the state's actual force. The Left opposition in the legislature alleged that the Congress Party was the master manipulator behind the scenes and Shiv Sena merely a pawn in a larger political game between the Union Party and the state government.[25]

What became clear, however, were the essential features of Sena's politics of violence, which persists to this day in Mumbai. First, the violence was framed as retaliation against perceived injustices or simply defense against aggression, indeed merely a primitive, elementary execution of natural justice—as Pradhan put it, above: "Whatever is mine is mine, and what is yours is yours." Second, the violence was portrayed as spontaneous and popular, and therefore uncontrollable. It was said to be a natural reaction of ordinary people. "The responsibility for the consequences doesn't lie with us," Thackeray said at the peak of the violence in 1969. "The people can't be faulted for today's happenings."[26] Thackeray uttered almost the very same words at the beginning of the anti-Muslim pogrom in January 1993. Third, the violence was seen as purifying, capable of creating clear and sharply defined lines between friends and foes in the maze of compromises and half-truths of a pluralist and complex public culture. Fourth, the Sena's violence had no precise or consistent targets. Rather, it was intended essentially to be performative, to establish the Sena as a spectacular, public force. As Eckert perceptively puts it in her account of Shiv Sena's legitimization of violence: "Thus public violence, and also the riots, become the mise en scéne, the enactment of the Sena's claims" (Eckert 2000, 172).

In other words, the Sena's spectacles of public violence are neither an effect of the movement's intrinsic nature nor of the social environment out of which it grew. It is the very generative and performative core of its being. It is through the ritualized destruction of property, the attacks on the police, the hurling of stones, the shouting of slogans that sainiks are produced, their identities affirmed and stabilized. It is this "ritualized violence," driven by the imperative of public assertion and performance, that is Sena's raison d'être; without the perpetual illusion of movement, action, and impatience, there would be no bond between Thackeray and the sainiks; indeed, the Sena would cease to exist.

RAJKAARAN IN THE SHADOW OF CONGRESS

Despite a well-rehearsed official denouncement of politics as dirty and unworthy, Shiv Sena has been engaged in electoral politics from its inception. Electoral politics was a sine qua non to get access to substantial resources and patronage by holding public office, just as many Shiv Sena leaders were keen on carving out a position within the political elite in Bombay and Maharashtra. Until 1969 Shiv Sena's relation with Congress was quite amicable both in the Bombay Municipal Corporation and the Legislative Assembly, despite many Congress politicians having officially denounced Shiv Sena, especially after its violent campaign in connection with the Belgaum issue. After the Congress Party split in 1969, a turbulent period followed in which Shiv Sena, for short periods or on single issues, was aligned with virtually all parties in the Legislative Assembly and the Municipal Corporation.

The sustained, though informal proximity to the Congress Party has, throughout Shiv Sena's tumultuous life, proven to be valuable for the consolidation and survival of the party. A persistent rumor regarding the formation of Shiv Sena is that both the former chief minister Vasantrao Naik, a friend of the Thackeray family, and the Congress strongman Vasantdada Patil tacitly supported the formation and growth of the Sena because of its potential for destroying the Communist hold over labor in the 1960s and 1970s. For obvious reasons this has never been verified, though several senior leaders confirmed the friendly relation with Congress in the early years of Shiv Sena's existence. The fact remains that shifting Congress administrations generally viewed Shiv Sena as a useful ally and applied a "velvet glove" with regard to restricting its public actions, despite its admitted involvement in multiple violent excesses. Since his arrest in 1969, Thackeray has not been arrested again nor has he been indicted for inciting communal enmity, which is a felony according to the Indian Penal Code. The latest example of the Congress looking the other way was the absence of any measures against the Sena during and after the January 1993 riots in Bombay.

In 1974 Shiv Sena formed an official alliance with the Congress Party in connection with municipal elections in Bombay. This act prompted Thackeray's old friend, G. V. Behere, editor of the Hindu nationalist journal *Sobat*, to write an article entitled *"Senapati aur Shenapati"* (Shena means cow dung in Marathi), in which he questioned whether Thackeray deserved the loyalty and admiration of young people in Maharashtra, calling Thackeray a commoner who deserved to be dumped in a dustbin.[27] A few days later, sainiks attacked and humiliated Behere. As a result of this episode, many more of Shiv Sena's sympathizers turned away from the movement, but still Thackeray insisted on the alliance with Congress.

Shiv Sena supported Indira Gandhi's imposition of a state of emergency from 1975 to 1977. It remains unclear whether this move was linked to genuine support for a benevolent dictatorship, which Thackeray had been advocating for years, or to fears of repression from the state machinery. The fact is, however, that Shiv Sena maintained its legal status and its leaders stayed out of jail since it complied with many of the local Congress Party's demands, such as unconditional support for Murli Deoras, a Congress stalwart but also a Gujarati and thus unlikely to be admired by the rank and file. This decision, however, caused severely damaging rifts within Shiv Sena, and several leaders and many activists left the party in disgust. The movement's support of the Congress also damaged the popular base of the party and remains an embarrassment for the leadership.

In his otherwise glowing account of Shiv Sena, Purandare is rather sarcastic in his treatment of this period. He talks about "a loss of face" and reproduces a speech by Thackeray from 1982 in which Thackeray tried to explain his stance during this period. Thackeray, for once involuntarily humorous, explained that he was not afraid of being jailed but that the then chief minister of the state, "Shankarrao Chavan [who is rather obese—T.B.H.], was sitting on our head, so to say. I was suffering from a toothache at the time. . . . I could not even speak." But, assured Thackeray, "we had not in any way mortgaged our self-respect even during the Emergency. We were studying the Indira regime."[28]

In the State Assembly elections in 1978, after the Emergency was lifted, Shiv Sena decided, in another display of political opportunism, to support the Janata Party against the Congress. Janata refused to make any adjustment of electoral seats with Shiv Sena, and the party was marginalized and failed to win even a single seat in its erstwhile strongholds in Bombay. Until the early 1980s, Shiv Sena remained marginal, had no presence in the streets, and survived only on its still functioning networks of patronage and shakhas in Greater Bombay. According to longstanding Shiv sainiks, this was a period of great frustration and bewilderment in the party. In some speeches Thackeray would praise socialism and the Soviet economic system, while in others he would attack his old foes in the Communist trade unions. When the historical textile strike commenced in Bombay in 1980, Thackeray took a decisive stand against the workers (Sardesai 1995, 130).

Shiv Sena's proximity to the Congress Party has left many traces in its style of everyday politics. When engaging in "normal," nonheroic political negotiations of patronage and compromise at the local level, Shiv Sena has often appeared indiscernible from Congress in its methods and rationales. It is no accident that almost every defector from Shiv Sena since the 1970s has joined Congress, just as disgruntled members of Congress on many occasions have found a temporary home in Shiv Sena. Dissident sainiks have neither joined leftist parties nor their alliance partner since 1988, the right-wing Bharatiya Janata Party, whose program suggests close ideological affinity. However, BJP's tight-knit organizational culture and ideals of ideological consistency, discipline, and self-restraint are far removed from the average sainik's combination of political pragmatism, aggression, and "actionism."

In 1979 Shiv Sena began negotiations with an unlikely ally, the Muslim League and its leader, Banatwala, and in February 1979 the two parties formed an electoral alliance. On that occasion Thackeray gave a speech at the Mastan Talab in Nagpada in the heart of central Bombay, where he praised the Muslims. He assured his audience that Shiv Sena had always been friendly to Muslims and deplored the fact that Muslims had never trusted Shiv Sena:

> Whatever we have done for our Muslim brothers has not been reported in the papers. . . . We invited all but no one heeded our call. Our sincerity was doubted. . . . Today the entire Muslim population lives in hutments. Who is responsible for this? Why have Urdu boards been put up only in Muslim areas? Why not in all of Bombay? . . . I am very happy that today green and saffron flags are fluttering together.[29]

Several of my informants in Nagpada remembered this unlikely alliance and also recalled this and other meetings held by the two parties in the densely populated areas of Bombay. An Urdu journalist from the area told me: "In those days Thackeray was desperate, he would do anything to survive, but no one took him seriously then, we were just a bit puzzled. . . . I think Banatwala was the one who lost in this strange alliance." The alliance did not even last a year and did not produce the results at the State Assembly elections that both parties desired, neither party winning even a single seat.[30]

TRIUMPH OF THE ORDINARY

In its first decade Shiv Sena voters represented a cross section of Marathi speakers as well as many Hindus from other language communities, drawn from almost all caste groups and from most income groups, except the very low and the very high (Gupta 1982, 110–11). The social profile of the Shiv Sena voter did not differ substantially from that of voters for the Congress or the Communist Parties (Joshi 1970, 978). But those representing Shiv Sena as candidates, shakha pramukhs, and local leaders have, since the late 1960s, been young men from slum areas or lower-middle-class backgrounds—many of them without stable employment and with only a limited education.

More than any other organization in the city, Shiv Sena promoted men from such modest backgrounds into public prominence. Some of the prominent leaders came from higher-caste communities (Kayastha and Brahmans) and many were Marathas, but comprising the ranks of the organization were many members of lower-caste groups, predominantly from Marathi-speaking communities. Men from similarly upwardly mobile strata, though representing all language and religious groups but with similar desires for recognition and prominence, also achieved more visible positions in the Congress Party in the same period. This reflected a transformation of the social complexion of the entire political world in Bombay and further questions the thesis of Shiv Sena as a vehicle for particular class interests. If Shiv Sena was a vehicle for anything, it was for a democratic revolution that introduced a new type of popular leadership and of "plebeian" politics into Bombay's political culture.[31]

It is ironic that an organization like Shiv Sena, whose leader openly advocates authoritarianism, became central in the affirmation of Bombay's lower middle class and working class in the 1960s and 1970s. This affirmation, rooted in the larger mobilization of the linguistic movement in the 1950s, claimed a political voice, public visibility, and, perhaps more important, political "property rights" to the city based on its numerical strength and allegedly purer Maharashtrian cultural heritage. Shiv Sena sought to use its emerging urban identity—culturally still more removed from the rural hinterland—to ensure its right to belong to and inhabit the city. In this period Bombay experienced a broad cultural expansion involving the increased use of city space, of its beaches and squares, by impoverished groups, the assertion of a vigorous working-class culture and of mass entertainment (Heuzé 1995, 228–36).

Shiv Sena contributed decisively to this massive extension of urban space through its spectacular enactment of huge rallies and religious festivals, its network of shakhas, its citywide newspapers, signs, and blackboards displaying a variety of slogans and pledges. But the Sena never attempted to stop, purify, or redefine this cultural expansion. Instead, it aspired to further these complex sociocultural currents of Bombay by posing as the staunch defender and voice of the ordinary, culturally conservative Hindu family desiring order and respectability. As I will take up in the concluding chapter of this book, those who search for Shiv Sena's secret and coherent vision or design will search in vain. For the truth of Shiv Sena, and of similar populist movements elsewhere in India and beyond, is that they truly believe in the virtues of "the ordinary" and detest any visions, designs, art forms, or lifestyles of communities that threaten the cherished routines of what they regard as predictable and imaginable.

CHAPTER 3

"Say with Pride That We Are Hindus": Shiv Sena and Communal Populism

SHIV SENA AND THE CITY

A complex relationship exists between Shiv Sena and the city of Bombay. Although Shiv Sena celebrates the social world of the ordinary and the poor, over the years most Shiv Sena mayors and municipal corporators have aimed at creating *Sundar Mumbai*, beautiful Mumbai. They have launched beautification schemes, ousted pavement dwellers from the inner city, and promoted infrastructural development in the city. For decades the Shiv Sena leadership and its substantial middle-class constituency have shared a dream of a clean, orderly, civilized city, free of the constant over-flow of slum dwellers and migrants. But until 1995 Sena had neither the capacity nor a program to develop Bombay in this direction.

Shiv Sena's effective power, understood as its capacity to effect changes in institutions and conduct, is widely dispersed and localized in a multi-tude of informal networks in slums and middle-class areas. This structure, and the marginal position of parliamentary politics in the organization, impedes sustained political efforts within the civic administrative institu-tions. Instead, the Shiv Sena thrives on this diversity and only occasionally engages in concerted, spectacular campaigns, often according to the whims of Bal Thackeray. These campaigns did contribute, in the 1980s, to a deepening of the antagonistic relations between Hindus and Muslims in Bombay by transforming the energy and frustrations of ever growing numbers of young, unemployed men into anti-Muslim aggression.

Over the last few decades Bombay's social composition has shifted from one structured on class—namely, a large, industrial proletariat, a middle class, a small elite, and an amorphous slum population existing outside or on the fringe of the organized economy—into an incredibly complex mélange of social and cultural groups. The middle class has expanded rap-idly, and today there are more affluent people in Bombay than ever before. The working class has been disintegrating both as a sociocultural environ-ment and a political constituency, whereas the unorganized, informal, sec-tor has grown enormously. Gérard Heuzé argues that Bombay's social world has become increasingly bifurcated. On one side is the large, orga-nized world of the upwardly mobile and aspiring middle class and elite—

striving to retain the ideals and social parameters of modernity and order. On the other side is the informal world of the *zopadpattis* (slums) and chawls (working-class residences), where self-employment, marginalization, and exclusion are the fundamental social conditions (Heuzé 1995, 235–36).

Social strategies of the middle class for mobility or to consolidate one's status have given rise to powerful drives for education and employment for the younger generation engaged in a competitive labor market. The middle-class world is also increasingly marked by conspicuous displays of consumption and status, as well as a profound fear and contempt for the impure and violent world of the zopadpattis, an environment the middle class so painstakingly worked its away from. The expansion of middle-class residential areas along the railway lines into the Thane District north of Bombay is one manifestation of the effort of the middle class to escape congestion, high rents, and proximity to the slums. The entire real estate market, for both housing and rentals, is governed by a range of speculative mechanisms that has produced extremely high prices, what Appadurai calls a "housing-related hysteria" preyed on by a "huge disorganized army of brokers and dealers," and a veritable regime of rumors, blackmail, and "nervousness" which together form an unreal "spectrality of Bombay's housing scene" (Appadurai 2000). These pressures, compounded by Bombay's economic growth in the 1980s, made the middle class highly receptive to Shiv Sena's xenophobic rhetoric and promises of order, clarity, and heavy-handed governance.

In Bombay's vast zopadpattis and plebeian neighborhoods, fragments of the non-Brahman ideology, the socialist ideology espoused by the once powerful trade unions and the Communist movement, as well as the active Dalit (former untouchables) movement had firmly rooted a societal imagination organized around a "paradigm of rights" vis-à-vis the government and authorities. These were not notions of civic rights as defined in early modern Europe but rather straightforward ideas of entitlement, of claiming services, care, and protection, and so on.[1] For decades slum dwellers had demanded, even expected, provisions of services, political concessions, basic foodstuffs, civic amenities, and so on. For all these years these relations between government agencies—more broadly, the city elite—and those living in the slums were governed by a certain condescending, at times absent-minded, paternalism. This discourse and practice, which Gérard Heuzé aptly termed *ma-baap'ism* (*ma-baap* meaning mother-father) affirmed a hierarchical and unequal distribution of socioeconomic resources, cultural appreciation, self-respect, and one's ability to think and act appropriately.[2] *Ma-baap'ism* did not seek to change social conditions but merely to ameliorate the prevailing conditions and extend benefits to the poor through a network of local brokers and government schemes.

India's democratic revolution gradually undermined the idiom and practices of *ma-baap'ism*. The authority of politicians, government institutions, the police force, and the judiciary has been questioned because of their perceived—and real—corruption and criminal activities. The hitherto unarticulated social resentment and frustrated hopes for social mobility among still broader sections of Bombay's poor and marginalized population have grown into anger and defiance of authority. In Bombay of the 1980s, the so-called *dada culture*, which enjoys a long history in Bombay and other Indian cities as a popular model of authority and power, acquired new prominence as a style of public and political conduct, as *dadaism*. Dadas have been important figures in working-class neighborhoods— as protectors, brokers, and providers of services, jobs, and opportunities to men in the neighborhood throughout the twentieth century. A dada's status at any time depended on his performance and how powerful his connections were in political parties, the administration, the police, and so on. As in the case of the legendary dada Keshav Borkar of the 1920s and 1930s, networks of dadas were often used against striking workers and included in the mobilization strategies of political parties (Chandavarkar 1994, 200–211).

Dada literally means grandfather in Hindi but is used colloquially to mean elder brother and as a metonym for a criminalized subculture. Dadas are not always simply criminals, however, but often persons from the plebeian world who are physically strong, run small businesses, and have ties with a multitude of networks reputed for their personal integrity, courage, and honor. Dadaism is a style of exercising political and social power and protection that invokes images of a masculine, assertive, often violent local strongman, whose clout lies in self-made networks of loyalty rather than in institutionalized action and discourse. It is a style of conduct that appeals particularly to young men from the zopadpattis. It positions the young man aspiring to dada status as a protector of his family and kin, of women in particular, and as a man of honor who may be trusted by those who are loyal as much as feared if he is betrayed. It is a culture, indeed a style of personal conduct and reputation, that pervades the criminal world as well as the vast array of unauthorized activities taking place in the slums; moreover, it has become more noticeable in the public realm. Hence the commonplace observance of the "lumpenization" of Bombay.

Shiv Sena did not create the dada culture but, more than any other organization, it brought this long-standing plebeian discourse of masculine assertion into the public and political realms. Shiv Sena built on, internalized, and twisted this sociopolitical force in various ways. It gave historical legitimacy to manliness and violence, for example, Shivaji and the mythical Maratha bravery; it made a populist political idiom of the defiance of public authority as a way to protect fundamental cultural values and the chastity of women; it created a vehicle for collective action, for example, the networks of shakhas; it embodied a generalized cause to fight for; and, finally, it promoted a charismatic leader who, in dramatic and colorful language, could turn the feeling of marginalization into a sense of power and potency merely by virtue of numbers and by being a plebeian—simple, muscular, and courageous.

Shiv Sena became still more "dada-ized" as its political dadaism added its own distinct flavor to various social and cultural practices in Bombay's low-income neighborhoods. One of the most prominent institutions in the lives of young men in Bombay are the *Mitra Mandals* (Friends Associations), informal youth clubs and meeting places, found in the thousands all over Bombay. Many of the mandals are run or patronized by political organizations, local politicians, and dadas, and some enjoy a more independent status. The mandal is often merely a small house or room where young men meet daily to play cards and chat. Mandals often organize local functions and collect funds for religious festivals[3]—a practice systematized by the Shiv Sena shakhas. Though often sponsored by powerful groups or individuals, the mandals do function to some extent as a sort of free space for young men, a refuge from the compulsions of everyday life. Herein is nurtured the masculine culture of self-assertion, loyalty, and notions of honor and respect.

The gymnasiums and body-building clubs one finds today throughout the city emerged from the tradition of *akhadas*, which, for the past century, played a prominent role in Bombay's working-class culture. Akhadas, associated with martial prowess and admiration for the masters (*Ustads*) of the arts, have their roots in traditional country wrestling and are especially popular among Marathas in the Deccan. In India's urban colonial settings, akhadas became important meeting places for men to cultivate a sense of community and a fighting spirit (Alter 1994). In Bombay, middle-class youth also considered akhadas respectable places to meet, but after the communal riots in the city in 1929, akhadas became divided and often were hotbeds for conflicting communal sentiments, sponsored and patronized by renowned dadas (Chandavarkar 1994, 216–18). Like the mandals, gymnasiums provided manpower for political organizations, not least of all in the anticolonial struggle, and functioned as prestigious arenas where local patrons competed for influence and public standing.

Shiv Sena's shakhas and communal populism to some extent aggregated and politicized these masculine communities, and, in the organization's earlier phase, gave these communities a certain public esteem. Thus the vast number of young men participating in the Mitra Mandals—be they political or not—continue to be a receptive audience to Shiv Sena and to comprise a reservoir of recruitment for the movement.

This development has neither erased Shiv Sena's earlier features nor made dadaism the dominant form of social discourse and organization in the zopadpattis of Bombay. Clientelist networks and paternalism remain the leading forms of power relations both in the low-income areas and within Shiv Sena itself. The high regard with which certain popular practices at the organization's lower ranks are held has not displaced the conventionalist and conservative thrust of Shiv Sena's leadership, most of whom belong to Bombay's current parvenu elite eager to consolidate their new prominence and to be recognized for their elite status. There is indeed a cultural gap between the old, cosmopolitan strata that has dominated Bombay for more than a century and the new upcoming, wealthy strata of builders, politicians, film dons, and real estate developers. As Katzenstein et al. (1997) points out, which my own observations from interviews confirm, Shiv Sena leaders are generally not well-educated, few have been outside India, and most have grown up in a rather provincial, culturally conservative lower-middle-class environment.

The shift from ma-baap'ism to dadaism as the movement's preferred public language nonetheless signifies what seems to be an irreversible step in the larger process of democratic revolution, a process Shiv Sena has been skillful in capturing and manipulating for its own program of communal populism. This achievement, along with Shiv Sena's successful straddling of different social imaginaries, provided, as I demonstrate below, an essential precondition for the party's expansion and electoral success from 1985 to 1991 in Maharashtra.

GARVA SE KAHO HUM HINDU HAI
(Say with pride that we are Hindus)

After a long period of relative calm in the Bombay region, violent clashes between Hindus and Muslims began to reappear in the 1970s. The riot in Bhiwandi in May 1970, the most serious since Independence, was precipitated by a prolonged period of tense, escalating activity on the part of both Hindu movements (RSS , the Jana Sangh, and Shiv Sena) and Muslim organizations (Jamaat-i-Islami, the Muslim League, and the Majlis Tameer-e-Millat [MTM]). Because of the intense circulation of rumors in these political and religious milieus, the riots immediately spread to Jalgaon, a provincial city in northern Maharashtra, and Mahad, a town in the district of Kolaba. For this district, which for generations was intimately linked with Bombay's industrial labor market, news of the riots in Bhiwandi (broadcast on All-India Radio) had a devastating effect—an instantaneous, if short-lived, reenactment of the choreography of riots well known to the district. Hindus attacked and burned Muslim shops; Muslims retaliated; men, armed with spears, knives, bottles, and sticks, clashed in the streets; and the police opened fire, wounding several rioters on both sides.[4]

A commission of inquiry, chaired by Justice D. P. Madon, was set up to chart the causes of the disturbances and to apportion responsibility for the destruction of life and property. The commission's findings paint a clear picture of the riots as the outcome of a long-standing complex of economic contradictions between Muslim weavers and Hindu traders, interwoven with escalating competition over public space and identity in conjunction with the annual religious processions from Moharram to Shivaji Jayanti, a competition fueled and organized by communal organizations throughout the 1960s. The Madon Commission report severely criticizes the police for their feeble effort in preventing the riots, openly accusing the police of a clear anti-Muslim bias in their suppression of the disturbances. Not only were three times the number of Muslims killed and wounded than Hindus, the police arrested more than 2,000 Muslims but only 300 Hindus (Ghosh 1985, 188–89).

Like in other parts of India, anti-Muslim rhetoric proliferated in Maharashtra in the early 1980s. The pride in being a Hindu was fueled by, among other things, the enthusiasm that Khomeini's revolution in Iran in 1979 engendered among younger Muslims in different areas of the country. According to many Hindu informants with whom I have spoken over the years in the Bombay area, the mere sight of bearded, traditionally dressed, and highly visible Muslim youths in Bombay created an impression of Muslim fanaticism, which reactivated well-established myths of the Muslim threat to India.

In the same period, the practice of using loudspeakers to call people to the mosques for prayer spread to small mosques in the towns and villages. Many Hindus felt provoked that the Muslim community was becoming so "audible." Radical Hindus whom I met in Bombay and elsewhere in Maharashtra alleged that this practice had been encouraged by the "permission" given it by the chief minister, A. R. Antulay, a Muslim from coastal Konkan.[5]

A number of militant Hindu organizations took shape in Maharashtra in this period. One of these, the *Maratha Mahasangha*, sought, on the basis of militant rhetoric regarding Shivaji and the supposedly superior Maratha martial spirit (*patilki*), to propagate the idea that Marathas were the natural, rightful rulers of Maharashtra. The movement gained some foothold among groups of workers such as the *mathadi* porters in Bombay, in provincial cities, and in the affluent sugar belt in western Maharashtra.

In the same period a more activist organization, the *Hindu Ekta Andolan*, was formed by militants who believed that the BJP, in its liberal incarnation in the early 1980s, was ignoring the interests of the Hindu community and what they saw as growing Muslim influence in Bombay and western Maharashtra (Chousalkar 1989, 37–89). Though limited in membership, the organization succeeded in arranging a number of high-profile, anti-Muslim campaigns in the early 1980s in several provincial towns of western Maharashtra.

In 1982 the Ekatmata Yatra campaigns,[6] which the RSS organized throughout India, sparked a series of minor riots in Pune and Sholapur, and created tensions in many other places. The next year more riots broke out in the power-loom and textile center of Malegaon in northern Maharashtra, after young Hindus, in front of the Jama Masjid in the town, had celebrated the Indian victory in the World's Cricket Cup. This ignited widespread rioting and arson throughout the town. Not unlike in Bhiwandi, the consistent migration over the years of Muslim weavers from north India and their incipient economic success had changed the city's economic and demographic profile and added a distinct Muslim character to its cultural life.[7]

In 1984 Bhiwandi once more became the site of the most serious riots in the state thus far. These were intimately tied to Shiv Sena's pursuit, from 1984 on, of an intense anti-Muslim rhetoric and radical anti-Muslim strategy. Bal Thackeray formally announced the movement's new communal style in a starkly anti-Muslim speech at Chowpatty Beach in Bombay in April 1984, in which he repeatedly used the derogatory term for Muslims, *landyas*,[8] and called them "a cancer on this country. Its only cure is operation. . . . Oh, Hindus, you take weapons in your hands and remove this cancer from its very roots."

An article in *Marmik* claimed that Muslims "demand 33% representation in the armed forces. The motive behind such a demand is clear. . . . There will be no hesitation to inviting the armies of Muslim countries . . . under the pretext of defending the Muslim community." In *Sobat*, a Hindu nationalist weekly published in Pune, the editor wrote on 6 May 1984: "The Mussalman openly commit atrocities and treason, and openly express their loyalties to other Muslim countries. . . . Their aim is to convert the entire Hindustan into Islam. The only option we are left with is either to embrace Islam or destroy Islam." This rhetoric allowed the already existing myths of antinational and treacherous Muslims to be expressed ever more directly.

A few weeks after Thackeray's speech, Shiv Sena, Hindu Mahasabha, Patit Pawan, and other organizations formed the Hindu Mahasangh, an outfit designed to fight against the alleged Muslim aggression. In an uncanny replay of the events of 1970, one of the first actions of the Hindu Mahasangh was to organize a large procession through Bhiwandi on Shivaji Jayanti. Such processions had not been allowed in Bhiwandi since the riots in 1970, but the state government, led by Vasantdada Patil, a member of the Congress Party known for his sympathy toward Shiv Sena, allowed the march to take place. In an interview he justified his decision in this way: "Representatives of the Muslims told me that they did not have any objections. . . . No, I don't remember their names. I also learned that even if permission were not given, Shiv Sena, BJP, Patit Pawan, etc., would take out the procession. I told them they could do so but that the procession should take a different route and timing."[9]

The riots began on 17 May 1984 after a minor provocation, the placing of a saffron flag on top of a mosque. As the rumor of the disturbance spread, stone throwing, stabbing, and fighting broke out almost immediately in several places in the city. At this point an otherwise localized riot took on a new dimension, as Shiv Sena decided to intervene. During the first night of the confrontation hundreds of Shiv Sena activists from Bombay were transported on trucks to Bhiwandi, and so began the systematic looting and burning of Muslim houses, shops, and factories.

In the following days this pogrom spread to Thane City where several Muslim areas were attacked, their houses looted and burned. At the same time attacks were launched on Muslim settlements and slums in many of the industrial suburbs north of Bombay, spreading rapidly to central Bombay as well. The violence continued for ten days, until the army was called in to restore order.

Abundant newspaper reports, as well as interviews with individuals who had either witnessed or participated in the riots, confirm a pattern to the uprisings: active and systematic involvement of Shiv Sena, passive or active complicity by the local police forces, and a conspicuous lack of determined action by the state government. In keeping with the official routine in the event of a riot, Mrs. Gandhi and Rajiv Gandhi made a brief visit to Kamathipura in central Bombay to show their concern, where Mrs. Gandhi announced that a ban on Shiv Sena should be considered.[10] Official figures put the deaths at 278, the wounded at 1,115, and the arrests in army "clean-up" operations at a staggering 11,453. Thousands lost their homes and property, and the actual figures may well be higher than those the government indicated. Clearly the majority of victims were Muslims, although a substantial number of Hindus suffered in Muslim retaliations and in the local settling of scores that followed.

For Shiv Sena, the 1984 riots in Bombay, Thane, and Bhiwandi remolded its somewhat corroded image in Maharashtra into one of a staunch, courageous defender of Hindus fighting against alleged Muslim aggression. Indeed, several of Shiv Sena's founders in Aurangabad expressed to this author that the events in Bhiwandi and Bombay in 1984 confirmed that Shiv Sena was the only force capable of reversing what they saw as decades of Muslim dominance in the Aurangabad region.[11] Thus the ground was prepared for Shiv Sena's comeback in Maharashtrian politics from 1985 on.

WORLDS APART

The riots exacerbated the feelings of marginalization and isolation already rife among Muslims in Bombay. The discrepancy between the benign rhetoric of Muslim leaders in Congress, often derogatorily called *sarkari* Muslims (government Muslims), and the continued de facto exclusion of Muslims from white-collar jobs in the government and the industrial sector widened the gap between ordinary Muslims and their self-professed leadership. It was as though the credibility of a paternalist ma-baap authority collapsed much earlier within the Muslim community in Bombay than in other communities in the city. After the 1984 riots this gap was filled by the self-made Muslim underworld dons and smuggler kings, such as Haji Mastan, Karim Lala, and Yusuf Patel, who had risen to dominant positions in Bombay's underworld as the flow of migrant labor between India and the Persian Gulf made smuggling a hugely profitable business. These self-made dons—already popular heroes in the streets of Muslim neighborhoods—had, since the early 1980s, looked toward broadening their social recognition and indeed were quite successful in projecting themselves and their men as protectors of the Bombay Muslims.

Mastan and some associates had declared that they were "reformed" and had formed a political organization, the All-India People's Secretariat. During the May 1984 riots, rumors alleged that this organization was distributing weapons and explosives to Muslims in various parts of Bombay. As violence once again erupted in late June 1984, the police, acting swiftly, arrested and detained Mastan and most prominent leaders of his organization, as well as eighteen Shiv Sena shakha pramukhs and a few higher-ranking Shiv Sena leaders, such as Madhukar Sapotdar, under the National Security Act. Mastan, Karim Lala, and others were charged with manufacturing and distributing explosives at a factory the police claimed to have found in the Muslim neighborhood of Nagpada in central Bombay.[12] The Bombay police also testified to having filed cases against Shiv Sena leaders for making inflammatory speeches. However, in a manner typical of the Bombay police, none of these cases ever made it to court and most detainees were soon released on bail.

The open nexus between certain Muslim leaders and the underworld only confirmed the stereotypical view of Muslims, especially among the Hindu middle classes. Undoubtedly the riots in 1984 fueled the "dada-ization" of Bombay. Shiv Sena emerged as the champion of Hindus, promoting its own political dadaism through informal networks in both the city's slums and middle-class areas. At the same time Muslim underworld dons, whose power often was wildly overestimated by Hindus and Muslims alike, emerged as informal leaders in the Muslim community. The humiliation of the Muslims in the city and the absence of local leadership also allowed hitherto marginal political and cultural leaders a larger audience than before. Men like G. M. Banatwalla, Parliament member elected from Kerala and leader of the communal party, the Muslim League, managed to promote himself as the senior-most Muslim leader in the city. Further, Syed Shahabuddin, the emerging Muslim firebrand from north India who successfully encouraged Muslims to be more assertive in their public stance and defend themselves against Hindu majoritarian aggression, took up the Muslims' plight in Bombay. Revivalist and conservative organizations like the Jamaat-i-Islami and the Tabligh Jamaat also began to acquire a larger audience through their relief work among the thousands of Muslims affected by the riots.

This communalization and "dada-ization" of Bombay's political landscape were crucial prerequisites for Shiv Sena's victory in the 1985 Municipal Corporation elections in Bombay, where deep splits within Congress gave Shiv Sena an unexpected opportunity to win political influence. After years of political marginalization, the party emerged as the largest in the Municipal Corporation and ruled Bombay for the next seven years. This was a genuine surprise, considering that earlier the same year Shiv Sena had only won a single seat in the State Legislative Assembly with a meager 1.13 percent of the popular vote (Joshi 1995, 16). A triggering factor for this victory was undoubtedly the provocative, but false, remark by the then chief minister of Maharashtra, Vasantdada Patil, about secret plans in Delhi to make Bombay a Union Territory and move the state capital to another city. This rumor boosted Shiv Sena's odds in the election considerably, not least because the primary adversary, Murli Deora, was a long-standing Congress leader and, most important, a non-Maharashtrian businessman known for his excellent relations with Indira Gandhi (Sardesai 1995, 131).

Shiv Sena's hardened stance and political victories added to widespread anxiety and frustration among Muslims in Bombay, and gave impetus to the unexpectedly enthusiastic response to the protest voiced over the verdict in the Shah Bano case in 1985, a verdict seen as encroaching on the Muslim Personal Law.[13] Some of the largest and most spectacular demonstrations against the verdict were organized in Bombay. An editor of an Urdu daily, who was among those who called for the agitation, attributed this to a new sense of self-confidence among Muslims:

We were surprised by the magnitude of the response we got. Lakhs [a lakh is 100,000—T.B.H.] of people took to the streets. It was not just this verdict. . . . It was more a feeling that just because some Muslims were beginning to do well in Bombay and Bhiwandi, some political forces wanted to stop us, to turn the Hindus against us. So basically this was the reason.

These protests obviously provided an opportunity to demonstrate against the ruling party, a party that had failed so conspicuously to protect the Muslim community in Maharashtra despite its long-standing loyalty to Congress. The worlds of the Hindus and Muslims seemed to drift apart in the 1980s, leaving the Muslims more isolated both economically and socially, a subject I discuss further below.

Shiv Sena's success in the municipal elections and sudden control over the vast resources of the Bombay Municipal Corporation caused surprise and considerable disarray within the movement. In the next two years, the Shiv Sena leadership focused on consolidating its political structure and its networks of clientelist relations, now made more accessible because of the party's attainment of institutional power. Shiv Sena's new prominence in the political field also enabled it to strengthen its trade union wing, the Bharatiya Kamgar Sena, which, in the ensuing period, grew to become one of the dominant trade union organizations in Maharashtra. In 1985 the party also formed a women's wing, the Mahila Aghadi, led by a central pramukh, Sudha Churi. The women's wing was not an independent body with its own units but was designed to work as a women's division taking care of such problems as domestic violence, divorce, the plight of widows, and so on, within each of the more than two hundred shakhas Shiv Sena had established in Bombay by the late 1980s.

In Shiv Sena's older middle-class strongholds, the Mahila Aghadi worked as a support structure for the Sena, arranging meetings for ideological training (*shibirs*), support functions during campaigns, and separate activities for women and children during the large religious festivals. In the zopadpattis the organization had, to varying degrees, been devising separate programs for women supporting income-generating activities and demanding the opening of creches, which the state government had promised to provide to enable women to take on more permanent employment.

In many cases the Mahila Aghadi proved rather effective in staging these types of demands because the organization directly made use of Shiv Sena's "nuisance-value" as a compelling argument vis-à-vis employers, government officials, landlords, and others. Indeed, the pramukh of Mahila Aghadi made an obvious allusion to Shiv Sena's popular philosophy, that "being a Shiv sainik means half the job is done," in the following statement: "If a husband who, say, is unwilling to pay maintenance is brought to our shakha and told to pay, do you seriously think he will refuse? If we lead a *morcha* (demonstration) to a police station demanding the arrest of a husband or in-laws involved in a dowry death, do you think the police will refuse us? Come on, we are part of the Shiv Sena."[14]

During this period an increasing number of young enterprising men from small towns throughout Maharashtra approached Thackeray and other party leaders seeking entrance to the organization and permission to start local shakhas in far-off towns in rural Maharashtra. Circulation of Shiv Sena's weekly magazine, *Marmik*, was encouraged and greatly expanded, but it was only in 1987 that Shiv Sena had accumulated enough manpower and money to boost its image and structure throughout the state.

The most effective instrument proved to be Bal Thackeray's extensive tours and mass rallies all over the state. Thackeray's reputation was already well established but the extraordinary attendance by the populace at these mass rallies, even in provincial towns and rural areas, broke all previous records. At the same time Shiv Sena's larger units were given financial assistance and backing from Bombay to consolidate their local networks and to contest local elections wherever possible. But the organization's rapid expansion at this time was largely owing to the large number of itinerant, impatient younger men in the villages and towns across Maharashtra.

NON-BRAHMAN'S, OTHER BACKWARD CLASSES, AND ANGRY YOUNG MEN

Unlike in northern India, no major political party in Maharashtra succeeded in welding caste communities into a distinct OBC (Other Backward Classes)[15] constituency. In the late 1980s a Janata Dal politician and former Dalit Panther leader, Arun Kamble, advocated a strategy of "Kunbi-ization" of the Maratha caste in order to undermine, even dissolve, the hitherto solid base of Congress in the dominant caste. But Janata Dal's dismal electoral performance in Maharashtra, even at the height of its national success in 1989, indicated that the rhetoric of a distinct OBC identity was relatively ineffective in Maharashtra.

One reason was that the Maharashtra government, already in 1967, had identified 183 communities as "educationally backward classes" (EBCs). In 1978 this list grew to 199 communities, and the state government implemented a policy of reserving 10 percent of educational seats and government jobs for these categories. Another reason was that the political leaders, whose power and legitimacy in the Maharashtrian countryside depended vitally on the continued non-Brahman equation of Shudra and Maratha, had sensed the danger of their power and legitimacy being depleted. The 1931 census, which still serves as the official guide regarding the size of castes and communities, defined Maratha-Kunbis in two ways: In the more inclusive version the caste cluster comprised 40 percent of the population, whereas in a narrower definition it comprised only 30 percent. The percentage of OBCs would therefore vary accordingly, between 29 percent and 38 percent of the population.[16] Of critical importance to Maratha leaders was to ensure that the widest definition of Marathas prevailed, and to minimize the size of the OBC communities.

The Maratha Mahasangha (All-Maratha Federation), founded by Annasaheb Patil, a Congress Party member, embarked, in the early 1980s, on an anti-Mandal campaign among its constituent communities, especially the union of porters in Bombay known as the Mathadis. The Mahasangha promoted the Maratha caste myths and attracted young marginalized Maratha-Kunbis through a martial and clearly chauvinistic rhetoric stigmatizing Dalits and Muslims. The organization, at times close to Sharad Pawar's breakaway party, Congress (S),[17] quickly established a record of communal violence and collaborated closely with Shiv Sena on several occasions. The organization feared that the Mandal formula would further marginalize poor Maratha-Kunbis and bifurcate the caste cluster into Kunbis and high Marathas. The association never had much success outside Bombay and certain areas in western Maharashtra, but its existence and campaign indicated that at least some political leaders from the Maratha caste felt the need to counter the rising assertiveness of OBC groups in the political arena (Chousalkar 1989, 84–89).

The homelessness of many OBCs was compounded by the de facto closure of the Congress Party as a road to upward social mobility and access to resources. Internal elections had not been held in the Congress Party since the early 1970s, and most of the nominations for powerful posts in the party took place by proxy or through familial ties. Local Congress leaders made sure that their relatives were placed in a number of key positions in the party. Furthermore, Panchayati Raj elections had not been held since 1979, and the elected representatives from the panchayat level and higher had for years simply been granted automatic extensions. This immobility in the political structure consolidated the dominance of established, older, and rather conservative interests at the local level and excluded an expanding group of young, politically ambitious men from influence and positions.

In 1986 Sharad Pawar decided to dissolve his party, the Congress (S), which he had founded when he broke away from Congress in 1978, and return to Congress. This stalled many promising political careers, because many of Pawar's local leaders could not be absorbed into Congress. Further, Pawar's return especially deprived the younger and ambitious Marathas of their focal point and symbol of Maratha independence and strength, which was embodied in the person and career of Sharad Pawar.

In the 1980s fairly large numbers of young men from both the Maratha-Kunbi cluster and a variety of OBC communities had been educated in the mushrooming colleges and educational institutions in the smaller towns and cities of the state. Many of these young men, semi-educated and underemployed, had, during the period of economic growth in the mid-1980s, established themselves as minor businessmen and contractors. As newcomers they faced difficulty penetrating the tightly knit clientelist networks governing the political administrative setups and cooperative institutions, where business depended on the brokerage of connections, contracts, and official permits. These young men found themselves in the almost classical condition of harboring rising, but unfulfilled expectations, their social mobility blocked by what seemed an impenetrable and complacent political establishment.

In Bombay similar groups of self-employed men became important bearers of the emerging dada culture, which, in a somewhat diluted version, had sifted down to smaller towns and villages. In most of these small towns and villages there emerged groups of young businessmen who ran small shops (electronics, cold drinks, video libraries), minor contracting firms, country bars, transport businesses, and similar undertakings. They remained at the fringe of the organized and clientelistic economy, their status marginal in terms of economic power and social position. These groups were often divided along communal lines, young Marathas and OBCs on one side and, on the other, younger Muslims traditionally occupied in retail and commerce. The former group, engaged in business competition with obvious communal dimensions and marginalized from power and social recognition, became the group from which Shiv Sena recruited many activists and local leaders.

Shiv Sena did not appeal directly, however, to OBC communities and never tried to style itself as a political home for the lower castes. The organization's rhetoric remained largely within the established discourse of the Maratha caste and the unique character of Marathi speakers in terms of its historical and mythical references. The party's aggressive style, its hammering away at injustices allegedly done to oppressed Hindus, and its antiestablishment rhetoric made it attractive to the large groups of young men from OBC communities. Shiv Sena's militant opposition to the assertion of Dalit consciousness, especially by the Mahar community of neo-Buddhists, also added to its popularity among young Marathas and OBC youths.

For years Chagan Bhujbal was Shiv Sena's mayor of Bombay. He had been associated with Bal Thackeray and Shiv Sena from the organization's infancy. He was a Neta and had served for years as an able fund-raiser for Shiv Sena. With political power firmly entrenched in the Bombay Municipal Corporation in 1985 and the vast financial resources this opened up,

Bhujbal became a central figure in Shiv Sena. He extended the organization's economic base deeply into the lucrative real estate and construction business in greater Bombay and oversaw the expansion of clientelistic networks to other cities in the state such as Pune, Nasik, and Aurangabad. Bhujbal was also the central and energetic organizer of Shiv Sena's expansion into the rural hinterland. Later, he was put in charge of the distribution of candidacies among Shiv Sena candidates for the 1990 Legislative Assembly elections, a process involving, within Shiv Sena or the Congress Party, the payment of substantial sums of money from candidates to party coffers. Bhujbal is from the Mali (gardener) community, which had been categorized as OBC. He was touted as a genuine OBC leader, and his adept maneuvering secured him substantial political clout among many of the new MLAs—mainly Marathas and OBCs—elected on Shiv Sena tickets in the 1990 State Legislative Assembly elections. During this period, Bhujbal and his OBC followers were constantly paraded as irrefutable proof of Shiv Sena's popular and non-Brahman character.

One of Bhujbal's most prominent gestures toward defining OBC identity occurred in connection with a controversy regarding the official publication, in 1987, of Babasaheb Ambedkar's older work, *Riddles of Hinduism*, a highly critical text of Brahmanical Hinduism that pointed out theological inconsistencies in the ancient scriptures. The Maratha Mahasangha was first to take up the issue, demanding that the text be withdrawn, and the Congress government gave in with little resistance. Quite predictably this provoked Dalit organizations for which Ambedkar is the preeminent icon. In November 1987 Dalits held one of Bombay's largest demonstrations ever, demanding that the government reverse its decision. The government conceded defeat and published Ambedkar's text.

The Dalits' successful show of force on the streets of Bombay provoked Shiv Sena. As a result, the party called for a rally in January 1988 in an advertisement entitled "An Insult to Hindu Religion." The following statement in the advertisement clearly alluded to the impurity of Dalits: "Only those Hindus who have unadulterated blood in them should join this morcha [demonstration]. Come from every direction of Maharashtra and join with saffron flags."[18] Massive numbers of sainiks and supporters showed up, and in the following weeks both Dalits and sainiks took to the streets. Sainiks organized public burnings of the book and engaged in violent clashes with young Dalits in several areas of Bombay. Young Dalits damaged the memorial for the "Mumbai *hutatmas*," which Sena had erected at Flora Fountain Square; in response, Bhujbal performed a religious purification ceremony of the damaged structure. Although Bhujbal claimed that he had nothing against Dalits, the message was clear: OBCs were the defenders of Hinduism against its enemies, the Dalits. Ambedkar's work was not withdrawn, but Shiv Sena's tough stance on the issue earned it popularity among caste Hindus and OBCs. Most important, its popularity spread to the Marathwada region where Dalit radicalism was well established and where riots in 1978, over the proposed renaming of Marathwada University in Aurangabad to Babasaheb Ambedkar University, was still fresh in people's memories.

Another dimension of the proliferation of anti-Muslim stereotypes among communities classified as OBC was the somewhat vague community identity of OBCs. Because Muslims were a distinct minority, their self-identity had always been clear, their boundaries only sharpened by Hindus' stereotypical views of them and the stigmas held against them. In contrast, the OBC groups had never, before the Mandal Commission, been organized around a common identity or name and had never been viewed as a unified group with common interests and representation. Often defined as residual groups, political elites within the OBCs had long been in search of a distinct identity as well as a stable source of patronage and political inclusion. In the Maharashtrian context, the naming of these groups as "OBC" could not produce an effective identity and only seemed to aggravate the groups' long-standing sentiments of marginality and political homelessness. Thus Shiv Sena's anti-Muslim and communal rhetoric offered a clear enemy—the imagined menace of assertive Muslims and Dalits—and thus clarified, at least temporarily, the meaning of an OBC identity as being unequivocally Hindu.

THE DISCOURSE OF COMMUNAL POPULISM

Shiv Sena's ideology is almost exclusively produced and articulated by Bal Thackeray. Speeches and articles of other Shiv Sena leaders and legislators are more or less imitations of Thackeray's style, both in their themes and manner.[19]

Thackeray's style is conversational; he conducts imaginary exchanges in ordinary language, to a predominantly male audience. Much of his oratory is based on rhetorical questions or references to accusations from his opponents and his replies to these questions. He does not develop arguments but constantly jumps from one theme or question to another, making the kind of associative leaps typical of everyday conversation. He sprinkles his speeches with anecdotes, jokes, and historical myths—twisted or exaggerated for his purpose.

Thackeray relies heavily on mythical parables and metaphors, evoking arresting images of his opponents, of the threats Hindus face. The metaphors are constructed around the theme of violence, bravery, and manliness versus cowardice, weakness, impotence, and bizarre behavior. For example, he refers to the Congress government as a "*Shikandi* government."

Shikandi, from the epic *Mahabharata*, is a cowardly eunuch, who dresses and behaves like a woman and attacks the hero from behind. Thackeray is famous for his innovative play on words; he toys with the ambiguities of language, dissecting and reassembling phrases to suit his own purpose. For example, the term for socialists is *samajwadis*, *samaj* meaning community and *wadis* meaning adherents or followers in Marathi; by removing "*sa*" from the beginning of the term, Thackeray refers to socialists as maj-wadis, "maj" meaning arrogant in Marathi. Hence he derides socialists as arrogant intellectuals who actually despise the common people they claim to represent. In a 1989 editorial in *Saamna*, entitled "One Hundred Blows of a Sonar (Goldsmith), One Blow of a Lohar (Ironsmith)," socialists are alluded to as the effeminate Sonars, whereas Shiv sainiks are the masculine Lohars, the real men.

Finally, Thackeray is famous, as mentioned above, for constantly going over the limit of what may be said in public. He uses street language, slang, extremely abusive, yet often amusing language when ridiculing and imitating Muslim and Congress leaders. Thackeray routinely abuses Muslims in a language normally used only in highly informal settings (calling them "rats," "poisonous snakes," *landyas*, "traitors") and openly advocating that all Muslims go to Pakistan.

Thackeray's defense of Mahatma Gandhi's murderer during the 1991 election campaign, calling him a hero, and his admiration for Hitler's "determination to oust antinationals from Germany," have been widely discussed. But one glance through the editorials of Shiv Sena's mouthpieces, *Marmik* and the daily newspaper *Samna*, as well as his election speeches, reveals that such transgressions are regular features of Thackeray's writings and utterances. Addressing a large crowd in Aurangabad in January 1998, of which I was a part, Thackeray mocked and imitated Sonia Gandhi's broken Hindi and called her an "unauthorized structure" in reference to her Italian background, using the colloquial term for shabby, makeshift buildings in Indian cities. Probably the only reason Thackeray has not been legally charged for defamation more often is that he and Shiv Sena would turn such charges into major public events.

Although other political figures use many of these populist techniques, I believe that what sets Thackeray apart from these other politicians in Maharashtra, if not all of India, is that he combines these techniques with a total disregard for convention. Thackeray's peculiar technique transmits an intimacy and confidence in people that results in their basic acceptance of popular idioms, prejudices, and truisms. He never asks his audience to change their ways or to embark on some new endeavor; he merely tells them to assert themselves, to be proud of who they are, namely, Hindu men who are strong because of their number and superior culture. Thackeray's message of self-respect feeds on elevating the lower castes and the "ordinary" and is highlighted by his use of street jargon and abuse to which Thackeray, by virtue of his position in the political elite, bestows a certain legitimacy.

A standard approach used by Indian politicians, including those from BJP, is to address their audiences as *ma-baaps*, meaning parents, patrons, and well-wishers of the humble politician before them. They ask for votes, they promise to make a number of improvements, and they disavow power as a goal in itself. This, to Thackeray, is hypocritical. Instead, he addresses his audience as "brothers, sisters, and mothers." He makes it a point never to be humble, and he ridicules hollow promises. He portrays himself as a proud man who speaks his mind. He asks his audience to do the same: to stand up as men, be proud of who they are, believe in themselves. While Shiv Sena is helping and protecting women, men must gather their strength and join the Sena (the army). Indeed, Shiv Sena does protect but only those worth protecting—the proud, the bold, the assertive.

This dada discourse is supported and validated by Shiv Sena's loose and informal character. Anyone is free to call himself a Shiv sainik, to start a shakha. He merely must meet two qualifications: First, he must accept, unconditionally, the leadership of Thackeray, the Senapati (commander-in-chief) and show loyalty (*nishta*) to the power Thackeray assigns the pramukhs at various levels; and, second, he needs to be aggressive and assertive in order to be accepted by other Shiv sainiks.

Thackeray's speeches and writings revolve around three themes. One theme is frank opposition to the Congress Party, an assessment of the party as corrupt, lacking in development, and betraying the electorate. A second theme outlines what one might call "communal common sense," which represents Muslims, and to a lesser extent Dalits, as conspiring against Hindus, as being antinational, violent, and so on. The third theme is more subtle and revolves around sexuality and the creation of self-respect, masculinity, and strength in Hindu men. It ridicules Congress and intellectuals as effeminate, demonizes myths of Muslim potency, and challenges young Hindu men to "stand on their own two feet."

These themes, always interwoven, may be seen on three psychological levels: first is the openly contested ideological space of interparty rivalry, then communal common sense and myths, and finally a deeper subjective layer of young men's ambiguous, sexual identities. In this association of politics with sexuality lies, as in the communal discourse of the wider Hindu nationalist movement, an important explanation of the appeal of communal populism. The main difference between the Shiv Sena, the RSS, and the BJP in this respect is not in their demonizing and expunction of the Muslim threat, but in their remedies (see Hansen 1996c). The RSS speaks at length in high-caste idioms of "purification," "character building," and the sublimation of mental energy into physical strength. Shiv

Sena, on the other hand, speaks of physical violence as a way to purify society and to restore masculinity.

Here I quote some examples of the style in which Thackeray ridicules his political opponents. On the eve of the municipal elections in Aurangabad in 1988, he alluded to the shameless and effeminate behavior of Congress leaders:

> The politicians have turned democracy into a brothel. The job of spitting *paan* and calling the passerby has started. For that voluptuous Vilasrao [Vilasrao Deshmukh, the Congress candidate] was squatting in Aurangabad. Middlemen like Jadhav and Pawar were searching for customers. All this is going on in the face of democracy. (*Marmik*, 1 May 1988)

In an election speech during the 1990 Assembly election, Thackeray ridiculed the empty promises of Congress leaders:

> In Sangli there was a shepherds conference [the *dhangar* community— T.B.H.). Rajiv Gandhi was specially invited. Because he was told that unless he went there, the goats would not come. So Rajiv Gandhi went there, but the goats did not turn up. . . . The shepherds were given assurances "we will start a wool-project!" (Speech in Marsi, 4 February 1990)

Elsewhere, Thackeray accuses Rajiv Gandhi ("a nice chubby boy") for being non-Hindu and non-Indian. He alleges that Christian conversions have increased since Rajiv Gandhi's Italian wife arrived in the country. And he jokes that the "throne in Delhi is so sticky now after one family in power for so long, that one should clean it properly in Dettol [a well-known strong disinfectant—T.B.H.]" (Speech in Nagpur, 19 August 1989)

Thackeray is even harsher on his local competitors from Congress such as Union Home Minister Shankarrao Chavan, derided for being submissive to the Nehru family, and Sharad Pawar, derided for his dark-skinned complexion—often seen as a mark of lower-caste origin—which Thackeray, in his speech, regards as a mark of treason.

> [To Shankarrao Chavan] Here in the house you give challenges, but there [in Delhi] you run to the latrine. Who has the time to keep a record of what you have done in the latrine. When Sanjay Gandhi was alive you lifted his chappals. And placed them at his feet. This is an insult to our great Maharashtra.
>
> [On Sharad Pawar] He was saying, "If I go back to Congress, I will apply coal tar to my face" [a sign of shame—T.B.H.]. Did he not say this? Coal tar is readily available. Even coal tar is ashamed, how to stick to his dark face. This man is coal tar incarnate . . . This man is Afzulkhan of Maharashtra.[20] (Speech in Marsi, 4 February 1990)

Muslims, and especially Muslim leaders, are ridiculed and abused in a language no other Indian politician would use. The themes persistently revolve around the growth of the Muslim population, "appeasement of Muslims," antinationalist activities, and the secretive, conspiring, and violent nature of Muslims. In this regard Thackeray presents a cruder, more hard-hitting version of the RSS's more convoluted communalism.

> In this country only Muslims have been given the right to utter the word *religion*. In every sentence the Muslims can chant Muslim. But Hindus do not even have the right to spell Hindu. . . . Along with Jinnah's Pakistan, Pandit Nehru created an internal Pakistan within this country. . . . These poisonous snakes [Muslim leaders—T.B.H.] who under the name of religion like rats nibble at our country, and like snakes bite the stone of liberty. . . . If by tightening the ropes around their necks we do not show them their place, then after 50 years no Hindu will remain on the world map. (*Marmik*, 26 February 1986)

Under headlines like "Capital Punishment to Shahabuddin" and "Hang Bukhari," both prominent Muslim leaders at the time, Thackeray wrote that these "snakes should be crushed" or "drowned in the sea." The weak cowards in the "eunuch government" do not dare to control the Muslims but let them reign freely and hatch conspiracies against India, Thackeray alleged.

> If armament is found in a mosque, or out of Gulf money marble stones decorate their walls and silver ornamentation takes place . . . the Government does not dare to question where the money comes from. The registrar of religious institutions dare not step inside a mosque to find out what exactly happens there. (*Marmik*, 31 May 1987)

> The cancer of Pakistan has spread. . . . Hindus live in their own country as refugees in a transit camp . . . an international plot is being hatched in some Muslim countries to inflame hatred against India under the name of Islam. But the wire puller is of this very country—Imam Bukhari—grown arrogant under the aegis of *Jama Masjid* [in Delhi—T.B.H.]. *Jama Masjid* has become a den of conspiracy. (*Marmik*, 3 January 1988)

Concerning the Muslim population growth, Thackeray alludes to prominent myths regarding Muslims, namely, that they are primitive, culturally backward, lazy, unemployed, and obsessed with sex:

> They have gone beyond 150 millions now. Why so much is our question? Go to cinema. Go to drama. What are you doing, sitting at home? We go to cinema, everything is in order, that is a fine family planning. . . . They do not have any other work! . . . You asses, haven't you been given Pakistan? Then go there! Lessen the burden on the land. (Speech at Dombivli, 6 November 1989)

The worst part of the assumed Muslim conspiracy seems to be the myth of the innate self-confidence and unity of the Muslim community. This self-confidence is, according to Thackeray, the ultimate insult to the population's Hindu majority. Commenting on the ease with which Salman Rushdie's *Satanic Verses* was banned in India, months before the book even became an issue in the rest of the world, Thackeray alleges that it was because of "Muslim shouting":

> But I think for Muslim fanatics, mere shouting is a sign of effeminacy. Therefore, slogans such as "We got Pakistan by fighting, we will take Hindustan by laughing" are to be heard in various places in India. (*Samna*, 16 February 1989)

Sexual undercurrents are noticeable in Thackeray's attacks on Muslims. It is the Muslims, after all, who obviously are the obstacles to a full and proud Hindu masculinity. It is they who are obviously "stealing the national enjoyment" by their very presence. In Lacanian terms, the Muslims in India are the *objét petit a* representing what is "lacking" in the Hindu, namely, weakness, effeminacy, and so on. The remedy Thackeray prescribes is to recover Hindu aggressiveness, restore the martial spirit of the Marathas. The recurrent references to *Shivshakti* (Shivaji power), to the myths and anecdotes of Shivaji, to the worship of the war goddess Bhawani all contribute to that theme.

In an election speech Thackeray refers to the legendary martial traditions of the Sikhs and tells the story of a historical figure of Punjab, Guru Govind Singh, who, before a battle, selected the most fearless boys for combat. Here he challenges secular intellectuals on the issue of women's bodies, asking them to "give their daughters to Muslims":

> Neither of these Sikh boys would complain even if their bodies were pierced through! I want such boys! . . . Where is our unity [these days]. Some self-styled progressives will blame me for talking about Muslims. Come, marry your son away, give away your daughter to them if your progressiveness is so overflowing.
>
> I am saying only one thing: Those who utter insulting words about Hinduism and our Gods and Goddesses—remember, we will cut off his tongue and his hand. . . . What the government is not able to do, you must do. *You will have to do it.* Otherwise, don't take the name of Shivaji in your mouth. Don't celebrate the birthday of Shivaji! (Speech in Marsi, 4 February 1990)

In Thackeray's universe the ideal ruler is not Ram. It is Shivaji's muscular anti-Muslim deeds that serve as the primary reference. Whereas the Vishwa Hindu Parishad, through fanciful historical engineering, pitched a mythological ram against a historical Babur in Ayodhya, Shiv Sena goes back to the innumerable battles between the Mughal emperors (especially Aurangzeb) and the Maratha Empire. Maharashtra's landscape is filled with remnants of fortresses and tombs constructed during this period when both Maratha and Mughal power were at their zenith. Thackeray refers extensively to this history and the many myths surrounding it, seeking to emphasize the significance of the Marathas' martial qualities. In an editorial after Shiv Sena's victory in the 1988 Municipal Corporation elections in Aurangabad, where many Muslim candidates were defeated, Thackeray reinvoked the historical battles, equating Muslims and Aurangzeb as follows:

> For three hundred years the ghost of this thirsty soul [Aurangzeb] has harassed this country. Barrister Mohammad Ali Jinnah was the last incarnation of this ghost. He succeeded in his plot and divided this country into two parts. On that occasion, Aurangzeb must have scornfully laughed underneath his tomb in Aurangabad. . . . After three hundred years, history has been repeated, and the *mard* [virile] Marathas have buried the ghost of Aurangzeb in the very soil of Aurangabad. (*Marmik*, 1 May 1988)

Hindutva is nationalism, and Maratha men (used as a metonym of Maharashtrian Hindus), given their historically proven courage and fearlessness, should, Thackeray asserts, be in the forefront of the "nationalist resurrection."

> We are asked, why did you turn to *hindutva*? We did not turn! It was in our blood from the very beginning. He who is Maratha, who is *Margattha* [stubborn, staunch] for *Shivrajya* [rule of Shivaji], is a nationalist. It is in our blood. Each and every cell in our body talks of nationalism. . . . [Addressing those who threaten to assassinate him, Thackeray says:] Hey, if you have courage then come, come on such an open ground [like here]! Why aim arrows from behind the skirts of your wife? These are Shiv Sena's *mards* [virile men], believing in face-to-face confrontation. (Speech at Nagpur, 19 August 1989)

In an editorial in *Saamna*, Thackeray comments on the case filed against Shiv Sena's Zilla Pramukh in Thane District for having attacked and disturbed an educational camp held by a socialist group in Thane. Shiv Sena alleged that the socialists were spreading anti-Hindu propaganda and that the leader of the socialist group had had to beg the local police—rather sympathetic to Shiv Sena—to file a complaint against the party. Here, socialist intellectuals are depicted as weak, effeminate, upper-caste intellectuals "caressing the beards of Muslims," whereas Shiv Sena is depicted as the robust, strong, and simple defenders of basic Hindu values:

> Reality was, that the Shiv sainiks just gave the slogan "Shiv Sena has come!" and the pants of these so-called progressives got wet. . . .) On this what can

one comment? We can only say: Get up, effeminate chap, get up! And hence-forth think a hundred times before throwing mud on Hindu sentiments. . . .) The glory of Hindutva is not in *Janva* [sacred thread worn by the upper castes—T.B.H.] nor is there any national interest in caressing of the beards of Muslims. This is our standpoint. (*Samna*, 11 April 1989)

As I have tried to demonstrate in these examples, the stylistic elements of Thackeray's discourse supports the construction of Hindu masculinity that lies at the heart of Shiv Sena's ideological and practical strategy. The Hindu man—who is a dada and not a pitiful object of benevolence—comes into being as he starts to talk straight, to act radically and violently, and to constitute his own will, both as a collective led by Thackeray and his lieutenants and as an individual who is active and enterprising. Commenting on the economic promises of Congress, Thackeray derides dependency on the government. "Do something! Start a shop or a business!" he challenges his followers, as he has done since the 1960s when he called on them to set up food stalls selling *vada pav* (a popular dish in Mumbai). The unassertive Hindu man is an effeminate weakling who allows himself to be exploited by Congress leaders and "effeminate intellectuals," which then renders Hindu society vulnerable to the expansion and violence of the Muslims. Hindu society creates itself through action, especially violent action. In that sense, Muslims are merely a tactical obstacle, namely, a community that blocks the full development of Hindu masculinity, and hence the economic and political development of Hindu society (India as Hindusthan), preventing it from becoming as great and as strong as other nations in the world.

Shiv Sena and the RSS both share the idea of Muslims as the "other," blocking national development by their "theft of national enjoyment"—what Zizek describes as preventing the enjoyment of a community and a history that they never actually had. The two parties also share the belief that activism, unity, and discipline are the qualities necessary to regain Hindu masculinity. However, whereas the RSS promises harmony, cooperation, collective organized activism, and reconciliation, Shiv Sena promises violence, strife, and conflict. Only by making sacrifices for the nation (Thackeray speaks of *Dharmayudh*—holy war), by demonstrating individual courage and aggression will Hindu masculinity, and hence Hindu society, recover from its present stage of effeminacy, derision, and disarray.

The major difference between the RSS and Shiv Sena at the ideological level boils down to their different attitudes toward the ambiguities of male sexuality in India, as analyzed by Sudhir Kakar. Kakar argues that male sexuality exists in a void between the notion of women as adorable, asexual mothers or lustful women whose sexuality must be controlled, on the one hand, and, on the other, the Brahmanical idea of sexual abstinence and the sublimation of bodily desire into spiritual energy as the highest mark of masculinity (Kakar 1989). Although I disagree with Kakar's generalizations about (national) culture and personality, his propositions about the paradoxes of male sexuality may have some relevance in the case of higher-caste Hindus.

The RSS basically accepts this latter structure of sexuality and prescribes organizational discipline and collective assertion under the appropriate moral guidance (namely, the RSS) as the way that sexuality—which is becoming increasingly free as family authority and traditions erode—can be controlled and sublimated into national strength and glory. In Lacanian terms, the institutional patriarchy of the RSS offers to heal the symbolic order, to institute a new and consistent "law," and to embody this new compelling order—to be the stern, yet caring "Name-of-the-Father."

Shiv Sena, on the other hand, seeks to expand the boundaries of male sexuality, drawing on the combination of an unequivocally masculine Kshatriya tradition and emulation of the image of strong, active, conquering men nurtured in Islam. It offers masculinity through violence—for example, through annihilation and humiliation of the Muslim "other," who has long deprived Hindus of their masculinity. In Lacanian terms, this is an attempt to "mind the gap" (that is, to reduce the "lack," which, according to Lacan, characterizes all subjectivity), as well as a strategy that allows Hindus to rage against the "thieves of enjoyment," to have a free run, to expunge the *objét petit a*, the Muslim. Shiv Sena's glorification of action and immediacy, in contrast to the RSS's notion of cultural essences, displays, in a rather naked form, the temporal and unstable character of subjectivity: If we do not continue our actions and attacks, we cease to be true Hindus. Further, Shiv Sena offers an "army" and leadership, a law and a father, under whose demanding orders one can recover one's masculinity, assert oneself, and subvert authority, all under the protective hand of Shiv Sena, never having to fear retaliation from those one attacks.

In short, Shiv Sena offers young, powerless, insecure men the opportunity to view themselves as strong, enterprising men, accepting of their male desires, able to control women and to command respect simply by their association with Shiv Sena. The Shiv Sena discourse invites these young men to become dadas. Undoubtedly the attraction of this identity construction is heightened by the fact that, unlike joining a criminal dada culture, joining Shiv Sena does not entail a sharp break with societal and moral authority. Indeed, one can become a political dada under the absolving canopy of Thackeray's leadership, couched in the rhetoric of honesty, social work, and the protection of cultural values.

MASS PRODUCING SAINIKS: ON THE
CAMPAIGN TRAIL, 1988–1992

From 1987 on, Shiv Sena began to expand more systematically into the interior of Maharashtra. Instrumental in this endeavor was the party's strident communalism and the many popular slogans that Thackeray's reputation and the weekly *Marmik* now spread throughout the state. The most popular of these slogans was in Hindi: *"Garva se kaho hum hindu hai"* (Say with pride that we are Hindus), which both captured Shiv Sena's departure from its former regional nativism and condensed the party's self-assertive plebeian mentality to which Shiv Sena gave a distinct and twisted voice in the public realm.

In 1988 Shiv Sena began publication of a Marathi daily, *Saamna* (Confrontation), whose striking headlines and inflammatory style won broad popularity in many cities and towns outside Bombay.[21] Realizing Shiv Sena's immense dynamism in these years, the BJP leadership initiated an electoral alliance with Shiv Sena. The agreement entailed a distribution of seats that favored Shiv Sena at the state level and the BJP in the general elections.[22]

In the 1989 election campaign the parties shared a commitment to *Hindutva* but otherwise pursued very different programs in diverse styles. Shiv Sena fielded a simple nine-point program containing a few loose promises to various disadvantaged groups but focused mainly on symbolic issues like the proposal to change the constitutional name of India from Bharat to Hindusthan.[23]

In that election Shiv Sena won four of the ten seats secured by the alliance. Despite the meager number of seats won, the result was significant for Shiv Sena, which, for the first time, acquired seats in Lok Sabha in Delhi. Before the 1990 State Assembly election Shiv Sena gave in to the BJP's demand for a common platform, which promised a clean, stable, and honest government, devoted to serve the people: "In short, the farmer will become the king, the consumer will be happy, and mothers-sisters will become fearless. This is the crux of our pledge." The platform contained a long list of populist guarantees such as the waiving of agricultural loans, remunerative prices on agricultural products, clean drinking water, improved educational facilities, cheap housing, better pensions, and so on. One of the more interesting promises was for 15 percent of educational opportunities and jobs to be reserved for the economically disadvantaged—a bid to preempt the Mandal formula of prioritizing on the basis of caste. The proposal for a 30 percent quota for women in all elected bodies was later passed in 1991. Shiv Sena's former nativist agenda surfaced in the party's demand to implement Marathi as the administrative language and to create a local Marathi television channel that would service the state.[24] Trying to outbid his competitors, Thackeray promised free and quick housing for four million slum dwellers in greater Bombay.

Shiv Sena used Thackeray's picture with its bow and arrow symbol in its ads, which, often imaginatively, made key promises and ridiculed Congress. A widely used advertisement depicted a pair of worn-out chappals, with the text: "Why Shiv Sena? The answer is given by this worn-out footwear in search of a job." The text continues: "Tolerated for 42 years. How much longer?" Then large letters spell out the slogan: "When tolerance (*Sahanshakti*) ebbs, *Shivshakti* (power of Shivaji) rises." And next to the bow and arrow symbol, the text reads: "Self-respectful minds acknowledge: Pick that bow, let the strike be perfect."[25]

Other slogans widely used in posters, ads, pamphlets, and wall paintings included "Hinduism Is Our Life—Saffron Flag on the Assembly Hall"; "To Blast the Traitors: Take the Bow and Arrow of *Shri Ram*"; "Each Hindu is Acid!"; and the old Maratha war cry "*Har Har Mahadeo.*" In an innovative move, Thackeray's speeches were widely circulated on cassettes and videotapes. A number of videotapes projected images of saffron flags waving in the wind, old castles on hilltops from the Shivaji era, flames, and huge enthusiastic crowds intermingled with fragments of Thackeray's oratory, with Thackeray depicted in heroic postures as a modern incarnation of Shivaji.

Because of the huge response evoked by the election campaign, the Shiv Sena leadership began to entertain hopes of a victory for the alliance. The election results were therefore a major disappointment, although the alliance did draw as many as 27 percent of the popular vote. Congress's victory was probably secured in the last moments of the election by mobilizing the considerable resources of the Congress machine, as well as making use of Thackeray's derogatory comments during the campaign. The election campaign had polarized Maharashtra's political field, leaving the Shiv Sena–BJP alliance a rather formidable political factor. Shiv Sena's senior leader, Manohar Joshi, became the opposition leader in the Legislative Assembly, and Chagan Bhujbal, the architect of Shiv Sena's expansion throughout the state, was not actually rewarded but simply given another term as mayor of Bombay. This created a rift between rural-based legislators from OBC communities rallying around Bhujbal and urban-based legislators rallying around Joshi, a Brahman teacher turned businessman in charge of a network of evening schools and private education, the *Kohinoor* classes, which had diversified into a chain of hotels and restaurants by the same name.[26]

The tensions between the two partners in the alliance were exacerbated on the eve of the 1991 general election when, at a meeting in Pune, Thackeray publicly praised Nathuram Godse's assassination of Mahatma Gandhi, saying: "Nathuram who was afire with the thought that this individual [Gandhi] stays alive, then the country will be divided again, did no wrong. He saved the country from partition. Hence we do not feel ashamed of him, but justifiably proud."[27]

Once Thackeray's statement was widely publicized, the shrewd tactician Sharad Pawar used the remaining election campaign to portray the alliance between the BJP and Shiv Sena as a reincarnation of the Brahmanical reactionary plot that killed Gandhi. The BJP was infuriated that Congress had been given this unwelcome chance to revive the old Brahman-Maratha antagonism that the BJP had tried to ignore. The alliance was unable to win additional seats, and tensions between the two partners grew in the following months. Violent clashes erupted between the student bodies of the two partners, the RSS-affiliated ABVP (Akhil Bharatiya Vidyarthi Parishad) and Shiv Sena's Bharatiya Vidyarthi Sena led by Thackeray's flamboyant and aggressive nephew, Raj Thackeray. In an angry reaction, Thackeray stated:

> Snotty nosed, whom are you challenging? . . . These snotty-nosed kids of ABVP reached out for Shiv Sena labeling it "Goonda Sena." . . . This is too much. In spite of the nuisance BJP is causing to us in many states, we tolerated it all for the protection of Hindutva (. . .) If these female camels are not restrained by their leaders, we do not care for the alliance. (*Sakal*, 3 September 1991)

The alliance was deeply fractured, and in early 1992 it collapsed under the weight of its internal contradictions.

A CRISIS OF AUTHORITY

In December 1991 members of Congress had persuaded Chagan Bhujbal and twelve Shiv Sena MLAs to defect and join the Congress Party. Bhujbal, in 1991, recognized the impossibility of his position. It was difficult for him to advance further within the Shiv Sena without clashing with other senior party leaders or without provoking Thackeray and thus jeopardizing his own personal following in Shiv Sena.

The pretext for his defection was a number of derogatory remarks Bal Thackeray made about the Mandal Commission and about caste-based reservations of jobs or education in general. Thackeray and other Shiv Sena leaders disapproved of the rising assertiveness of OBCs in general, and particularly of those within Shiv Sena. The prospect of Shiv Sena becoming identified as a lower-caste movement within its constituency (which already included a large number of OBCs) was at odds with the party's preferred self-image and particularly with Thackeray's worldview.

He envisioned Shiv Sena as a vehicle for the social mobility of Maharashtrians into prestigious posts in politics, business, and administration.[28]

Given the OBCs' impressive support of Shiv Sena and their receptiveness to the party's communal populism, Thackeray's insults to these groups seemed politically and tactically suicidal. Had Thackeray operated according to a common "electoral instinct," undoubtedly Shiv Sena would have consolidated itself among these OBC communities. However, he continued to oscillate between the "plebeian" and "respectable" discourse he had developed over so many years, which underlined a central feature in Shiv Sena's modus operandi, namely, that while it spoke in an ostensibly plebeian and popular idiom, the values and customs it conveyed typified the upcoming parvenu entrepreneurs from where its leadership was drawn.

The ideological fantasies of worthiness and respectability through which Shiv Sena operates tend to blind its constituencies to who they actually are while opening their eyes and expanding their imaginations as to who they would like to be. Obviously Shiv Sena's vision of respectability within the middle-class lifestyles of Bombay, which it transmits through advertisements, films, and magazines, is enormously attractive to younger people throughout the state. Adopting an OBC identity, asserting pride in oneself as a plebeian, in who one actually is, would have clashed with the dynamic, if precarious, fantasies of worthiness and respectability that are at the heart of Shiv Sena.

In Lacanian terms, one might argue that Shiv Sena's desire for recognition based on respectability—articulated as a right to recognition qua being Hindus—revolves around a paradoxical *jouissance* of the abyss of the plebeian and the rough. In the social existence of many upwardly mobile groups and individuals, the plebeian seems to occupy the place of what Lacan calls the "Real"—the fascinating and deeply troubling residues of existence that escapes symbolization, that is, that resists interpretation and must be concealed or encapsulated. Thus the plebeian is that element in the background and habitus of many sainiks that blocks or destroys any illusion of being a truly "cultured" person worthy of recognition. Shiv Sena seeks to glorify this plebeian lack of culture and education and turn it into a source of recognition qua strength and courage in the struggle against the Muslims, the Hindus' common enemy. At the same time any assertion of OBCs being ennobled simply because of their status as plebeians had to be excluded from Shiv Sena's discourse. This is the very reason why the assertion of Dalit consciousness provokes such violent reactions among Shiv sainiks: Dalits signify and compound what is lacking and impure in the social existence of all lower castes. The socially dominant higher castes' exclusion of, contempt for, and refusal to recognize these lower-caste groups, regardless of their affiliation with Shiv Sena, cannot be ignored and will always stand in the way of their being identified as true Hindus.

Thackeray's refusal to allow his organization to identify with its emerging constituency among the lower-caste groups, and his insistence on Shiv Sena's authority to represent and hence mold popular identities, further supports my argument that parties rarely reflect a preexisting interest or group; on the contrary, they create and reiterate the precarious boundaries of a group through the act of naming. This is analogous to the doubts as to the actual existence of the Maratha-Kunbi caste cluster discussed above. Identifying with the Maratha denomination is appealing because it promises power and strength to those who lack these qualities. Similarly, as mentioned above, Shiv Sena's constituency is not built on who people are or how they behave but rather on who they wish to become. Bhujbal's popularity among OBCs was not the result of his merely being from an OBC community but rather that he was an OBC man who had "made it" in Shiv Sena and had realized the dream of both respect and respectability.

The significance of the OBC denomination in this regard is that Bhujbal, from the mid-1980s, began to play on his background and vast network of contacts to establish a relatively independent group of loyal supporters—both OBCs and Marathas—within Shiv Sena. That this defection, in itself a routine practice in Indian politics, was represented as an OBC rebellion indicated that OBC communities, also in Maharashtra, had become the most contested stratum of the electorate. Although Marathas and Brahmans still dominate politics in Maharashtra, OBCs have moved closer to a political representation congruent with their actual share of the population.

The defection of Bhujbal and his group dealt a major blow to Shiv Sena's cohesion and political strength. The situation was complicated by the deep involvement of sitting councilors and local leadership in contracting, construction, and real estate, as well as crime and smuggling. For most municipal councilors, therefore, the stakes in local politics were considerably higher than before they entered the civic body. These increased risks in civic politics and the weakened authority of Thackeray and the Shiv Sena leadership after the split in the party made the distribution of tickets, especially for the Bombay Municipal Corporation, a virtual chaos. Many Shiv Sena men defected to Congress, which eagerly recruited disgruntled sainiks. Complicating matters further, many former councilors who were not given a ticket ran as independents in their wards.

Because of the high economic stakes in local politics, candidates with a criminal background became increasingly prominent within all parties, but Shiv Sena was the party with the most candidates with long criminal records. This was true in both Pune and Bombay but was most pronounced in Bombay, where several well-established gangsters, major slum-lords, and dadas ran on a Shiv Sena ticket.[29]

The defections, together with Shiv Sena's rather modest record of civic improvements in Bombay, lent to the party's major defeat in the local elections, both in Bombay and the rest of the state. As the turmoil in the wake of the elections receded, Thackeray felt a need to reestablish his authority and to purge the inner structures of Shiv Sena. In April 1992 the party underwent a major reshuffling. All shakha pramukhs in the greater Bombay region were removed along with several district supervisors, and distribution of responsibility was changed. In short, the organization's stamina was weakened and its potential for action severely hampered. For Thackeray, however, this was an essential element in revitalizing his undisputed leadership. As he stated in an interview: "I want to chop off the dead wood. . . . I gave a long rope to the sainiks, and it did not help at all. . . . I want to run the Sena according to my will, or I'll quit!"[30]

In the following months Shiv Sena ostensibly was trying to work out a new strategy on various issues. For one, Thackeray proposed that the Israeli intelligence service, Mossad, be invited to train and equip Shiv Sena's own antiterrorist squad in order to stop the bombings and killings in Bombay by the underworld. Thackeray claimed that the request came from the rank and file, who wanted more discipline and militancy in the organization. Although the proposal never materialized, it was an indication of Thackeray's desire to reinvigorate the organization according to its seasoned recipe: violence, militancy, and a direct, unmediated relation between Thackeray, the supreme leader, and the rank-and-file sainiks.

Frustrated by the lack of enthusiasm in Shiv Sena, Thackeray, in July in the daily newspaper *Samna*, announced his intention to step down as Senapati. The immediate pretext was a public claim by a former Shiv Sena leader that Thackeray had groomed his son, Udhav Thackeray, and his nephew, Raj Thackeray, as prospective leaders of the party.[31] Directly after Thackeray's statement became known, thousands of sainiks assembled in front of Thackeray's Bombay residence, Matoshree, and senior leaders arrived to persuade Thackeray to remain on as party leader.

Thackeray prolonged the suspense for two days, while the crowd grew outside his home and was joined by an army of journalists (and a social scientist), until he finally agreed to reclaim his post as "army commander." Reentering the scene with one of the majestic, heroic postures of which he is known to be so fond, he delivered a fiery speech, accompanied by thunderous applause, to a crowd of thousands of people gathered in front of his house: "I do not want to lead an organization of impotent people," he said. "I wanted to lead a party of courageous young men, and not just cowards who would sit and criticize. . . . I like to deal with fire, not with ashes. . . . I was pained that no Shiv sainik came forward to break the bones of a couple of MLAs who defected to the Congress along with Bhujbal."

After this carefully staged spectacle Thackeray was back in full command. With great theatrical effect, he had reaffirmed his authority and reestablished a direct link with the rank and file, and, in the process, had sidelined the intermediate leadership. By his actions, Thackeray had staged a classical enactment of the central mechanism of charismatic leadership, namely, he had reaffirmed the nonreciprocal relationship of affection between leader and followers. Thackeray needed and cared about the sainiks as a group but had no affection for any individuals among them, whereas the rank and file focused all their affection on Thackeray, wanting him alone to take care of them, punish them, and love them. By stepping down, even as a token gesture, Thackeray made it clear to all that he was indispensable to his followers and to the movement. His resignation left them without direction, confused, in the wilderness. Thus he forced the second-rung leadership and his followers to give him their unconditional loyalty. Only then would he consider them worthy of his continued care and protection.

In the following months shakha pramukhs were once again appointed under Thackeray's undisputed leadership. But it was half a year later, during the January 1993 Bombay riots, when the decisive moment arrived to re-create the party's inner cohesion by means of a spectacular and violent transformation of the organization's original aura.

How did these transformations of Shiv Sena and of Bombay's political culture manifest themselves in the city's different localities? How did local leaders, ordinary sainiks, and Shiv Sena sympathizers interpret the party's brand of dramatic politics and its many vivid changes and crises? To answer these questions and expand our understanding of Shiv Sena, let us turn to Thane City, one of Shiv Sena's oldest and most stable strongholds in the northern outskirts of Bombay.

CHAPTER 4

Thane City: The Making of Political Dadaism

THANE CITY is a fast-growing industrial city in the northern part of the greater Bombay area, forty kilometers north of Bombay's city center. The oldest and largest urban agglomeration in Thane District, Thane City is characterized by rapid and haphazard urbanization along the railway line stretching northward from Bombay. The city's population has grown rapidly since the 1960s, and today the Thane Municipal Corporation (TMC) has an estimated 1.2 million people.

The linguistic, religious, and regional complexions of the city reflect the different communities that have settled in and around the city at various periods. The older, central areas around the lake, in the business district, and near the overcrowded railway station are overwhelmingly Maharashtrian (Naupada, Tembi Naka, Charai, etc.), inhabited by people from nearby districts who have settled there for several decades. On the other side of the busy national highway leading to Bhiwandi and Surat, one finds Wagle Estate, stretching to the North and West. This area developed since the late 1960s as a mixed industrial and residential section inhabited mainly by low-income families, among them a sizeable group of north Indians. The same pattern holds true in the Belapur Road Industrial area stretching southward from the city, also inhabited by lower-income groups from various regions of the country.

In many ways these large, populous areas are extensions of the popular Bombay culture, yet they retain their own particular expressions and reinvent differences between groups and castes. There is a measure of animosity in many areas between Maharashtrians and north Indian *bhaiyas* (literally, "little brother," used derogatorily as "rural bumpkin"), whose rustic and supposedly uncultured influence, according to local Maharashtrians, destroys Bombay's cosmopolitan and liberal atmosphere. There are also a few Muslim areas in these industrial belts, for example, in Rabodi near Wagle Estate. A survey conducted by the Thane Municipal Corporation in the mid-eighties revealed that more than 30 percent of the city's population live in slums, especially in and around the industrial estates within city limits, while as many as 66.6 percent, namely, two-thirds of the population, lived in what is termed slumlike conditions.[1]

A network of Shiv Sena shakhas was started in Thane City as early as 1967. By the late 1960s there were more than thirty shakhas in the city, a concentration denser than anywhere in Bombay. The sainiks in Thane, as in the rest of Bombay, were young Marathi-speaking men of either lower-middle-class (white-collar) or working-class backgrounds. One circumstance that boosted Shiv Sena's early growth in Thane was its unanticipated success in electoral politics, which, in 1969, surprisingly catapulted a group of rebellious young men into the position of councilors. According to one of Shiv Sena's founders in Thane, the party insisted on changing the name of the councilors from "city fathers" (*nagarpithas*) to "city workers/volunteers" (*nagarsevaks*), "because Thackeray thought that one's mother, the city, should not have so many fathers." In accordance with worshiping the nation as a mother, so pronounced in the Hindu nationalist movement for decades, "Thackeray thought we should be servants of our mother, and we should therefore call ourselves nagarsevaks."[2]

Another reason why Shiv Sena prospered in Thane was the relative success of the local Shiv sainiks in providing jobs for young Marathi-speaking men in the rapidly growing industrial belt around Thane City. Further, several of the leading sainiks in Thane started a relatively successful cooperative milk business in the city, which provided employment to a large number of rank-and-file Shiv sainiks.

Shiv Sena's stronghold was among the Marathi-speaking communities employed in the area's industries and, like elsewhere in the Bombay region, the party's constituencies and organization began to change in 1980. Until 1980, Shiv Sena had solid backing from Thane's Marathi-speaking middle class because of the party's relatively successful management of the city during Satish Pradhan's long tenure as mayor. True to the demonstrative nature of Shiv Sena's politics, Pradhan erected a number of conspicuous landmarks in the city—such as a large sports stadium, a theater, and other facilities for the Marathi performing arts.

Sena's growing entanglement in the profitable real estate and building sectors, along with the expanding gray economy, soon made the party appear, according to one local advocate, "a boorish version of Congress." Still more councilors from Shiv Sena turned into builders cum politicians; underworld connections became ever more apparent; and the politics in the Thane Municipal Corporation turned increasingly violent and criminalized, with physical assaults, threats, and armed attacks characterizing the interaction between different parties and between factions within the same parties.

Shiv Sena began to rely increasingly on the support of lower-income sections and poor areas, from which it recruited most of its activists. As Sena leaders embarked on a strident anti-Muslim course during the 1984 riots in Bhiwandi—in which several small Muslim areas in Thane were attacked—the trend toward increased violence and a deeper entanglement with construction, real estate, and criminal environments became more pronounced.

A glance at the careers of the shifting Shiv Sena leadership in Thane reflects this "dada-ization" of the party. The first generation of leaders were businessmen, like Satish Pradhan, or fairly educated white-collar workers from higher-caste families, like Modhav Joshi, a Brahman and former Marxist, who to this day maintains that providing jobs should be Shiv Sena's prime concern, or Prakash Paranjape, another Brahman, graduate turned builder, and councilor for Shiv Sena since 1971. Pradhan and Joshi were zilla pramukhs and city pramukhs, respectively, until 1974.[3]

Hereafter the scene was taken over by very different types of men. One was Shabir Sheikh, a Muslim and former blue-collar worker with no formal education, and, according to widespread rumors, associated with underworld activities. Sheikh was district chief from 1974 until 1984. Later, in 1990, he was elected legislator from Kalyan in Thane District.

Sheikh fortified his career by being the most prominent and loyal Muslim in Shiv Sena, always projected as living proof of the party's broadmindedness. During his tenure Shabir Sheikh was the zilla pramukh instrumental in spreading Shiv Sena to Kalyan, Bhiwandi and, the rural areas of the district. His image as a hefty, fearless man to whom all the mythical, martial qualities of Muslims were ascribed, now with positive connotations ("He is our Muslim"), helped Shiv Sena strengthen its "dada-ized" image. However, except for his name, Shabir Sheikh is no more of a Muslim in terms of outlook and practice than any other Shiv sainik I came across in the course of my study. Apparently Sheikh had taken over the entire Shiv Sena discourse, on both Islam and Hinduism. He consistently used the terms *they, their*, and *them* when referring to Muslims but spoke of *we, our*, and *us* when referring to Hindus and Shiv Sena: "We will never respect the Muslims if they do not respect the country. Ask them to respect the national anthem, and we will allow them to put up loudspeakers on their mosques. This is our civilization, Hindu civilization. . . . Idol worship only symbolizes the god we want to worship, unlike Islam and other religions that are against idol worship."[4]

Another Shiv Sena leader whose career began in Thane City was Ganesh Naik, an MLA since 1990 in Thane's industrial belt. Naik belongs to the "*agri*community," which has considerable influence in Thane. The agricommunity owns most of the land in the area and, because of land sales for industrial and residential purposes, has developed into the district's single most powerful community. Though technically belonging to the OBC category, many agris today call themselves Marathas, and in the 1970s a group of agri businessmen founded the *Agri Sena*, a sort of militant caste association aimed at optimizing the influence of agris in public life. Because of its control over banks, real estate, and construction, the

Agri Sena became the center of political power, shifting its allegiance between Congress and Shiv Sena, its support for candidates and parties or stand on various issues always given due attention in the local press and in the local political equation. Naik began as a regular Shiv sainik in Thane City, gradually rose in rank, and finally was elected a member of the district's Zilla Parishad (District Council). He then built up a strong position as a maverick union leader in the industrial belt stretching from Thane City to New Bombay. Naik's *Shramik Sena*, like other Sena unions, is run along highly personal lines, largely functioning as a loose association of company unions held together only by the supreme political leader. According to Naik, the leader's function is to provide political "deterrence," which can be useful in local negotiations with the management. In return, the political leader establishes a certain loyalty that may yield votes and a reservoir of manpower and activists. While this pattern does not set Shiv Sena apart from the modus operandi of many other unions, Sena leaders generally have been more successful in converting union strength into political capital.

Like Sheikh, Naik is a self-made man with little formal training but well versed in the intricate connections between politics, real estate brokerage, and industrial investments that pervade contemporary politics in the greater Bombay area. Naik's position as a union leader has given him access to large numbers of employees in the private sector, as well as access to many industrial houses.

THE INVENTION OF DIGHE *SAHEB*

In 1984 Anand Dighe was made zilla pramukh of Thane District. Dighe had grown up with Shiv Sena in Thane. From a modest background and with no formal qualifications, he developed a strong emotional attachment to Shiv Sena and Bal Thackeray, who had discovered, early on, the extraordinary energy and determination of this quiet young man. Dighe, an extremely strong-willed man, became known as an able organizer and ruthless operator in the street fighting and semi-legal activities that were becoming ever more important in Shiv Sena. Only in his early thirties when he took over as zilla pramukh, Dighe has since developed into a kind of mythical figure to whom superhuman qualities are ascribed, including omnipresence and omnipotence. Dighe carefully cultivates this image of mystique and power. He is always on the move throughout the district in his jeep, and rumor has it that he never sleeps in the same place twice. His headquarters in Tembi Naka in central Thane has been made into a huge reception hall, where from fifty to one hundred people wait every evening, either to ask for or offer assistance or to express their thanks. Outside

Dighe's office, a group of young men stand guard, always ready to carry out Dighe's every order. Several of these young men try to imitate Dighe's hairstyle or his curly beard. His office, like a sanctum sanctorum, is located deep within the building, and one must pass through another small room before entering it. Inside the office are three or four telephones, *trishuls* (tridents), the compulsory statue of Shivaji, and images of Thackeray, with saffron flags hanging from the walls. Dighe himself resembles a typical dada: Dressed in white, he wears many gold rings, gold necklaces, and a heavy gold wristwatch.

The paraphernalia of mythical power with which Dighe so carefully stages his appearance is more than a mere political trick. It reflects the genuine aspirations and partially fulfilled dreams of many younger Shiv Sena leaders, mostly from poor families, for whom Shiv Sena provides an avenue to power, money, and status. Anand Dighe's life story, the fearful fascination that surrounds him today, represents the dream of every Shiv sainik, a glorious future in which he is transformed from a "nobody" to a local "somebody."

Dighe has also re-created Shiv Sena's image as a band of local Robin Hoods, protector of the common man, the great, yet humble, defender of a popular Hindu assertion. For their part, shakhas collect large numbers of schoolbooks and notebooks each year to be distributed to needy children or sold at concessional rates to other students. Many shakhas also maintain a small library containing the most common schoolbooks, and these are made available to boys affiliated with the shakha.

Since the 1970s Shiv Sena has frequently arranged blood donating drives, health camps, and a free ambulance service. These ambulances, conspicuously marked with Shiv Sena's symbol of a roaring tiger, have become tangible and highly visible manifestations of Shiv Sena's commitment to social work throughout the Bombay region and beyond. In addition to the symbolic value of the ambulances, which reaffirm the party's commitment to assist ordinary people, the blood donation campaign invokes a deeper connotation, namely, that young, aggressive Shiv sainiks are willing and able to sacrifice their blood for the good of the larger Hindu community. Thus the act of donating blood is perceived as an act of heroism—mediated by modern medical technology. Heuzé (1992) argues that this practice is driven by the notion that sainiks are "people of blood," true patriots whose young and virile blood can reinvigorate an otherwise effeminate and degenerated culture. This may be pushing the point a bit far. In my experience, the populist discourse of this patriotic "social service," at least in the minds of the rank-and-file sainiks, is predominantly a matter of donating clean versus contaminated blood. Besides, many other organizations and parties, including Congress, also conduct blood-donating drives with similar patriotic underpinnings. Among the Shiv sainiks I met, the most common reason for donating blood was to provide blood banks with clean, healthy blood and keep out contaminated blood—blood that was medically and ritually impure, and, moreover, regularly sold by slum dwellers and other marginalized groups.

Another highly publicized and effective populist technique has been Shiv Sena's frequent interventions in the market for basic necessities. When prices on sugar, oil, flour, and other essential commodities skyrocketed during strikes or shortages, Shiv Sena often forced shopkeepers to lower their prices. In several cases Anand Dighe simply appropriated stores from certain traders and sold their products at concessional rates in the market. During a prolonged transport strike in July 1992, Shiv Sena looted several storehouses in Thane and distributed sugar, flower, and oil among the poor. Such careful displays of plebeian heroism, not surprisingly, have created enthusiasm for Dighe in the slum areas and added to his mythical status in Thane.

From Shiv Sena's early days, religious festivals, as mentioned above, were the party's central loci of performative politics. The collection of funds and preparation for religious festivals have also long been central activities for young men in Shiv Sena shakhas. The party's wider practice of collecting funds from businessmen and shop owners through a combination of threats and promises of patronage has been very effective in Thane owing to Shiv Sena's local dominance in the Municipal Corporation, where business licenses and construction permits are issued. Given the party's strength and so-called nuisance value, many shopkeepers aptly regard these donations as protection money and a way to maintain good relations with Shiv Sena. The spectacular efficacy of Shiv Sena *bandhs* (closure of shops, markets, and transport) in the Bombay region in terms of closing down shops and offices does not necessarily reflect the party's popular support but is directly linked to this structure of funding and potential of violence practiced by local Shiv Sena networks.

The practice of donating even substantial sums to Ganpati mandals—whether under the aegis of Shiv Sena or not—has obviously boosted the size and opulence of the processions during the festival, and Shiv Sena has successfully appropriated the festival to the extent that the celebration has become strongly associated with the party. In the 1980s Shiv Sena began to promote the Navrati festival of the artisan gods as a more general celebration of the work place and professions. Originating in Gujarat but adopted to attract Gujaratis in Bombay to Shiv Sena, the festival has gained importance in the 1980s with the gradual "dada'ization" of Shiv Sena. With more direct appeals to a robust, masculine Hinduism, this celebration of the deeds of the ordinary man has become quite important.

For years Anand Dighe has sponsored a spectacular celebration of the Navrati festival in Tembi Naka. Although the Ganpati festival is organized and celebrated by hundreds of mandals throughout the city, in Thane the Navrati is a rather centralized affair, with Shiv Sena acting as the festival's public sponsor, organizer, and interpreter. Shiv Sena provides the food, lights, and entertainment, and is clearly the host of the festival. Like all celebrations, the Navrati serves as a meeting place for young men, a place to drink and dance to the loud tunes of Hindi films. For the Sena, it serves to amplify the party's message of a popular Hinduism, grand in gesture and scale yet simple and accessible to the common man, a way to enjoy the masculine community.

Another spectacular campaign arranged by Anand Dighe and his lieutenants is the annual march to a local Muslim *dargah* (tomb) on a hill north of Thane City. It is the Haji Malang dargah, named after the Muslim Sufi saint, Haji Malang Baba, who is buried there. For centuries the tomb has attracted thousands of pilgrims throughout the district as well as from Bombay and Konkan. According to the *District Gazetteer* of 1882, the Muslim Sufi came to Kalyan in the thirteenth century and became very popular: "On the Malangadh hill is held a fair in honour of Haji Abdul Rehman, an Arab Missionary said to have died 700 years ago, and whose sanctity is said to have gained him the favour of the reigning Hindu King Nal Raja, whose daughter he is said to have married. His fair is held every year at the *Magh* (January–February) full moon, and is attended by a large number of Hindus and Muslims from Panvel, Kalyan, Thana and Bombay. The fair last for four or five days."[5]

The dargah is just one of hundreds of examples of religious syncretisms centered on tombs of local saints, deities, and gurus, both Muslim and Hindu, throughout the countryside of Maharashtra. A Brahman family that has hereditary rights to this privilege manages the annual festival at the Haji Malang tomb. Many of the rites performed at the annual festival are distinctly Hindu. A specific caste (*bhois*) has the exclusive right to carry the *palanquin* used in the annual procession to the tomb; during the festival a sandalwood paste (*uti*) is applied to the tomb, food is offered, musical instruments typical of Hindu worship are played, and flags are unfurled. The tomb itself, however, is clearly Muslim in form and inscription. The trust managing the site, called the "Secular Trust," has for decades served as a near perfect incarnation of the official ideal of secularism: equal respect for all religions and peaceful coexistence of religious communities at the popular level.

From 1988 on, Shiv Sena—impressed by the effectiveness of the agitation to "liberate the birthplace of Ram" in Ayodhya in north India— claimed the Malangadh Hill as an ancient Hindu shrine (*samadhi*) of the Nath Panthiya (an esoteric yogic order of north India)[6] and claimed that Haji Malang was a Muslim conqueror who destroyed the existing Hindu shrine and constructed a fort and tomb on top of it. Since 1988 Anand

Dighe has publicly called for the "liberation of Malangadh." Every February, at the time of the festival, he calls on thousands of Hindus to gather at the hill and leads processions there to reclaim the site "back from the Muslims." During these campaigns Dighe has been arrested under the Terrorist and Disruptive Activities Act (TADA), and each year this has led to violent agitation and bandhs demanding his immediate release. Dighe's arrests and the campaigns for his release coincided with the election campaigns of February 1990 and May 1991. In 1991 the bandh following Dighe's arrest on combined charges of murder and disturbances at Malangadh turned violent. Trains were stopped, buses and buildings stoned, and more than two hundred people arrested. All leading candidates in the ensuing election for Shiv Sena and the BJP demanded his release and urged the public to take immediate action against the "chains on Dighe."[7] In a news article in *Samna* on the arrest of Dighe, an elderly woman was quoted as saying: "Dighe saheb is not only our god, but the god of the public. One who clashes with him will never be forgiven by god."[8]

With some success Shiv Sena has manufactured this recurrent conflict in order to project the party as the defender of a naive, good-hearted Hindu community, unaware until now of the Muslim "theft" of this ancient place of worship. Dighe's arrests each year have been effectively projected as proof of his fearless, martial nature. Despite the inevitable harassment at the hands of the police in their efforts to protect the "Muslim occupation of our shrine," as Dighe himself expressed it on one occasion, nevertheless, urged on by his (manly) conviction, every year he leads a procession of Hindus to take back the shrine. The Shiv Sena leadership and local newspapers have contributed to the public construction of Dighe as a "saint-warrior," a man whose convictions and fearless sacrifice always informs his actions, however questionable these actions may seem from the viewpoint of a hostile anti-Hindu government.

The continual conflict over the Malangadh Hill in Kalyan, besides being a high profile political performance, also demonstrated Shiv Sena's overall strategy to purge the everyday world of its ambiguous, syncretic meanings and replace these with more manageable symbols, namely, good versus bad, pure versus impure, Muslims versus Hindus in the latter's effort to claim their right to community.

Shiv Sena's representation of what it claims as a broad Hindu opposition to the name Haji Malang, and to the annual festival held there, denounced by sainiks as a treacherous, "pseudo secular" ritual, clearly affected popular perceptions. Increasingly the place has become identified as a Muslim site, although most of the devotees are Hindus, but not Hindus in the sense represented by Shiv Sena. Sena has represented Hinduism as a "thin," emblematic, external, activist creed—reduced to a symbolic backdrop and referential structure on which a frustrated masculinity can be reerected and on which fragmented social identities can be healed, their ambiguity purged.

The dada'ization of Shiv Sena in Thane in the 1980s meant that the party lost its stable hold of political power at the municipal level; that its middle-class constituency began to disintegrate; and that the position of party leaders in the business community and administration declined. This gave way to a more incoherent but more spectacular Shiv Sena, led by a highly visible, often dreaded task force of angry young men under the command of Anand Dighe, a man capable of conspicuous public action though less able to maintain the networks surrounding shakhas on which the earlier Shiv Sena organization had been based. As part of this same development, Shiv Sena's municipal councilors often became involved in the murkier compartments of the real estate market, the construction industry, the liquor trade, and entertainment.

Since Anand Dighe's rise in the organization, the older guard of Shiv Sena workers, recruited in the 1960s, has given way to a new type of sainik as shakha pramukh and councilor. These young men of limited education grew up with the party since childhood, are blindly loyal to Dighe, and are aggressive, often bearing firearms and knives. Manohar Gadhwe and Rajan Vichare, two municipal councilors in central Thane, both belonged to Dighe's personal cadre. Each represented, in different ways, the outlook and aspirations of the "dada'ized sainik."

Manohar Gadhwe was elected a councilor for Shiv Sena in February 1992. He was an unskilled worker at a large textile company, belonged to the *khatik* (butchers) branch of the community of shepherds (*dhangars*), and had been associated with Shiv Sena since the age of ten. When his electoral ward was reserved for scheduled castes and nomadic tribes, he was asked to contest the municipal elections, and, with the help of the former Shiv Sena councilor, he won with a large margin. Gadhwe, a big muscular man, regarded himself as a loyal sainik, willing and able to obey Dighe's every order.

> Since I was ten years old I was with Anand Dighe. We do all kinds of work as per the orders of Anand Dighe. In case of immediate civic problems we swing into action at the orders of Dighe. . . . With him it is less of politics and more of social work. . . . In this area we are a couple of hundred activists. Normally a person would spend eight—ten hours a day. If he is unemployed, he will be at Dighe's office doing whatever Dighe would ask him to do. After all, Anand Dighe would in the end see to it that he got a job. . . . Most of the activists are around the age of twenty-five. Some are employed, some are not, some have left education halfway. And some have a business of their own.[9]

Gadhwe took pride in being a loyal soldier. He regarded himself as a "social worker" whose duty was to serve the party and Dighe: "I do not know what Shiv Sena sees in me, but I will see to it that Shiv Sena grows because of my work." Like several other sainiks he carried a gun, since, as he said, "social work has become a dangerous business" and "one needs to protect oneself." Despite his new duties as councilor, which was to solve problems in the ward, he still hung around Dighe's office many evenings, chatting with old friends, awaiting orders from Dighe, and receiving directions concerning his work in the ward and in the Municipal Corporation. There was no independent shakha in his ward, as most of the activists belonged to Dighe's cadre, and Gadhwe did not feel that his status had changed much since his election as councilor. He lived according to the first principle of Dighe's cadre and Sena as a whole: *nishta* (loyalty).[10]

The councilor from the neighboring ward, Rajan Vichare, like Gadhwe, had been with Shiv Sena since childhood. Vichare came from a middle-class family but dropped out of a college in Bombay. He held various blue-collar jobs for some years until, in 1985, he became a full-time worker for Shiv Sena and was asked by Anand Dighe to start an independent shakha in the ward. Vichare is also a great admirer of Dighe: "I was influenced and guided by Dighe throughout. Today Dighe is a highly influential and highly respected man in Thane. He has created such an atmosphere in Thane that all decisions are made in consultations with each other. We play politics only in the Corporation. Outside we concentrate on social work for those who have voted for us."[11]

Unlike Gadhwe, Vichare had social ambitions. He constantly emphasized that his ward was a middle-class ward with educated people, and he himself, in the last five years, became a builder in the area. His newly acquired financial strength enabled him to construct a lavish shakha, which has become his office both in his capacity as councilor and as builder. The building is furnished with heavy chairs and decorated with a huge Shivaji statue, saffron flags, maps, and religious symbols. Vichare resides behind a huge desk, elevated at one end of the room, in a huge thronelike chair. One evening, soon after we met, I asked Vichare to call on some activists in the area for a group interview. I wanted to get an idea of how Vichare would like to be seen. That evening, a number of the most "respectable" people he knew from all over the city came: a pop singer, an official from the National Table Tennis Association, managers from local firms, and so on. None of them were actually activists or even lived in the area, but they all testified to Vichare's social standing and respectability.

Vichare had also started a mitra mandal that arranged religious festivals, and he was running a body-building center for local boys. The center was decorated with an interesting mixture of adornments: pictures of oil-glistening muscular idols of American extraction, saffron flags, and images of

Shivaji on horseback and the war goddess Bhavani. This body-building center, and the inordinate pride Vichare took in his position as its patron, in many ways symbolized what Shiv Sena provided its activists and supporters in Thane: a renewal of Hindu masculinity through a mixture of mythical references to a martial past, high-tech body-building techniques, and social respectability gained through money and self-made business, that is, becoming a respectable dada.

Vichare's attraction to Shiv Sena had to do with the simplicity of its message and Thackeray's forthright, honest style:

> We believe that first comes the nation, and if there is a nation, then the religion will survive, and we will be there only if there is religion. Shiv Sena is known to be in such a way, that if there is injustice we will fight it in a rather dashing way. Only Shiv Sena has the guts to talk about the problems and against what is wrong on an open platform. No other person does it as openly as Thackeray.[12]

Vichare's attachment to Shiv Sena has altered his life. He is acutely aware that his current position as a respectable dada—in tune with the middle-class complexion of his domain in both his style and discourse—was earned through Shiv Sena. Indeed, his entire identity is derived from his association with Shiv Sena. This is a sentiment he shares with many sainiks, and one that may explain Shiv Sena's continued coherence and staying power in spite of changing fortunes in the political field. Vichare summarized this succinctly: "In short, Shiv Sena is everything to me. I am there because Shiv Sena is there. If you remove the last four words from my name (Rajan Vichare, *Shiv Sena shakha pramukh*) my value is zero. I am recognized only as a Shiv Sena man."[13]

These sainiks are attracted to Shiv Sena by its performative style and egalitarian discourse that is less pervaded by caste and notions of purity than the distinctly high-caste idiom of the RSS and similar Hindu nationalist organizations. Shiv Sena's history and dynamism, in many ways, is based on its populist program of bestowing self-respect on ordinary people, regardless of their caste. Thus Shiv Sena directly engages a widespread quest for social mobility among ordinary people—a quest compounded by the slow structural forces of the democratic revolution.

However, Shiv Sena's ostensible egalitarianism pertains only to caste and to the abandoning of old habits—and embracing the new—so urgent among young men and women in the Bombay region. But in terms of class and authority, there is nothing egalitarian about Shiv Sena. Most sainiks dream of moving upward, becoming like Dighe or Vichare, wielding power and respect in the party's highly authoritarian system.

By transposing a plebeian quest for equality into the pursuit of upward mobility and social status, Shiv Sena is in tune with the broader social

processes of urban life. It is also in harmony with the social dreams of
those living in the plebeian sections of the zopadpattis and those among
the upwardly mobile lower middle classes. Most important, it is in syn-
chrony with the social ambitions and fears of young men, their style of
cherishing authority, action, and enjoyment, the fashion in which they
envision their future.

THE FRAGILITY OF PERFORMATIVE POLITICS

In the Shiv Sena organization in Thane, power gradually moved from Satish Pradhan to Anand Dighe, as the latter's militancy and almost suicidal
devotion to Shiv Sena won him Thackeray's attention and confidence.
Pradhan had established himself comfortably in the local power networks
and had become a major wholesale dealer of alcoholic beverages throughout Maharashtra. But, as many boys told me, Pradhan had also grown too
old and too settled to become a credible leader of young sainiks. His
wealth, influence, and independence made him unreliable in the eyes of
Thackeray, who was always wary of his second-rung leaders becoming too
powerful.

From 1984 on, Anand Dighe rose to prominence and power in Thane.
In this period he reinvigorated—and deinstitutionalized—the basis of
Sena's activism, displacing many of Shiv Sena's old hands in Thane. By
1991–92 Dighe had apparently become too powerful, and on several occasions Thackeray sarcastically nicknamed him the "King of Thane." At this
point Pradhan was remobilized to select candidates and distribute tickets
for the 1992 municipal election and, at the same time, was given a seat
in the Upper House (Rajya Sabha) in Delhi. Another dimension of this
balancing of forces between Thane's old and new leader was undoubtedly
the many criminal cases pending against Dighe, which severely impinged
his freedom of movement and hence his utility as a leader of Shiv Sena.[14]

The events that occurred after the 1986 municipal elections serve to
illustrate Shiv Sena's transformation in Thane. Before this election Shiv
Sena had dominated the Municipal Corporation (holding a total of sixty-
six seats). In keeping pace with the urban growth, the number of available
seats in the 1986 election expanded to eighty-five. Shiv Sena was still able
to win the seats it had controlled for years. After the polls, Shiv Sena
managed to construct a fragile coalition with independents and the BJP
and to win the mayoral post.

Three years later, local Congress men were able to persuade four councilors from the influential agri-community—elected for the BJP—and
some councilors from Shiv Sena to join the Congress Party. Shiv Sena
subsequently lost the mayoral post as well as its longstanding majority in

the Municipal Corporation. The Shiv Sena leadership did not take this lightly. As punishment for what he viewed as laxity and a lack of discipline, Thackeray forced all the Shiv Sena councilors in Thane to resign. This deprived Shiv Sena, and Satish Pradhan, who led the councilors, of all political influence while denying the councilors their profitable jobs as brokers in the construction boom of this period.

Instead, what emerged as the party's dominant modus operandi in Thane was Dighe's strategy of high-profile populist activism, "street politics," and liaisons with the murkier side of the business world. Anand Dighe also wished to avenge the humiliation Shiv Sena had endured in its old stronghold. He wanted to prove, once again, his unfailing loyalty to Thackeray by imposing strict discipline on the Shiv Sena in Thane. He even tendered his resignation to Thackeray, as a sign of repentance and shame, but Thackeray refused to accept his resignation.

A few months after his defection to Congress, the former Shiv Sena councilor Khopkar was murdered under mysterious circumstances. Rumors immediately spread that Anand Dighe was behind the murder, and Dighe did not explicitly deny it. Instead, he issued such statements as "The hand that keeps Shiv Sena away from power will be cut off." As if to confirm the Hobbesian idea of violence as the origin of power, sovereignty, and reverence, Dighe's new "secret" had an electrifying effect on the Shiv Sena organization, arousing fear and respect for Dighe, who was now arrested and imprisoned. A campaign demanding his release was launched, and one month later he was released on bail. The murder charges against Dighe increased his fame and mythical aura, and henceforth the question of his guilt or innocence became an important topic in Thane City. The murder case remains pending, and, along with Dighe's other actions at Malanghad, provides Shiv Sena with intense publicity and press coverage.[15]

The forced resignation of Shiv Sena's councilors from the Thane Municipal Corporation rendered the party rather powerless regarding local politics in the following years. Recognizing Shiv Sena's institutional weakness, the Congress Party in Thane worked systematically to reestablish its influence in many of Shiv Sena's earlier strongholds. Several new housing schemes were begun, a new hospital was built, civic amenities improved through a major loan from the World Bank, and so on. It was hardly surprising, therefore, that Shiv Sena was unable to make a mark in the 1992 municipal elections. The BJP had acquired some of Shiv Sena's earlier supporters in the middle class, and Congress had encroached on several of Shiv Sena's strongholds in the city's lower-income areas. The result was that Shiv Sena came out of the 1992 election with only twenty-five seats, the poorest showing since 1970.

The following example clearly illustrates the fragility of Sena's power, even in an old stronghold like Thane. For more than twenty years, the densely populated low-income area known as Chandanwadi had been a Sena base of support. The area comprises a number of older chawls, some upgraded hutment areas, and newer slums. The Sena shakha, painted in brilliant colors, is located next to the area's main road. For years this shakha had been famous for its spectacular mandap tableaux's during the Ganpatiutsav, and its many active sainiks were always seen around the shakha at night. Two brothers, emerging businessmen and close friends of Dighe, let us call them R and A, had long been the leading Sena men in the area. Sena's decline in the area started in 1989, with the forced resignation of the councilors and the party's loss of power in the Municipal Corporation. The two brothers began to quarrel, and Dighe decided to support one brother (R) against the other. The quarreling led to a certain inactivity and decline in the life of the shakha and in Shiv Sena's credibility as a broker and supplier of various services in the area. The shakha remained more or less dormant for several years. As a result, a young man named Pawar, from the southern end of the area, emerged as an aspiring dada with considerable success. In the northern end of Chandanwadi, dominated by *bhaiyas*, the north Indian owner of most of the land and an aspiring builder, Sheth, came forward as the new strongman. His main interest in local politics, as he readily told me, was to get permission to clear the slums and to construct high-rise buildings.

Supported by a rich maverick builder family in Thane—running hotels and bars throughout the district and acting as a major financier of the local Congress Party—Pawar soon emerged as a serious contender for power in Chandanwadi. Pawar started his own mitra mandal, which soon began to organize conspicuous celebrations of religious festivals. In the 1992 municipal elections Pawar linked up with Sheth and managed to win the seat as councilor in the ward. As a reward for this important victory, Pawar was given the post as member of the standing committee in the Municipal Corporation for a year, which enabled him to pay back his debt. Pawar readily admitted the logic of his appointment: "I was given this post in return for my victory in Chandanwadi. Since then I have issued many 'No Objection Certificates' to shopkeepers and builders in the area. They have also donated substantial amounts of money to the social work we carry out in our mitra mandal."[16]

This and many similar processes in other parts of Thane indicated how much the local sainiks' image depended on Shiv Sena's larger public image as well as on the party's capacity to sustain local activism and to deliver services. It also demonstrated that the party's capacity in both these respects depended more on its access to political resources than its public appearance and self-projections would admit. The mode of functioning and the logic of patronage governing Sena at this level closely resembled that of any political party in India.

By this time Shiv Sena's general crisis pervaded other Sena networks in Thane. Many shakhas lay idle after Thackeray's dismissal of all local leaders in an attempt to purge the organization. Dighe's central office still worked at full steam as a local *durbar* (court), where justice was meted out, advice given, and solutions reached and enforced according to the sainiks' notions of "natural justice." Another factor impeding the party's functioning at this time was the presence of Thane's police commissioner, A. S. Samra. Samra, reputed for his honesty, began to make so-called precautionary arrests of Dighe and other sainiks before "critical situations" broke out, and to put Dighe away for longer periods. "We have to demonstrate that our penal code applies to all Indians," Samra told me a few weeks after massive riots in Bombay, in January 1993, had not spread to Thane and Bhiwandi.[17]

This situation produced a feeling of despair, lack of direction, and disenchantment among rank-and-file Sainiks, and among councilors, now subjected to the often whimsical rule of independent maverick councilors on whose marginal seats Congress had premised its rule in the city. The most powerful posts in the Municipal Corporation were occupied by various well-known local dadas, such as the chairman of a local auto rickshaw association known for its violent clashes with business rivals. In Bombay and elsewhere, fist fights, shootings, and inter-gang rivalry among councilors began seriously to affect the functioning of the city administration.

THE PRODUCTION OF A HINDU COMMUNITY

In India, as elsewhere, the dissatisfaction with what is depicted as declining standards of public life seems to reflect discomfort with the loss of aristocratic or clerical aura of public persons. The "magic of ministry" cannot easily apply to an ordinary person elected to office. What is revealed, therefore, is a sometimes ugly, always unwelcome, representation of the profane and ordinary—vanity, greed, lust for power, and all the other acknowledged features of human conduct. The profanity of the elected representative and the political realm in general could, in Lacanian terms, be seen as the "Real" of democratic practice, the almost unbearable truth of the profanity of power. Yet, this is exactly the core of the "*jouissance* of politics": the pleasure derived from constantly revealing this profanity, of cynically "saying things as they really are." This specific *jouissance* of politics also provides the energy and momentum for recurrent populist discourses claiming to represent the real people, to reveal the profanity of politics,

and yet claiming to articulate the real grievances of the people, uncontaminated by representation, undistorted by mediators.

As in the case of egalitarian values and the notion of rights, Shiv Sena
has also enveloped and rearticulated this *jouissance* of politics. The party
has, with some success, projected itself as nonpolitical, as "80 percent social
work, and 20 percent politics," as one of Anand Dighe's favorite slogans
goes. Shiv Sena portrays politics as everything Shiv Sena is not: empty rhetoric, hollow schemes, self-enrichment, petty factionalism. By contrast, Shiv
Sena stages itself as living by direct visibility, rapid action, and personal
command and authority over workers. This obviously connects well with
widespread popular notions of politicians as self-seeking, corrupt persons.

Instead, Shiv Sena has created what I call performative politics, which
deal with everyday problems rapidly, visibly, and, though rarely aimed at
transforming institutions or practices, with some immediate effect. Hence
the party's provision of blood and ambulances rather than an efficient
police force preventing crime and road mishaps; hence the curbing of
petty *dadagiri* (dada power) by creating a more hard-hitting and well-
organized political dadaism; hence the pressure on municipal authorities
to solve problems advanced by Shiv Sena activists and local dadas rather
than efforts to create effective service provisions. These activities are at
the heart of Shiv Sena's politics of the spectacle.

The sense of Shiv Sena as being truly egalitarian and honest was expressed by an elderly woman, an enthusiastic supporter of Shiv Sena for
several decades: "In Shiv Sena there was no differentiation between rich
and poor like in the other parties; and no flair of casteism like the Jana
Sangh had in the case of the Brahmans, and which they showed in their
behavior. . . . We were enthusiastic about the party, that it would do something for Maharashtrians."

A housewife in Tembi Naka felt that Anand Dighe was outside the profanity of all other politicians: "At least in Thane we have Anand Dighe,
and he is the only man we can go to and get our problems solved. He
listens to us, to our plans, helps us and shows the way. Hence we admire
him. . . . What I like about Shiv Sena is its social work, that is, the relief
work every year when the *nallah* (swamp) gets flooded every year."

An elderly clerk in a large company in Bombay and an admirer of Anand
Dighe emphasized, in the same vein, that Dighe took no interest in such
lowly spheres as politics. To him this was a sign of culture and education.

Anand Dighe works selflessly. He is very calm and quiet and does not seem to
be interested in contesting elections. I think he is a graduate.

To a poor women from the *teli* caste (OBC) who lived in Chandanwadi,
the utility of Shiv Sena was practical and straightforward in matters of vital
importance.

They clean the gutters, get water connections, get us released from police custody, and sometimes Anand Dighe sends his men to force the employers to pay the regular salaries. Anand Dighe is fighting injustice on the poor people. . . . Shiv Sainiks sold sugar and potatoes cheap. Dighe also gave a cricket set to the children each year. And they stopped the black market racket in edible oil and sold the oil cheap.

The peculiar equation of Shiv Sena politics with social work was clearly expressed by a group of young sainiks at the shakha in Chandanwadi who explained to me that Shiv Sena's decline in Thane in 1991–92 occurred because too many members of the Municipal Corporation, who had been elected on Shiv Sena tickets, "had become mixed up in politics," that is, corruption and factionalism. These young men, all supporters of the local dada and of the sainik, R, also said that the worst aspect of the new Congress councilor in the area was that he had only won because he was a "totally political man . . . a dada, attracting the boys with liquor and meat." This type of politics, which had given up even pretending that the representatives were driven by elevated motivations, was a scandal that had to be corrected in order to restore the *jouissance* of politics—a joy that presupposes, of course, the existence of something larger, namely, a cause, a leader, a true people, the nation.

To the rank-and-file Shiv Sena supporter, ideological constructions of a higher purpose were, in most cases, rather straightforward notions of a majoritarian justice for Hindus and the warding off of the imagined Muslim threat to ordinary people.[18] A militant supporter of Shiv Sena living in a modest neighborhood in central Thane expressed it this way:

> People today are simply bothered only about one thing: where will they get safety? Shiv Sena is today the only fighter organization. The need of the hour is not to hold a stick in your hand [like RSS practice—T.B.H.] but to use it. . . . Considering today's situation in Bombay, one has a fear of being attacked and if any Shiv Sainik is watching that, he will come to rescue, and no one should have doubts about that.

Another Shiv sainik from the same area said that he had been a Congress supporter for many years until he saw that Shiv Sena was defending the Charai neighborhood during the communal riots in Thane in 1984. To him, everything boiled down to a Muslim conspiracy:

> I realized that all these riots—also the recent one—are instigated by foreign infiltrators—Pakistanis and Bangladeshis—together with Muslim builders and goondas. But now [January 1993—T.B.H.] they have been taught a lesson. Still here in India Muslims are better off than in Pakistan, That is why they keep on coming back. Today they are on high posts all over. We see it before our eyes.

Although BJP supporters at this critical time often talked at length about the "appeasement of Muslims," a common civil code, secessionism, and that Congress was to blame, most rank-and-file sainiks were far more blunt and direct, in the style of Thackeray; "who says what we cannot say." The enemy was not an abstract, Muslim domination subtly enacted through Congress but a tangible enemy who wished to kill Hindus. A young girl from the *dhangar* community claimed:

> During this riot [January 1993—T.B.H.] Muslims burned our Hindus alive. I was told that more than forty to fifty Hindus died in one incident in Jogeshwari. Riots take place where Muslims are in majority. They live in our Hindustan and they kill us. [Her brother interjects:] If you support Congress, then the entire state will come under Muslim flag.

According to the RSS, India's problems stem from the weakness and disunity of Hindus. If Hindus unite, then even the undivided India, *Akhand Bharat*, will reemerge. Most Shiv Sena supporters took a simpler view: The problem was the Muslims as a whole, and it could only be solved in one way:

> Let all the other community people go to their country, Pakistan, and let our people come here. Then it would be a real Hindustan. It will never be possible for the two countries to unite.

Shiv Sena supporters rarely couched their fear and distrust of Muslims in their discourse of overriding national loyalty. The bluntness of Shiv Sena's communal populism had become a virtue in itself. According to a retired clerk, the antagonism between Muslims and Hindus was foundational:

> It is simply that there is hatred against Muslims amongst us, and vice versa. You cannot expect that the eagle and the snake will stay together. . . . I do not feel like eating in a Muslim house, and hence friendships between Hindu and Muslim families will never be possible. . . . When I go to Bombay, I never go to a Muslim joint, because I fear they might use bull's meat. And, most importantly, cleanliness is lacking in their hotels, and their houses are so unclean that you don't feel like eating there.

At the time of my work in Thane in 1992–93 Shiv Sena had not only been able to recast popular myths of Muslims into a solid common sense among its own activists and supporters. Several families I interviewed were divided in their political sympathies, typically between Shiv Sena and Congress—a split that often ran along generational lines, with parents supporting Congress and the younger generation being pro-Shiv Sena.

What was striking, however, was that most of those with whom I spoke in these strongholds of Shiv Sena, regardless of whether they were Congress supporters, more or less openly shared the communal common sense depicted above. Especially after the razing of Babri Masjid in Ayodhya in December 1992 and the Bombay riots in January 1993, communal sentiments flared up in the entire Bombay region. Many of my informants were initially quite reluctant to touch on communal issues, but after these events took place it was as though an entire layer of moderation and civility were removed, and a more brutal language and sentiment appeared. An unmistakable mood of triumph and self-satisfaction was reflected in many of the reactions of ordinary residents in places like Thane to what they perceived as the Hindus' long overdue revenge against the Muslims. Expressions like "I was overjoyed," "I felt happy," "Justice was finally served" were typical responses to the razing of Babri Masjid. After the Bombay riots I heard "We taught them a lesson," "This was the wrath of the Hindu," "For once we Hindus paid them back in their own currency," even among people not affiliated with Shiv Sena or the BJP.

Clearly the Hindus believed that they had retrieved their national pride and their masculinity, which the Muslims had stolen from them. At least momentarily, in the heat of a sharpened antagonism, the imaginary "Hindu community" crystallized as an experienced reality. In those few days the mood crossed the boundaries of the average Hindutva supporter and enabled Shiv Sena to rehabilitate somewhat its otherwise battered image in the Bombay region.

THE RETURN OF THE KING

In the years that followed Congress tried to consolidate its fragile hold over the local political scene in Thane City. Its efforts, however, were constantly thwarted by incessant rivalries and "political entropy" that affected all political parties. Every ward and locality saw constant struggles and factional fights within and between families in which politics cum social work had literally become a full-time vocation. What drove this tendency toward entropy was, as elsewhere in Bombay and urban Maharashtra, the rapidly growing economic stakes in local politics. The booming market in construction and real estate, and the proliferation of corruption and brokerage at the municipal level that accompanied this prosperity, attracted a large number of ambitious individuals. As a result, each municipal election saw an increasing number of independent candidates; further, parties found it difficult in general to control their selection of candidates and the defection that ensued after the elections.

For these reasons the alliance between Shiv Sena and the BJP rarely could sustain itself at the local level before municipal elections, and Thane City was no exception. Preceding Thane's local elections in February 1997, Shiv Sena and the BJP were pitted against each other in open battle, including occasional violent encounters, in a chaotic election campaign in which almost one thousand candidates, mostly independents, were competing for the ninety-five seats in the Municipal Corporation.[19]

The background of this conflict was Anand Dighe's determination to regain his power and influence after the crisis between 1992 and the 1995 elections that had brought Shiv Sena to power in Maharashtra and secured the party's complete political domination in Thane. Ganesh Naik, Dighe's contemporary and competitor, had become minister and had also been entrusted the task of being Sena's "guardian" in the entire Thane district. Dighe needed to consolidate his position, and his method of doing so was to proclaim that Shiv Sena alone would win a majority in Thane, to cut down on the share of seats given to the BJP, and to "declare war on independents and defectors," as he expressed it in an interview.[20]

Dighe also decided to step out of the aloof role of "godfather" he had designed for himself and to circulate rumors several months before the election that he might run for the post of mayor. This rumor was something of a "public secret": Everybody heard about it, nobody really believed it, and yet it kept alive wild speculations about Dighe's intentions. In addition, his rather spectacular campaign throughout the city resuscitated some of the former enthusiasm of Shiv Sena activists.

While Dighe campaigned in the name of party discipline, Congress candidates in Chandanwadi, among them N. Pawar, embarked on a protest against the alleged demolition by city authorities of a small Ganesh temple in the neighborhood. Using the techniques that Sena had honed and made common currency, Pawar declared a bandh in the area, stopping traffic on the main road and asserting that he and other candidates would fast indefinitely until the city administration issued an official apology. It is interesting that neither Shiv Sena nor the BJP even commented on the issue, which, in any case, seemed to have no major impact on the election result.

Shiv Sena emerged from the election as the largest party in the Corporation and realigned itself with the BJP to keep the many independents out of decisive posts in the city administration. "The people respected our stand on corruption. I had spoken out against widespread corruption in the corporator cartel, and we initiated an inquiry," Dighe said.[21] The goal had been achieved. Dighe's status as "King of Thane," a "messiah of the poor" as an admirer put it, had been affirmed both formally and informally. However, it was a victory won within the Hobbesian theater of power that seems to govern local politics in urban India. Dighe was now compelled to assert his dominance—to act as a sovereign, to control the political entropy, the proliferating violence, and the general "dada'ization" of city politics that he himself had been instrumental in creating and perpetuating.

CHAPTER 5

Riots, Policing, and Truth Telling in Bombay

"LET BOMBAY BURN!"

Immediately after the demolition of the Babri Masjid in Ayodhya on 6 December 1992, angry Muslims took to the streets all over India. Some of the most violent confrontations between demonstrators and authorities took place in Bombay, where the police force clamped down, with considerable brutality, on Muslim protests and the ensuing clashes between Hindus and Muslims. Within a few days close to two hundred demonstrators, mostly Muslims, had been killed and hundreds wounded. The general tension in the city was exacerbated as Moreshwar Save, a Shiv Sena MP from Aurangabad, and Bal Thackeray publicly ventured to take credit for the demolition, claiming that five hundred specially trained Shiv Sena storm troopers had led the assault on the old mosque.[1] This claim was untrue; indeed, a group of high-ranking Shiv Sena leaders actually arrived in Ayodhya too late even to witness the demolition.

While the police shot at and arrested Muslim demonstrators, Shiv Sena was allowed to conduct large public celebrations of the demolition, even to construct a makeshift *hutatma* (martyrs) column in the Marathi-speaking area of Dadar listing the names of Hindus killed in the December 1992 riots. Shiv Sena also began the so-called *maha aartis*, mass prayers performed in front of temples as a show of strength against Muslims as well as a way to boost confidence among Hindus. The maha aartis were clearly political demonstrations, as Hinduism has no such tradition of public mass prayer; it was a symbolic response to the Muslims' Friday prayer, regarded by many Hindus as a public show of strength. Accompanied by extensive press coverage, and under the protection of police and army personnel, Shiv Sena leader Pramod Nawalkar led the first maha aarti on December 11, a Friday, at a time coinciding with the Muslims' Friday prayer throughout the city. By the end of December the Shiv Sena leadership decided to launch a regular campaign, and hundreds of maha aartis were performed all over the city well into January 1993. Despite these events, banning Shiv Sena, or even just curbing its activities, was not considered at this point, although former Sena leader Bhujbal strongly recommended such a move (Sardesai 1993, 191). Thackeray's response to a ban on Shiv Sena was highly belligerent: "I think this ban should come—it must come so that when tomorrow our government comes, we can ban Congress with ease. Yes, I will welcome a move to ban us." Commenting on the riots, he said: "If our people should not retaliate then they should really wear bangles."[2]

The Congress administration seemed willing to protect Shiv Sena for fear of a massive Hindu backlash in the polarized climate that existed in December 1992. As a result, the communal division was given a free run and escalated in the streets of Bombay as hundreds of maha aartis and Muslim prayers became the loci of communal tension. All through December 1992 minor incidents of stabbing, arson, and violence occurred almost daily throughout the city.

On 8 January 1993 a Hindu family was burned to death by unknown arsonists in the Bombay suburb of Jogeshwari. On the same day Thackeray called on Shiv sainiks to defend Hindus, and, by means of the evening newspapers and Shiv Sena's blackboards all over the city, word spread within hours.

Over the next four or five days groups of Hindus, often led by sainiks, rampaged the city, systematically looting and burning Muslim shops, houses, and businesses. Many apartments, cars, shops, and hutment areas were marked in advance based on electoral rolls and information from the civic administration. Shiv Sena targeted Muslims in a concerted and, to some extent, prearranged attempt to intimidate them and drive them out of Bombay. The official death toll quickly exceeded 800; more than 150,000, mainly Muslims, fled the city; and more than 100,000 took shelter in hastily erected refugee camps in Muslim areas in central Bombay considered relatively safe for Muslims. Other narratives, however, as well as evidence presented before the Srikrishna Commission, indicated that even in these so-called safe areas there was widespread arson, confrontations with the police and Hindus, as well as stray killings.

The Bombay police assumed several opposing roles in this anti-Muslim pogrom involving thousands of people all over the city but most cruelly displayed in the city's widespread slums and hutment areas; at times the police were passive, at times complicit bystanders, at times even active participants. I was in Bombay during the riots and, on several occasions, witnessed looting and arson while nearby police constables either ignored what was happening or actively protected the rioters. Radio communication between a local police headquarters and field units revealed the repeated use of grossly abusive language regarding Muslims. Police officers instructed constables in the field to "let the Muslims be roasted." Ironically, because these tapes had been illegally recorded, they were later disallowed as legal evidence. In November 1995 Olga Tellis, one of the journalists behind these disclosures (now a Thackeray supporter) told me that nothing significant had been recorded on these tapes. Some leftist groups had blown the whole incident out of proportion, she assured me. "Besides," she said, "it was the Muslims who started the whole thing. They asked for trouble, and they got it. Since then, they have behaved themselves."[3]

The riots quickly got out of Shiv Sena's already ineffective control and catalyzed a series of smaller, localized incidents; older scores between individuals and criminal rivalries were settled in the atmosphere of violence and lawlessness that had engulfed the city for more than a week. During this week the government, and military contingents deployed in the city, were either defunct or passive, newspapers were erratic, and radio and TV broadcasting remained either silent or reported misleading accounts of what was actually occurring. As in other similar riots, a network of terrifying rumors and wildly exaggerated threats from the Muslim world and reports of the misdeeds committed fed into the collective anger and fear that raged in the city.[4]

This climate gave birth to the most inflated rumors that fed into the fear of a forthcoming Muslim retaliation. There was talk of marauding gangs of Muslims roaming the streets at night to avenge their dead and to rape Hindu women. Driven by guilt and fear, middle-class Hindu men armed themselves and patrolled their neighborhoods at night. Another rumor was that large arms shipments were to arrive at the coast as assistance to the Muslim underworld from alleged secret patrons in Pakistan and the Persian Golf. At night, hundreds of cars, with headlights glaring, and massive crowds of Hindu men, most of them armed, assembled on the beaches, staring over the dark sea, preparing to ward off imaginary attacks.[5]

As in other riots, rape was a regular feature of the atrocities committed, both by mobs and smaller groups. As in earlier riots, women were seen distributing bangles to men who did not participate in the riots. Reports also circulated of Hindu women actively assisting in the gang rape of Muslim women, as well as in arson and looting.[6]

Popular involvement in this riot was more extensive than in any previous riot in the Bombay region. The theater of lawlessness and chaos provided an opportunity for local dadas to assert themselves, prove their capacity, establish their reputation. To many observers in the local press, the massive involvement of the ostensibly civilized middle class in the kind of violence typically associated with the lower classes was particularly shocking and ominous. Whereas earlier riots had mainly been played out in low-income areas, now systematic attacks were being launched on middle-class residential areas, including the burning and looting of homes and property belonging to Muslim professionals and middle-class families. For many upwardly mobile Muslim families, the hope that education, money, and respectability would earn them acceptance from Hindu colleagues was shattered. Many prosperous and upwardly mobile Hindus also saw these new spatial dimensions of the riot as threatening to their way of life and sense of security.

Most of the city's elite and intelligentsia immediately placed the main responsibility for the violence on Shiv Sena. Thackeray was more than eager to assume this responsibility and to play his favorite part as the establishment's whipping boy. In keeping with Sena's well-rehearsed construction of violence as natural and spontaneous, Thackeray claimed that the riots were "justified self-defense," expressing a "spontaneous anger on the part of Hindus." He denied the existence of any major Shiv Sena master plan behind the events and argued that the sainiks only tried to further the Hindus' interests wherever they could. There is little doubt, however, that Shiv Sena leaders organized maha aartis all over the city, compiled lists of Muslim houses and shops, and prepared its activists for the ensuing confrontation. The leadership was clearly looking for a cause and a pretext to revitalize Shiv Sena's battered image and to reenact the movement's "original effervescence" after its electoral defeats and protracted crisis in 1991–92.

However, a closer scrutiny of the events from mid-December 1992 to the end of January 1993 does not suggest the unfolding of any larger design. During this chaotic period, Shiv Sena merely acted according to the daily situation in various areas of the metropolis, seeking to attract media exposure through radical statements and public performances, such as the maha aartis and the *hutatma* column in Dadar. Once the riots began, Shiv Sena's leadership was both unable and unwilling to control the situation. Sainiks were simply given free rein, and the police force—especially the lower ranks generally supportive of Shiv Sena—was paralyzed by contradictory political signals from the state government.

Shiv Sena's modus operandi before and during the riots supports the observation made from above that the Sena's activities spring from popular sentiments in various situations while seeking to give these a twist, boosting, wherever possible, the organization's image of being aggressive, uncompromising, and hard-hitting. Given the pent-up anger, fear, and sense of triumph in Bombay's deeply polarized atmosphere after the first round of riots—where mostly Muslims were killed by the police—a second round of riots, without the Sena, could easily have taken place. But Shiv Sena sharpened and aggravated tensions, adding organization and ideological eloquence to the events. Thackeray at this time was the man most interviewed in Bombay. Fully enjoying the situation, and appreciating preferential treatment from the media, he proliferated radical communal statements, only further exacerbating tensions. At lower levels, Shiv Sena leaders worked overtime to whip up communal sentiment and to mobilize as many sainiks as possible in order to prove their loyalty to the

Senapati. At the local level, young boys again flocked to the shakhas, which, in the heat of the moment, had become magnets drawing in angry, frightened young men, criminals with their own agendas, even respectable middle-class fathers determined to defend their home and locality against the assumed threat from the Muslims.

The combined effect of all these events was to elevate Shiv Sena once again as a powerful force in Bombay, perceived by many as the ultimate defender of the Hindus. Shiv Sena's image as an irresponsible group of *goondas* (criminals) had in some ways been confirmed, yet, among the city's Hindu middle class, the party was viewed as a reliable defense against the Muslim menace. "They are bastards, but they are *our* bastards," as one Hindu journalist put it. On this score, Shiv Sena undoubtedly commanded more respect than the BJP.[7] While leaders of the BJP and RSS in Bombay continued to project themselves as responsible, democratic, and moderate, thousands of activists and sympathizers of the Hindu nationalist movement participated in maha aartis and in the riots under the banner of Shiv Sena.[8] Dilip Karambelkar, the editor of *Vivek*, a Bombay-based RSS magazine, told me: "Eighty percent of the Hindus in Bombay were emotionally involved in the riots—on the Hindu side."[9]

In March 1993 a group of people, mainly Muslims affiliated with criminal networks in Bombay, arranged and executed a series of bomb blasts that killed hundreds of civilians all over the city in a single day. The blasts wrecked bus terminals as well as the city's stock exchange. A few weeks later, consignments of arms and sophisticated explosives were recovered in several places along the Maharashtrian coast. The police, as well as Hindu nationalist organizations, immediately alleged that the Pakistani intelligence unit, ISI, had been involved in the bombings by assisting local underworld networks in Bombay.

Regardless of the factual complexities surrounding the bombings, it soon became widely assumed to all that the bomb blasts were the Muslims' answer to militant Hindus. "Don't mess with us" was the message allegedly sent by the legendary Dawood Ibrahim, now elevated to the status of stern godfather, along with his gang, on behalf of the Muslim community. "God knows that I don't approve of the killing of innocent women and children," a Muslim friend of mine remarked some months after the bombings, "but after the bomb blasts we could again live with some dignity—we could again look our Hindu colleagues in the eyes." A Muslim teacher from Nagpada told me, in 1993:

We all felt horrible during those four months [December 1992 to March 1993—T.B.H.]—all over you would hear these derogatory remarks about Muslims, you felt the hostility all over, in the trains, in shops, in my school. I recall riding on a train when a group of Hindu women spotted me and started talking quietly. One said "We Hindu women should also do something. Look at that Muslim woman there—one should throw her off the train." . . . All this stopped after the bomb blasts—not because they accepted us, but because they feared us.

Five days after the blasts, Dawood Ibrahim's former residence in central Bombay was itself bombed by the police in retaliation against the expatriate underworld figure. The rubble was then fenced off from the public, and the area seems still to radiate a mystical power. Several years later, when doing fieldwork in the area, I was advised not to go near the ruin at night, and, on several occasions, young men showed me pieces of Italian marble tiles they had stolen from the lavish bathrooms of the former residence. For these young men, these scraps of tile were highly prized symbols of their courage to have entered the ruins, said to be under the surveillance of Dawood's men, as well as venerated objects, symbolizing the power of this local dada who had become a legend larger than life. (I shall return to this subject below.)

THE MYTH OF THE STATE

After the riots, many public figures bemoaned the shattering of their dream of Bombay as the anvil of a national modernity where new secular identities would arise from factories and institutions. These concerns seemed symptomatic of a wider, inexplicable anxiety concerning a kind of mythological vision of the state, an image of the state as a distant, uncertain, yet persistent guarantor of social order, justice, and protection from violence. The shattering of this overriding myth appeared in different guises to different groups and communities.

For the Muslims, who had born the brunt of police brutality and ethnic rage from militant Hindus in both rounds of violence, the riots marked the final step in a long process of political marginalization. For years, the police force, as well as the mainstream press in Bombay, had consolidated images of the city's Muslim areas as inherently criminal dens of drug peddling, smuggling, and violence, peopled by clannish, fanatical, and hostile Muslims. Many Muslims blamed the Congress Party for the riots and the expansion of the Hindu nationalist forces. Having been wholly identified with state power for decades and perceived as the ultimate protector of secular practices and minorities within the Indian state, the Congress became the target of Muslim anger and frustration. Leading Congress ministers were present in Bombay during the riots, among them Union Minister of Defense Sharad Pawar. Although the army and the Rapid Action Force were called in, both performed their duties in an embarrassingly ineffectual fashion and were unable (or unwilling) to curb the violence. Throughout the conflagration, the supreme jurisdiction over the city remained with the police commissioner and the local authorities, while the central government refrained from taking any action despite the proliferation of violence. Moreover, the anti-Muslim bias among the city's police force was well known to most Muslims. This became more obvious than ever during the riots; when Muslims were demonstrating, police officers shouted the order, "Shoot to kill," but they generally used milder forms of riot control against Hindus crowds.

These circumstances gave rise to a host of rumors and conspiracy theories. According to most of my informants in the Muslim neighborhoods in central Mumbai during the winter of 1996–97, their vision of the upper echelons of the state bureaucracy and the Congress Party as sites of justice and protection had given way to a radical sense of isolation and betrayal. Several Muslim leaders and high-ranking police officers have stated, in retrospect, that the atmosphere among Muslims in the city that first year after the riots was so tense and their sense of frustration and humiliation so aggravated that more organized urban terror may well have emerged. In this regard, the official report of the Srikrishna Commission inquiring into the riots stated that "a grand conspiracy was hatched at the instance of the notorious smuggler Dawood Ibrahim Kaskar, operating from Dubai, to recruit and train young Muslims to vent their anger and wreak revenge by exploding bombs near vital installations and also in Hindu-dominated areas so as to engineer a fresh bout of communal riots" (Srikrishna 1998, 60). Justice Srikrishna praises the effective police investigations that revealed this conspiracy (61) but fails to mention the vital role that corrupt customs and police authorities played in facilitating the import of explosives and weapons needed in the operation.

"We have never been accepted by them and we never will," a young Muslim graduate who lived in the northern suburbs told me in 1995. "For me, these riots all of a sudden made me see clearly what I had refused to see earlier. They have always hated us. In school we are taught that Shivaji is the greatest warrior the world has seen. When we did sports, the teacher divided us into two teams, Hindus on the Shivaji team and we Muslims on the Aurangzeb team. . . . We never thought about it but now we know how they look at us."

Among the substantial sections of the Hindu middle classes and the slum dwellers, having supported Shiv Sena and its allies, the shattering of the myth of the state emerged in an altogether different form. Here, what materialized was a rather triumphant sense of having "taught the Muslims a lesson," of overruling and defying the state, of celebrating an ethnic-majoritarian justice opposed to what Hindu nationalist leaders had decried as the state's "pampering" and protection of minorities. During these heated months in 1993, it seemed that earlier, more restrained and guarded modes of naming and talking about Muslims gave way to an open enunciation of the most radical xenophobic statements and fantasies that circulated widely from rickshaw drivers to respectable family doctors.

After the riots, Shiv Sena began to consolidate its position and to rebuild its organization. At the 1995 elections, which brought Shiv Sena to power in the state of Maharashtra, the party completely swept the polls in the metropolis. Despite compelling evidence of increasing levels of corruption, open contempt for the legal process among Shiv Sena's leaders, disregard for democratic procedures, and Thackeray's celebration of having his own "remote control" of the government, the Sena's popularity remained unaffected for several years. Amid mounting evidence of corruption at the highest level, the party once again swept the polls at the 1997 municipal elections in Mumbai and several other cities in the state (see Hansen 1998, 148–62).

As I shall discuss further below, Shiv Sena's hold on Mumbai over a longer period may indicate a transformation of the state's image. The aura of the state as a site of neutrality, harboring a measure of predictability based on impersonal rules and legislation and technical expertise that the colonial and postcolonial state had constructed and maintained, seemed no longer to hold the same meaning as before. In a complex society traversed by discourses of rights and entitlements, where public spectacles and democratic procedures are generally adhered to, the state must still appear as a set of institutions and practices with special features and authority that cannot be fully owned or controlled by any political formation. As we shall see, Shiv Sena and other political forces in Maharashtra were forced to realize that the state, in order to be effective, had to retain a unique image distinct from, and elevated above, the wider society.

The state is a name given to various practices and institutions of government, not only as an analytical concept but also as a locus of authority invoked and reproduced by an endless range of interventions—from validating documents and checking motor vehicles to prohibiting certain substances or encouraging particular forms of behavior that serve the public health, and so on. In other words, the state is an organizing concept through which people in Mumbai, in India as a whole, and in other societies as well imagine the cohesion of their own society, its order, its sovereignty but also its secrets, its sources of violence, its evil, and so on.

In the history of the Western world, the idea of the state emerged as a site of sovereignty, a symbolic center of political will and power over partisan interests. According to this tradition, a state needs to govern but must also reproduce something more, an imaginary dimension that separates the actions of the state from those of any other agency. To generate legitimacy, more is required than the hegemonic imposition of categories and epistemic regimes. The state must be endorsed as the symbolic center of society, the arbiter of conflicts, the site of authorization, the sole agency with the right to delegate power as well as to "write society"—to author laws, a constitution, rules, certificates, and so forth.

Ernst Kantorowicz has shown with great subtlety how a legal-political theory of the "King's Two Bodies" developed in medieval Britain. Here, political authority was constructed as a dual structure—on the one hand was the notion of a sublime, infallible, and eternal King (the Law) and, on the other, the profane, human, and fallible king (the giver of laws). On the sublime dimension of royal authority, Kantorowicz quotes Blackstone: "[The King] . . is not only incapable of *doing* wrong, but even of *thinking* wrong: he can never mean to do an improper thing: in him is no folly or weakness" (Kantorowicz 1957, 4). As Lefort points out, the efficacy of this construction flows precisely from the simultaneous separation and unity of these two bodies, from the combination of the profane and the sublime in the eyes of the subjects:

> It is the image of the natural body, the image of a God made flesh, the image of his marriage, his paternity, his liaisons, his festivals, his amusements and his feasts, but also the images of his weaknesses or even his cruelties, in short, all the images of his humanity, that people their imaginary, that assure them that the people and the king are conjoined. (Lefort 1998, 245)

This union of the two bodies was later reconfigured as the nation, the people, and the leader took the place of the sublime-abstract body and made governance of the empirical and profane people possible in the name of this higher principle (254). Lefort argues that with the advent of democracy this mythical and original source of power becomes radically empty, since it can only be temporarily occupied by representatives of the people, of the nation, and so on (17). These representatives stand for the people by occupying exactly that which seems more permanent and enduring: the central legislative institutions of the state.

In the eyes of political forces nurturing projects of domination, conquest, or transformation of societies, the state seems indispensable. Only within this elusive apparatus can one find and develop the technologies and rationalities that makes governance, social transformation, planning, and regulated social engineering possible. The myth of the state has historically been constructed in the Western world to give body to notions of universal justice and forms of knowledge, reason, and authority that exceed any single party, ethnic group, or class. This is indeed a mythical construction, and, as Foucault pointed out, effective governance takes place in a vast and amorphous terrain of small arenas and micro processes often extending beyond the state (Foucault 1991b). I will submit, however, that governance and legitimacy of the state are not identical and that they necessarily must draw on different symbolic registers. Public and performative dimensions of governance and sovereignty remain critical to the construction of "stateness"—spectacles, political rhetoric, symbols—as well as the pertinence of the "Law," of public legal processes, and so on.[10]

I suggest that the imagination of the state be seen as being marked by a deep and constitutive split between its profane dimensions—the incoherence, brutality, partiality, and banality of the technical sides of governance, as well as the rough and tumble of negotiation, compromise, and naked self-interest displayed in local politics. These features stand opposed to sublime qualities imputed to a more distant state, that is, the opacity of the secrets and knowledge of the higher echelons of the state, its hidden resources, designs, and immense power, as well as the illusions of higher forms of rationality or justice believed to prevail there. The repertoire of the state's public performatives—from stamps to military parades to imposing architecture—serves to consolidate this imagination of the state as an elevated entity. To paraphrase Durkheim, the celebrations of the rationality and power of the state are examples of how modern societies worship themselves and their own social order.

If we keep in mind this duality of the state, we may see the full significance of why political forces and agencies of the state felt the need to launch various initiatives in Mumbai in order to create mechanisms for reconciliation, or at least cohabitation, between Muslims and Hindus after the riots. I argue that these initiatives were launched to reassert the state's authority—partly by reorganizing techniques of governance but also by reconfiguring the state's legitimacy and authority in order to retrieve a myth of the state without which a democratic state cannot govern—not even if this state is headed by a government that nurtures the most antidemocratic form of majoritarianism, as in the case of Shiv Sena.

Before proceeding to the complexities of contemporary Mumbai, let us briefly consider whether and, if so, how such a line of reasoning derived from medieval Western political thought can be made relevant to contemporary India. Does modern India embody any sublime dimensions at all of the state and political authority? Should one adopt instead a *longue durée* perspective and inquire into how older registers of kingship and the relations between Brahmans and Kshatriyas are played out today?[11] Undoubtedly notions of honor, patronage, and the appropriate behavior of the landowning aristocracy and dominant castes in various parts of India have shaped the construction of politics there in profound ways. As we saw above, the ethnohistorical imaginary remains a very active factor in shaping political identities in contemporary Maharashtra. These cultural repertoires seem insufficient, however, to capture the range of meanings evoked by the term *sarkar* (government, state) in contemporary India.

First, colonialism brought about a deep and important break with what Kaviraj has called the "majesty and marginality of the state in precolonial India" (Kaviraj 1997a, 233). As we saw above, it broke and reduced the power of local jagirdars and notables, and ruled instead with an unprecedented intensity through relatively uniform regulations dispensed by a permanent structure, the district administration that to this day forms the backbone of the state administration. Initially, the position and functions of local district collectors were undoubtedly understood within local vocabularies of respect and deference, but, over time, colonial rule added new and enduring rules and codes to the meaning of *sarkar*.

Second, in spite of deeply segmented and competing notions of power, leadership, and legitimacy in postcolonial India, its public culture has produced a large reservoir of shared symbols, languages, and references—from war heroes to politicians and film stars to sports teams, cultural events, brand names, and styles of consumption shared across the breadth and length of India, as well as across caste and class. This national, or at least nationwide, culture has systematically been promoted by the state whose crucial role in producing a national imaginary can hardly be overestimated, as Khilnani has pointed out (Khilnani 1997, 19). People live with, and mix, a range of cultural registers, and so do those aspiring to political leadership. Sharad Pawar likes to style himself as a modern version of a fierce Maratha warrior, and Bal Thackeray enjoys imagining that he is a modern incarnation of Shivaji. But these and similar invocations of the aura of aristocracy, the purity of high birth, or the wisdom of religious texts are only some of the cultural registers through which political leaders try to invoke a sublime and exalted authority.

Education, command of English, and competence in the world of science and administration constitutes equally, if not more, powerful registers of authority and sublime qualities. The bureaucrat, the planner, the scientist, the member of the Indian Administrative Service—the heavily mythologized steel frame of the state—all occupy crucial positions in contemporary political imaginaries, not least of all the large middle class. The bureaucrat was, until recently, the hero of modern India, and until the 1970s was depicted in Hindi films as a man of character and insight.

Until quite recently this modern nationalist aristocracy—lineages of high-ranking bureaucrats, scientists, and politicians—were referred to with awe and respect. The mark of these ideal national citizens who manned the bureaucracy was precisely their combination of moral integrity, commitment to the larger abstract nation, and deep technical insights. The authority of education, especially English medium education, remains crucial among ordinary people as well, where it often generates more respect than wealth. Many ordinary people in India still attribute considerable authority and sublime qualities to such institutions as courts, to

judges, to senior bureaucrats, and so on. This testifies to how effectively
the modern nationalist elite in India throughout this century has made
education, science, the rule of law, and the role of the public sector into
core signifiers of the modern nation.

Complementing older registers of public conduct, this nationalist register has evolved into a complex web of public languages and political imaginaries that shapes discourses of the state and boosts rumors and stories of
the transgression of rules, of corruption, and of the abuse of governmental
authority. It is worth remembering that it is the sense of violation of the
state's imputed idealized, sublime qualities that makes such stories worth
telling at all. Ordinary Indians are undoubtedly less in awe of the state
than they were a few decades ago, but the state is still regarded as indispensable in terms of public order and of recognizing communities, leaders,
or claims of legitimacy and authenticity. Bureaucrats, judges, and officers
are called on every day to authenticate, inaugurate, and authorize, in brief,
to act as transient incarnations of authority and symbols of the state. These
manifestations of the state's authority may well be a structural effect of
governance, as Tim Mitchell contends (Mitchell 1999, 89–91), but they
are also important public performances that need to be studied in their
own right.[12]

Below I illustrate the divided representation of the Indian state as both
sublime and profane by first analyzing judiciary initiatives, especially the
construction and impact of the Srikrishna Commission's inquiry into the
1993 riots and bombings and the proceedings of the special TADA court
investigation of the bombings in March 1993.

Second, I discuss how the government maintains public order in central
Mumbai, and how the police and nongovernmental organizations
(NGOs) established the so-called *mohalla* committees in these areas in
1994. Further, I examine the trajectory of these initiatives and how they
impacted on local perceptions of state and authority in the context of the
strained everyday encounters between police and Muslims in the city.

THE SRIKRISHNA COMMISSION: CATHARSIS
AND THE POLITICS OF TRUTH

A few weeks after the January 1993 riots, the government of Maharashtra
decided to set up an Inquiry Commission headed by the High Court
judge, Justice Srikrishna. The massive evidence of Shiv Sena's and other
political parties' blatant involvement in the violence, and abuse of authority by the police, clearly required that the government, in order to reestablish its authority in the eyes of minorities, human rights organizations,
and the broader public, had to demonstrate its commitment to justice.

The commission began its work in June 1993 with a mandate to establish "the circumstances, events and immediate causes of the incidents which occurred in the Bombay Police Commissionerate area in December 1992 on or after the 6th December 1992, and again in January 1993, on or after the 6th January 1993." The commission was further authorized to identify "individuals, or groups of individuals or any other organization" responsible for the riots, as well as to assess the effectiveness of the Bombay police in handling the situation (Srikrishna 1998, 1).

The commission was supposed to work like a public hearing and initially called on "all persons having knowledge about facts touching upon the Terms of Reference to come forward and file affidavits before the Commission" (Srikrishna 1998, 2) and also called on the police and the government to submit their versions of the events in the city. As many as 2,126 affidavits were filed: 2 by the government, 549 by the police, and 1,575 by various individuals and organizations. After several attempts by the state government to obstruct and delay the information, the commission's report finally appeared in August 1998, five and a half years after the riots. It was left to the state government to decide whether the massive evidence gathered by the commission should be made available to the advocate-general in order to allow the state to institute criminal prosecution.

Public inquiries into serious conflagrations, major policy failures, or disasters such as famines or revolts have been conducted in India since the 1870s. The inquests of the colonial state were normally carried out by civil servants, who interviewed police officers, victims, witnesses, and so on, to establish the factual circumstances and to apportion responsibility. In the independent postcolonial state, these techniques of governmental self-diagnostics continued but acquired new moral and political dimensions as they became intensely occupied with rooting out harmful practices and with reforming society by means of reforming the state. As Visvanathan notes in his discussion of corruption inquiries in the 1950s and 1960s, "Public administration was [now] the home science of the modern state. The state was not seen as something gargantuan, a huge organism or a giant machine, but as something tentative" (Visvanathan 1998, 15).

With the Shah Commission's probing, in 1977, into the excesses of the Emergency imposed by Indira Gandhi, a new and more openly cathartic mode of inquiry was created. The need was felt to clarify the extent of the damage caused by authoritarian rule as well as to redeem the state apparatus. The Shah Commission resembled a hearing, investigating submissions from victims of the state's excessive use of powers as well as from responsible bureaucrats and politicians. Everyone who appeared before the commission was allowed legal representation, and the commission, in its style and proceedings, sought to be as similar as possible to those of a courtroom.

In comparison, the Srikrishna Commission was more like an open tribunal. The proceedings were made public, and interested organizations and parties were called on to be represented through legal counsel along with the commission's own official advocate. A number of organizations and parties were represented before the commission between 1993 and 1997: the Shiv Sena and the BJP, both ruling the state during most of the commission's tenure; the All-India Milli Council, a coordination group for a number of Muslim organizations; the Jamiyat-E-Ulema (Council of Islamic Scholars); the Communist Party of India (until 1995); and a variety of human rights associations, such as the Lawyers' Collective and the Committee for the Protection of Human Rights. The commission could order any public servant to testify, whereas ordinary citizens appeared of their own free will. The same voluntary principle applied to those elected for public office, but, given the public nature of the hearings, public figures felt pressured to appear and to be cross-examined.

The hearings began as a systematic inquiry into the events that unfolded during the critical period in the city's twenty-six police districts that had been involved, and later focused on background factors and the role of specific public agencies, especially the police force. Based on independent investigations and affidavits from citizens and police officers, the commission and the counselors representing the interested parties called and cross-examined witnesses of various sorts and loyalties. After each witness was cross-examined, Justice Srikrishna drew his conclusions regarding the chain of events, their cause-and-effect relationships, and these brief summations of his judgments, along with a substantial bulk of written material, formed the essence of the final report.

Obviously the material presented to the commission was intensely politicized, just as the hearings, which were covered by the press, often became rhetorical platforms for the counselors representing the various parties. The commission tried, admittedly with some self-consciousness, to extract or approximate the truth from a series of political interpretations. The task of positively establishing who did what to whom, and when and how it occurred was exceedingly difficult, often having to rely on inferences rather than clear-cut evidence. Let us glimpse briefly into how material was presented before the commission.[13]

RECONSTRUCTING TRUTH AFTER THE FACT

Just as the state government was deciding to set up a commission of inquiry in February 1993, Bombay's commissioner of police during the riots, S. Bapat, was transferred, and A. S. Samra, a highly respected officer, was brought in to reform the Bombay police. Samra had successfully prevented the massive riots in Bombay from spreading to Thane and, as a Sikh, was widely assumed to be neutral in the Hindu-Muslim conflict. This move, and the wording of the commission's mandate, made it clear to many police officers that the state government was prepared to place the bulk of responsibility on the police force. Hundreds of police officers, who had been in command at police stations at the time, began writing lengthy affidavits explaining their actions and perceptions during the riots.

The two handfuls of such affidavits to which I managed to get access ran along similar lines. They each began with a long, often rosy account of the officer's career, his specific distinctions, often pointing to the officer's acknowledged skills in handling "mobs." One officer referred to his lengthy experience in the police stations in Bombay's mill district where, on many occasions, he had dealt with demonstrators and "violent mobs." Another gave an account that ran close to ten pages of all the demanding posts he had been assigned—ranging from Dharavi, the biggest slum in Asia, to Agripada, described as one of the most "notorious trouble spots in Bombay," and rendered a virtual catalogue of situations he had dealt with in these locations: mass meetings, Hindu-Muslim violence after cricket matches between India and Pakistan, religious processions turned into "rampaging mobs," and so on.

Armed with these credentials, the officers then turned to describing the areas where they were posted during the riots. One officer described the Muslim-dominated Dongri area in central Bombay as dangerous and unpredictable:

> This locality has a long history of communal riots [that have] been occurring here at frequent intervals since 1893. . . . Though by and large the residents are peace-loving citizens, incidents of antinational character committed by a few mischief mongers tend to cause sudden escalation of tension. The area has earned such a notorious reputation that the police machinery has to be alert round the year. However, it is not always possible to predict how and to what extent a situation can deteriorate.

The accounts then presented vivid and detailed descriptions of the events and of the officers' actions, the orders issued, the number of rounds fired, and so on. What emerged from these narratives was a picture of chaos, drama, and confusion: a city exploding in random and unintelligible violence, looting and arson breaking out behind police lines as the officers dealt with one situation after another, as new reports arrived of police vehicles being stoned and attacked by rioters in other areas. These stories all described a police force not properly prepared for such situations, reflecting as well the officers' fear of mobs that, in accounts from Muslim areas of the city, were intensely hostile to the police force.

In the cross-examinations most officers defended their actions and asserted the need for public order. One officer maintained that when Hindus were ringing the temple bells on December 6 (the so-called *ghanta naad* promoted by Shiv Sena) to celebrate the demolition of the mosque in Ayodhya "it was treated as a religious activity exempted under the ban order of the Bombay Police Act." A senior inspector from the Nagpada police station admitted that although he was aware that sainiks made highly provocative speeches in connection with the *ghanta naad*, "it did not then occur to me to take any action."

The lawyer representing the Milli Council asked an inspector to justify his calling the Muslims the aggressors. He replied: "Muslims were aggressors because they came out in large numbers [and] they did resort to violence. The police had to take effective action and the Muslims who were on the streets had to bear the brunt of the police action." According to this officer, the questions of why events took place, which people were shot, and so on, were irrelevant to policing. Their job was to restore public order, and anyone who got in the way might be shot.

The issue of whether the police used excessive force against Muslim rioters was discussed at length at the proceedings. One police officer defended the immediate use of "extreme force," that is, shooting directly at rioters to kill them: "I do not think that it is always necessary to use graded force when dealing with a situation of violence. If extreme force is resorted to, at the very first stage, in order to put firmly down the riots, I would consider it justified."

Affidavits from ordinary constables revealed a less orderly story, filled with the horror of advancing mobs: "The mob did not respond to our tear gas. . . . On the contrary, they indulged in heavy stone throwing . . . [and] then someone fired a gun at us." An elderly constable related how he was attacked with a sword and how his colleagues withdrew into the police post: "I was then left alone in the hands of the mob, I was terribly frightened. . . .) Someone attacked my face and neck with a sword."

Most of the constables' accounts reflected both fear and incomprehension, as if the rioters were a natural calamity, displaying aggression toward the policemen that the officers themselves did not connect with their status as police. Instead, many of them depicted themselves as the victims of the riots. Judging from my conversations with policemen, this was not an attempt to exonerate themselves or their actions. None of the policemen I spoke with denied that they had killed or wounded rioters. To them, it was done in self-defense, the only way they could respond to the dreaded mobs. The officers shared a common experience of being unjustly targeted while doing their job, of being hated by the local people, of detesting these same people themselves, and of being stabbed in the back by political leaders. This appeared to be their strongest bond, a sort of negative esprit de corps. In summarizing the police officers' low morale, Justice Srikrishna wrote: "The police, by their own conduct, appeared to have lost moral authority over the citizens [who] appeared to evoke no fear. . . . The criminal elements were emboldened to hurl a crude bomb at the Police Commissioner and hack constables to death without fear. The police developed a psychological fear about attacks on them" (Srikrishna 1998, 34).

Most of the evidence presented to the commission, however, was affidavits submitted by victims and bereaved families (mostly Muslims), social workers, local organizations, journalists, and many others who did not share the perspective of the police. There were harrowing accounts of the brutality and rage of groups of men attacking Muslims both in the streets and in their homes, assaults often led and organized by local sainiks; and there were frightening accounts of the anti-Muslim bias among the police in their so-called clean-up operations. A young man who worked in a Muslim-owned bakery recounted the following before the commission:

> Commandos in light uniforms and bulletproof vests entered the building. I peeped out from my hiding and saw Samshad standing, two commandos pointing their guns at him. He folded his hands and sat down near the commandos and pleaded that he was a Bhaiya [from Uttar Pradesh]. One of the commandos kept saying that Samshad was a Pakistani, the other said that he was Kashmiri. . . . I concealed myself again, then I heard firing and it became quiet. I saw Samshad writhing in pain, blood flowing out. He said his prayers for a minute or two, and then he was quiet.

However, the testimonies that elicited most interest from journalists and others attentive to the proceedings were those from leading police officers. V. Deshmukh, former leader of the Special Branch (SB) in Bombay was the first high-ranking police officer to appear before the commission. Deshmukh, a well-spoken man with intellectual inclinations, appeared humble that day in mid-February 1997 as he stood in his uniform in the dock in the large spacious room in the Bombay High Court.

Deshmukh was more frank in his admission of the failures of the SB than anyone had anticipated. He explained the lack of intelligence work with the fact that he, along with many others, "was led to believe that the government would protect the mosque [in Ayodhya]." He said that he was well aware of Shiv Sena's capacity for violence, that the party "had incited hatred against the minority community" and that "maha aartis were started by Shiv Sena in late December 1992 with the purpose of forcing the minority community to give up their *namaz* (prayer) on the streets." He also stated that the SB knew all the central persons of communal organizations in the city but chose to do nothing since he and other police officers were reassured that nothing would happen in Ayodhya. According to Deshmukh:

I had assessed that arresting activists and leaders of the Shiv Sena would result in further communal violence. . . . The tension that developed in areas under Shiv Sena influence following a rumor that Bal Thackeray would be arrested was not a factor that affected my assessment. It was based on what had happened on previous occasions.

In his cross-examination of Deshmukh, Shiv Sena's counsel, Balakrishna Joshi, followed the course he had pursued throughout the hearings. Instead of challenging the evidence of Shiv Sena's involvement (which would have been a futile exercise), Joshi focused almost exclusively on alleged Muslim aggressions and attacks on the police and on Hindus. During the riots, rumors were rife that Muslims collected arms in mosques and that loudspeakers on mosques were used to incite attacks on Hindus. But Deshmukh stated that the SB never recovered any weapons from mosques.

Questioned by the commission's counsel, Vijay Pradhan, Deshmukh admitted that he had not recommended any preventive arrests to be made in early January, although it was common knowledge that Shiv Sena was inciting its followers in ever growing maha aartis.

> *Pradhan*: Were you aware of a closed-door meeting for the entire Shiv Sena leadership on 29 December 1992 [alleged to have been the time when Shiv Sena's subsequent attack on Muslims was planned—T.B.H.]?
> *Deshmukh*: Yes, Sir, we were aware of that meeting being held.
> *Pradhan*: Did you get information about what happened at that meeting?
> *Deshmukh*: We were informed that the agenda concerned collection of funds for riot victims.
> *Judge Srikrishna*: Would such an agenda in your opinion need closed doors?
> *Deshmukh*: No. The SB received reports on December 10 that *masjids* (mosques) maybe were used to instigate violence, but issued no instructions in this regard . . . nor did it act against two Muslims who gave provocative speeches in November 1992.

Deshmukh's reaction here revealed that he subscribed to the widespread notion of communal violence as simple retributive justice, where a killing on each side cancels each other out and makes the two sides even. The grave failure of the Security Branch to monitor Shiv Sena could, in this view, be counterbalanced by its equally serious leniency toward Muslim communal organizations. One non-action made another non-action plausible and permissible. Shiv Sena's counsel pursued this line in a subsequent attempt to exonerate Hindu policemen by claiming that particular Muslim police officers had acted in a partial and anti-Hindu manner during the riots. No conclusive evidence was produced, and Srikrishna dismissed the allegations.[14]

The perception that Muslim aggression justified police brutality and later Hindu retaliation also informed the testimony in the following weeks of Shreekant Bapat, who was Bombay's police commissioner during the riots. Bapat was widely believed to be sympathetic to Shiv Sena and the BJP and had submitted a 175-page affidavit. For a week he was cross-examined by five counselors, among them a Mr. Hudlikar, who represented the police force. Hudlikar was generous in his questioning and gave Bapat ample time to expand on what he had stated in writing. Bapat was particularly adamant in his rejection of the charge of having an anti-Muslim bias: "According to me, the larger number of minority community casualties during December 1992 can be explained on the basis of the much greater aggression of the minority community mobs," he said. After this question was pressed further by Mr. Muchalla, lawyer for the Milli Council, Bapat said angrily: "It is not true that action against the minority community in December 1992 was wholly unjustified." Muchalla then confronted Bapat with police statistics that clearly showed that also in January 1993, when Hindus led by Shiv sainiks were the undisputed aggressors, most of the victims of police firings were Muslim. Bapat replied: "I cannot comment on that."

The commission's own counsel then took over and asked Bapat why his affidavit made not even a single mention of Shiv Sena's by then well-established role in the riots. Bapat replied: "If there is reference to Shiv Sena, it should be there. If there is no reference, there is none." He continued, "The police is concerned with offense, not with political affiliation."

At this point Justice Srikrishna lost patience and asked Bapat why the issue of organizations' involvement in the riots was omitted. Visibly disturbed, Bapat gave his assurance that the police, before the riots, "had taken action against organizations known to be violent."

> *Srikrishna*: If this was done, why is there no reference to organizations in your affidavit?
>
> *Bapat* : We had no material at hand at this point in time indicating that any organization was involved in the riots.
>
> *Srikrishna*: Were you not aware that Shiv Sena leaders claimed that their volunteers had demolished the Babri Masjid [a news item that had been splashed across the front pages in most of the country's newspapers a few days after the demolition—T.B.H.]?
>
> *Bapat* : No, I was not aware of such statements being made.

Here the judge sighed, leaned back in his chair, and said, "Thank you, Sir."

THE POLITICS OF BALANCING GUILT

The evasiveness and obvious irresponsibility of leading policemen who appeared before the commission, as well as the ordinary policeman's apparent lack of understanding of the social world he is supposed to protect, testified to how ill-equipped the police were to perform their basic task of maintaining public order. The interpretation of communal riots in terms of apportioning and balancing collective guilt and responsibilities among faceless and abstract communities, which emerged from the commission hearings, clearly reflected a dominant and widespread modality of politico-moral discourse. However, it did not produce adequate evidence for the prosecution of individuals who may have committed actual crimes. As Mumbai's former police commissioner, A. S. Samra, told me emphatically a few days before he was appointed:

> Our penal code and our idea of justice revolves around the idea that individuals commit crimes and are punished, whereas political parties as a whole do politics. There might be individuals within these parties who commit crimes, even leaders, but they must be punished as individuals. . . . What can we do to an organization? Ban it? That is difficult to do more permanently in a democracy.[15]

When appearing before the commission in April 1997, Samra reiterated this point of view, declining to name particular organizations responsible for the violence. When Justice Srikrishna pointed out that a range of organizations such as Shiv Sena, Vishwa Hindu Parishad, and various Muslim groups were listed in the Maharashtrian government's "Guidelines to Handle Communal Riots" issued in 1986, Samra said: "It is true that they were active in social activities, but it did not come to my notice that they as organizations indulged in illegal acts. Some of their members have done so."[16] Like other high-ranking police officers, Samra appeared rather eager to protect the police corps. In his deposition, Samra depicted the police as protectors of society, conveniently blaming the riots on Dawood Ibrahim and other criminal networks and "landgrabbers." According to Samra, these criminals felt threatened after the municipality and the police force cracked down on illegal constructions the previous year, and "they hit back by exploiting the feelings of the people after the demolition of the Babri Masjid."[17]

Despite such statements, the public nature of the proceedings of the Srikrishna Commission turned it into an ongoing tribunal that inadvertently exposed the complex links between political parties, the state, and the legal system. This became particularly evident as the main perpetrator of violence, Shiv Sena, assumed office in the state government in 1995.

The principal area of contention between the government and the commission concerned the release of documents and files related to the inquiry. The commission had to seek permission from the advocate general for the release or declassification of documents. In some cases, such requests were refused on the basis of "state interest" or some other compelling reason, but, for the most part, the state, in principle, could not claim privilege over the required documents and refuse to hand them out (according to the Public Inquiry Act). After the Hindu nationalist coalition government came to power in Maharashtra in March 1995, twelve of the more than twenty cases pending against Thackeray for violence-inciting rhetoric were either withdrawn or classified, that is, considered to be a security question and hence not subject to public prosecution or scrutiny by the commission. After a protracted legal tussle, the state government ultimately agreed to hand over the files of four of these cases to Justice Srikrishna.[18]

The commission was now able to demonstrate that for years no government agency had dared to take action against Thackeray and that Sena leaders had openly threatened previous Congress governments to withdraw the cases. Police Commissioner Tyagi stated that if the government were to decide to withdraw the cases "in the interest of communal peace and social justice," that would be understandable and the police force would have no objections.[19] It should be noted here that Mr. Tyagi, after his retirement from the police force in 1997, was nominated as a candidate for Shiv Sena in the 1998 general elections but failed to win a seat.

When Shiv Sena and its ally, the BJP, came to power in Maharashtra in 1995, the new government began a process of obstructing the course of the investigation. Papers and documents were not released or were delayed. As mounting evidence pointed to the Shiv Sena's crucial role in both rounds of violence, and to the many links between the party and the police force, the government decided, in January 1996, to dissolve the Srikrishna Commission. Although, in a strict sense, the state had the legitimate power to dissolve the commission, and indeed Shiv Sena had sworn to do so during the 1995 election campaign, there were few precedents for such an act and certainly none involving such blatant mala fide intentions.

Clearly, however, the issue of legitimate authority was at stake. Could the state actually sustain a credible mythology of impartiality when, in such an unmitigated manner, it exercised an apparent ethnic and majoritarian form of justice? In the ensuing debate, activists, intellectuals, and political figures argued that the commission should be reinstated in order to consolidate communal peace and harmony; questions of justice and prosecution of the perpetrators of violence played only a minor role. After pressure from the short-lived BJP government in Delhi in May 1996, the decision was made to restore the commission but with an expanded mandate. Now, its deliberations were to include the March 1993 bombings "to give a clearer and more comprehensive picture of the patterns of violence and civil disturbances in the city," as argued by the advocate general.[20] The inclusion of these bombings was a rather transparent attempt to deflect the course of the investigation, but nonetheless the move enjoyed considerable support in the public debates that followed. This public acceptance was an indication that the dominant, official interpretation of the riots as irrational excesses committed in extraordinary situations spontaneously, and with equal participation, by faceless Hindus and Muslims and not by organizations or specific individuals had gained widespread currency. The government's decision authorized the formula of a "balanced and equally apportioned guilt," namely, that every murder a Hindu committed was ethically neutralized by a corresponding atrocity committed by a Muslim. This notion of retributive justice, exploited by both Shiv Sena's counsel and the Sena-led government in order to exonerate the party, was, in other words, being slowly imposed on the commission.

The contrast was glaring between the slow, contested, and often academic nature of the work of the Srikrishna Commission and the simultaneous prosecution of those accused of the March 1993 bombings. In the weeks following the bomb blasts, more than two hundred people, mainly Muslims, were rounded up and detained under the stringent TADA (Terrorist and Disruptive Activities Act) legislation. As many as 189 persons were accused of participating in the conspiracy. The majority of detainees were subjected to the most humiliating and brutal forms of interrogation, and only a few were granted bail. Even those accused of playing a minor role in connection with the arms consignments that landed on the coast of Maharashtra in February 1993 were imprisoned for more than two years before being released for lack of evidence. A new high-security TADA court was erected in Mumbai, and the police displayed unusual diligence in producing and gathering substantial evidence in the cases. Before the case was taken over by the Central Bureau of Investigations in Delhi, the Bombay police had charged all the accused with one of the most serious offenses in the Indian Penal Code: "waging war against the state." These charges were withdrawn only after a much-delayed intervention by the attorney general (Visvanathan 1998, 127–28). The majority of evidence gathered by the Bombay police to indict these large numbers of innocent people on flimsy grounds at best was either irrelevant or inadequate. By contrast, the police did not even question the corrupt police and customs officials who had made the entire import of advanced explosives into Mumbai possible.[21]

The proceedings of the TADA court, which have been closed to the public because of the allegedly sensitive nature of the evidence, have progressed at a brisk pace. The prosecution has been targeting individuals, while the Shiv Sena government, on several occasions, has explicitly stated that the process be speeded up against what it calls "Muslim gangsters" responsible for the blasts. Some of the accused have been sentenced to ten or twenty years of imprisonment, while a number of key suspects, allegedly connected in some way with Dawood Ibrahim, are still absconding. Although the case is still not over, it appears unlikely, given the strong political pressure on the TADA court, that those sentenced might expect a new trial or that the government would be willing to concede that many were convicted on questionable grounds.

DIAGNOSTICS, PRESCRIPTIONS, AND STATE SPECTACLES: THE REPORT OF THE SRIKRISHNA COMMISSION

The status and authority of a report from a commission of inquiry is precarious. It is not simply a report put together by experts or some research commissioned by the government. Whether or not the government in power agrees with the conclusions, it is inevitably an authoritative statement on the matter under scrutiny. However, the government is not compelled by law to implement or even accept the commission's findings and recommendations. The complicated and contested trajectory of the Srikrishna Commission had, more clearly than any other commission I know of in India, been the scene of an often spectacular clash of radically different notions of the state. In one corner was a decent High Court judge of impeccable moral integrity, supported by human rights activists and large segments of the press, defending the idea of the state as impartial, above society, and committed to a universal form of justice. In a second corner were the administrators and the police employing their armory of techniques to delay, obstruct, or influence the inquiry in order to protect their own secrets and to cover up their failings. And in a third corner were the political forces governing the state, committed to a majoritarian notion of retributive justice, bending and threatening the administration to serve their own ends. Although public in form, this debate on the authority of state power remained within the state, both in terms of its mandate, resources, methodology, and authority. The debate involved neither a citizen's tribunal nor an independent investigation.[22]

I argue that both the Srikrishna Commission and the TADA court should be regarded as state spectacles, public displays of the state as a producer of impartial and universal justice. At the same time, these two proceedings—one indicting Hindus and the police, the other "Muslim goondas"—represented another kind of spectacle, that of the discourse of retributive justice. Both investigations were marked by a crucial duality inherent in the state. The Srikrishna Commission revealed numerous examples of the profane side of state power: the deplorable quality of policing and police intelligence; the partial, biased, and brutal conduct of the police force; the government's blatant attempts to obstruct the proceedings and to prevent powerful politicians such as Bal Thackeray from being prosecuted; and so on. At the same time, the commission's very existence; the tenacity and integrity of Justice Srikrishna; and the public exposure of misconduct, corruption, and liaisons between politicians and the police force also provided a kind of public catharsis.

In this latter capacity, the commission has become a symbol of the resilience of a higher, more benevolent form of justice, and thus a sign of the permanence of the sublime dimension of the state. In a sense, the state's inherent duality was also represented in the very choreography of the proceedings: Before the bench was a string of counselors seeking to extract their own particular, intensely politicized claims of truth from the stream of witnesses passing through, while the judge, positioned three feet above the others, concluded each cross-examination with a summation intended to extract a reasonable and plausible truth—the negotiated truth—from the maze of interpretations before him.

The final report from the Srikrishna Commission adopts medical terminology. As if he were a medical doctor, Justice Srikrishna diagnoses a "communal malady" and prescribes a possible cure:

> Communal riots, the bane of this country, are like incurable epileptic seizures, whose symptoms, though dormant over a period of time, manifest themselves again and again. Measures of various kinds suggested from time to time dealt with symptoms and acted as palliatives without effecting a permanent cure of the malaise.

The judge argues further that until there is a complete change in the social outlook and level of education, "communal riots must be treated, perhaps, as an incurable disease whose prognosis calls for suitable measures to contain its evil effects (Srikrishna 1998, 4). In keeping with this diagnosis, the judge is brief in his examination of the causes behind the riots, admitting that they come from complex dynamics of demography, class, and the political discourses of organizations. Bombay had the unfortunate combination of an increasingly impoverished and isolated Muslim community and a set of very aggressive Hindu organizations (25–29). Srikrishna is emphatic in its statement that "[no] known Muslim individuals or organizations were responsible for the riots," and is equally emphatic in pointing out that Shiv Sena was not responsible as an organization per se but was accountable only in so far as "the attitudes of Shiv Sena leaders [, as reflected in] the doctrine of "retaliation," were responsible for the vigilantism of Shiv sainiks (30).

Justice Srikrishna regards communal riots as incurable and notes, in a more poetic vein, that because "the beast in man keeps straining at the leash to jump out" (Srikrishna 1998, 63), effective measures are of paramount importance. Most remarkable in the report is its diagnosis of the structure and shortcomings of Mumbai's police force and its recommendations to remedy these (31–62). Srikrishna paints a gloomy picture of a complacent, biased, disorganized force where even the most common routines such as the filing of cases, physical training, or discipline are incoherent or entirely absent. Returning to his diagnostic mode, he offers the following summation: "Despite knowledge of the fact that the force had been infected by communal virus, no effective curative steps were taken over a large period of time, as a result of which communal violence became chronic and its virulent symptoms showed up during the two riot periods" (35).

The report's entire tone maintains this measured distance to the interested parties and gives critical and considered summaries of the events unfolding around each police station. The judge examines the depositions by leading police officers and political leaders, including former chief ministers and the former minister of defense, Sharad Pawar. Reading through these pages evokes a vivid picture of the theory of the state to which Srikrishna subscribes. The tone is not legalistic but moral. He is highly critical of the lack of adherence to rules and regulations in the police force and even more critical of the ostensible lack of commitment and moral outlook among leading police officers and many political figures.

Clearly Srikrishna believes that a sense of duty toward the nation and an ethical view of life must be the basis of the state's representatives. His formula—"the higher the rank, the deeper the commitment"—echoes the dominant discourse of the postcolonial nation-state in India. The idea of the state as a moral entity, enunciated once again in an official document, remains precisely the most unattainable goal and therefore the most precious and sublime dimension of the state.

Representation of the state was slightly different in the TADA court. Here, the rhetoric of secrecy and the practice of classifying even the most banal piece of evidence, supposedly in the state's interest, contributed to a sense of urgency that something greater was threatening the nation. The Mumbai police eagerly boasted of the enormous bulk of materials it had gathered in order to generate a similar illusion of the effectiveness and ubiquity of the state's knowledge and its capacity for taking on public enemies. The profane dimension in the court proceedings was equally obvious in the brutality and partiality of the police investigations and in the harshness of its treatment of the detainees. Unfortunately, however, the serious nature of the crimes committed, the alleged connections of the "Muslim gangsters" to Pakistan, and the secrecy surrounding the case meant that these obvious abuses and human rights violations never generated the kind of public concern and debate that surrounded the Srikrishna proceedings, not even in the English-language press. In a conversation in 1997, a liberal Hindu businessman expressed quite succinctly to me how the scale of knowledge and violence at the disposal of the state acquired sublime dimensions: "Many of the accused in this case are well-known criminals. They have committed a terrible crime—even Muslims admit that. We should not be soft on them. . . . Besides, there are so many things we are never told. The government has a lot of information it cannot disclose."

The deep divide between the social worlds of Hindus and Muslims traversing the city today not only seems to have affected people's sense of justice but also the public interest in these two proceedings. Many educated people from all communities have taken a keen interest in the Srikrishna Commission. A string of independent reports and documentations of sufferings and abuses have emerged from NGOs and civil rights activists. My impression from discussions and interviews over the last four years is that many ordinary Hindus approve of a balanced apportionment of guilt and responsibility for the riots. This formula provides a convenient nonlegalistic framework that enables ordinary citizens to categorize riots simply as events without actors, as unfortunate aberrations from the normal order. To most ordinary people I met, the commission of inquiry appeared as a somewhat inconsequential sign of the state, a manifestation of authority that simply was expected to restore the public order that had been upset by the riots. But the rhetoric of the state as a moral entity, as well as the legal intricacies of the proceedings, were mainly directed at the educated, literate middle class, always the primary constituency and concern of the postcolonial state.

Among ordinary Muslims in the parts of central Mumbai that I got to know, the commission figured less prominently, although Justice Srikrishna was praised as a "secular person," in the sense of being highly educated, impartial, and critical of Shiv Sena. There were hardly any protests among Muslims when the commission was disbanded in January 1996. For some, this only confirmed that "the whole thing was an eyewash. Do you think they would ever allow themselves to be exposed?" as one young man from Madanpura said to me. Others felt that taking up the issue again would only open old wounds. "Will the inquiry bring back our sons and husbands? What is the point? Just leave us alone," one elderly Muslim woman told a journalist at the time.[23]

The Muslim social world of Mumbai is not only spatially separated from that of Hindus but is also demarcated by a local Urdu public sphere consisting of newspapers, journals, and local cable TV. To the average Hindu, conversant in Marathi and Hindi, this world is closed, even threatening, and the Urdu press is routinely accused of spreading anti-Hindu propaganda. Such accusations were also presented before the Srikrishna Commission but were never substantiated. Rather than being a vehicle of sectarian ideology, however, the Urdu press seems to be strongly introverted and preoccupied by issues internal to the Muslim community. It was not surprising, therefore, that the TADA case was thought to be more important and given more concern than the proceedings of the Srikrishna Commission. Muslim organizations documented the harsh treatment of the predominantly Muslim detainees under TADA—an act that in itself has become a symbol of the state's inherently anti-Muslim bias. Calls for dismantling the TADA laws altogether have, for some years, been high on the agenda of local organizations and Urdu newspapers, as well as often raised in the campaigns of local Muslim politicians. As we shall see, the TADA proceedings resonate with a long tradition of enmity between Muslims and the police in the popular neighborhoods of central Mumbai.

GOVERNING THE MUSLIM *BADMASH*

Colonial rule in India organized its objects of governance into two categories: on one side was the huge mass of ordinary people, peasants and artisans, in brief, subaltern groups regarded as irrational, passionate, and traditional, and therefore in need of firm governance as subjects of the colonial state. On the other side were the educated middle classes, the literate elites in provincial towns, the landlords, the "natural" leaders of sects, castes, petty kingdoms, and religious communities, who were considered amenable to reasoned persuasion and negotiation. These latter groups were the pillars of colonial rule, entrusted with the local administration below the district level, revenue collection, the management of affairs internal to communities, and so on.

The uncontrollable religious sentiment among ordinary masses was a constant worry to the colonial officers. During the riots in Bombay in August 1893, the press, the police, and officials all agreed that the riots were caused by the *badmash* (rogue) of the slums who incited the "lower classes." After suppressing the riots with a heavy hand, the police commissioner called a meeting of "representatives and respectable members of the communities" to discuss how these citizens could control and influence their communities and thus limit the corrupting influence of the badmash on the lower classes (Krishnaswamy 1966, 29).

As industrial capitalism developed in the Bombay region in the first decades of the twentieth century, the mill districts and the so-called popular neighborhoods developed quickly. These areas were marked by densely populated chawls and a sprawling, tight-knit web of economic relations, associations, and leisure activities. They were structured overwhelmingly by class, although communities of caste and religion also played a crucial role (Chandavarkar 1994, 168–238). Muslim weaver communities (*ju-laha-ansaris*) from Uttar Pradesh acquired a good position in the textile mills and settled in neighborhoods in central Bombay already known as predominantly Muslim. The Pathans from the Northwest Frontier—the most martial of all Indians, according to the colonial theory of "martial races"—occupied a crucial position as moneylenders and acquired a repu-tation for effective and hard-nosed servicing of debts and interests. The Pathans and their position in the growing underworld were increasingly seen as a menace to Hindus as well as Muslims (Chandavarkar 1998, 194).

On the surface, the protracted riots in 1929 were triggered by violence between Pathans and Hindu mill workers, but they were actually born out of a rather more complex conflict as well as by the prolonged strikes in the city's textile mills in 1928–29. For several decades the Bombay police had attempted to decipher the dynamics of the working-class neighborhoods they tried to regulate but with little success. They relied on a theory of "hooliganism," namely, that, "generally speaking, it is not the ordinary resident with a home and an occupation who keeps the police and the military busy. It is the riff-raff, the scum of the city that gives the trou-ble."[24] During the prolonged disturbances in 1929, the "hooligan" again "personified the collapse of order," as described by Chandavarkar: "Anxie-ties about 'the other,' fortified by social prejudices harboured in ordinary times, now acquired an awesome and menacing shape. . . . The hooligan became the universal embodiment of 'the other'" (Chandavarkar 1998, 174). These events further entrenched the anxieties regarding the "roughs" from the working-class neighborhoods in the eyes of the police, the elite, and respectable citizens, paving the way for the emergence of the Muslim badmash as the most dreaded figure in the city.

The 1930s and 1940s saw an incipient isolation of the Muslim working class both economically and in terms of urban space—a process that be-came even more pronounced after independence. The naval strike in 1946 in Mumbai, launched against the British, quickly spilled over into a riot between Muslims and Hindus and left 250 persons dead and more than 1,000 wounded. Concerns were expressed regarding the "alarming degree of instigation by goondas," which, according to an editorial in the *Bombay Chronicle*, meant, "the widespread involvement of domestics and paupers in looting and arson."[25] Newspaper editors were critical of the brutal con-duct of police and troops in quelling the riot. To counter the authorities, activists of the Indian National Congress launched "People's Peace Bri-gades," volunteers dressed in knickers, white blouses, and caps, who pa-trolled the streets in open lorries and sought to intervene among the rioters and stop the violence. Police officers did express concern over the large number of casualties among these volunteers.[26]

After the riots, Congress formed an inquiry committee and urged the police to cooperate. Police Commissioner Butler felt threatened by the political interest in the work of the police and was unwilling to comply. Testifying before the Municipal Corporation, Butler issued an unveiled threat: "You must trust your police. If you push me down, if you don't stand by me, so help you God." The tough line of the police against "goondas and troublemakers" from the lower classes was supported, however, by several members of the Municipal Corporation. One of them, Mr. Sabawala, stated: "No government that does not fire and resolutely restore order, ceases to be called a government."[27]

The Congress Party also proposed to make the Peace Brigades in the city permanent committees open to "all responsible political and social organisations," as suggested by S. K. Patil , the legendary Congress leader in Bombay.[28] After a few months, these brigades had disintegrated, and the focus of political and public life shifted to the impending independence and the intense competition for office and position this generated. It was indicative, nonetheless, of the public climate at the time. The complete alienation of Muslim politicians and public leadership at this juncture resulted in the Muslims hardly being involved at all in the peace making; instead, it was a matter discussed among Hindus and between the Congress and the colonial authorities.

Since independence, the Muslim community in Bombay has been marked by increasing socioeconomic isolation. This has been accompanied by intensified policing in Muslim areas where there are more police stations and *chowkis*—police posts on strategic street corners built of stone and, as in the colonial period, equipped to be barricaded and turned into a bunkerlike structure—than other areas in the city. Clearly the Muslim areas today are viewed and treated as "security problems," as dens of crime and mafia activity, just as some of the Pathan areas used to be regarded. As we saw in the depositions from police officers at the Srikrishna Commission, these are areas where the "police machinery must be alert around the year." Despite assurances that the police had changed their minds about the Muslims after the 1992–93 riots, the infrastructure of the police in these areas has expanded considerably in recent years. Thus the relation between the police and younger Muslim men especially remains extremely strained and hostile, and everywhere there are testimonies of random arrests, beatings, and insults meted out to young men. The practice of making "preventive arrests" of people the police term "notorious characters" or just "rowdy young men" before festivals, elections, and so on, is widespread and generally accepted.[29] To say that for young Muslims in these areas the police force is an ever present, dreaded representation of the state as a hostile entity is no exaggeration.

The police force in Mumbai is overwhelmingly Hindu, and its members have been recruited from the same social environment and caste communities from where Shiv Sena emerged. In the predominantly Muslim areas in Mumbai where I worked, I frequently went to two police stations and met officers and constables there, as well as in their chowkis. Within each of the compounds, which were considered the strong arms of the secular state, one found two or three small temples devoted to Ganesh or Hanuman (the monkey god associated with courage and the fighting spirit). These had been financed by donations from officers and constables and had been constructed within the past decade. "Some of us have questioned whether it is appropriate," one Christian officer told me, "but my superior simply replied that if there were more Christian officers and constables, he wouldn't object to us having an image of Virgin Mary in one corner of the compound."

I must have appeared unconvinced by this demonstration of the secular orientation of the police, because, a few days later, another policeman offered to take me to the police station in nearby Dongri, another "notorious trouble spot," as he described it. Here a Muslim *dargah* (shrine) had been built inside the police compound already in 1923, and later a small Shiva temple had been placed beside it. After the 1993 riots, a senior police inspector initiated renovation of the *dargah* and invited both Hindus and Muslims for cultural programs involving *qawwali* songs and Hindu *bhajans* (devotional prayer songs). "This initiative has really improved the relations between the police and the general public here," the police officer claimed.

In talking to policemen I got a clear sense that the "sociology of the hooligan" that earlier had informed police work in Bombay had now evolved in the Muslim neighborhoods into a certain "sociology of Muslims." This matrix of knowledge was based on an admixture of stereotypes and rumors, many of them modified versions of those circulating in the neighborhoods. Consider the following example based on the stereotype that Muslims continually divorce their wives. One officer explained: "One reason for the high level of crime is all these young boys who grow up without a proper father—this is because there are so many divorces and the men just leave their families behind."

Anyone with even a rudimentary knowledge of Muslim personal law, however, knows that, according to this legal complex, children belong to the father, and even poor fathers only in extreme cases would abandon their sons (though maybe their daughters), as sons are crucial to their father's social standing and future prospects in life. The following off-the-record statement by a young, inexperienced officer testified to the gap between the social worlds of the predominantly Hindu police force and the Muslims in these areas:

> In the beginning when I came here, I was nervous when we went on patrol, especially at night. This hostility was something I never experienced before . . . but then after some time I started to look them right in the eyes and pretend that I was indifferent to them. I also learned more of the dirty language they use around here. . . . That helped a lot. Now I get answers to my questions and I feel more respected.

Postings at these stations are considered strenuous, full of hard work and danger, but also a source of considerable rewards and bribes from the brisk flesh trade and drug economy in parts of central Mumbai. As a rule, officers are rarely posted more than twelve to eighteen months in one police station, whereas constables typically serve two to three years or longer. The police departments depend vitally, therefore, on their networks of neighborhood informants, networks that are created and maintained through an ongoing flow of *hafta* (literally, weekly; a colloquial term for regular bribes) and other economic transactions.

This bears a striking resemblance to the methods and discussions of colonial policing. Chandavarkar has shown how the poor quality of policemen recruited into the city's police force was a constant worry for the colonial authorities.[30] Bombay was a difficult place for the police to regulate, densely populated, full of hooligans and prostitutes, as well as other temptations. The authorities were always concerned with the poor quality of information they received and had an uncanny sense that, in fact, they did not know what was happening in their areas. The Director of Criminal Intelligence wrote to the Home Minister in 1908, immediately after a strike had once again taken the authorities by surprise:

> The ignorance of the Bombay Police as to the agency and methods used for engineering the strike is nothing short of appalling. . . . Many of the constables live in the chauks from which the worst natives come. Yet no information. They are all Ratnagiri men together and of course in league. (Quoted in Chandavarkar 1998, 197)

As Chandavarkar shows, for decades the minds of leading policemen were occupied with worries regarding "mob violence," when and how to exercise the proper measure of power when confronted with furious mobs possessed by irrational sentiments. As anticolonial campaigns and industrial action picked up after 1919, the police were beset by constant dread that they were dealing with inadequate forces and equipment, sitting on a cauldron of popular resentment that could erupt at any time. In response, British officers developed a theory of using excessive force in colonial situations out of necessity, a force strong enough to prevent disturbances from developing further. J. C. Curry, a senior police officer in Bombay, noted that "these circumstances [inordinate tensions—T.B.H.] render it compellingly necessary for authority to be armed with wide powers for which no need exists in other more homogenous countries" (quoted in Chandavarkar 1998, 219). As discussed above, such notions of policing an unpredictable cauldron and the use of excessive force are still widespread in the Bombay police force.

In his deposition before the Srikrishna Commission, the Special Branch chief in Mumbai revealed that a "Communal Riots Prevention Scheme" has been in existence for the last thirty years, according to which police stations in sensitive areas are supposed to keep track of communal organizations capable of violence, to monitor the leaders of these organizations and networks, and to arrest these individuals whenever the situation demands.

Indicative, however, of the distance between the police leadership and the lower ranks was that virtually none of the sub-inspectors and responsible officers at the police stations scrutinized by the commission were able to define precisely the criteria for identifying individuals as "communal goondas." Leading police officers had also shown little interest in implementing this scheme. Instead, provisions for carrying out preventive arrests were often employed simply according to the whim of commanding officers or at the request of local political forces.

One senior police officer told me that on 8 December 1992 all police stations were told to round up the "communal goondas," but no arrests were made, he said, because, in most cases, "these Muslim mobs were leaderless." If nothing else, this reflects the police officers' limited knowledge of, and unwillingness to interfere with, the activities of the local goondas, who, whether Muslim or Hindu, often command the vital flow of money and power in the neighborhoods.

In December 1992, when the central government asked the Bombay police to submit all its available intelligence reports on Shiv Sena to the Union Home Ministry to consider imposing a ban on the organization, the police officers advised against it. They insisted that if a ban were imposed, the force would not be able to guarantee the city's safety and security. The leading officers did not threaten the political leaders as directly as Butler had in 1946, but the message, "Bombay cannot be ruled without us," was similar.

The depositions before the commission also revealed many ties between the police force and local political organizations, particularly Shiv Sena. Clearly the police could not destroy the intricate web of *hafta* and the tacit understandings between local operators, builders, and local dadas on which the daily police work depended. These networks were highly fluid, multidimensional, often transgressed lines of caste and religion, and operated on the basis of rumors and gossip. To claim that someone was a police informer or was paid by the police was a trivial element of tacit warfare between such networks. The status of "informer," therefore, was never certain knowledge and the claims of police that someone "works with us" was often as strategic as the rumors afloat in the *biraderi* [kin group, clan] networks.[31] I only was able to meet the public friends of the police, men who traded openly with them, drank with them, fixed various problems for the officers, and were free to walk in and out of the police station. Many of these "helpers" were men at the margins of powerful networks, small traders, some with criminal records or from low-status families.

An interesting paradox of the relation between a brutal, incompetent, and biased police force and the Muslim communities in central Mumbai was the reconciliatory gestures and signs of respect that Muslims displayed toward leading police officers. During the Eid Festival in early 1994, leading police officers, determined to renew their relations with the Muslim community, waited outside several of the large mosques in central Mumbai. As the congregation left the mosque after prayer, the officers distributed flowers and greeted hundreds of men and boys. Rumors of this gesture quickly spread, and soon the officers were surrounded by crowds, hesitant at first but increasingly enthusiastic. I heard many accounts of this incident, which, despite its obvious banality, "had a soothing effect. It made the process of reconciliation that followed possible. What impressed people was that these were not local officers from our police station but the top brass people who stood there," as a local imam of Madanpura explained to me.

In the following years new connections developed between leading police officers and Muslim leaders. For decades, the relation of patronage and recognition between the Congress government and the Muslim community had been ritually confirmed when Congress leaders and ministers were invited to honor cultural events and religious festivals in central Bombay. After the riots, a strong sense emerged of having been betrayed by Congress, and dignitaries were not invited to any events or festivals in 1993–94. With Shiv Sena and the BJP coming to power in 1995, the sense of alienation from political parties in power became even more pronounced.

"We don't regard these people [Shiv Sena] as worthy representatives of the Indian state. They may be ministers of my state, but they are not my ministers. Why should we honor them by inviting them here?" said Maulana Kashmiri, a well-known conservative figure whom I interviewed in 1996. Instead, leading police officers were invited to honor religious functions, not because they were trusted but because these officers, owing to their seniority and rank, represented the state, not the government. In this capacity, they confirmed the official recognition of the Muslim community as integral to the larger Indian society—a function that, needless to say, was critical at this juncture.

Another dimension of this paradoxical relation between Muslims and police was the way that local politicians and businessmen in central Mumbai strove to reestablish a good relation with the police force, not tacitly as a decade ago but as publicly as possible. One found, for instance, well-constructed police chowkis displaying plaques saying, "Donated by the honourable Shri . . . member of the Legislative Assembly" or small constructions at street corners providing shade for police constables and exhibiting conspicuous ads for the local shops, restaurants, and firms that sponsored these structures. Why these donations to the police? One influential politician known for making such donations said rather bluntly:

> In 1993 we paid the price for our bad relations with the police. We Muslims have always blamed the police for everything, we never tried to understand their point of view. Now I realize that working with the police is the way to prevent another riot here. I represent this area—it is my responsibility to protect my people. . . . Before, I was treated with suspicion when I took a complaint to the police. Now all that is much easier.[32]

Today Patel has emerged as one of the more powerful operators in central Mumbai, because he has forged these links with the police and recognizes that in his area the foremost representation of the state are the police. Not that the police necessarily control the neighborhoods, as there are other contenders for sovereignty over these areas—criminal networks as well as religious and ethnic organizations. Patel's point seems to be that having the police as a strong presence in the area makes it easier to work with them.

A similar reasoning seems to inform the East-West Airlines, one of India's largest private airlines and widely regarded by the police, as well as independent observers, as one of Dawood Ibrahim's more successful enterprises.[33] In 1995 the company sponsored a police chowki in a Mumbai suburb, and it is likely that several others of the newly erected chowkis are funded by members of Dawood's networks,[34] supposedly the largest criminal organization in South Asia (more on this below). These donations symbolize "the new and warm relations between the public and the Bombay Police," declared Commissioner Tyagi in 1996.[35]

STATE SPECTACLES AND POLITICS IN THE MOHALLA

In 1994 *mohalla* committees were set up throughout the city in the areas that had been affected by the riots. These were launched to create "communal reconciliation" in the city and to facilitate the future governance

of the urban territories in central Mumbai. As we saw above, peace committees are hardly a novelty in the city; they are as old as communal disturbances themselves. After the riots in Thane in 1984, which had also affected large parts of Bombay, peace committees were formed in a number
of mixed neighborhoods in Bombay such as Mahim, Bandra, and Byculla.
Over the years, however, they had evolved into platforms for local politicians who saw the committees as an opportunity to forge ties with the
police and to strengthen their position in the neighborhood. None of
these committees played any role in preventing violence in 1992–93, and
they were dissolved quickly thereafter.

Police Commissioner Sahani, known for his inclination toward what
one officer described to me rather disapprovingly as "intellectual policing," launched the initiative after a period of intense deliberation among
leading police officers and a range of NGOs in the city. These deliberations
had involved a series of unprecedented initiatives: Police officers were told
to cooperate closely with social activists and to attend long sessions where
riot victims gave detailed and moving accounts of their experiences during
the riots, describing their loss of children and spouses at the hands of the
police. The police were also instructed to sit through week-long courses
on Islam and Muslim culture conducted by people such as Asghar Ali
Engineer, a well-known activist and vocal critic of the police force.

The plan of action implemented in 1994 called on the police to form
mohalla committees at every police station in the so-called problem areas,
areas that almost exclusively happened to be those with a substantial Muslim population. The initiatives shared many affinities with similar techniques of governance employed over the past century: bodies of concerned
and respectable citizens from all communities in a neighborhood were
called on to take responsibility for action, to soothe angry sentiments, and
to assist the police in taking preventive actions. Just as important, the
committees aimed at "re-creating confidence in our institutions and in
our democracy among the Muslims in this city," as expressed by one of
the driving forces behind the initiative.[36] When the mohalla committees
were set up in 1994 they mainly recruited members from the Muslim
middle classes. Many of the members were people highly respected in the
locality, individuals often involved in volunteer work and accustomed to
being in close contact with state institutions. As a young progressive advocate known for her controversial support of divorced Muslim women and
her active participation in the committee in Nagpada stated: "The fear of
the intentions of the police was the biggest problem, and then the fear of
attending meetings inside the police compound itself. Only educated people who knew they enjoyed some respect among constables and officers
were willing to do that in 1994. You can imagine how the atmosphere
was at that time."[37]

The police officers broadly assumed that Muslims, especially the poor and uneducated badmash, were the main problem. According to the police, riots started when such people were incited and manipulated by local political leaders and their imams. The police saw the committees as a way to "de-politicize" the neighborhoods and to contain communalism, that is, to reduce it merely to occasional outbursts of irrational social behavior and, most important, to reduce the political manipulation, which, among the police (and many social scientists) in India, is considered the primary cause of the riots. Members of political parties and politicians elected in the area were not admitted into the committees. Based on their earlier experiences, the police wanted to retain firm control of the committees, to keep politics away "in order to curb the divisive effects of partisan interests," as one high-ranking officer put it. The objective was more ambitious this time around, for, as he said, "We want to create a new leadership among Muslims."

The police wanted to bypass and exclude the established brokers and dadas in the mohalla and instead have "civilized citizens" represent the Muslims; that is, they wished to include Muslims who, according to the standard assumption central to governing India for a century, had, by virtue of their education, abandoned primitive beliefs and become amenable to reason and persuasion. In the committees, these representatives would act as "super citizens," and, through them, the entire community would be addressed and governed. This reflected a pragmatic strategy of managing the badmash, but it also affirmed the state's privilege and special license, represented in this case by the capacity of the police to invest authority in certain persons rather than others.

In their initial phase, committee members told me, the meetings were tense and serious. A retired judge who served on a mohalla committee related: "In the beginning, all the top officers from the station were present at the meetings. On Fridays, when the streets were full of people assembling for the Friday *namaaz* (prayer), we would all come out with the officers and stand around the crowd, very alert, watching passersby and making sure that no one made any provoking moves. There were tense moments, but I think we were successful."

As political attention faded in 1995–96, the committees were subtly transformed. On the initiative of Tyagi, the new, flamboyant police commissioner, the committees were enlarged from a maximum of fifty members per police station to as many as two hundred members.[38] Many of these members were the "marginal men" whom the police used to gather knowledge of the neighborhoods. These men desired recognition and some standing in the community, and so the police rewarded their loyalty by conferring on them the official status of community representative. The expansion of the committees by this inclusion of larger groups of people had several effects.

First, the social prestige formerly associated with being a member of the committee was immediately reduced, since people like "Y," a "rag merchant" who had become rich by buying from and exploiting the rag pickers in the area, was included in the Nagpada mohalla committee. Y, a hefty man, was known for his violent temper and for carrying a long whip as he ordered his many workers around. He was feared but not respected. Another new face was "A," a supplier of all kinds of goods to the police. He walked in and out of the station, was always servile to commanding officers, always joking with the constables. He had a small office in the building opposite the police compound, with nothing but a table, a telephone, and a chair. From there, he boasted, he could fix anything: "Just tell me, you are my friend, I will get it for you." "S" was another new member, a lecturer at a local college with political ambitions. He had been with the Muslim League, later with the Congress Party. "Now I am a social worker. I work only for the community." S traveled around with a couple of muscular young men, men who answered his cell phone, brought him cold drinks, drove his car, men he claimed to be students.

As the campaign for the Municipal Corporation elections in Mumbai commenced in January 1997, many members of the mohalla committees tried to convert their newly achieved visibility and public standing into a bid for political careers. As a consequence, these committee members, strictly speaking, had to be excluded because they had been "polluted" by the political world. This was of little consequence, however, as many political figures had already begun to attend the meetings after the enlargement of the committees. On several occasions, prominent political figures not only attended meetings but even presided over functions organized by the mohalla committees. Very few of the politically involved ever left the mohalla committees, and the still more infrequent committee meetings at the police stations began to resemble public functions, often lavishly hosted by "helpers" and friends of the police.

Another result of the expansion of the committees was that certain police stations assumed new functions of brokerage and the fixing of local problems that paralleled those of the local politicians they had sought to marginalize. An officer at the Agripada police station told me enthusiastically about his new found role as fixer:

> Now many people come to us with their usual problems—sewage, water, telephone connections, school admissions, etc. For us it is very easy to solve—we just make a few phone calls. When I present myself to these lazy bureaucrats

at the Municipal Corporation, things start to happen. . . . [nodding toward a line of people waiting in the compound] So, as you can see with your own eyes, people have gained confidence in us. They can see that we actually solve their problems.

These mohalla committees, and the new friendliness asserted by the police, have indeed reduced the tension in these areas, but they have neither removed the mechanisms producing communal enmity nor the organizational structures that perpetrate the violence. On the contrary, the mohalla committees, in many ways, have only provided the police with a new set of techniques for controlling "trouble spots" through a network of underworld operators, liaisons with political figures, direct interventions in public services, and so on.

WHITHER THE STATE?

The way the badmash in Bombay has been treated over the past century demonstrates how the postcolonial state continues to represent itself as a locus of a higher rationality above and beyond the masses. Both the Srikrishna Commission and the mohalla committees were interventions and spectacles to support this style of governance. In both cases, the "sublime" dimensions of the state—fairness, rationality, tolerance, and justice—were the ideal representations of governance to the preferred audience of the postcolonial state, the educated middle class.

As relative peace began to prevail in central Mumbai, middle-class society—the high-ranking officers, the educated, and the activists—withdrew from the mohalla committees and more everyday and profane forms of governance and networking took over. The public spectacle of the Srikrishna Commission also came to an end, and its report can be found in limited circulation in libraries and among curious intellectuals and political activists. It then fell on those most strongly indicted by the report, the Shiv Sena and the Mumbai police, to decide whether the commission's recommendations regarding police reforms should be implemented. In other words, the political world in Mumbai was back to "business as usual."

In the September 1999 elections for the State Legislative Assembly, Shiv Sena lost some of its former electoral strength in Mumbai, and a more centrist coalition, which included the Congress Party, formed the new government. Nevertheless Shiv Sena remained a force to reckon with in the city and state. When the new government, in July 2000, declared its intention to prosecute Bal Thackeray for his role in the 1992–93 riots, Shiv Sena leaders threatened that Mumbai would burn. As had occurred so often in the past, once again the police advised that arresting Thackeray would not be in the interest of public order and communal harmony. In other words, Shiv Sena still remains the most powerful organization in the city. These events clearly beg the question as to whether the state spectacles analyzed above were able to resuscitate the myth of the state. I shall return to this question in the final chapter.

CHAPTER 6

In the Muslim Mohalla

NEIGHBORHOODS like Nagpada, Mominpura, Madanpura, and Kamathipura in central Mumbai were once integrated parts of the mill districts in Bombay. A large proportion of the adult population was employed in or around the large mills and smaller industrial plants and workshops. Today these names evoke quite different connotations—crime, prostitution, and gang war—but are also associated with Muslims and myths of the Muslim badmash. Dramatic changes have indeed taken place in connection with the decline and closure of the mills and the restructuring of industrial employment in Bombay since the 1960s.

Local residents tell stories of the deterioration, isolation, and erosion of the city's cultural and moral fiber, all of which seem to conform to the ethnic-religious segmentation of Bombay since the 1960s. Compared to the settlement patterns of religious communities in cities like Hyderabad, Lucknow, and Delhi, Bombay, before the 1992–93 riots, was marked by a relatively high degree of ethnically mixed neighborhoods, with the Muslim population scattered over many smaller areas in the greater Bombay region.

The riots changed that decisively. Many Muslims who had lived in the "pockets" of Hindu majority areas fled to areas where Muslims were in the majority, such as Nagpada and its adjoining neighborhoods, and stayed there even after the riots had subsided. The highly differentiated Muslim sects and communities in the city have undoubtedly become more spatially concentrated today than ever before. In many Muslim areas, extra floors are added to existing buildings to accommodate families; small workshops are installed on rooftops and in high-rise buildings, often causing additional damage, noise, and pollution in these already congested areas. The density of hutment and pavement dwellers is high in these areas and grows yearly. The struggle to maintain a livelihood is obvious in the congested streets that are practically blocked by hundreds of mobile stalls selling cloth, fruit, brassware, and so on.

In this chapter I explore the changes in the Muslims' identity strategies in Mumbai. I argue that Muslims, having been marginalized from the organized industrial sector, have developed compensatory strategies for self-employment. In the cultural and political fields, Muslims, tormented by Shiv Sena's aggression, have been torn between a strategy of "community purification," advocated by religious organizations, and another strategy of "plebeian assertion," promoted by small entrepreneurs and local strongmen linked to the Samajwadi Party, which, since the mid-1990s, has sought to represent the Muslims in Mumbai. Finally, I explore some recurring themes and structures that emerge in the stories and rumors regarding the reign of the Muslim underworld in Mumbai.

TALES OF CLASS AND COMMUNITY

The working-class culture of central Bombay in the early decades of the twentieth century was structured by a repertoire of different identities and loyalties played out in various social domains—sometimes as peaceful cohabitation of the same social space, at other times as competition and open conflict (Chandavarkar 1994, 168–238). Caste and community were articulated at the workplace through an elaborate division of labor, where some groups successfully claimed certain functions with reference to their hereditary occupation. This was true of the Muslim *julaha-ansari* weavers, for instance, who, in the mills in Mominpura and Jacobs Circle, successfully claimed the more advanced operations in the weaving shed as their exclusive domain, even obtaining an almost aristocratic position among the workers, including the right to hire their own casual laborers (*badlis*).

Other groups like the Marathas from Konkan won a similar position in other mills owing to their organization and numbers. But, as Chandavarkar (1994, 168–238) argues, the deployment of caste in the case of specialized functions or marriage practices neither precluded joint "class action" across caste and community when it came to industrial disputes nor frequent and close social interaction in the streets, in the many different *akhadas*, and in other leisurely activities.

The positions of Muslims vis-à-vis various Hindu communities in Bombay developed historically in contradictory patterns. From the latter half of the nineteenth century, the economic position of the elites within the Bohra, Khoja, and Memon trading communities became rather strong and their political influence considerable (Engineer 1980, 142–64; Masselos 1973, 132–72). In the predominantly Muslim neighborhoods of Bhendi Bazaar, Umerkhadi, Dongri, and in the mill districts, ever more migrants arrived each year from the villages of the Deccan, from the Konkan coast, and from north India. Conforming to broader trends of nationalist politics and communal mobilization, religious festivals and processions became occasions for the manifestation of political identities and the contestation and coding of social space in these neighborhoods. In some cases the city experienced disturbances and violence, for example, as in the countrywide impact of the Cow Protection campaign that triggered the 1893 riots in the city and in the case of the early history of the Ganapati festival in Bombay in the 1890s; in other instances, such as the Moharram festival, the political intensity was markedly lower, and the Hindus were broadly involved in the festivities (Masselos 1976, 1982).

Naturally, the broader dynamics of the formation of communal identity from the 1920s to the 1940s throughout India deeply affected Bombay, and conflicts and mobilization ignited by strikes and industrial action were sometimes transformed into communal conflicts. The case most well known was the 1929 riots, where resentment against Pathan moneylenders and Muslim workers hired to break a strike was condensed into protracted communal riots (Chandavarkar 1994, 422–25). In the following years the city experienced a series of smaller riots as tension mounted. Elements of the Muslim leadership and political activists felt even more alienated by what they viewed as the Congress Party's hidden agenda of Hindu majoritarianism, and thus they forged still more intimate ties with the Muslim League (Hasan 1985, 102–120).

Despite the communalization of city politics in the 1940s, there was no massive exodus of Muslims from Bombay to Pakistan after 1947. A more systematic inquiry of the Partition and post-Partition events in Bombay still awaits its author, but, according to the modest number of family histories I have gathered, those who left the city were mainly *ashraf* (noble) Muslims of north Indian descent and various minor trading groups who remained marginal in relation to the well-established economic elites among the Memons, Khojas, and Bohras. Large sections of these communities chose to stay in Bombay, hoping to maintain their position in the regional economy and to retain their well-entrenched position in the local hierarchies of rank and status.[1] Among ordinary Muslims, the option of going to Pakistan remained remote and beyond their economic capacity.

The Muslims' position in the industrial workforce was not particularly marginalized in the first half of the twentieth century. Konkani Muslims were well established among the laborers in and around the docks, and *ansaris* (weavers) held a fair, if numerically negligible, position in the textile mills. According to an authoritative study from the 1950s, the workforce in the textile mills included only 5 percent and 1 percent, respectively, of Muslim men and Muslim women (Gokhale 1957, 116).

For decades, the labor market for weavers had been divided into a highly mechanized though labor-intensive mill sector and a sector organized into small units that primarily used hand looms (Gadgil 1942, 185–93). With the evolution and spread of small power looms from the 1940s on, the entire textile industry underwent profound restructuring. The combination of technological innovation and competition from textile sectors in other parts of the country led to a progressive trimming of the workforce in many mills. At the same time, the increased availability of electricity in and around Bombay meant a rapid growth in the power loom sector from the late 1950s on. Some mills closed while others increased their efficiency, adopting synthetic fibers and new production methods. From the 1970s on, a considerable number of power looms were moved to places like Bhiwandi and Malegaon north of Bombay, where the cost of both space and electricity was substantially lower than in Bombay proper.

These trends in the textile industry and the labor market affected the Muslims in central Bombay more directly than many other groups because of the concentration of ansaris there. According to the older textile workers and union activists with whom I spoke, Muslim workers were among the first to be laid off from the mills in the 1960s, and even more were laid off in the 1970s. As job opportunities became scarcer in the mills, older conflicts and prejudices between the various communities were revived—a process exacerbated by the growing influence and popularity of Shiv Sena's unions in the Bharatiya Kamgar Sena. According to several informants, one of these conflicts had to do with the threading of the large looms in the weaving shed, an operation that was often done by ansaris and required that they wet the cotton thread with their mouths. Non-Muslim workers would then regard the cloth as polluted and would refuse to touch it. One veteran organizer in the union movement told me that the management of the mills preferred to steer clear of such conflicts:

> The management wanted to avoid such problems, and in many unions this silent process, where you got rid of Muslims, just went on without anybody interfering . . . nobody took their side. Many felt uncomfortable with these communal sentiments, you know, felt that we should not talk too much about it—in the interest of unity. . . . Today we can see that these communal sentiments really paved the way for the Sena and for Datta Samant's goonda methods [getting] into the workers movement.[2]

Madanpura began to develop as an industrial area in the 1950s. After an initial conflict between the newly organized weavers in Madanpura and the Bombay Municipal Corporation regarding the installation of power looms, the weavers were granted special permission to install power looms.[3] This marked the beginning of the area's development into a dense, small-scale industrial region with hundreds of small factories and workshops. Many of those who owned the plots and controlled the installation of electricity had previously held relatively secure and well-paid positions in the mills—often as jobbers or in positions requiring specific technical expertise. The compensation they had received from the company after being laid off had often been invested in buying a number of power looms and installing electricity. In some cases families would send one of their sons to the Persian Gulf to earn money for the family, while their other sons would be given technical training in some skill other than weaving. As one owner of eight power looms, a former mill worker, explained: "I have been working in the mills all my life. Now I work harder and earn less even in my old age. I don't want my sons to live a life like that. They must advance further—educate themselves, go abroad."[4]

Most of the small workshops in Madanpura are also the intermediate homes for many of the workers employed there. Workers are often recruited through biraderi networks back in their native villages and adjoining areas in Uttar Pradesh. Many are ansaris who now carry out diverse functions but also work as mechanics, blacksmiths, and carpenters; a number of others are employed in the workshops for nine to ten months a year. Many of the married men return to their native villages during the harvest season to look after their land and their family, whereas the younger, unmarried men typically remain in Bombay. There are no unions in the area; most of the employees work for uncles or more distant relatives and, in many cases, are allowed to sleep in the workshop. Some owners take their role as head of an enlarged family rather seriously, and it is not uncommon that elderly women from the neighborhood are hired to cook and take care of the young men in the workshops.

For decades, the pattern in this labor migration was for laborers to try to accumulate enough money to acquire a small room in the vicinity in order to bring some of their family members to Bombay. The 1993 riots seem to have reversed this trend, however, at least for a while. Many of those who had fled the city in the dramatic days of January 1993 were migrant laborers who returned with their families to their villages in Uttar Pradesh. Only the men returned, as some of them perceived that Mumbai was no longer a safe place to bring their family. From the perspective of some local union organizers, this lack of attachment to the city and its people was a major obstacle in improving working conditions:

> These workers who come from Uttar Pradesh or Tamil Nadu they are thinking that this is not our mother country. Our country is Tamil Nadu or UP. So, whenever any crisis or conflict comes about they just run away from Bombay. They don't belong to Bombay city. . . . They are working in the looms, sleeping there, eating there—they never get out of Madanpura except when they go back to their village.[5]

The following two examples illustrate the type of small entrepreneurs who dominate Madanpura today. Before the riots, several major businessmen, mainly Gujarati Hindus, owned workshops, ran wholesale businesses, and marketed the area's products. Today few Hindu owners remain in the area, as most of their businesses have been purchased by people who returned with savings from years of employment in the Persian Gulf.

A. A. was sacked from Hindusthan Mills in 1979, after having been with the company for more than thirty years. The amount he earned in his last years was respectable. After long delays, he received 45,000 rupees as compensation for being laid off. At that time he went to Saudi Arabia, where he worked for two years as a cleaner in a military camp. He was treated well, he said, but felt lonely and wanted to return to his family. He spent some of his money on old power looms that he and five employees have been operating for the last ten years. His employees were all from his native Uttar Pradesh, and so his business was, in his words, "really a family business." He worked in the shop every day for more than ten hours, anticipating that in another two years he could sell his looms and retire. He wanted to send his son, who had been trained as an air-conditioning mechanic, to Saudi Arabia, but that would require an investment of about 50,000 rupees. Once his son was in Saudi Arabia and began to earn money, he planned to retire.

S. K. worked in the maintenance department of a textile mill for fifteen years. There he maintained and repaired the looms, acquiring excellent skills in all kinds of metal work, fitting, and so on. In 1978 he was fired. He was immediately able to get another job in Bahrain, where he worked for the next eight years as a plumber, at a time, he said, when "earnings were very good, much better than today. In those days, I earned more than an engineer in India." He lived in a modest room, only going back to see his family three times during that period. After his return, an old colleague told him that he was selling his power looms but needed someone to rent his workshop and his electricity supply. S. K. rented the place, bought some old machines, and began producing buckets, washbasins, trays, and other metal products. He has eight workers now and no longer works in the shop himself. Instead, he concentrates on finding good raw materials, new products, and so on. He wants his son, who studies engineering at the local college, "to take over the production and turn it into a proper factory, and maybe relocate it to Navi Mumbai."

These stories may well be read as testimonies to the entrepreneurship of ordinary Muslims coping with the hardships they faced after having been squeezed out of the textile mills. On the other hand, they are also disturbing narratives of the Muslims' increasing isolation from the rest of the city, in both socioeconomic and political terms. This has also transformed the composition of central Mumbai's population from one that previously included a considerable number of Christians, some Jews, and a variety of older, urban Muslim communities to one that is predominantly Urdu-speaking with a distinct north Indian complexion. Older residents in the area complain that the *bhaiyas* have taken over the neighborhood and given it a more rural quality: "These people still think they live in a village"; "They spit, shout, and throw things around." Within their grumbling lies the old distinction between the civilized and refined manners of those who arrived a generation earlier and the allegedly unsophisticated and unpolished manners of the newcomers. A local advocate spoke disapprovingly of a "UP'ization" of Nagpada and Mominpura, as if an alien, arcane, and sectarian form of community life had replaced the more refined, enlightened forms of modern urban life.

One of the more arresting images of this transformation of Nagpada and Mominpura from working-class areas with many Muslims into Muslim areas with many workers is that of the *Awami Idhara* (the Peoples House), created in the 1950s by cadres of the Communist Party of India and union activists. Located opposite the now closed Khatau mill, next to a newly renovated and enlarged mosque that overshadows the modest two-floor Idhara, the building seems like a historical remnant left over from an era that has irreversibly passed. Behind the building, rows of hutments cling to the dilapidated walls of another abandoned industrial plant. The poor families residing in these huts are from Bihar and Uttar Pradesh. Some of the men work as *badlis* (casual laborers) in Madanpura, and many of the women are domestics in middle-class homes in nearby Byculla.

Across the road is where, some years back, the conservative and revivalist organization, Jamaat-i-Islami Hind, opened its regional headquarters for Maharashtra. Inside the Awami Idhara, a group of elderly activists—retired mill workers, clerks, and civil servants—maintain impeccable order and, together with most of the local newspapers, run a small but very well-organized library and reading room. Local CPI units hold their meetings in the building, and, upstairs, female activists conduct children's programs and evening classes for women.

A caretaker of the Awami Idhara, whose family, for generations, were jobbers in the mills, lamented the younger people's lack of interest in broader social causes:

> Look at us here. We are all retired. We grew up with the unions and the mills. There we were respected because of the skills we have in our community [as ansaris—T.B.H.] when it came to weaving. But now it is all closed, and all there is left are these power looms you have seen in Madanpura. Some are owned by our members. But who will come after us? Young people don't want to be weavers; they want to go to Saudi Arabia and make money. I can understand that. . . . But our cause suffers, our culture here is dying.[6]

Another example of the disappearance of an older, popular culture in this part of Mumbai may be found only a few minutes away from the Awami Idhara at the large YMCA sports compound. Inside the building is an old wrestling pit, where one might find a few young men wrestling in the coarse sand, their bodies and hair glistening from oil. Next door, occupying most of the building, is a modern body-building center with lots of machines and mirrors, full of youngsters sporting fancy hairstyles and admiring their bulging muscles. A. Khan, a former coach and *pehlwan* (wrestler) in the *akhada* (gymnasium) and a former respected *ustad* (master), with many championships behind him, has trained young men from the area for fifty years. He describes how this Mominpura akhada once provided the most important leisure activities in the area. In his day, he explains, a good pehlwan commanded tremendous respect among the young mill hands. Today, however, no one bothers to pursue this goal because, in order to be a pehlwan, one must practice several times a week, in fact preferably every day, must observe a strict diet, and so on.

> In those days, even the young toughs from Kamathipura would come and do exercise. But in this day and age, where fights are settled with guns and bombs, who cares to be a good fighter. . . . Besides, when you are a pehlwan you don't look strong, but your body is like a steel spring. But today fellows like them only do it to impress the girls in Bandra.[7]

Khan is referring to the groups of young men who arrive in expensive clothes in new Marutis from the prosperous suburbs to do their weekly exercises in the gym. Here they pay less than one-fourth of what they would pay in middle-class neighborhoods. The young YMCA caretaker remarks that the gym cannot afford to say no to these boys "from the outside," because the interest in sports and physical exercise has largely disappeared from the neighborhood. According to the old Ustad, this has to do with the general decay in society and discipline, with materialism, and, above all, with the misconception among many young people that they can simply return to the Middle East, work for some years, and then return to Mumbai and do nothing—or, even worse, as Khan says, "that one can go idle and remain so just because one has a brother in Dubai."

LABOR MIGRATION AND NEW ASPIRATIONS

The history of migrant labor in Bombay is inextricably linked to the booming oil economies in the Gulf and Bombay's historical role as supplier of raw material, goods, and enjoyment to the entire region surrounding the Gulf. In the late 1970s, labor migration to the Gulf was a true economic bonanza because of the relatively high wages paid to even unskilled laborers in construction and sanitation, and the lack of effective regulation of immigration. An elderly carpenter related:

> My cousin and I went there believing that we were supposed to do carpentry only, as the agent had told us, but we were put up on the open roof of our rich employer's house and made to do everything in the next two years. . . . We did not object. . . . We put a small wooden shed up there. . . . After all, in those two years we made as much as we could have done in ten years here in Bombay. . . . Young people cannot do this today.

Labor migration was a way to escape from the underpaid jobs in small-scale industry and an alternative to the many jobs lost in the textile industry. It also provided an avenue whereby younger people could escape from their ancestral, lower-caste profession as a weaver and instead accumulate enough money to open a shop or start a small business.

Small travel agencies and manpower agencies emerged, many of them subcontractors for the larger agencies that had obtained official authorization from the consulates of various Gulf countries to receive a certain quota of visas. A related sector of "trade testing centers" also appeared, where applicants could test their skills and be issued a certificate. In addition, hundreds of hostels provided accommodations and amenities to the many thousands of applicants and migrants passing through the city every year.

Given the relative lack of higher education among Muslims, especially those of north Indian descent and an ansari background, many of the better-paying jobs went to Hindus. However, Muslims constituted the bulk of both the skilled and unskilled laborers. Among the older, urban Muslim trading communities of Bombay, migrant labor did not appear equally attractive to younger educated men. Both the Memon and Bohra communities had rather elaborate systems of trusts and educational institutions that ensured a relatively high level of education among most men in the communities. Besides, the tradition of running independent businesses rather than engaging in government service or other types of employment remains strong among both Bohras and Memons. One young Bohra trader claimed that this has to do with the specific Bohra interpretation of Islam that forbids any Bohra to take up employment except if he is forced to do so by external circumstances. To be employed is shameful, he went on, "and it does not make any difference even if you work for a pious Saudi Muslim."[8] Instead, the trading communities of Bombay made the migration industry into a rather lucrative business. Most of the major manpower agencies are run and managed by the city's older trading communities.

Despite the relatively low rank of Muslims from Bombay and elsewhere in the labor markets around the Persian Gulf, the difference between the earnings in India and those abroad was so substantial that the flow of money from the Gulf contributed to a certain dislocation of social hierarchies back in Bombay. The drop-out rate from high schools and colleges grew, and I heard stories, undoubtedly exaggerated, of college classes being left half-empty in the mid-seventies. Initially it was primarily young men from families with some financial resources and education who went abroad to exploit the new opportunities, hoping that their investment in a ticket and a visa, as well as having to endure the hardships of manual labor considered unworthy for college men, would be more profitable than pursuing the meager opportunities in Bombay. In the seventies this strategy was generally successful. Larger numbers of lower-income families began to develop similar aspirations toward a certain middle-class lifestyle and began sending their children for a higher education. This made established social hierarchies of rank and status more fluid and contested.

In the 1980s immigration laws became more stringent in many of the Gulf countries, and Arab employers began to squeeze salaries. Unskilled labor from countries like Bangladesh (reputed to be extremely cheap and docile) and the Philippines (thought to be more dependable and flexible in terms of job functions than South Asians, that is, willing to clean toilets or do other "dirty" jobs) began to replace Indian labor in many fields.

Arab employers now mainly recruited skilled labor and technical manpower from India, and it became exceedingly expensive for unskilled laborers to acquire a labor contract. Throughout the 1980s, as competition became sharper, recruitment agents began to ask for higher fees and bribes from applicants. After the Gulf War in 1991,[9] the entire market for migrant labor experienced a dramatic slump. Many manpower and travel agencies had to close as Saudi Arabia and the smaller Gulf states began deporting illegal migrants back to India and Pakistan in substantial numbers. Lately, in another attempt to limit immigration and to strengthen its religious-national authority, the Saudi Arabian government decided, in 1996, only to allow Muslims to obtain work permits in the country. Today, however, India's educated Muslims are less interested than earlier, because opportunities have expanded in India after initiation of the liberalization policy and because the gap between salaries in the Gulf countries and India has been reduced.

Today, migration to the Gulf is only considered attractive to skilled or technical manpower, whereas regular manual laborers are often underpaid, insecure, too expensive to hire, and vulnerable to all kinds of fluctuations in immigration practices. Very few men from Mumbai are willing to take such jobs, and, as one agent told me:

> We don't want these Bombay fellows. They are troublesome, pick up fights with their employers, and they are particular about the jobs they do. They behave like little *rajas*. . . . People from the south, especially these Muslim fellows from villages, are very good—very simple, quiet, and hard-working. They are very popular with the Arabs.

While the option of regular employment in Mumbai's large industries virtually disappeared, social expectations intensified considerably among a younger generation who had grown up accustomed to the flow of money and consumer goods from their family members in the Gulf. Manual labor was still considered respectable ten to fifteen years ago, but the drive for education and the influx of poor laborers from the villages in north India has made this an improper option today for a young man from an established Mumbai family. Instead, doing "business"—running a small firm or shop in Bombay or in the Gulf—is the more suitable course if the family's rank in the internal hierarchy is to be maintained. It is thus symptomatic that an old carpenter's son, who went to the Gulf in the 1970s, today works as a mechanic in a large foreign company in Saudi Arabia and that the sons of a communist secretary of one of the weavers' cooperatives in Nagpada both work in foreign companies in Jeddah in Saudi Arabia.

In Gardner's account of a single village in the Sylhet District of Bangladesh, the differentiation between "londoni" families with members in Britain or the Gulf and those without tended to transform hierarchies of rank and honor in a direct and conspicuous manner because of the absence or weakness of other alternative paths to social mobility and financial strength (Gardner 1995, 98–161). This was clearly not the case in Mumbai, where migrant labor was an important but not dominant avenue to upward social mobility.

However, in lower-income areas like Nagpada and Madanpura, where most inhabitants are first- or second-generation migrants from north India, labor migration to the Gulf was indeed central to the livelihood of many families, as well as to their prospects of achieving higher social status. Two factors were particularly important: First, and most significant, young men from modest family backgrounds but with good earnings in the Gulf could hope to get a bride from a family of somewhat higher status. This applied not only to the son who actually worked in the Gulf but to his younger brothers as well. In other words, young men who worked hard in the Gulf not only honored their entire family but could also hope to get a beautiful wife—"a really good bride with some education and good manners—someone who has been to convent school," as one unmarried Gulf migrant described his dream to me.

The other dimension concerned the style in which wealth was accumulated and displayed. A technician or an engineer working in a regular company in Saudi Arabia could make enough money to support most of his family. The explicit demand of bringing home gifts to all branches of the family was a grudge many of the migrants held against their own families, especially brothers and cousins. "They go idle, take food, watch TV, and enjoy themselves, without doing a thing. Some of them may get a good wife just because of me. They never think of thanking me or just acknowledging me. They just enjoy," as one migrant put it bitterly.

As I began to identify and talk to migrant families in Nagpada and Madanpura I often encountered the rumor, prevalent among those who did not migrate, that many of these families had ceased to be respectable, that they were ridden with conflicts, and so on. Many stories circulated of deceit in migrant families—infidelity, lack of moral fiber, brothers and fathers sleeping with the wives of absent men, women indulging in improper behavior when beyond their husband's or father's discipline—all the while receiving substantial amounts of money. This discourse of moral decay, dissolution of families, and excessive consumerism obviously grew out of gossip and envy. But underneath were anxieties produced by the displacement of hierarchies of rank, status, and respectability between the hitherto dominant (*ashraf*) Muslims and the ordinary (*ajlaf*) Muslims, who, for decades, accepted the cultural leadership of the ashraf families. The new flow of money enabled lower-status families to wear expensive clothes and to flaunt the consumer goods they received from relatives in ways that higher-ranking families considered both improper and vulgar.

The construction and narration of the migration experience was complex, however. Although established elites in these neighborhoods deplored some of the new forms of social mobility that migration had made possible, at the same time the Arab world often construed the migration experience as an act of purification that brought one closer to Islam and to a larger Muslim community. But these constructions were fraught with contradictions. The layoffs and deportations in the Gulf countries since 1996 have made it clear to most migrant workers that settlement in the Arab countries is less desirable than they had hoped and that migrant labor simply provided a temporary source of income and savings that might enable one to start a business or buy a house in Mumbai.[10]

IN THE NAME OF THE COMMUNITY

Well until the 1970s the trading communities formed the economic and political elite in Bombay's Muslim neighborhoods. In the last decades religious figures, political leadership, as well as writers and intellectuals active in the Urdu public sphere have increasingly been of north Indian origin. This tendency, along with the continuous cycle of labor migration between villages in north India, has increasingly made lifestyles, religious leanings, and political identities of northern India integral parts of Bombay's Muslim world. The impact of culturally conservative north Indian Muslim sensibilities and identities was amply demonstrated in conjunction with the agitation surrounding the Shah Bano case in 1985.

At this juncture in the 1980s liberal Muslims feared that such manifestations of identity only reinforced the stereotype of Muslims as conservative and pre-modern in outlook and would harm the Muslims in the long run. These same liberals had also feared a conservative introverted backlash after the 1993 riots, but they were in fact proved partially wrong—as though the catastrophe had destroyed the older notions of community. Instead, identities among Muslims in contemporary Mumbai seemed suspended between two distinct, yet intertwined, positions: on the one hand, a largely conservative and at times radical quest for internal purification and unity of the Muslim community, of self-enclosure and withdrawal from political, legal, and economic dependence on the larger society; on the other hand, a more pragmatic strategy bent on "plebeian assertion," articulated around the entrepreneurial spirit and lifestyles emerging from small industry and informal businesses. This latter tendency was linked to the Muslims' assertion into the political field through the Samajwadi Party, which attracts lower-caste Hindus and many Muslims in north India and which recently made significant electoral gains in Mumbai.

Both these strategies of identity have tried to maintain the distinction between "politics" and "culture"—the first pillar of Indian secularism. At the same time, the "plebeian" tendency and the desire for recognition among ordinary (ajlaf) Muslims also tend to challenge the second pillar of Indian secularism—the representation of communities through educated elites. This latter tendency has exposed the paternalist spirit intrinsic to the exhortations of a singular Muslim identity and has led to a more visible enunciation of plural Muslim identities.

PURIFYING THE COMMUNITY

Central Mumbai was home to an impressive array of religious entrepreneurs, most of them claiming to speak for the community. They all wished to purify the community's inner life, to unite the different sects and interpretations of Islam, and to make the community more independent of the larger society. All these initiatives and organizations sought to derive their own legitimacy from an ideal, but impossible, separation of culture and politics.

One of the several "Ekta" (unity) initiatives was the Ulema Council, led by maulana Kashmiri, a man known for his close and longstanding ties to the Muslim League, the once influential Muslim political party, which he recently abandoned. Explaining why he created his influential and "nonpolitical" organization, the maulana said: "This organization was founded in order to promote the interests of the Muslim community as such. . . . All the different groups sacrificed their political interests for the larger welfare of the community." While unequivocally defined as a community organization above politics, another of its spokesmen emphasized that "our greatest contribution has been to wean people away from Congress and to ensure their defeat now in two elections." The council obviously saw its political role as representing the community, but it derived its authority from its members' nonpolitical credentials, their religious expertise, and their generally high status.

The Ulema Council also promoted itself as a community authority with more capacity for interpreting Muslim Personal Law than any court. One member of the council stated:

We tell the people—if you have a domestic problem, please don't go to court—let us sit together and we will solve it. Why should we go to them [the courts]—you know judges call for all these things, everything depends on evidence, cross-examination, circumstantial evidence, etc.—we have our own laws and we are capable of solving our own problems.

The council claimed that its efforts have led to reduced divorce rates because couples attend counseling sessions provided by the council or go to imams in the local mosques. Lawyers and social workers in the area strongly contradicted this claim, however, arguing that divorces (*talaq*) have become an increasing social problem as the practice of getting a new and younger wife, or a second wife—always a mark of status among the ashraf Muslims—had become more broadly embraced as a sign of upward social mobility. At the same time, public criticism of the talaq practices had become quite troublesome because these practices, and their associated stereotype of the polygamous Muslim, have occupied a central position in Hindu nationalist rhetoric over the last decades.

To a group of preachers dispatched from the famous madrasah in Deoband in north India, the central institution in developing a scriptural and conservative form of Islam in South Asia since the nineteenth century, the upholding of Muslim Personal Law was also of paramount significance: "In Islamic countries Muslims are safe—here we need the Personal Law to protect ourselves. It is after all not just a law; it is the word of God. . . . It has to do with the customs of the community, it deals with very personal matters. It cannot be encroached upon." According to these preachers, the problem was not talaq but the lack of moral fiber among Muslims, their "indulgence in pomp and splendor," particularly in Mumbai, where, in the words of a preacher, "TV is taking over the functions of the family, sexes are mixed in educational institutions, and respect for elders has broken down."

According to these Deobandi preachers, the Muslim Personal Law should be the pillar around which Muslim unity can be re-created. Deobandi Islam, being the "natural form of Islam in the subcontinent," must be at the center of this endeavor because it is a more "correct form of Islam." As one preacher put it, "We don't want to change the political system such as the Jamaat-e-Islami does" (more on this below). But the goal of the Deobandis was not merely unity but also doctrinal purity and a pedagogical effort to displace and refine the Islam practiced by the common ajlaf Muslims. As another preacher stated: "Besides, we are much more educated. Our Islam is more refined than that of the Bareilvis who embrace all sorts of primitive practices and worship deceased *pirs* [saints] owing to ignorance and superstition."

A few hundred yards away, the All-India Tabligh-e-Seerat also claimed to work for Muslim unity, but, contrary to the cultural accent of the Deobandis, President Syed Ashraf argued that, in the present situation, it was imperative that religious authorities intervened more directly in politics. They should infuse a "purer spirit" into politics and thus create a more "decent generation of Muslim politicians, people who are actually willing to work for Muslims, to get Muslim ministers, to reserve jobs for Muslims, more Urdu schools—ours is the second largest language in the country—more public investment in Muslim areas, and so on."

One cannot, after all, separate politics from other aspects of life, Ashraf argued, and his organization was created in 1989 to give the "majority of Sunni's in this country a voice in the nation's politics. . . . We declared that we are saying good-bye to Congress and instead we supported the Janata Dal." Syed Ashraf is a spiritual leader among the many Bareilvy Muslims in Mumbai—the amorphous, folksy, but also conservative variety of Sunni Islam wherein many *sufi* practices, such as reverence for saints, remain important elements.[11] The Syed made it clear that the contemporary rethinking of Muslim strategies of identity and public representation must imply a subversion of conventional hierarchies between Muslim sects:

> Politics has for such a long time been the monopoly of Deobandis and for Wahhabis [a purist form of high Islam dominant, for example, in Saudi Arabia—T.B.H.] [that] now it is time that we, the Bareilvis, who are 85 percent of all Muslims in India come out and stake our claims for political influence and demonstrate that we no longer can be taken for granted, neither by Congress nor by the so-called Muslim leadership.[12]

The subversion of older and elitist representations of the Muslim community by the growing public assertiveness of Bareilvy Sunni Muslims was subsequently brought out in a violent clash in the city between Deobandis and Bareilvis in front of the large Jama Masjid, the primary mosque of the Deobandis, on 18 January 1998, leaving two dead and several injured. The immediate cause was a disagreement over the exact date of the beginning of the holy month of Ramzan that subsequently determines the date of the celebration of Eid, the most important Muslim festival. The Deobandis began their fast one day before the Bareilvis, and this caused deep anger and frustration because it was seen as yet another sign of the arrogance of the Deobandi clergy. Matters deteriorated when, at a meeting called to sort out differences, the Deobandis demanded that the Bareilvis fast an extra day after Eid so that the Deoband interpretation of dates and rituals could go unchallenged. The following day, members of the groups clashed. Political leaders from both the Janata Dal and the Samajwadi

Party promptly took the side of the Bareilvis in the conflict. The result was a meeting, held shortly thereafter, where the two sides agreed on a truce which ensured that both communities would celebrate Eid on the same day.[13]

In newspapers and public discussions, the sectarian clash was denounced as yet another example of the divisive effects of politics on the inner cohesion of the Muslim community, and political leaders were widely blamed for instigating splits among Muslims. Paradoxically this criticism only confirmed the impossibility of separating "culture" from "politics," and demonstrated that any articulation of a sense of community inevitably was shot through by political identifications. That Bareilvis no longer accepted the theological and political leadership of Islam's "high" forms was, to my mind, not merely an outcome of the support they received from powerful political formations. Rather, it was one of several effects of a broader assertion of ajlaf (non-elite) modes of being Muslim, cherishing somewhat conservative and strongly patriarchal notions of Islam. But, as I have indicated, the imaginings of a united and pre-political religious community as a reservoir of morality and purity also remained crucial in these otherwise earthy and robust discourses on politics and identity.

More unequivocally antipolitical notions of purification of the community informed the fast growing Tabligh-e-Jamaat, a worldwide organization propagating a pious lifestyle among Muslims.[14] A local Tabligh worker outlined the regenerative, quietist project of the Tablighis in the following way:

> We are missionaries through our own examples, by showing that it only is by turning to the Creator you can realize your human nature. Without the Creator you are only worldly desire, greed, and lust. . . .) We are not political people—we show that through total sacrifice and devotion you can turn criminals and pickpockets into respectable citizens.

Mohammad Talib describes the Tablighi "mode of being in the world" in this way: They believe firmly that Muslims need to anchor their own identity in their own selves and their immediate environment—disciplinary practices relating to the body, the family, and the neighborhood—rather than in "external" symbols such as the Muslim Personal Law, the status of Urdu, or other conventional markers of Muslim identity in India. The enemy of Muslims is not the state or the Hindus but *naf*, the desires and drives of the "lower self," and the internal divisions and lack of devotion among Muslims (Talib 1997, 32–51). The antipolitical stance of the Tabligh-e-Jamaat is, in other words, both more radical and more introverted than any of the conventional postures promoting unity among Muslims in the public sphere and the political world. The Tabligh-e-Jamaat has expanded its influence in India's larger cities like Mumbai over the last five years. In 1997 the organization held its largest *Isthama* (gathering) ever in the subcontinent, when hundreds of thousands of Muslim men assembled in Mumbai for a series of functions, collective prayers, and so on. The Shiv Sena government welcomed the opportunity to facilitate the Isthama so as to proclaim a noncommunal profile. Tablighi practices fed into more enduring models within South Asian Islam of how high status and upward social mobility were displayed through outward signs of piousness and purism, for example, women wearing *burqahs*, sons being sent to madrasahs, the undertaking of pilgrimages to Mecca [*haj*], and so on. As the political domain has increasingly become occupied by individuals from lower-caste communities, whom many respectable Muslim families so despise, the Tabligh-e-Jamaat provided a public articulation of Muslim identity and sensibility that appealed to the educated Muslim middle class.

A similar combination of social mobility and a turn to scripturalism was at play among upwardly mobile ansari weavers turning to Al-i-Hadith, the scripturalist, Wahhabi-oriented sect that stands for a simplified interpretation of Islam and emphasizes a return to the basics of the Koran and the Hadith. Of the three mosques in the Nagpada/Madanpura area where I worked, one was regarded as belonging to the Al-i-Hadith and its followers. The Al-i-Hadithis are often the owners of power looms, traders, or people with some education but of an ansari background who have strong convictions and keenly wish to put distance between what they regard as their new, purer, and stricter practices and the broadly Bareilvy-oriented religious practices of the majority of ansaris in the area.

This model of social mobility and scriptural sectarianism was obviously linked to migration from, and extended contacts with, Benares in north India, a leading center for weaving as well as an important hub for the Al-i-Hadiths in South Asia. As Searle-Chatterjee has shown, the Al-i-Hadiths have been active in Banares since the 1950s, but it was the urban development there and the increased flow of remittances from labor migrants in the Gulf that enabled more ansaris to prosper and hence consolidate their new status through their involvement in the Al-i-Hadith sect (Searle-Chatterjee 1994, 83–93). This pattern parallels the effects of labor migration on rank and social status in the neighborhoods of Nagpada. Overall, however, these cultural changes are undoubtedly driven more by the broader process of social mobility afforded by Mumbai's economic development and the remittances from migrants than by any direct influence of Islam or Middle Eastern cultural practices.

One of the religious entrepreneurs who tried most directly to address the issue of Muslim unity and to "renew and adapt Islam to the modern age," as people claimed, was the Islamic Research Foundation, a well funded, smoothly run organization in central Mumbai managed largely by one man, Dr. Zakir Naik, who has traveled widely as an Islamic preacher since 1993.[15] The foundation has library facilities, lecture halls, book-shops, and so on. The well-trained staff addresses both visitors and disciples as "brothers" or "sisters." Naik and some of his assistants deliver public addresses to the men in the lecture hall, while the women watch the lecture on a TV monitor in a separate hall. Topics include "Islam and Modern Science," "Islam and Christianity," and "Islam and Secularism." The talks are conducted in English and videotaped to be broadcast every Saturday and Sunday on several of the extensive cable networks in Mumbai's Muslim neighborhoods. According to Dr. Naik, the goal is to "concentrate on the educated Muslim youth who have become apologetic about their own religion and who have started to feel that their own religion is outdated."

> We want to remove common misconceptions about Islam. . . . We want to show that unlike other religions there is no contradiction between Islam and modern science. On the contrary, there is not a single verse of the Koran [that] opposes established scientific facts. It may conflict with certain theories of science, but none of these, like evolution, has been scientifically proved, and they change all the time. . . . Many of these facts were anticipated in the Koran. [The] Koran speaks, for instance, of Big Bang already fourteen hundred years ago.

Naik may have only a few hundred people in the crowd when he speaks, but videotapes of his talks are widely and effectively circulated. That he is medical doctor and scientist who can recite by memory both the Koran and Hadiths (commentaries and interpretations of the Koran) in Arabic, Urdu, and English and travels to America and Europe to debate Islam with theologians has made Naik quite a star in central Mumbai. Having seen his talks repeatedly on TV, it became obvious that fragments of his arguments, his examples of the social and cultural evils of the West, his direct and confrontational promotion of the truth of Islam vis-à-vis the West, constantly reappeared in conversations with people in the locality, especially those with some education.

The strategy of purifying Muslim practices in order to renew and reinvigorate the community found an even more radical form within the Student Islamic Movement of India (SIMI). This student organization, which resembles Jamaat-e-Islami ideologically, is a rather clear-cut revivalist Islamic movement that is a relatively marginal force in India but plays a certain role in Pakistani politics.[16] Its main goal is *Tarbiyah* (character building) and the development of a dedicated cadre of *ansars* (helpers) who are morally regenerated through intensive studies of the Koran, Hadiths, and Islamic scholarship in history, ethics, and other fields. This perpetual training should enable its members "to shun everything evil, to live righteous lives, to be modest, shun alcohol, TV watching, obscene movies, and other evils creeping into our society," as one young SIMI activist explained the ethics of what he termed an "Islamic revolution." The SIMI is both radical and youthful, and attracts college students who are more intellectually inclined—often extremely bright with excellent academic prospects and outstanding self-discipline. The organization has a few thousand members in the Mumbai area, where it achieved a breakthrough as a result of a large conference it organized in 1991, which attracted fifty thousand participants. One young SIMI activist from a modest family background in central Mumbai, now a successful student of natural science at one of the elite colleges, told me:

> I spend all my time studying. In the daytime I study natural science. I am taught Darwin's evolution theory, the big bang theories, and theoretical physics. I learn it but I don't believe any of it. In the evenings and Saturdays we study our own SIMI syllabus, and we discuss the Islamic teachings of how Allah created everything.

By the end of 1996 SIMI launched a campaign against all forms of nationalism, for a new "Khilafat," a new sense of universal brotherhood through the worship of God. One element of the campaign was explicitly directed against politics in general and democracy in particular. SIMI had been under police surveillance for "antinationalist activities" since 1991, and the organization was one of the first to be suspected after the bomb blasts in March 1993. An intelligence officer told the magazine *Blitz* that "only leaders of an organization like SIMI can possess the requisite psychological and ideological motivation to engage in acts of subversion."[17]

Democracy, SIMI argued, is inherently divisive, as it leaves room only for the representation of particular interests and excludes any higher truth. SIMI advised activists and supporters to abstain from any political participation such as voting, and so on. One SIMI pamphlet read: "God and not the demos has the right to rule. . . . The Prophet has given guidelines for a proper political system, and man-made laws are never very helpful to mankind. God who has created mankind knows better its true interests." Like its parent organization, the Jamaat-e-Islami, SIMI carefully avoided any references to internal sectarian divides among Muslims. The main concern was the Muslim Umma as a whole and the generation of an Islamic ethics fit for modernity. The organization published elaborate career-planning materials for its members and sympathizers, and it encouraged hard work and discipline in order to qualify for leading and powerful posts in the state bureaucracy and the private sector. SIMI, as well as the Jamaat-e-Islami, deplored what they saw as "lax discipline" in India, the decline of public ethics, soaring crime rates, the erroneous attitudes toward work preached by trade unions, and overindulgence in sex. Much like the Hindu nationalists and other radical conservatives, they advocated stronger government and the protection of family values, admired China for its discipline and developmental results, and praised women who embraced their proper role as mothers instead of demanding equality. In one publication, SIMI described women's enfranchisement as an "evil innovation" that upset the proper balance between the sexes.

The SIMI and the Jamaat-e-Islami clearly catered to the same antipolitical sentiments as the Tabligh-e-Jamaat, and shared a similar distaste for the chaotic, transient, and increasingly plebeian nature of the political world. Although both organizations took a high-profile stand on public policies and were extremely critical of the government, and although Jamaat-e-Islami issued guidelines to its members on how to vote, the main thrust of their work remained informed by the classical and elitist project of piety and organization (*tabligh* and *tanzim*), which has marked Muslim identity politics in South Asia for more than a century.[18]

PLEBEIAN POLITICS

Another way of approaching the questions of politics, community, and culture also emerged in central Mumbai. It was not one coherent ideological project but rather dispersed approaches to social mobility and family strategies aimed at education and respectability among the large groups of ordinary ajlaf Muslims, who, until a decade ago, largely held manual jobs in mills and smaller industries.

A result of this, and the not unfounded perception that Muslims, especially after the 1993 riots, were unable to get jobs in the government or the private sector, many younger educated Muslims now tried to start their own businesses. One effect of this new bid for social success is the declining enrollment of students in the extensive Urdu school system run by the Bombay Municipal Corporation.[19] Boys especially are now enrolled in private English medium schools, and several teachers in these schools complained about the intensive workload and the immense pressure put on these boys from *ajlaf* parents: "Now, we get many parents from modest backgrounds who save everything they have just to keep one boy in our school. . . . Their expectations to these children are completely unrealistic. Many times boys are beaten when they return home with modest marks," one teacher from one of Nagpada's English medium schools remarked. As elsewhere in India, instruction in English has become the single most important key to escaping the life in the mohalla. Among Muslims, this tendency also undermines the older, once influential strategy among Muslim leaders to establish Urdu as a primary language of instruction as well as a signifier of identity for Indian Muslims.

The shadowy sector of smuggling, drug peddling, and serving as local toughs to collect rent, debts, and "donations" also provides conspicuous avenues to money and recognition in these areas. The unemployment rate among young people is staggering, and hanging out with the local dada or aspiring to become a dada is a very visible, though far from cherished, part of the daily experience of young boys and men in these neighborhoods. The local dadas provide effective role models and often material access to signs of the good life displayed in the maze of commercials and TV serials pumped out around the clock by enterprising cable operators here and in other parts of the city. These signifiers range from cellular phones, Maruti-Gypsy jeeps, air conditioning, visits to bars and the nearby Kamathipura red-light district, and, not least, a measure of respect and recognition in the local hierarchies. As the son of one of the local fixers and fighters told me:

> People will tell you that my father is a criminal, that he is not a good Muslim. But none of them will dare to challenge him face to face. And they all come here when they are in trouble. To be a dada is to have this reputation, to command this respect.

His father, I, had come from a north Indian village as a child and later became the best *pehlwan* (wrestler) in the Mominpura akhada; gradually he established himself as an able and tough fighter and trader who, as his college-student son put it, in the now global American street jargon, "took no shit from anybody." Inevitably he became involved in a conflict with one of the reigning dadas and ultimately killed him in a knife fight. He seemed reconciled with this act, had served time in prison, and was well aware that this act, which, according to him, was "wrong but necessary," was crucial to his current reputation. Today he is an efficient broker, a successful businessman, and president of the local unit of the Samajwadi Party in his area. His is a truly ordinary but effective success story in a social environment where the narratives of the deeds and misdeeds of gangster kings provide a fascinating and ambivalent representation of the flip side of the Muslim community.

This is particularly true of Dawood Ibrahim, the expatriate gangster king of Dubai who grew up in these neighborhoods in central Mumbai. Over the years his mythological status has grown into an enormous self-perpetuating narrative of a mystical hero that incarnates much of the stigmas, stereotypes, and fears associated with Muslims within the Hindu middle classes, the press, and the police. Dawood is feared and respected because of his courage and power. He has become a hero, whose status as the radical evil of all Hindu dreams makes him an icon among young toughs. "It is better to be respected as a dada than to be neglected as a fool," as one of them told me. To have a "reputation" for being affiliated with "Dawood's men" is an ephemeral, cherished, yet deeply ambivalent mark of importance and identity in the streets. In the eyes of religious activists and respectable families of some status, Dawood is the very symbol of the inner rot and contamination of the Muslim community, the epitome of material greed and unrestrained desire. However, I was told many times by local leaders, as well as ordinary people, that dadas perform important functions. A local resident in Bohri mohalla, Dawood's "native territory," put it succinctly: "We have to respect these people—in times of crisis who else will fight for us in the street? There the nice advocate or doctor is no good. . . . But that does not mean that we trust them; that is something else."

But according to I, the hope that Dawood or other big men will help Muslims is naïve. Muslims must fend for themselves, he felt: "One who thinks should think about himself, he should have guts in himself. . . . I have no hope of receiving help from Dawood. According to me, everyone should have guts, believe in himself, they should think of themselves as Dawood." The new prominence of dadas and ajlaf Muslim entrepreneurs, in local politics as well, has been articulated only to a limited extent within the network of institutions, trusts, and associations that make up the cultural establishment of the Muslim community. Instead, most of these men have established themselves and their credibility through extended kinship structures, biraderis, and other informal relations of trust, trade, and patronage. In other words, they have emerged from social environments whose ethos of action, violence, and male honor are strikingly similar to those that form the basis today of Shiv Sena's hold on popular neighborhoods in other parts of the city.

The popularity of Mulayam Singh and the Samajwadi Party among Muslims in Mumbai should be seen in this light. The Samajwadi Party moved into Mumbai in 1994 through alliances with a number of prominent Muslim business people, as well as extensive informal networks of small-scale operators in the so-called informal economy, who subsequently provided much of the funding and key personnel for the party's hastily erected organization in the city. The reputation of Mulayam Singh and his party had long been known, but only after 1993 and the riots in Bombay did the party emerge as a realistic alternative to the Janata Dal or the Congress.

The party's Mumbai president is a major businessman, who was imprisoned for one year for alleged proximity to Dawood Ibrahim and the conspiracy behind the 1993 bombings; many of the party's local leaders and elected representative are known as local fixers, brokers, and businessmen. Some religious figures denounce it as a "goonda party" and prefer wish to keep a safe distance away; to them, the party behaves almost too shamelessly, even in the realm of rough-and-tumble politics. Some local party

leaders like to portray themselves as men hardened by the life in the mohalla, undaunted by the treacherous and often violent world of politics,
men who need no excuses or religious sanction for their political work.
Or, in the words of a local candidate running for the municipal elections:
"If you want to fight in politics, come with us. If you want to be a pious
Muslim only, then go to the masjid. We are not religious people, we are
in politics."

This representation of the Samajwadi Party as a resolute and plebeian
organization, needing blessings from neither religious authorities nor
leading community figures, is, however, riddled with ambivalences. One
example is the fact that maulana Kashmiri and his Ulema Council of
learned people were backing the Samajwadi Party, as were several well-
known and well-educated individuals known for their affiliation with the
communal Muslim League. Local supporters often cited this fact as proof
of the legitimacy of the party's claim to represent Muslims. Similarly, the
party's resolute stance in favor of the Bareilvis in their conflict with the
Deobandis in January 1998 demonstrates that the party in no way wishes
to be regarded as indifferent to religious sensibilities.

This oscillation between the party's claims to represent both a broader
plebeian identity and the Muslim community was evident in the party's
election campaign for the February 1997 local municipal elections in
Mumbai. Most candidates deployed two distinct, though intertwined,
discourses: on the one hand, they promised to protect the Muslim community and the dignity and self-respect of Muslims. As one campaigning
MLA repeatedly asserted: "Our demand is simple—we want identity."
Here, the party's leader and at the time Union Minister of Defense, Mulayam Singh, and his secular credentials (understood as his commitment to
intercommunity balance), namely, his opposition to the Hindu nationalist
party BJP in north India, was advanced again and again as the Muslims'
guarantee for physical security in Mumbai. At a public meeting in late
February 1997, Mulayam Singh addressed a large crowd in Nagpada. He
promised that the Hindu nationalists would "not be allowed to touch the
seat of power in Delhi," and, with well-rehearsed bravado, swore that he,
both as minister of defense and a man, would guarantee the safety of Muslims in India. At the rally a young man I knew approached me and said,
triumphantly, "Who said that we Muslims are not in the mainstream? We
are right here in the mainstream with the defense minister of India."

The other discourse the candidates deployed was one of plebeian assertion, an identification of ordinary Muslims as small folks, marginalized,
impoverished, and unjustly neglected by the Congress, the state, and the
Muslim leadership. This signified a clear-cut transformation from the
older, often paternalistic enunciation of community among Muslims discussed above, by which religious leaders demand respect and recognition

as Muslims, as the other large community of the Indian state. The following statement by another local Samajwadi candidate exemplifies how Muslims were increasingly viewing themselves: "We have to look at ourselves, see who we really are. We are no longer *rajas* or big people, we are as poor as the backwards [lower-caste Hindus—T.B.H.], and even worse." It was significant that many of the party's candidates in these neighborhoods proudly referred to themselves as ansaris or julahas, the Muslim weaving community that forms a substantial part of the population in these areas.

Several prominent residents in the area strongly deplored this as an attempt to divide the Muslims along caste and community lines just to win the election. However, the articulation of "lower-caste" or ajlaf identities among Muslims had been developing for some time. Muslim communities that fell within the category of other backward classes (OBCs), which formally entitled them to certain benefits and reserved jobs in many states in India, had organized themselves in north India for a while. The ansari association was created in Mumbai in the 1960s to affirm a long-standing strategy among the ansaris, both inside the Union movement and within their own organizations, to gain recognition as workers and artisans worthy of respect from both the ashraf Muslims and the Hindu communities. In 1990 the julaha/ansari association in central Mumbai petitioned the chief minister in Maharashtra for recognition as a backward community, and hence eligible for reserved seats in educational institutions, for scholarships, and so on. In their petition, the association argued that their community, known as julahas and not even recognized as proper Muslims until the nineteenth century, had adopted the name ansaris, or helpers (referring to those who helped the Prophet) in an attempt to earn proper recognition from the Muslim elite and from society at large. This had not worked sufficiently well, the petition argued, and so it was the community's wish to reassert its original name and have the state government recognize that all ansaris are also julahas, and hence entitled to "the grants and concessions available to the backward classes of society." Although clearly instrumental in their motivation was to partake in the resources flowing from the government, this document nonetheless signified an emerging horizontal fissure in the hitherto dominant representations of Muslim identity.[20]

This strategy coincided with a broader tendency among ansaris in other parts of India where the Mandal report had initiated similar efforts toward redrafting the community's identity strategy in distinctly non-ashraf terms. The mass gathering of ansaris in Delhi on Independence Day in 1996, where demands to be included in the OBC formula were loudly and clearly voiced, is but the latest articulation of this new strategy of recognition (see Engineer 1996).

As the Samajwadis moved into Mumbai in 1994, this new strategy was indeed realized by means of a carefully planned alliance between the party leadership, who had long worked with local Muslim leaders in Uttar Pradesh, and a group of businessmen and local leaders among the Muslims in Mumbai. Some leaders of the Samajwadi Party in Mumbai are former Congress men and some are associated with the Muslim League; at the local level, however, the party has, with considerable success, generated its own network of local supporters and leaders, often among small businessmen and established brokers and dadas in the Muslim neighborhoods. Judging by the election campaign for the 1997 municipal elections, many of the candidates in places like Madanpura and Nagpada were ansaris who clearly used their community background when arguing that Muslims had to align with lower-caste Hindus in order to protect their community and, in doing so, to assess realistically the Muslims' situation rather than retain outdated "beliefs in our own superiority," as one candidate expressed it. In other words, the julaha-ansari identity had been recoded as a sign of difference and backwardness, enabling it to align with the broader "plebeian" identity strategies promoted by parties like the Samajwadi.

The general style and self-representation of the Samajwadi Party in Mumbai draws on ordinary plebeian language that achieves credibility by the reputation and masculinity of its local party leaders. Samajwadi leaders and activists stress the party's fearlessness, its cadres' willingness to confront Shiv Sena, the Congress, anyone. Clearly the party does not wish to be viewed merely as a "Muslim" party but seeks to carve out a public profile that will attract ordinary non-Brahman Hindus. As the Mumbai president told me: "We are a secular party. We will create a Hindu leader, a Maharashtrian Hindu, a Maratha, and under his leadership we will work. We are ready to confront the communal forces."

The Samajwadi Party was indeed successful in carving out a place for itself in Mumbai's 1997 municipal elections, winning a considerable number of seats in Muslim areas. In the 1998 general election, the party decided to make a pragmatic electoral alliance with the Congress Party in Maharashtra; as a result, the ruling Hindu nationalist coalition suffered a resounding defeat in several of Mumbai's central constituencies that Shiv Sena had come to regard as its home turf. This seemed to confirm that the Samajwadis' brash and masculine style could effectively counter Shiv Sena's confrontational and violent political style. This new configuration of political identities also challenges the dominant paternalistic discourses of Muslim identity in the city. This is not because the Samajwadis necessarily promote a more "progressive" or liberal form of Islam; on the contrary, they seem to espouse rather conservative notions of gender and honor. The novelty is that more plebeian, less "respectable," and less educated Muslims, often representing popular forms of Islam, now represent and speak for Muslims—not in their capacity as a cultural community but as ordinary and "small people" of the mohalla who have only themselves to trust.

THE BEAST IN THE BELLY: DADAS IN THE URBAN IMAGINARY

The term *super cop* was popularized in India during the protracted dirty war between Sikh militants and the Punjab police in the 1980s. The first holder of the title, Julio Ribeiro, devised the "bullet for bullet" strategy to exterminate the militants systematically. Since 1996 Gopinath Mundhe, BJP's home minister in Maharashtra, framed a similar policy toward the of Mumbai's underworld. On a TV show in March 1997 Mundhe announced: "The police now retaliate if gangsters open fire. Do or die is our motto." In the following months, newspapers regularly reported on how gangsters were "eliminated" almost daily, often in encounters set up and provoked by the police. Government-friendly papers had charts drawn up to show graphically the number of dead gangsters per year, with a pedagogical breakdown of their affiliation with the gangs of Dawood Ibrahim, Arun Gawli, Amar Naik, Chhota Rajan, and others. The chart represented the police as a faceless head with a cap, while the gangster was pictured as a man with a fancy hairstyle, sunglasses, a black shirt with a long collar, and a beard—normally the sign of a Muslim. Police officers noted with satisfaction that the "bullet for bullet" strategy worked and that even some of the gangs' so-called *super numberis* (number-two men) were killed.[21]

This "war against crime" received widespread endorsement among ordinary people, not least of all journalists, who were instrumental in producing the dominant and widely disseminated discourse on crime in Mumbai. The underworld was constructed as a known topography of highly organized gangs locked in deadly rivalry over territory and business opportunities. When one reviews the newspaper reports on crime and the underworld over the past decade or so in Mumbai, it is evident that the journalists' predominant source of information was police officers. Furthermore, rarely do the journalists question the authenticity of the police narratives nor that the independent investigations of journalists are mainly directed at communal conflicts where innocent people have been killed or wounded. Moreover, the treatment of criminals, especially "hardened criminals," by the police and the judicial system is of limited interest to organizations monitoring civil rights and governance in the city.[22]

Many journalists clearly accept the police narrative that if only the police had more resources, were subject to less political interference, and were governed by a more strong-willed judiciary, then the thin, khaki-clad line of professional and dedicated policemen would win the war on crime and restore order in the city. One journalist, Ketan Tanna, referred to the mafia gangs, with their international connections, as "NRI dons" backed by Pakistan, and likened them to terrorists. "Not many realize that encounter killings are the natural way of dispensing justice to hardened criminals who, if caught, invariably seek or jump bail. Most of these gangsters owe their allegiance to either Dawood or Gawli." To Tanna, this very allegiance, or the rumor thereof, meant that these criminals deserved to die.[23]

The Mumbai police obviously view this war on crime as part of a larger effort to create a new image of the police as an effective and citizen-friendly force. When the new police commissioner, Mendonca, assumed office in August 1997, he ordered the police to play a more active role in assisting ordinary citizens while continuing their hard line on criminals. "If we deal with gangsterism effectively, that itself will improve our image," Mendonca stated. He also assured the public that "the common man is not affected by the activities of these criminals"[24] and need not worry about safety. In this he echoed the chief of the Crime Branch, who, a few months earlier, had stated that "Mumbai is the safest city in the country, perhaps in the world."[25] Judging from my own experiences and many conversations with people in Mumbai over the years, the city is indeed not regarded as a dangerous place in terms of everyday occurrences. Few people hesitate to walk the streets or sit alone on a train in the evening, and their homes are not fortified with bars against a possible burglary.

Instead, people's sense of danger or, more precisely, their anxiety about the absence of safety, is of an intangible nature, relating more to the fundamental opacity and mystery of the multilayered life in the metropolis. In this respect, the problems of knowledge and policing in colonial Bombay discussed above have remarkably continued into contemporary Mumbai. Commissioner Mendonca expressed it concisely: "Security problems are unique in Mumbai because of the large floating population. Anonymity is the highest compared to any other city. . . . This has a direct bearing on the crime rate. Wherever anonymity is high, criminals are always very active."

To colonial police officers, the "hooligan" was the favored representation of this anonymous chaos, and in the postcolonial city the Muslim badmash assumed a similar role as a relatively tangible symbol of the frightening and fascinating chaos and anonymity, namely, the opacity around which the urban imaginary essentially is organized. More recently, it was the hard core of the Muslim badmash—the hardened criminal, the mafia don—who became the ambivalent, frightening, but also ultimate symptom of Bombay's urban modernity. In the figure of the gangster is condensed, and exaggerated, everything fascinating in urban existence: the effortless command over the complex urban landscape, hedonism, lavish consumption, a fascination with technology, flashy clothes, classy women, ruthlessness, individuality, and so on. All this makes the criminal deeply provocative, and at the same time the antithesis to family values, decency, and civic norms. In other words, the criminal is the perfect object to invoke in any discourse of order and discipline. The ubiquity of the underworld is therefore central to the claims of the police to be the defenders of society against chaos; it is posited as the chief obstacle to creating a rational city, the underlying cause of communal riots, the basis of corruption and dishonesty in the world of politics, and so on.

Space does not permit a fuller exploration of the discourse on crime in Mumbai, which, given its centrality to the topic at hand, surely merits a study of its own. But here I want briefly to sketch how the contemporary mythology of the mafia gangs—epitomized today in the figure of Dawood Ibrahim—came into being since the 1970s as a metonym of Bombay's Muslim world. I do not raise the question of "what really happened." I have no positive evidence of events or guilt—all I have are narratives, rumors, allegations, and stories. But, indeed, very little of what is known of the underworld in Mumbai has ever been based on positive evidence, court cases, convictions, and the like. When a gangster is killed in a confrontation, the police state that he was a "close aide" or "associate" of a certain gang. The allegations of police officers are readily accepted and reported by journalists as sufficient proof of the guilt of those killed or held by the police. Dozens of people perish at the hands of the police either in encounters or while in custody without any shred of evidence of their misdeeds. The powers accorded the police under such laws as the "Maharashtra Prevention of Dangerous Persons, Slumlords, and Bootleggers Act" (MPDA) or the "National Security Act" are indeed broad. I am not suggesting that such individuals are indeed innocent or that criminal networks do not exist in a multitude of forms. I am merely observing that what the press and the police term "notorious criminals" from their "charge sheets"—people who are rarely tried, much less convicted—and their sudden deaths are essential elements in the larger narrative that places crime, the evil of the gang world, corruption, and communal politics at the heart of Mumbai's urban modernity.

FROM SMUGGLERS TO *SUPARI* KILLERS: ON RUMORS AND NARRATIVE FRAMES

There has always been a wide range of activities in Indian cities that could be characterized as semi-legal or illegal. But the line between illegality and legality is anything but self-evident. As anyone familiar with the organization of social life in Mumbai's popular neighborhoods knows, local fixers and men of local eminence who broker contacts between ordinary people and authorities and who extend help of various sorts have always been essential in the networks of dependency, exploitation, and debt that organize life in the slums and chawls. These men are always paid in cash or kind, and they are able to arrange the protection of residents; others extort money on a regular basis. They are also money lenders, patrons of religious festivals, people who donate money to orphanages, education, and political parties, who settle local disputes, and so on. These local, eminent figures are deeply ambivalent. Both loathed and respected, they are sort of indispensable parasites within local moral parameters. Ubiquitous, informal, and impossible to fix within the boundaries of formal law, these men and their networks constitute elementary units of popular urban neighborhoods. They embody the opacity of urban life, and some of them, and some of their activities, also form units of "criminal rackets"—gangs of slumlords, bootleggers, extortionists, and smugglers.

Knowledge has always been the main obstruction to policing in Bombay, as we saw above. Exactly when the term *gang* became the dominant model through which police, officials, and the press tried to understand the hidden side of the city is unclear. However, in the 1970s, a complete terminology and set of narrative frames derived from the American gangster mythology became ever more popular in descriptions of Bombay's underworld. The gang world was divided into four distinct mafia syndicates, each defined by a specific territory and headed by a don whose life story, lifestyle, and personal qualities, spread both by rumor and intensive press coverage, became the "talk of the town."

The most flamboyant of these characters was Haji Mastaan, a former coolie in the Bombay docks, who, through the 1970s, had emerged as the king of contraband—cigarettes, cloth, electronic goods, gold, and so on. This hedonistic chain smoker with artistic and spiritual inclinations, or so the myth went, had never been convicted. In the late 1970s he declared that he was reformed, had beaten his drug addiction, and had gone into real estate and the financing of films, although indirectly. As he told a journalist: "[Financing] would mean taking interest and according to Islam that is *haraam*. I wouldn't do it."[26] He also initiated a social organization, "The All-India Milli Secretariat," involved in educational and social work, and he liked to pose as the gray eminence of the Bombay Muslims. He also turned to religion; in Urdu his name means "the most devoted pilgrim," and he styled himself as a kind of godfather, affectionately known as Baba, an arbiter of conflicts among the new, more aggressive breed of young hotheads emerging in the early 1980s.

Karim Lala, the don of Dongri, bore the myth of the violent and shrewd Pathan with distinction. Originally from the Northwestern Province of Pakistan, but a resident of Bombay since the early 1950s, Lala was known, by rumor and newspaper reports, to specialize in extortion, servicing debts (a "typical" Pathan job), *supari* (contract killing), and real estate. Arrested and charged with innumerable crimes since 1955, he has never been convicted. Portraying himself as an honest businessman with various economic interests, he is a keen follower of a spiritual leader among the Pathans, Khan Abdul Ghaffar Khan, also known as the "Gandhi of the Frontier," as well as a supporter of the Pathan struggle for autonomy in Pakistan. He is known as a staunch supporter of the Congress Party and has met with most of the national leaders, freely admitting that, as a private person, he has donated money to the party coffers. Throughout his career, Lala cleverly played on his status as an incarnation of evil in the Marathi and Gujarati press. Obviously enjoying the publicity, he ridiculed the police and his critics and portrayed himself as a dignified, pious, and respectable citizen in a series of interviews with the English-language press.[27]

The former associate of Haji Mastaan, Yusuf Patel, a Muslim from Gujarat, was known as a major builder and owner of real estate. Like the other dons, he also claimed to have reformed himself and become a god-fearing legitimate businessman. Not as charismatic as the others, Patel, in his own way, portrayed the stereotype of the enterprising Memon trader with extensive and closed networks of associates.

The fourth don, Vardharajan Mudaliar, was the unassuming Tamil king of Dharavi and the vast south Indian colonies in Matunga and Sion. Colloquially identified as Vardha, he was known to have made his money on the sale of illegal liquor, extortion, and smuggling. At the same time he was one of the most respected community leaders in his area, a major patron of temples, a keen supporter of non-Brahman political and cultural organizations, and the man whose advice, protection, and opinions were sought by thousands. His modest home was known as the preferred informal court for the settling of disputes and the resolution of conflicts, and for decades he was said to be in a position to make and unmake political careers. Vardha was the perfect prototype of a slumlord and gangster. Mani Ratnam's breakthrough film, *Nayakan* (Hero/star), released in 1987, explicitly depicted Vardha's life and career through the narrative prism of the Corleone saga.

In a way these dons incarnated all that respectable citizens of Bombay considered evil and dangerous—Muslims, slums, south Indian criminals. But it was also a somewhat familiar world where the evil forces were localized phenomena that did not affect everyday life. This changed in 1983–84, when bloody rivalries between various "gangs" led to a series of highly publicized execution-style murders in public places; Dawood Ibrahim's brother, Shabir, was one of the victims. The murders were avenged in a highly dramatic style by daring contract killings in broad daylight in the Bombay High Court in front of the judge and police officers. This drama provided material for a series of popular writings and semi-fictionalized accounts of the romantic and dangerous world of the mafia.[28] It also made the narrative frame of the mafia saga credible. An editorial in a leading newspaper read: "Unless something drastic is done, Bombay will soon begin to resemble Chicago of the thirties and forties."[29]

These murders started a new era of more professional gangsterism and the formation of new gangs armed with automatic weapons and cellular phones, as well as drug dealings linked to international cartels. The legend of Dawood as a new, more brutal, more powerful, more sophisticated type of underworld don was born, only to be nurtured by Dawood's move to Dubai in 1985. From there Dawood controlled his growing empire, ranging, the police claimed, from real estate to film, drugs, and gambling. The standard picture of Dawood henceforth became that of a don dressed in a flashy white playboy outfit, sporting sunglasses, on a boat or at the race track, always with a cellular phone in his hand. The quintessential gangster had become a part of the wealthy, high-tech NRI Indian who emerged in the 1980s as the symbol of both modernity and India's backwardness.

The period after the 1984 Bhiwandi riots also saw police officers, political leaders, and writers launch a powerful theory that communal riots were instigated by the (Muslim) mafia as a reaction against the actions of upright police officers or against the bright light of investigative journalism (!) so loathed by the dons. One reporter wrote:

> The communal riots that rocked Bombay . . . brought into the open for the first time the tremendous reach and influence that the mafia dons had acquired over the years. . . . The police crackdown on the underworld last year brought the dons together . . . and a meeting of the four dons took place in March to map out a strategy. What followed a couple of months later was the worst riots ever to rock Bombay.[30]

This became a popular theory that is heard today all over the city. The reasons for its popularity are obvious: It invokes a scenario of conspiracy, a summit of evil forces as the cause of riots; it conveniently excludes the hazy world of politics, removes the heavy hand of Hindu nationalist organizations in instigating the violence, and puts the blame squarely on the Muslim badmash; it exonerates the police force and thus produces a fantasy of the city as "almost normal" except for the "cancer" of the Muslim underworld that produces these unintelligible outburst of chaos and violence. Again, the "hardened criminal" is the somewhat empty signifier that makes the opacity of the urban landscape intelligible.

As we saw above, attributing full responsibility to Dawood for the 1992–93 riots, interfering with links to the Middle East and Pakistan through his residence in Dubai, and Shiv Sena's determination to link the riots and the 1993 bombings to a single conspiracy all fit into the theory of a causal link between the underworld and the (Muslim) instigation of riots. In an uncanny resemblance to the pattern established in 1984, it was alleged that the riots had occurred a week after the demolition of illegal buildings in central Bombay in late November 1992. Leaders of the Muslim League had allegedly instigated the destruction of these buildings precisely to arouse disturbances and resentment. According to this theory, the riots that followed the demolition of the Babri Masjid on 6 December 1992 were nothing but the response of Muslim underworld figures and communal politicians to the "clean-up" operation in Bhendi Bazaar by supposedly upright officers of the Municipal Corporation.

Despite its popularity among the Left and the Right, among intellectuals and journalists, this theory has never been substantiated. The particular incident was investigated by the Srikrishna Commission in March 1994,[31] but no causal links between this and the ensuing riots were found and Srikrishna made no mention of this in his report on the riots.

According to the local legend told in his native mohalla, Dawood Ibrahim's career started in the 1970s when he and some other boys stole two bales of gabardine cloth from Haji Mastaan's storehouse and sold them. Later they formed their own gang, called "The Young Party," and fought minor battles with other local gangs. As the legend goes, Dawood became leader of the gang when he killed a man in a row over a girl. This was also when Haji Mastaan discovered his "talents," after which Dawood worked for him for many years. However, the violent events in 1983 and the "gang war" following it marked the point when he broke away from "Mastaanbhai," who spoke out against the killings, and came into his own. Now he emerged as a more modern type of gangster, who abandoned old conventions of pride and restraint and entered the international scene, becoming more cynical and ruthless, expanding his scale and ambitions.

Dawood's story paralleled the rapid changes in Bombay at the time, its booming real estate market and its entry into the larger markets of the world. His story also corresponded to the progression of the Corleone saga—the change from the older, straightforward, more dignified ways of the "family" to the more brutal, businesslike, and less principled ways of the younger generation. Dawood was not merely a smuggler, like "Mastaanbhai"; he was the shadow leader of the "D-company," as he and his networks became known. In a sensational interview with a journalist in 1988, Dawood portrayed himself as an unhappy man who took "the path of revenge" against his brother's killers because of his own sentimentality (*jazbati*), and thus he had to flee Bombay.[32] He saw himself as a businessman, but admitted his guilt for avenging his brothers death. "Whatever has happened was done by God," he said. During the interview, he lived up to his status by spouting semi-philosophical statements about his personal beliefs: "I am a student looking for the secret of survival in this world. I hold the belief that life should be lived with pride and dignity and that it should not be a life of servitude but one of freedom. . . . I am a human being. I don't want to be so sweet that people swallow me completely."[33]

Dawood's networks and reputation in Bombay grew wildly in the 1980s, as did the stories of his deeds and whereabouts. Dawood's sophistication became almost an object of pride and admiration in newspaper articles about him, proof that Bombay was not only India's primary city but that it was also home to India's most advanced underworld. He, or his various companies, owned many buildings in central Bombay, among them his own former home in Bohri mohalla. Rumor had it that the home was lavishly decorated, but no one had actually been inside.

Since the late 1980s, Dawood and his supposed wars with former friends like Chhota Rajan or rivals like Arun Gawli—once a friend of the Thackerays whom Bal Thackeray referred to as "our Hindu gangster," have been at center stage in Mumbai's underworld. The structure of four major syndicates, each headed by a don, comprised of people who once were friends but now compete and occasionally cooperate remains essentially as it was in the era of Haji Mastaan—hardly surprising considering that the source of all rumors and narratives about the underworld remains the city's police officers.

The main difference is one of scale. That Chhota Rajan is said to operate from Malaysia, and Dawood from Dubai, Karachi, and elsewhere, has added a more menacing aura to the underworld. No longer is Dawood merely a young dada from central Bombay. A former college friend of Dawood put it succinctly when he said to me in 1997: "Today Dawood is not a man, he is a concept; you can attribute anything to his name and people will believe you. . . . Before 1993, anybody here would love to be seen as a friend of the D-company; today people don't take his name in the mouth. They don't dare to do that anymore." This schoolmate found it strange that Dawood had become a gangster. "He was never a leader. He was quite arrogant you can say. A bit *jhagdalu* [one who fights often] and possessive. But definitely not a leader. . . . I think Dawood is a creation, not a person."

Little evidence exists of Dawood's activities; even his role in the bombings is shrouded in mystery because most of the information is classified and is within the realm of central intelligence gathering at a national level. It is widely assumed that he works closely with ISI, the independent Pakistani Intelligence Service, but little information exists in this regard, except for statements from police officers and the Home Ministry. Since the BJP took office in New Delhi in 1998, Home Minister Advani has stepped up the rhetoric against Pakistan, calling it a "terrorist state." In 1998 a report from the Home Ministry estimated that ISI had been responsible for the deaths of no fewer than thirty thousand Indians since 1988, and, moreover, that the intelligence service operates a network of as many as nineteen thousand agents throughout India. As one senior bureaucrat of the ministry stated: "There are few crimes or plots unearthed in India where either Dawood or the ISI do not have a role to play."[34]

Apparently Dawood, who for years served Shiv Sena and the government and police force of Maharashtra so well as a universal force of evil, has now become nothing less than a national menace, a security threat more damaging than many a neighboring state. The boy from central Bombay has indeed made it big.

CHAPTER 7

Living the Dream: Governance, Graft, and Goons

*"Shivsainik is like a burning torch. He shall burn
the evil and he shall also show the path of life
to those who are struggling in darkness."
(Slogan at the Shivsena Rajyapramukh Parishad,
18–19 November 1995)*

I HAD CALLED the secretary in advance, and he had assured me that the minister indeed remembered me and looked forward to meeting me again. We had met three years earlier in his office and later in a shakha in the town of Kalyan north of Mumbai. At that time Shabir Sheikh was MLA for Shiv Sena and still active in the trade union Bharatiya Kamgar Sena. Now, in November 1996, he was minister of labor in the Shiv Sena/ BJP government. When I entered his newly decorated office in the Mantralaya building in Mumbai, many others were there as well. They were sitting in five rows—well-dressed union representatives, elderly men holding half-torn brown envelopes, some with rugged faces looking as though they had stepped right out of a small village—all facing a huge desk. On the desk were five telephones—one massive in size, old-fashioned, and shining in imitation gold, the others made of plastic. Above the desk hung a photograph of Thackeray, staring down at all of us. The photograph was huge, at least five feet by eight feet, so none of us could avoid his gaze, at the same time demanding, arrogant, and somewhat bored. Below was a quotation by Thackeray: "We are Hindustanis and therefore Hindus. That is the belief of our party. We love Hindustan more than ourselves."

The minister was receiving people in the side office. An elderly peon, a skinny man in a blue safari outfit, was guarding the door, discretely entering visitors' names on a list, whispering that the minister would be free before long. He was the man in charge; he knew the etiquette, the routines, the workings of the huge building, and we all depended on him.

But he was not happy with the situation and was sending disapproving glances toward the big desk in front of us, where four young men in expensive new clothes were sitting, standing, almost lying across the desk, fighting joyfully over the phones that did not stop ringing. They joked and laughed loudly, making coy remarks on the phone, talking about who they should call and occasionally, rudely, asking the elderly peon for local numbers in the building. He mumbled the numbers in a low voice, embarrassed in front of the waiting crowd. Apparently they were calling friends elsewhere in the building, and obviously took pleasure in humiliating the peon. They were enjoying their sense of importance, their playful performance, that they were in control, sitting on top of the big table in front of the many people who all sat silently, watching them. I thought I recognized one of them from the shakha in Kalyan, and I nodded and smiled at him. He looked at me and directed the peon to go talk to me. "Oh, I just wanted to ask if these boys are from Kalyan like the minister," I told the peon. "I don't know, Sir, all I know is that they are sainiks," he said. "Do they work here?" I asked him. He shrugged. "They are with Mr. Sheikh, that is all I can tell you," he replied, and walked back to his desk at the door.

I finally had a brief conversation with the busy minister. Yes, he was proud that the Senapati had appointed him minister. It proved that the Sena was not anti-Muslim, only against "antinational" Muslims. He considered himself a staunch nationalist. "I am an Indian first, a Maharashtrian next, and then a Muslim," he said. Sheikh had little to say about specific policy measures or strategies in his field, except reducing the use of casual labor and creating more regular jobs, always a Sena agenda. He gave vague and evasive answers to my questions about the role of unions in restructuring public-sector undertakings, the retrenchment in the textile industry, and other burning issues. All he worked for was to bring more jobs to Maharashtra, he said, and it was unimportant whether the investors were foreign or Indian. "But we still believe that Maharashtrians should have their fair share of the good jobs. This is our state, our city, why should we not enjoy?" as he put it.

As I left the office, it struck me that this question "Why should we not enjoy?" and the sight of the young sainiks displaying their right to roam the offices and corridors of Mantralaye, the symbol of government in Maharashtra, touched something central to what Shiv Sena was all about. Shiv Sena does not harbor any project of social transformation, of creating a different society, even less of fashioning the "new man," the disciplined *bharatiya* citizen that RSS and the wider Hindu nationalist movement try to produce through organization and ideological training.

Rather, Shiv Sena's program has been and remains centered around creating a certain public attitude among Maharashtrians and Hindus in general: an attitude of assertiveness and self-confidence toward authority and toward forces perceived as "antinational." "Shivsena aims at moulding the youth into a formidable force for fighting evil," reads one official party goal.[1] At the same time, the party is driven by a powerful quest for recognition of the social and cultural world of the Marathi manus, the ordinary Maharashtrian, and to secure jobs in government and the more organized labor market. Whereas the former is seen as the performative dimension of the Sena, the latter is often regarded as the party's more important driving force. My argument throughout these pages has been that politics played out as public performance in the streets and neighborhoods of Maharashtra was always at the heart of Shiv Sena. As the party gained power and triumphed, it also experienced a "loss of the loss," namely, the loss of its claim of being marginalized and shut out from the establishment that, for decades, had been so essential to the movement. Losing this claim rendered the Sena even more dependent on its continued capacity for public performance.

My experience in Sheikh's office epitomized the realization of both the party's dream of assertiveness and of recognition. Both Sheikh and the sainiks did exactly what they and the ordinary people they claimed to represent could not have dreamed of doing a few years earlier: to be at the center of power, to be recognized as influential, people to whom even polished bureaucrats, with their refined manners and language, had to show respect.

But probably the more significant part of this incident in Sheikh's office was the young men's idleness and playfulness, their less than respectful attitude toward the many people waiting to see the minister. Although the sainiks had arrived at the seat of power, had achieved the public recognition they so desired, they actually did not know what to do with it, except simply enjoy it, live the dream. But as we saw in the preceding chapters, the dreams and desires Shiv Sena tapped into so effectively were deeply split between the wish to achieve respectability and social recognition and the yearning to rebel against convention, to become manly, assertive, bold, self-respecting—in other words, to achieve the state of mind of the ideal sainik.

Shiv Sena had assumed political power in Maharashtra in March 1995 based on the party's rapid growth throughout the state in the preceding years and its successful campaign against the ineffectual performance and corrupt practices of the ruling Congress Party. Shiv Sena's program, however, was as vague as always, offering voters few concrete promises. Predictably the easier course was to carry out the more cosmetic, symbolic elements of its program, such as changing the name of Bombay to Mumbai, rounding up alleged Bangladeshi illegal migrants, and introducing military schools (sainik schools) in every district in the state. Far more difficult was carrying out the larger schemes, such as a slum redevelopment program in Mumbai, the *zhunkar-bhankar* program for the poor that promised "a meal-a rupee-a-day," or curbing the power of the cooperative sector in the countryside.[2] However, the lack of a larger vision as well as the difficulties in initiating and implementing structural reforms are not unique to the Shiv Sena/BJP cabinet in Maharashtra. What is unique is that Shiv Sena could not possibly have had a larger vision nor developed a more consistent policy because of the specific style in which Bal Thackeray exercised control over the party.

Thackeray chose to remain outside any formal power structure in order to retain a position from where he could enunciate all the gestures of opposition—to government policies, to the judicial system, and, more broadly, to the "establishment"—a strategy that remains vital to the continued production and reproduction of sainiks. After the Sena had been in power for only a brief period, it became clear that the party's two motivating forces, respectability and self-respect, were not necessarily compatible, each referring to rather different symbolic registers and requiring often conflicting commands to the sainiks. Manohar Joshi, as chief minister, became the ultimate symbol of Shiv Sena's quest for respectability and the ascendancy of its leadership into Mumbai's parvenu elite. Thackeray strove to remain a law onto himself so as to retain his enormous authority in the party structure and his hold on the imagination of millions of people in the state. He remained the producer, the authorizer, and the incarnation of the somewhat obstinate sainik style of defying authority. I argue that Thackeray's much maligned, and much discussed, "remote control" of Shiv Sena lies at the heart of the somewhat ambivalent bias that makes the Sena and the identity as a sainik so attractive.

WHAT DO YOU SEE IN ME?

How might one explain the continued efficacy of Thackeray's openly irresponsible leadership, the longing among the many followers and admirers in Mumbai for his unrelenting commands, the enjoyment of his idiosyncratic utterances? Let us turn to Hegel's classical reflections on the relationship between master and slave.

In Alexander Kojéve's reading of Hegel's master-slave dialectic, he emphasizes that what the slave admires is "the desire of the desire of the other," that is, the master's recognition (*annerkennung*) of the slave's humanity, and thus his desirability. The slave asks the master, "See me for who I am," and thus constitutes his own identity through this confrontation with the other. In Kojéve's dramatic and teleological reading, slaves, that is, ordinary human beings, move history and are the truly creative figures by means of their tremendous drive toward recognition and freedom. The masters, that is, the elites, the aristocracy, for their part, are doomed, as they have nothing to strive for; the recognition they crave, though easily achieved, is worthless, because it is given by slaves and thus only reproduces the master as he already is (Kojéve 1969, 45–55).

As Lacan has pointed out, this compelling logic of identity is destined to be incomplete. The subject in the encounter is born to desire the other, and thus its identity depends on the character of this desire, that is, the gaze of the other, understood here, in Lacanian terms, as the symbolic order: authorities, dominant discourses, social conventions, and so on. This gaze, namely, the other's desire, cannot be fully understood, and therefore the subject is bound to be one of radical uncertainty. Zizek argues that this uncertainty, which defines the subject, suspends it between anxiety and desire. "Anxiety is aroused by the desire of the Other in the sense that 'I do not know what *objét a*[3] I am for the desire of the other.' What does the Other want from me, what is there—in me more than myself—on account of which I am the object of desire of the Other?" (Zizek 1993, 71). What is posed to the other is therefore not "see me for what I am" (because I cannot know) but rather the probing and anxious question, *ché vuoi?* "What do you see in me?"

Subjectivity is bound to take shape in this gaze, or desire, that cannot be fully understood, and the answer to this dilemma is what Zizek terms "anticipatory identification"—that we become what we think we are in the eyes of the other. Instead of waiting anxiously for a symbolic mandate to arrive, to be hailed and thus become the subject, as Althusser [1984] would have had it, human beings often anticipate the signs by which the other knows, and desires, them: "Anticipatory identification is therefore a kind of preemptive strike, an attempt to provide in advance an answer to 'what I am for the Other' and thus to assuage the anxiety that pertains to the desire of the Other" (Zizek 1993, 76).

The Shiv sainiks are indeed haunted by the anxiety of fathoming what respectable society, the "establishment," sees in them—ordinary men from a social world stained by the slums, the zopadpattis. Does society view them with contempt, respect, or fear? The sainik's self-image is bound to be split: on the one hand, respectable society expects him to behave in accordance with acceptable rules and conventions now that he is part of the establishment; on the other hand, Thackeray, the Senapati, does not require conformity with such norms and conventions, commanding instead that sainiks be self-respecting, assertive, and at the same time unconditionally obedient to his leadership. Thackeray, by his example and rhetoric, affords them their self-respect and courage. In other words, the sainik is subject to two opposing gazes, two different symbolic registers, two distinct "anticipatory identifications": one is to be respectable, to indulge in the enjoyment (*maza*) of one's newfound status, to play by the rules; the other is to remain angry, to display courage (*sahas*) and manliness, to be the opposition.

But the latter is a precondition of the former. Sainiks have arrived in power and command respect precisely because of their aggressive attitude and forthrightness, namely, their plebeian dada style. Thus they display their loyalty to Thackeray by anticipating and delivering what he expects of them. As the shakha pramukh in Thane stated, "Without the Shiv Sena I am nobody."

Thackeray is the demanding father who expects loyalty and submission, who rules through the anxiety his gaze and presence instills in sainiks, especially the intermediate leaders who constantly doubt themselves, wondering what he sees in them. Yet by asserting his independence, his capacity for violence through the loyalty of his sainiks, he offers a sense of freedom, of recognition, within the more established institutions. The anticipatory identification of sainiks—in Sheikh's office, in the streets, and elsewhere—is exactly to act as plebeians in the eyes of "the establishment" and thus to fulfill the role they have been assigned. Because of their association with Shiv Sena, they can self-consciously and with self-respect, and even with a measure of enjoyment of their own "nuisance value," bear the stain of the zopadpatti—the unpredictable and indelible threat of violence that defines them. This ugly stain of violence is also what makes the Shiv Sena so desirable and fascinating to the respectable middle class, a sign of the "unrepresentable" Real around which the sainik anticipates his identity regardless of whether he actually lived in a slum or ever even carried out a violent act.

On the surface Shiv Sena promises freedom, enjoyment, and self-respect to the ordinary Maharashtrian. Thackeray draws liberally on the non-Brahman tradition of Phule, or the left populism of Comrade Dange, when he ridicules the pompousness of the Brahman cultural establishment and "high society." The celebration of action, youth, the future, modernity, and strength promises a break with the conventions of the older generation, the political establishment, and the rural tradition. Through his oratory and style, Thackeray celebrates urban modernity, Mumbai's modernity, and promises young men that to be a sainik is to become a modern urban subject: the impatient, mobile young man who has no time for pretentious leaders, lazy bureaucrats, self-important intellectuals. A sainik is, and will always remain, wild at heart. Thackeray styles himself as the perfect example of someone who is feared and respected because of his mettle.

The sainik's sense of freedom and self-respect is illusory, however. His confidence is tenuous, attained only through submission to the paternal and unpredictable law of Thackeray. The sainiks' rebelliousness never subverted moral and social conventions. Thackeray remains, in many ways, the traditional master commanding total and abiding loyalty. Shiv Sena does not want to transform society. Sainiks and their leaders merely want to muscle their way into respectable society through violence or just the threat of aggression. The truth of Thackeray's power is not that he is respected because of his fortitude, inventiveness, or personal courage, but because he has many thousands of loyal followers and an assumed capacity to create havoc in the city. He has repeatedly demonstrated his will actually to let his sainiks loose on what he regards as enemies of the Marathi manus, and more recently against intellectuals, newspapers, and writers. Except for the confrontation in 1969 over the Belgaum issue, however, the Sena has never confronted the state or established centers of power. The violence of sainiks is anticipatory identification—attempts to become real sainiks, ablaze like an inferno, by fighting. The brutality of sainiks does not grow out of desperation or poverty; it is nourished by Thackeray's command to let go of restrictions and social conventions, to act out frustrations and desires without bounds. In *The Moor's Last Sigh*, Rushdie captures the attraction of this violent milieu when the Moor, while beating up the workers in the textile district on behalf of Mainduck, reflects: "We crave permission to openly become our secret selves. . . . I found for the first time in my short-long life, the feeling of normality, of being nothing special, the sense of being among kindred spirits, among people-like-me, that is the defining quality of home" (Rushdie 1995, 305).

When Shiv Sena came into power in 1995, the threat of violence had to be tamed, and the two desires driving sainiks and the Sena, respectability and self-respect, had to be reconfigured. Here, I wish to consider briefly the two faces of Shiv Sena as played out during the party's tenure in the state government. First I examine the construction of Thackeray as both a mystical and admired figure, the most powerful man in Mumbai, and then analyze some of the more significant policies of the Shiv Sena/BJP cabinet. I conclude with a discussion of the fragmentation of sovereignty and state power in Mumbai during Shiv Sena's tenure.

"THE I OF THE STORM"

Six months after assuming power in Maharashtra, Shiv Sena held a large convention, Shivsena Rajyapramukh Parishad, in Mumbai for leaders at many levels of the party organization and associated wings. The aim was clearly to streamline the organization and the party's profile in the face of the many new tasks involved in ruling the state. Shiv Sena has never published elaborate manifestos or programs, and even its election proposals have generally been brief, built around a handful of simple demands. But before the convention a pamphlet was issued in which the aims and outlook of the party were outlined for the first time in many years.[4] Throughout this brief document runs Shiv Sena's central and ambivalent command: Make your own law in order to obey the Law, that is, the lofty commands of the community of Maharashtrians and the nation, Hindusthan, as enunciated by Thackeray.

The pamphlet begins by stating, "Shri. Balasaheb Thackeray is our only hope." It claims that Shiv Sena "was founded for achieving Social Moksha. Shiv Sena strives for the good of the entire society." It states further that "Yesterday was of the older generation but 'Tomorrow' welcomes you; it belongs to you." Considering that the meaning of Shiv Sena lies in action and violent performance, it is not surprising that the section in the pamphlet on aims and objectives is literally devoid of any concrete content. The only specific demand is that young people are taught Marathi, Hindi, and English—which is already the case for most middle-class children in Mumbai and urban Maharashtra. As in the 1960s, Shiv Sena denounces *rajkaaran*, and "believes more in social activities than in active politics." Its emphasis is on developing "a strong, upright, and cultured youth aware of responsibilities and duties," and "willing to do any sacrifice to the Motherland." The tasks of the youth are not specified; it is merely emphasized how important it is to "remove depression" and "to blow confidence" in the youth. The program exhorts sainiks "to abide by laws that protect national interests" but not necessarily to abide by the law per se. It is more important to "fight corruption, mal-administration and red-tapism."

In the first years of tenure of the Shiv Sena-led cabinet, Thackeray, on several occasions, demonstrated his determination to act as a law onto himself outside the governmental structure. Although previously Thackeray's contempt for democracy and his preference for dictatorship (*tokshahi*) had been of little consequence, it now interfered in the affairs of government and frequently put Shiv Sena ministers and MLAs in an embarrassing and difficult position of having to serve two masters. Thackeray intervened in the highly controversial Enron case and forced his own chief minister and the entire cabinet to work out a compromise with the American power company.[5] As we saw above, Thackeray has often shown his disrespect for the judicial system. Whereas most other political leaders testified before the Srikrishna Commission, Thackeray displayed only contempt; he made sure that the government withdrew or classified twenty-four cases pending against him for using his writings and rhetoric to incite violence; he offended several judges; and he refused to appear before a Magistrate's Court in Mumbai in 1996 regarding an attack on the offices of Mahanagar, whose editor, Nikhil Wagle, had consistently opposed the Sena for more than a decade. Further, he has often publicly denounced his own ministers and has made highly offensive statements about BJP leaders, social activists, and anyone who criticized the unprecedented amassing of wealth by the entire Thackeray family.

All this Thackeray has done with impunity and without remorse, fully aware of his unique position as father figure and master to many thousands of young sainiks and sympathizers, whose affection for him seems only to grow with every rule and convention he violates. Thackeray's wit, his obvious irresponsibility, and the sheer violence of his rhetoric has placed him in a position to do whatever he wants. Although he grants only illusory freedom to "his boys," they are able to experience the freedom, arrogance, and fearful fascination of the Sena by following Thackeray's celebrity status and the awe he inspires among large sections of the middle class. Thackeray has wisely exploited fully the new, more brutal, and less convoluted rhetorical style that dominates Indian politics and public debates in the 1990s. With his powerful, unrestrained style, his lack of any bourgeois pretension, Thackeray has acquired a larger audience than ever before.

Nowhere was this brought out more clearly than in the eight-page feature item celebrating Thackeray's seventieth birthday, sponsored by a string of major companies and published by respectable mainstream newspapers like *Times of India* and *Economic Times*. The feature, clearly targeted toward an educated, middle-class readership, was entitled "The I of the Storm" and included an illustration across the upper part of the page of Thackeray in a silk kurta below a drawing of the seventeenth-century fortress that is the Sena's urban signature.

In the interview, Thackeray said that he "will fight to the end" against his critics and opponents, but, as always, he remained vague when it came to any larger goals. He spoke at length about the need for "a strong regime in India" and that "this city cannot be kept clean by putting up posters. Nothing happens till you crack the whip." He predicted a civil war and stated his credo: "Life is harsh. Each to himself, that is the way it is. War alone and not national integration will bring Indians together." He hoped that the army would feel compelled by a sense of duty to take over the rule of the land. He openly criticized his own government for its lack of dynamism, for not making quick decisions, for letting itself be slowed down by compromise and consultations. "Take the decision—I don't like feet-dragging. I am with you. I will face the consequences. What more do you want?" he stated, clearly addressing Chief Minister Manohar Joshi, essentially asking, since his master supports him, why is he so afraid?

Elsewhere in the interview Thackeray states that because he is not in a formal position of power he does not feel restrained in terms of what he can say or who he can attack. His prerogative of irresponsibility, both in rhetoric and actions, which is the source of his power, was evident when he stated: "My strategy is simple. I will finish off those who are out to finish me. I don't care if we lose power. Restraint or propriety is a good quality, in small doses though. Remember, I belong to the Thackeray clan. My father has taught me to fight injustice. I will do just that."

The feature item carried many of Thackeray's best cartoons over the years, as well as articles by friends, colleagues, and his son, Udhav, being groomed to take over ultimately for his father. The obvious intention was to portray Thackeray as a great personality, a serious journalist, and an artist. One section showed a series of pictures of Thackeray, "in the company of fellow artistes." Portrayed as if paying tribute to his art, India's most famous singers and artists are shown with Thackeray. Under a picture of Thackeray with Amitabh Bachchan, arguably the biggest superstar ever of Hindi cinema, the text ran, "Stalwarts from their respective fields."

In a tribute to Thackeray, Chief Minister Joshi wrote that he has no problem with Thackeray's shadow leadership of the government. With uncanny precision, Joshi described how, over thirty years, he has been guided in the Sena by the seemingly perpetual force of anticipating Thackeray's wishes: "Some of Balasaheb's views are very firm and most be treated with utmost respect. I have now developed a gut feeling about Balasaheb's precise expectations, and that guides my actions." He went on to praise Thackeray's openness regarding his desire to control the government and found it fair considering that Thackeray was the one who made the conquest of power possible. With almost touching sincerity, Joshi admitted that he was no match for Thackeray, the master: "I have never seen a public speaker who starts addressing the audience as 'My Hindu brothers and sisters and mothers' and is greeted with thunderous applause. It is a great sight to watch. I have tried it out, but the response was simply not the same." Joshi admitted that, like all the others in the Sena, he depended profoundly on Thackeray's favors. Praising Thackeray for removing caste as a factor in the Sena, Joshi conceded that only because of Thackeray could he, a Brahman, become chief minister in a state where caste plays such an important role in politics and public life.

Over many years the aura of the Thackeray family has been developed methodically by frequent reports on the family's activities, its inner affairs, as well as by rumors that flow quite freely. Thackeray has been grooming his soft-spoken son, Udhav, to be a second-rung leader, along with his nephew, Raj Thackeray, who uncannily is the mirror image of his uncle, in looks, style, and manners, and currently heads the newspaper *Saamna*, as well as the student organization BVS.

Thackeray remains indispensable, however, and his face, his statements, and his speeches still constitute the party's main assets in election campaigns. Most of the newspaper ads Shiv Sena used in the 1997 elections for the Brihanmumbai Municipal Corporation featured a large picture of Thackeray, hands lifted, eyes staring insistently, as though making every effort to get a point across. The campaign was successful, and Shiv Sena secured a major victory in the elections on the promise of cleaning up and beautifying the city. The main reason for its success according to post-poll analyses, however, was that a large share of the non–Marathi-speaking voters in the more affluent western suburbs also voted for the Sena.[6]

Thackeray's remote control and the dual leadership structure of the Shiv Sena almost collapsed in March 1998 when the results of the general election were declared. The Shiv Sena-BJP alliance clearly had performed badly, and had lost votes and seats in Maharashtra to Congress. Thackeray was furious and blamed the chief minister and other top Sena leaders for being ineffectual and soft on Sena's adversaries. He announced that he would resign, "step aside for some time, but remain a watchdog." He was unhappy with the government's performance, he told the press, and said that, "Mr. Joshi has to be careful." In an uncanny repetition of the resignation drama staged by Thackeray in 1992 (see chapter 3), thousands of ordinary sainiks gathered outside Thackeray's residence begging him to stay. "We want Shri Thackeray, not power," the slogan went. The assembled sainiks shouted abuses at the many Sena leaders who arrived, and some shakha pramukhs and councilors were physically assaulted, "to punish them," the sainiks said, "for their nonperformance, which had caused the Senapati such pain and anger." Thackeray once again affirmed his position by demonstrating that he was indispensable to the party and the intermediate leaders. Joshi retained his post as chief minister by once more submitting to Thackeray's will, stating that "Balasaheb is like a father to me."[7] Their relationship was damaged, however, and later, in 1998, Joshi was forced to resign his post to a new, less experienced but apparently more loyal leader, Narendra Rane.

Rane seemed to be all that Joshi was not. Joshi was an accomplished, affable communicator, an urban and polished Brahman, and a respectable member of the new business elite in Maharashtra; in brief, he represented Sena's respectable face. He was on good terms with most leading figures in the political and economic elite, a suave and smooth operator, and therefore not entirely dependent on Thackeray's goodwill. Rane, on the other hand, was a Maratha from the Konkan region, Sena's old stronghold, who, with a secondary school background, had found a clerical job in the state government in Bombay. He had been a loyal sainik for thirty years and had slowly risen in the ranks by hard work, loyalty, and a talent for administration. He owed his success to his loyalty to the Thackeray family, as well as to the fact that he, unlike Joshi, was a real sainik. He had been a part of street politics in his hometown as well as in Bombay for many years, and there was a charge against him for being involved in the murder of a Congress leader in his hometown. Although Rane had been cleared of the charge, the accusation in itself testified to his having been involved in the "real thing"—street violence for the sake of defending and expanding Shiv Sena's turf at the local level. Thackeray's choice of Rane, the "real face of the Shiv Sena," as one journalist put it,[8] was undoubtedly a gesture of affirmation toward the rank-and-file sainik. Drawing in a former street fighter to occupy the chief minister's chair also signaled an end to moderation and well-behaved mainstream politics. It seemed that Thackeray wanted to return to a more confrontational strategy in order to sharpen the profile of Shiv Sena, which, on many policy issues, was almost indistinguishable from its alliance partner, the BJP.

WHY CAN'T MUMBAI BE BEAUTIFUL?

Before the 1997 election for the Brihan Mumbai Municipal Corporation, many newspaper ads featured Thackeray's insistent gaze, his questions to the readers: "Why can't Mumbai be beautiful? Why can't the plague, malaria, and polio be stamped out forever?" Many ads concerned the Sena's achievements in improving the city's infrastructure, and others repeated the old Sena slogan, "Clean Mumbai, Green Mumbai." According to the Shiv Sena, Mumbai was plagued by pollution, both physical and cultural pollution. The first was caused by an inadequate infrastructure and the constant influx of new migrants, and the second by "antinational" elements, foreign cultures (Western and Muslim), and "degenerate" works of art emerging from the leftist and liberal milieus in Maharashtra that never recognized Shiv Sena or Thackeray and were intensely resented by the Sena leadership.

It is noteworthy, however, that elements of the leftist opinion in Maharashtra is deeply rooted in the cultural populism of Samyukta Maharashtra Samiti and thus harbors certain ambivalence toward Mumbai as a cultural site. To many Marathi-speaking intellectuals, the cultural essence of Maharashtra is located in the countryside, and they criticize Shiv Sena for its "Mumbai-centrism." As late as 1997, in the municipal elections of that year, left-leaning leaders of the Janata Dal recirculated a new version of an old rumor in Maharashtrian politics: that Shiv Sena had a secret plan to turn Mumbai into a new Hong Kong and make it a separate state, as in the case of Delhi.[9] This time around, however, the rumor did not greatly affect the voters.

The diagnosis of the excesses and pressures of urban living are by no means the Sena's invention. It represents a widespread sentiment in the city, reflected in frequent violent outbursts of anger and desperation when the overcrowded suburban trains break down or when buses and cars are caught in massive traffic jams. The public is generally supportive when municipal authorities occasionally carry out heavy-handed demolition drives against "unauthorized structures" (not least in the Muslim parts of the city) or new slums. So, too, is there general approval of the systematic killing of gangsters, or supposed gangsters, by the police in deadly "encounters."

In 1986 members of the Lion's Club published a book entitled *Bombay 2000 A.D.*, which was prefaced by a quotation from Hegel: "Only the modern city offers the mind the grounds on which it can achieve awareness of itself." In the foreword, Chhagan Bhujbal, then Shiv Sena mayor, promised to work for a "clean Marathi Mumbai," which included clean footpaths and green space.

One of the book's contributors, Prem Vohra, a businessman, states: "Let us first admit and realize that these slum dwellers are as much human beings and Indians as those of us who stay in blocks and apartments." He asks: "Should they be forcibly driven out of Bombay . . . and deported to a 'no-mans land' below the Himalayas?"

Although Vohra seems to reject such draconian measures, the rest of his text belies his apparently civilized attitude, as he paints a picture of the ultimate urban nightmare of the respectable middle class:

> By the year 2000, 50% of Bombay's population will be slum dwellers. They will be cooking in the open, urinating, defecating and even procreating in the open! Filth, stench, dirt and human excreta right at your doorstep will be the order of the day. . . . There will be hundreds of slum dweller's own private armies, and paramilitary groups to protect their huts from demolition.

Even worse, Vohra foresees that the slum dwellers will use the judicial system to protect themselves: "There will be hundreds of court cases, from the small court up to the Supreme court—multiplying election after election." Vohra proposes that a special task force of administrators and policemen be set up to "remove and eradicate the existing slums," and he proposes that NGOs, apparently belonging to civilized society, are given police powers (Vohra 1986, 241).

This resonates all too well with the official discourse a decade earlier, during the Emergency period. Indira Gandhi stated in August 1975: "We must restore the pride in everything Indian. We have to clean up the country. If your house is dirty, you just don't leave it like that. You clean it up with a duster and a broom."[10] The broom was obviously to be the Congress Youth, whose members were given identification cards and invested with police powers in order to enforce the Maintenance of Internal Security Act (MISA), which Mrs. Gandhi saw as a primary weapon against "adulteration, corruption and fascist forces" aimed at creating a special Indian type of "participative discipline."[11]

In Bombay, this license given to the police force and Congress Youth to remove everything that could be seen as abnormal, annoying, or polluting led to a halt on all new construction, slum clearances, and rather absurd attempts to police bus queues, making it a punishable offense to step out of line while waiting for the bus.[12] The heavily censored newspapers celebrated the new discipline, and a long article in *Times of India*, entitled "Taming the Bombay Babu," reported in great detail how new disciplinary measures were now implemented in the municipal administration. In an almost textbook engineering of panoptic surveillance, superior officers were now placed in elevated, centrally located offices with glass walls, enabling them "to keep an eye on the Class III and Class IV staff," the lower-ranking bureaucrats who presumably were more prone to laziness than their superiors.[13]

Shiv Sena's leadership, the lone supporter of Mrs. Gandhi's policies, had, since the 1970s, supported and encouraged these visions of cleaning up Bombay and turning it into a modern, elegant, bourgeois city. The party had done little during its seven years of dominating the municipal administration, but in the 1995 election campaign for the State Legislative Assembly, promises of ridding Bombay of its overcrowdedness and renewing the city were high on Shiv Sena's otherwise rather vague program.

Immediately after the new cabinet was sworn in, a host of fanciful projects were suggested by Shiv Sena leaders, who enthusiastically flirted with the idea of making Bombay the center of a new "Asian Tiger," with Gujarat and Maharashtra as "special economic zones." In spite of BJP's skepticism regarding Shiv Sena's enthusiasm for urban planning, a series of infrastructure projects that could modernize Mumbai's strained and congested traffic system were presented. More than fifty major projects of "flyovers," a system of underground metros, new express ways, and so on, have been proposed since April 1995. In May 1996 a special Road Development Corporation was formed to boost the construction of new roads in the Mumbai area and elsewhere in the state.[14] The government also initiated the planning of a large new airport; there were discussions of a helicopter service in the city, and hovercrafts were put in operation as an alternative, if exceedingly expensive, means of traffic around the peninsula. Indicative of the urban imaginary that shaped these policies was that the railways, which are the most vital means of transport for most people in the city but are presently overloaded and in a rundown condition, were given less attention because of the massive problems that expansion and renovation of the rail system would entail. An estimated thirty thousand slum squatters live along the railway, and many have acquired legal rights on their plots. Thus any expansion of the tracks or acquisition of new land is an exceedingly sensitive issue.[15]

The most striking feature of these plans, however, was the extent to which they were marked by a distinct upper-middle-class view of the overwhelming part of the city, namely, vast expanses of slum or ordinary neighborhoods that one must drive through on new expressways, drive under on a new metro, fly over in helicopters, or avoid altogether in hovercraft services that would take the upper middle class from their homes in the western suburbs to the city center without even having to pass through the congested city.

The infrastructure in Mumbai has indeed been improved, and a sorely needed expressway between Mumbai and Pune is under construction with substantial involvement of private investors. The Shiv Sena/BJP cabinet has undoubtedly invested much more in the Mumbai area than had any of the previous state governments. But Shiv Sena was unhappy with the slow pace of many of the projects and complained about the obstacles created by court cases instigated by environmental groups against the new projects, bureaucratic routines, and the unhurried and meandering procedures of democratic decision making. Having just returned from a tour in East Asia, Joshi was full of admiration for the Chinese and Malaysian way of handling infrastructure and reform. "Here in India we have this habit of harassing each other, going to court, the press writing against politicians—in all this the people suffer. We face problems because of a democratic structure, or maybe because of corruption."[16]

The most ambitious part of this transformation of Mumbai was the slum rehabilitation scheme envisioned by Thackeray to remove the massive slum areas in the city and thus resolve "the major problem of dirt," as Thackeray put it. Given the very high costs of rentals and real estate in the city, Thackeray proposed, already in 1991, that the government raise the so-called FSI-index, that is, allow entrepreneurs to construct taller buildings and more densely in the slum areas, provided that free housing was made available to those who lived there. The additional space would then be rented out at normal rates, which would fully finance the cost of providing free housing to slum residents. The plan attracted considerable support from slum dwellers, as well as from builders who envisioned enormous possibilities. Thackeray acknowledged that a gray market might emerge if poor slum dwellers were to sell their new flats even before their completion, and thus the addition of hundreds of thousands of houses and flats would encourage the influx of new residents, making Bombay even more congested. "But," as Thackeray said, "we have our methods to prevent this. Already municipal officers have been instructed not to recognise any new *zopadpattis.* We don't want to add to our problems by allowing more immigrants to the city. We have to clean the system in a dictatorial manner— it is the only way."[17]

Before the scheme was implemented, the minister of housing, Chandrakant Khaire, stated that it was meant predominantly for Maharastrians and that "aliens"—Pakistanis and Bangladeshis—would never be given access to the plan. The selection would be based on the 1995 electoral roll but had to ensure that the projected four million people who were to benefit from the scheme would be those who had lived in the slums for a certain period time.[18] A new, high-powered Slum Rehabilitation Authority (SRA), chaired by the chief minister, was established to launch the large project, the biggest of its kind anywhere in the world. The SRA was invested with considerable powers, such as short-listing companies and suppliers qualified to undertake the construction of the thousands of projected high-rise buildings. Given the lack of precision in the identification of residents in slums, where neither houses nor plots carry numbers, and considering the rate of illiteracy, the SRA was given the final authority to determine whether a person was eligible for a free apartment under the plan. Detailed instructions were issued to the slum dwellers regarding the step-by-step procedures they should adopt to attract a builder and architect, and to acquire the SRA's full approval for the project. The rather detailed and technical procedures obviously presupposed that slum dwellers were given assistance either by the builder, social workers, or local people with worthy reputations and educational qualifications.[19]

From the outset the greatest obstacle to the plan's success was that the value and attractiveness of various slum areas differed enormously, which presented a problem in attracting builders willing to build in Dharavi, the largest slum in India, possibly in the world, and other slum areas because selling relatively expensive flats in these areas later on would be difficult. As soon as the plan was announced, these problems immediately surfaced: Swarms of builders of dubious repute approached residents of slums in attractive areas, offering their assistance in setting up the required housing cooperative, or, posing through straw men as NGOs, trying to lure slum dwellers into phony contracts. The inflated real estate prices in the city meant that the stakes were enormous for the lucky builder, and rumors circulated that high-ranking Shiv Sena leaders were using the SRA to shower favors on those who were friends of the party and of the Thackeray family. One lawyer estimated that the potential profit for builders who provided housing for the thirty thousand slum dwellers in the central Colaba area alone would be around 600 billion rupees.[20] Another unfortunate consequence of this scheme was that a number of more low-profile, less-expensive, but also more feasible programs to upgrade the slums were being terminated in the flurry of publicity that surrounded the launching of this new project.[21]

After two years, the results of the project were dismal. One building with fifteen flats had been completed, and the minister of housing had handed over the keys to the owners at the Dassera Festival in October 1997. Chandrakant Khaire, Shiv Sena's minister of housing admitted that preventing these flats from entering the market had been a problem: "The SRA has decided that these flats can only be sold after ten years. We have decided to put a metal plate in the apartment with government seal and the names of the legal residents to make sure that no one else occupies the place. The SRA can control it, it wants to, you see."[22]

Another ten thousand flats were being built, and the construction of another sixty thousand flats had been approved but not yet financed nor had permission been given to begin building. An SRA official concluded that at this rate it would take more than fifty years to clear the slums, even if no one else ever arrived in the city.[23] An important reason behind the failure of the scheme was that real estate prices in Mumbai decreased by more than 40 percent in less than a year. This slump, or rather this normal-ization from an inflated level in the early 1990s, completely undermined the considerable profit margin in the real estate market that had made the SRA concept feasible in the first place. Consequently few builders were willing to start projects under the SRA. In July 1998 the government established the so-called *Shivshahi Housing Corporation* with the aim of subsidizing and providing capital for the SRA projects. Although houses are being built and some two thousand apartments have been handed over to former slum residents in 1999, there is no indication that the pace of SRA projects has increased dramatically.

This particular scheme and the emphasis it placed on the private sector's involvement seemed to substantiate the accusations against Shiv Sena/ BJP of serving the interests of entrepreneurs and builders and of being more concerned with the physical dimensions of the city than with the lives of the poor. There is little doubt that the slum that is cleared today will likely resurface somewhere else tomorrow as long as the fundamental problems in the economy and the structure of the labor market continue to produce large numbers of low-paid casual employees and domestic workers. This will not necessarily damage Shiv Sena's image and might even lend more credibility to its proposals of "influx control" and similar measures to lessen the burden on Mumbai. Shiv Sena's central proposition to slum dwellers has indeed been rehabilitation: to lift them out of the slums into respectable high-rise buildings, into a city with expansive ex-pressways, high-tech transportation, and white-collar employment. Al-though Shiv Sena's rhetoric, profile, and constituency may be popular, its visions and the identities it offers, as noted above, have never been derived from the world of the zopadpattis. As we saw in the case of Shiv Sena's appeal to lower-caste groups, the party's attraction is that it offers its voters and supporters glimpses of what they may become—respectable, modern, and middle-class—while blurring what they actually are.

The issue of cleaning up Bombay was not limited to the slums. The clearing of footpaths, the removal of beggars, and deportation of the al-leged forty thousand illegal Bangladeshis living in the city had also been high on the Shiv Sena/BJP agenda for a long time. Immediately upon coming into power, the cabinet initiated a limited but widely publicized action whereby approximately one thousand persons without proper papers were rounded up in central Bombay in July and August of 1995 and ushered out of the state on trains, this in accordance with the colonial "Foreigners Act" of 1946 that places the burden of proof on the suspect. It was alleged that many of those rounded up in 1995 and in the following years (approximately eight hundred to one thousand a year during Shiv Sena's tenure) were actually Muslims from West Bengal and Bihar, who, as Indian citizens, had every right to remain in Mumbai. When raiding the footpath dwellings, the police had demanded passports, school records, or birth certificates, none of which these impoverished people, whether Indian or Bangladeshi, would ever have had.[24]

The government also announced that all beggars in the city would be deported back to their native state (regardless of whether they had indeed been born in Mumbai). This was a somewhat ironic response to a similar policy that the BJP administration had initiated in Delhi, whereby fifty-two Marathi-speaking beggars, or pavement dwellers, were sent to Bombay. This measure, as reported in the *Indian Express*, was intended "to reduce the increasingly sinister menace of beggary, intimidating citizens, and intruding on private property."[25] Clearly both Shiv Sena and the BJP, once in power, wished to continue this ousting and expunging of all signs of the poor and the plebeian from Bombay and other cities, whether in the form of Muslims or those living in the *zopadpattis*, namely, all who were seen as encroaching on the comfort and physical security of the middle class.

MORAL MUMBAI

As India's quintessential urban territory, never having been domesticated by a hegemonic vernacular elite to the extent that had occurred in colonial Calcutta, Bombay was always indecipherable and opaque, in constant flux and movement, truly cosmopolitan in its embodiment of so many foreign cultural fragments. The ambivalent attitude toward the foreign/modern/urban was not confined to Maharashtrian regional sentiments but characterized, albeit in complex ways, the wider matrix of Indian nationalism and notions of an Indian modernity. The big city was always mysterious, unknowable, but was also the theater of modern disciplinary power. Compared to the village, urban spaces were objects of intense governance. The classical debates in India on how a proper civic sense, a public ethos, and a feeling for the discipline engraved in the layout of the city could be imparted to its proper citizens, as well as to its more unruly slum dwellers, have always abounded regarding the use of urban space, as Kaviraj (1998) has pointed out.

It was not surprising, therefore, that the great Indian experiment of authoritarian rule, the Emergency, was played out, first and foremost, in the country's urban territories. The excesses committed by Sanjay Gandhi and his Youth Congress storm troopers in Delhi have been well publicized, if thus far undocumented in detail,[26] but similar scenes were also enacted elsewhere in the country. The Emergency's cultural dimensions have been less publicized, and one finds a number of uncanny parallels between the preoccupation of restoring "cleanliness," morality, and purity to the Indian culture during the Emergency and the contemporary cultural policies of Shiv Sena (and the BJP).

A few weeks after the imposition of the Emergency in 1975, police in Puri held Indian hippies in custody and forcibly shaved them and cut their hair; days later these actions were repeated in Bombay. Bombay's police commissioner stated that he was contemplating adding long hair to the list of punishable offenses, explaining that "most of the young people with long hair are drug addicts. This measure would add to our running campaign against drug peddling, *matka* (gambling), and prostitution." Only a month later this same commissioner told the press, with pride, that "matka is dead. We have sent thirty thousand criminals and people involved in gambling [to] prison." Quoting police sources liberally, the article graphically describes the secret, seedy world of matka and drugs in Bombay.[27]

The linking of foreign-induced amorality (long hair) with indigenous forms of amorality was clear. A similar connection was also articulated, in a slightly more complex form, in a series of articles run by *Times of India* in August 1975, which described the raids of houses and flats in posh neighborhoods in Bombay's western suburbs and in Pune by tax and custom authorities to recover black money and illegally imported goods. "Survey of Bombay Flats Reveal Vulgar Lifestyle," read the newspaper headline on August 3. All the articles gave detailed, curious, and morally outraged descriptions of the interiors and lifestyle to which they bore witness. Although not stated explicitly, clearly the assumption was that such amassing of wealth was not only amoral and antinational but was probably also illegal and linked to foreign smuggler rackets, and, in any case, led to an excessively hedonistic, that is, Western, non-Indian, lifestyle. The depictions of these wealthy tax evaders were cast in a mold that resembled the later fascination and contempt for the "notorious gangster" and underworld figure as condensed signifiers of urban amorality. Most striking was the outrage focused on the "intimate enemy," one of "our own," who, by his or her overindulgence in foreign and amoral habits, such as sumptuous urban living and decadence as well as alleged ties and affection for everything *videshi* (foreign), had in effect betrayed the nation.

Compared to most other political and public figures in India, Thackeray and his family and most of the Sena leaders have for years been quite forthright about their self-indulgence, their love of "Bollywood" films, fancy cars, beautiful women, the good life. As I have argued above, Thackeray's image as someone who speaks as a self-confident "Bombay wallah" and lives a life of glamour, rubbing shoulders with film stars and other celebrities, is an important element of Shiv Sena's appeal as a party that is assertive, urban—and ordinary. In these respects, Thackeray is as far removed from the ascetic cultural purism of the Rashtriya Swayamsevak Sangh as is conceivable in India.

Shiv Sena's endorsement of the pleasures of modern consumption, however, makes the Sena neither liberal nor tolerant. On the contrary, the Sena has always thrived on intolerance toward the alien, the impure, has always harbored a strongly anti-intellectual tendency, a strong desire to endorse and promote the virtues of the ordinary, the pleasures of popular culture. Thackeray has never aimed at an ideologically consistent stance against anything foreign, nor has he supported the styles of "patriotic consumption" advocated by strong forces in the RSS. To Thackeray and most Sena leaders, the criteria separating the tolerable from the intolerable seems to concern whether the issue can be seen as "antinational" (e.g., Muslim/Pakistani) or as offending widespread moral sensibilities among ordinary Hindus in Mumbai.

The party's attitude toward the film industry exemplifies this. Shiv Sena's involvement in the film industry is wide-ranging and complex. It concerns the "Motion Pictures Unit," *Shivsena Chitrapat Shakha*, which organizes employees in the film industry, a number of directors and actors who produce Marathi and Hindi films and are closely involved with members of the Thackeray family who invest in their films, as well as Cable Sena, a recent association of smaller cable TV operators in the Mumbai area.[28] The director most explicitly associated with the Sena is N. Chandra, who became famous in 1985 with the film *Ankush* that celebrated how four unemployed men, through their violent defense of women and their neighborhood against local gangsters, experience a metamorphosis and become a law unto themselves, only "to be hanged in a manner reminiscent of India's freedom fighters."[29] Chandra, a self-avowed supporter of Shiv Sena, continued his depiction of violence and poetic justice among Bombay's low-life in the hugely popular film *Teezab* (Acid) (1988), subtitled "A Violent Love Story." The film became famous for its detailed depictions of violence and the hit song of that year, *Ek do teen*. In 1991 Chandra produced the film *Narasimha*, featuring the muscular star Sunny Deol as a criminal and cop killer who is reformed and turns into an almost messianic avenger. Here, and in later films, Chandra excels in technically sophisticated celebrations of how poor and marginalized figures of the

urban jungle are redeemed and purified through acts of justified violence—an enduring element in the Sena ideology.

The most famous of the film personalities associated with the Sena is
the Maharashtrian actor Nana Patekar, who made a name for himself in
Chandra's *Ankush*. Like Chandra, Patekar has a penchant for the aesthetics
of excessive violence and is known for his many roles as the violent avenger,
a mixture of Dirty Harry and Rambo but not without his moral faults,
cleaning up the underworld or the corrupt, decadent world of big business
and high politics. Patekar is the closest one gets to a film icon of the
ideal sainik, the assertive, no-nonsense man from a modest background, a
man of action unburdened by the moral qualms induced by education and
refinement.

Indicative of Sena's attitude toward Bollywood productions is that no
Sena leader has joined the almost ritualistic moral condemnation of the
excess of violence and indecency in contemporary movies that has become
so common among politicians, commentators, and other public figures in
India in the 1990s.

So far it has only been films with more artistic ambition that has stirred
the wrath of Shiv Sena. Mani Ratnam's film, *Bombay*, angered Thackeray
because of the film's depiction of his role in the 1993 riots. He threatened
that his sainiks would burn down theaters showing the film and insisted
that certain sections be edited out. Ratnam gave in to Thackeray's demands and cut the film, perhaps, as Guneratne suggests, because of the
enormous publicity the controversy gave the film (Guneratne 1997,
180).[30] Months later controversy raged over Salman Rushdie's caricature
of Thackeray in *The Moor's Last Sigh* (1995). Thackeray, admitting he had
not read the book, said "I don't want to read books and spoil my thinking." Still, he maintained that because Rushdie depicted him as having
instigated riots in the city the book would be banned in Mumbai. ("I did
not start the riots," he said. "My job is to protect the Hindus").[31]

In 1998 Deepa Mehta's film, *Fire*, which, among other things, deals
with an erotic relationship between two women, was targeted by Shiv
Sena's women's organization, *Mahila Aghadi*. Activists attacked cinema
halls where the film was screened in Mumbai. In Gujarat, Bajrang Dal
activists followed suit, and the film was soon vilified in many parts of
the country as being "alien to Indian culture." Chief Minister Joshi in
Maharashtra publicly congratulated the women activists for their determination to defend Indian culture and morality. Thackeray demanded that
the film be censored and reiterated his anti-intellectual stance on the public depiction of lesbian love:

> In the name of art and intellectualism you cannot corrupt tender minds. To-
> morrow it might start in all ladies hostels. It is a sort of social AIDS. . . . It is

all right for hi-fi society-wallahs to sit in their AC-cabins and discuss democracy. But do they know what the public sentiment is all about? . . . If they pass the film, I'll invite the Pakistani cricket team . . . extremists from Pakistan. . . . I'll ask the Bangladeshi government to send more and more Muslims to our country.[32]

Here the chains of equivalence between various forms of betrayal were made abundantly clear: to allow such pollution of Indian culture was tantamount to betraying the nation, a betrayal equal to fifth-column activities on behalf of the neighboring countries. Thackeray, of course, played up the fact that the leading actress in the film, Shabana Azmi, was both a Muslim and a well-known leftist activist. Thus Azmi, the director, the entire artistic milieu was clearly playing the crucial role of the intimate enemy, the traitor in our midst.

To my mind, Shiv Sena's continual need to identify and expunge this internal enemy perhaps explains the apparent paradox that the Sena's leadership sponsored and publicly attended a Michael Jackson concert in November 1996. The party's entire leadership and all its MLAs attended in front-row seats, with some, however, using cotton earplugs. Considering that columnist Vir Sanghvi wrote at the time that Jackson was "known as a crotch-grabbing alleged paedophile," why would the Thackeray family wish to be associated with this person and his show? As Sanghvi claimed, the family attended as a pragmatic manipulation of votes and sentiments to attract the youth and because Jackson allegedly donated forty million rupees to the Sena.[33]

The clue was revealed in a statement Thackeray made in 1998 when he complained about the young "soft drink and pop generation": "Michael Jackson came and went back. This culture of the hi-fi generation is going to remain. Don't make outside cultures your own. Let them remain to be seen and discussed and stay where they belong."[34] To Thackeray and the Sena leadership, what is foreign is neither dangerous nor repulsive in itself; it may even be an attractive and desirable entertainment or experience, especially when represented by the most famous and richest pop star in the world. Only when foreign influence becomes implanted in the minds and practices of the nation's citizens, turning them into something new and provocative, into internal aliens and thus impurities in their own city and community—does that influence pose a threat. What gives rise to anxieties among average middle-class families is not Michael Jackson per se but the rapid development of a hedonistic youth culture, which is symbolized, above all, by MTV, which, in the last few years, has become associated with all sorts of damaging influences on India's youth. This culture of the youth threatens to create a larger gap between parents and children than ever before and has, in a sense, become a condensed sign of the rapid transformations experienced in India's urban worlds since the opening of India's economy and market to global products and media.

This concern may also explain why Shiv Sena's minister of culture, Pramod Nawalkar, adopted an ever more purist line in terms of trying to discipline Mumbai's public culture and to weed out what he regarded as immoral practices. For example, he ordered discos and rock concerts in Mumbai to close early; he branded public kissing on the stage among musicians and artists as "obscene"; he ordered rock groups to submit their lyrics for perusal by bureaucrats in the Ministry of Culture; he ordered bars to close early and not to hire female dancers; and so on. These measures undoubtedly were attempts to exploit the anxieties of millions of parents who worried about the new youth culture, about what it might do to morality, authority, and the chastity of their daughters.

In other words, Shiv Sena tried to assume a new role of being the defender of Indian culture without falling into the anti-Western, anti-urban, anti-modern positions so well rehearsed in India. The Sena's target was neither consumption nor capitalism. As with Sena's resentment of artistic refinement, the crux of the matter was the rejection of "urban excess"; immoderate enjoyment and overt sexuality marked the intimate enemy. In this case, it was Westernized upper-class youth in discos and rock concerts who were forgetting the virtues of plain old Bollywood songs and entertainment, that is, the conventional and ordinary forms of enjoyment of the Marathi manus.

IN THE NAME OF THE STATE

In chapter 5 I posed a question: How had Shiv Sena's style of governance and Thackeray's assertion of his "remote control" of the government and his contempt for the judiciary affected the larger myth of the state as a site of justice, sovereignty, and as the symbolic center of society. We may now be able to provide at least a few tentative answers to this question by asking a more fundamental one: How is public authority constructed and reproduced in Mumbai and Maharashtra in the 1990s?

As Foucault reminds us, the classical notion of sovereignty was "the right to take life or let live." If someone defied or transgressed the law of the traditional master, he "could exercise a direct control over the offender's life: as punishment the latter could be put to death" (Foucault 1984, 259). The sovereign exercised power both by taking life and by refraining from doing so. To Foucault, this was characteristic of a power that was external, extractive, and deductive, the power to seize a portion of everything, including life itself. Modern forms of power, by contrast, were regulative and inseparable from wider society. Modern bio-power "was a power to foster life or to disallow it to the point of death" (261), a power that was exercised through shaping, maintaining, and disciplining the life of entire populations. Sovereignty was no longer symbolically displayed as the right to take life in trials and on the scaffold but was exercised in the minutiae of regimented prison life and the administration of asylums. Individual transgressions of the law were increasingly viewed as symptoms of a larger ailment in the population and thus something that called for treatment and prophylactic measures rather than punishment. "Hence capital punishment could not be maintained except by invoking less the enormity of the crime itself, than the monstrosity of the criminal, his incorrigibility, and the need to safeguard society. One had a right to kill those who represented a kind of biological danger to others" (261).

This move from sovereignty toward bio-power undoubtedly represents a general tendency in the development of governmental technologies, of the institutionalization and routinization of governance by its implication in everyday forms of conduct, to the extent that it ceased to appear as regulation and commands. But as I pointed out in the discussion of the Srikrishna Commission, the Foucauldian perspective tends to underestimate the importance of public spectacles in the construction and transformation of sovereignty into its modern form, the assertion of authority as legality, regulated by law and procedures of adjudication. It also underestimates the continued foundational importance of violence in the reproduction of legitimacy, obedience to the law and the claims to sovereignty—that is, the right to be laws unto themselves—made by communities and leaders. Both the spectacles of the state and other continuous displays of sovereignty—the ability and will to take life and to punish—are important in a situation like that in Mumbai, where bio-political forms of government are less hegemonic and more precarious and contested than in the Western societies analyzed by Foucault. What I propose is simply that systems of governance and claims to sovereignty are deeply fragmented in contemporary Mumbai. The state commands no self-evident monopoly of violence and thus no self-evident authority to affect the rule of law. Instead, we see competing centers of power—Shiv Sena, the "underworld," the police force—exercising competing claims of sovereignty and employing different registers of bio-power, and thus different claims to "stateness."

As discussed above, the roots of this fragmentation can be found in the colonial state and in its distant and ineffective forms of knowledge and government intervention in the life of ordinary city dwellers. Further, the postcolonial state failed to make its objects of governance properly known and ordered into a manageable population. Populations continued to be bifurcated into a disciplined, governable segment of middle-class and other proper state citizens and a large mass of amorphous and obscure, partly unknown and unknowable, humanity in the zopadpattis. The opacity of the slum world also haunted Shiv Sena's slum rehabilitation scheme.

Modern bio-political governance did produce, nonetheless, an unprecedented clarity in terms of ethnic, religious, and caste categorizations and provided new languages of contention and rational regulations that settled in the political world of democracy. Here they became resources in the language of rights, demanding the collective well-being and entitlements of groups, worrying about the pollution of health and the culture of entire groups, the peril of social evils, of declining norms and foreign contamination in the Muslim neighborhoods and slum areas, to name but a few. In other words, these political languages drew on the rationalities of modern bio-power regulating health, reproduction, and bodies. But interspersed among these political languages, such as that of the Shiv Sena, were also the registers of blood, kinship, and honor, invoked by the power that, in Foucault's words, "spoke through blood, honor and the triumph of death" (Foucault 1984, 269), that is, sovereign power, but referring now, as we saw, to the abstract law—the law of the nation and a history marked by Shivaji's "original" violence.

Violence is at the heart of the sacred and is therefore indispensable to the construction of community and of the power of the sacred king, argues René Girard (1977). Communities are created and affirmed through "generative violence," of which the ritualized sacrifice of a victim who is made to be the symbol of all evil and transgression that the community seeks to expunge is the most elementary and recurrent feature. As Girard puts it: "In the evolution from ritual to secular institutions, men gradually draw away from violence and eventually lose sight of it; but an actual break with violence never takes place. That is why violence always can stage a stunning, catastrophic comeback" (307).

If violence is at the heart of the sacred, is it not equally central to the assertion of sovereign power? Girard argues that it is precisely the foundational character of violence that accounts for the continuities between the concept of the sacred king in premodern or archaic societies and the more political character of monarchy in the early modern period, as in Hobbes's notion of sovereignty as a covenant founded on a contractual submission to a stronger power. The cause of sovereignty and the awe and fascination surrounding sovereign power remains, in other words, the capacity for violence, the will and determination to take life or to let live. Violence may be justified in various ways, it may invoke different ethical registers, have different aims—from enforcing obedience to a master to hygienic and prophylactic rationalities—but the terror, awe, and surplus of meaning contained in violence, or in the threat of violence, can never be fully contained or explained (Balibar 1998). Even in thoroughly governmentalized societies, where the operations of power are dispersed, habitual, and rationalized, violence remains a phenomenon that resists symbolization, something that is beyond us and therefore terribly fascinating. Hence the attribution of sublime qualities and sovereignty to the dispensers of violence—be they police officers, spies, soldiers, or criminals. And hence the fascination of those who assert their own law, their archaic claim to sovereignty which they perform through acts of violence, in the midst of an otherwise complex, discrete, and internalized web of modern disciplinary power.

Girard's argument that the killing and exorcising of the "surrogate victim," the marginal member of the community—known and yet unknown—that symbolizes the weakness, sinfulness, and transgressions of the community, is not a logic that belongs to archaic societies alone. Indeed, it is a logic that resonates only too well with Shiv Sena's careful selection of intimate enemies that represent the "urban excess," both loathed and desired by the sainiks.

Girard's depiction of the attraction of the sovereignty of the sacred king also has an uncanny resemblance to how Thackeray likes to see himself:

> The king is both very "bad" and extremely "good." . . . The king's subjects may feel ill at ease in his presence, awed by his sheer superabundance of power. Nevertheless, they would be terrified if they were deprived of his presence. . . . The absolute can be likened to fire: too near and one gets burned, too far away and one gets nothing. Between these two there is a zone where one is warmed and heartened by the welcome light. (Girard 1977, 269)

Shiv Sena operates both inside and outside the formal apparatus of the state, and it oscillates between the two modalities of power we have identified: the bio-political governance of various targeted populations and categories in the name of maintaining the economic, social, and cultural well-being and purity of the proper (Hindu) population in Mumbai—slum rehabilitation, the deportation of alleged foreigners and beggars, the flushing out of immoral practices in the city.

The other side of Shiv Sena is Thackeray's exercise of sovereignty within the party, his remote control, the removal and humiliation of ministers at his whim, as well as the translation of some of his idiosyncratic predilections into cultural policies. What appears as idiosyncratic and as a lack of ideological consistency in Thackeray's thinking are, in effect, recurrent affirmations of his status as a sovereign, as a law onto himself.

What makes Thackeray unique is that he asserts sovereignty as a person and a leader, as well as making the more conventional claim of sovereignty on behalf of his followers, his party, the Maharastrians, and sometimes the Hindus as a whole, as, for example, when he claimed that he had every right to defend Hindus by killing Muslims during the 1993 riots. The discourse of retributive justice, that every killing of a Muslim is justified and ethically neutralized by violence done to Hindus, is at odds with the sovereignty of the modern state as the sole dispenser of legality and violence, as it paints a picture of two sovereign communities locked in conflict onto death. To make this discourse credible, Shiv Sena needs the myth of Dawood as the secret leader and avenger of the Muslim community, its "monstrous double," so to speak. The Hindu community also needs protectors and avengers, and Shiv Sena is only too happy to perform this role as the Hindus' necessary "monstrous double," relieved of the burden of moral injunctions. In the discourse of communal conflict, the register of blood and honor completely replaces the bio-political proposition of the strict governance of a diverse population.

As we have seen, this challenges not only bio-political rationality but also the idea that only the state can claim sovereign power. The last few years have seen a string of conflicts between Thackeray and various state institutions that illustrates how much room there actually is for assertions of different forms of sovereign power within the formal edifice and jurisdiction of the Indian state. In 1995 the Supreme Court of India upheld a verdict of the Bombay High Court that held Thackeray guilty of misusing religion to spread communal enmity during a local election campaign in Bombay in 1987. Thackeray was thus violating the election law. The consequences that followed the guilty verdict were unclear, and the case has been pending in the Election Commission for years. Some demanded that Thackeray be barred from holding public office; others felt that he should also be disenfranchised in elections for a period of time. Thackeray's many powerful friends were able to protect him for a long time, but, in July 1999, the president of India decided to disenfranchise Thackeray for a period of two years.[35] Here the logic of the state prevailed, whereas it had failed to indict Thackeray for the far more serious crime of his responsibility in the 1993 riots in Mumbai.

Another example was the much-debated conflict, in early 1999, over whether the Pakistani cricket team should be allowed to play in India. Thackeray was against the apparent détente that was under way at the time between India and Pakistan, and he ordered activists to Delhi to dig up the pitch where the match was scheduled. Sainiks also vandalized the Wankhede Stadium in Mumbai and attacked the office of the Board of Control of Indian Cricket in Mumbai. Sena activists were arrested after these activities, and Thackeray was outraged: "What is the use of having a Shiv Sena government if our cadres cannot be protected from arrest?" he was reported to have shouted at Chief Minister Joshi. The conflict evolved into a long drawn-out war on nerves between Thackeray and the BJP, which was representing the Union government. Here, too, the logic of the state prevailed, and Thackeray was forced to "allow" the Pakistanis to play.[36] However, as we saw above, more examples exist of Shiv Sena and Thackeray actually getting their own way through what some opponents call "extra-constitutional power"—that is, the exercise of sovereignty within the state.

It is possible, though, that Thackeray's very aggressive posturing before and during the 1999 election campaign, as well as the assertion of his own sovereignty, which, a few years earlier, had earned him so much admiration and support, had gone too far and actually contributed to the party's defeat in the elections, both for the Lok Sabha and the State Legislative Assembly.

As we saw in chapter 6, Dawood and other expatriate gangster kings, such as Chhota Rajan, a former associate of Dawood, also established themselves as sovereigns in their own right. According to sources in the Home Ministry controlled by the BJP, the gangster syndicates are increasingly being co-opted by the Pakistani intelligence organizations in what is termed "their relentless covert assault on the country."[37] The underworld is depicted in the press and through stories and rumors as a more covert, more sinister, and far more powerful type of sovereign power than Shiv Sena, not least because of these alleged links to foreign powers. The underworld is often the variable that solves most puzzles and difficult equations, a truly "empty signifier" that has very little substance but enormous flexibility and can stand in for an astonishing range of phenomena as an almost perfect intimate enemy who has turned into an antinational monstrous double with lethal high-tech weapons.

As Mumbai's dynamic economy creates new sources of wealth, new forms of crime accompany it. Extortion has become the new profitable line of work in the black economy and has sent shock waves through the business world. But the practice of business people giving donations (*khandani*) to local associations or to political parties and local strongmen for protection or to purchase favors makes it difficult to establish when requests for donations become outright extortion. Mumbai's police force apparently feels no need to change its conceptual and practical approach to the underworld. It remains structured by a number of identifiable gangs, and the success of the police force in preventing crime is still measured by the number of alleged gangsters killed in "encounters," now released to the press in neatly ordered statistics indicating the relative loss of men from each of the city's four main gangs, faithfully reported by the press.[38]

This complacent awareness of the underworld was upset somewhat by the emergence of reformed gangster Arun Gawli, once a friend and aide of Sena leaders, as a political figure heading his own *Akhil Bharatiya Sena*, based in Mumbai's old mill districts. With a program that promised jobs and housing to young workers and the city's unemployed, Gawli's party appeared to mimic the Shiv Sena of the 1960s, and Gawli clearly anticipated that his reputation as an underworld "don" would provide a following of young men seeking identity, protection, and a future. Only six months later, in August 1997, Gawli headed a demonstration of approximately seventy-five thousand people against the failed employment policies of Shiv Sena.

Gawli's methods of mobilization resembled Shiv Sena's initial techniques: dispensing quick justice in the neighborhoods, assisting in solving local problems, helping young men get a job, donating ambulances, and so on. Like other reformed gangsters, he was trusted neither by the police nor the press and was always referred to as the so-called reformed don. Gawli has made every effort to promote himself as a devout but noncommunal Hindu (his wife is Muslim) and a true family man. He has told women whose husbands physically abuse them to write to him and his wife, and they will personally deal with every case. His most notorious resolve is to "wipe out Dawood, if only the police will let me do it."[39]

In some ways, however, Gawli was too human, too tangible for his contenders and the police to handle. His physical appearance—a well spoken, tiny, but athletic man with large melancholy eyes staring sadly from the pages of all the newspapers—did not conform to the image of the typical gangster king. It was indicative of the relatively fixed framework of knowledge administered by the police that after the initial attention paid to him, and the many rumors of Gawli's continued criminal activities and extortion, shared liberally by police officers, both the police and the press lost interest in what turned out to be just another local politician and social reformer.

Not so with the Muslim gangsters who more faithfully performed their role as the "evil sovereigns" destabilizing the city. In March 1999 Milind Vadiya, a Shiv Sena leader described in the Srikrishna report as a key person in attacking Muslims during the 1993 riots in Mumbai, was shot and wounded outside his residence in Mumbai, as part of an ongoing battle between Hindu and Muslim gangsters and their aides and networks. The police force and the press suggested that a protracted war with communal overtones had been fought for years between two of Dawood's former lieutenants—Chhota Rajan, a Dalit; and Chhota Shakeel, a Muslim. What was at stake in this rivalry remained hazy, as always, but it seemed that a new communal grid had been added to the explanation of crime in Mumbai. Whether or not this was true, the more interesting fact was that for the first time a Muslim gangster, Chhota Shakeel, in a rare interview, explicitly presented himself and, by implication, the networks of his boss, Dawood, as the self-styled protectors of Muslims in the city.

Shakeel and his men claimed that they wanted to stop the revenge killings carried out by Chhota Rajan against people alleged to have been involved in the March 1993 bombings. Although, since 1993, Dawood had
been assigned the role of the "evil sovereign" of the Muslims, it had never
been confirmed before; it also remained unclear as to whether this was
merely a way to exploit Dawood's ready-made authority. In the interview,
Shakeel admitted responsibility for the attempt on Vadiya's life and then
turned to themes of revenge and honor: "Chhota Rajan wants cheap popularity. No one has given him the right to kill innocent people. We have no
option but to retaliate. We will respond by killing more Shiv Sena and BJP
workers." Defending one's own people and one's religion is noble and
human, Shakeel said, but he added that Chhota Rajan had ulterior motives
and referred to Rajan's Dalit background and lack of manners and culture
to explain why he lacked a proper ethos. "He was making holes in the
plates when he was eating. He wanted to portray himself as a white-collar
person, but he cannot wipe the stains from his white collar."[40] Shakeel's
statement was almost too good to be true, as it seemed to affirm all existing
knowledge of the character of the Muslim gangster world—inherently
communal but also stylish, highly urban, brutal, and white-collar.

As noted above, Mumbai's police force operates according to a rather simplified but robust understanding of the underworld as being governed by
a few gangs and its rather vulgar concept of the Muslim world in the city.
The rationalities guiding the work of the police are informed by notions
of bio-political governance, however unsophisticated in their content, that
target the entire Muslim population as a problem: attempts to identify and
weed out the bad elements, to create a new leadership and self-governance
through mohalla committees; preventive arrests; keeping an eye on "history sheeters" (persons with an alleged criminal record); encouraging
games and sports among the youth to create alternative activities; and so
on. The construction of the "notorious criminal" as a dreaded figure beyond redemption, as a symptom of a disease that must be eliminated in
"encounters" for the good of society, is also a wholly bio-political construct. The most surprising and disturbing feature of the policies and
knowledge of the police was that their understanding of the city had acquired a position as the official, almost uncontested truth. But there are
also more overt political angles to this consensus.
    In the 1980s allegations of links between Muslim gangsters, communal
organizations, and Muslim politicians became numerous and customary
in the press. Ties between Muslim builders, communal politicians, and
the mafia simply became standard knowledge eagerly disseminated and
corroborated by the police. As we saw in chapter 6, some of the recent

success of the Samajwadi Party among Muslims in Mumbai has been based on its forceful and self-conscious play on these stereotypes, an anticipatory identification embracing the positions of plebeians and dadas they already had been assigned. Aided by journalists, the police have continued to vilify Muslim political figures and to reiterate their connections with the underworld.

The police have long accused Abu Asim Azmi, the Samajwadi Party president in Maharashtra, of having (unspecified) links with Dawood Ibrahim. Although Azmi had his name cleared in the Supreme Court, successive police commissioners have continued their allegations. Ignoring the Supreme Court verdict, Commissioner Mendonca stated in an affidavit to the High Court in Mumbai in 1997, "I submit that Azmi has a criminal record and is in close association with Dawood Ibrahim, as per police records. He was accused in the serial bomb blast case and is involved in the scandalous shoe scam case."[41] It should be added that Azmi has not even been formally charged in the latter case. But the crux lies in the phrase "as per police records." The Mumbai police consistently play on, and affirm, the common assumption that they know more than what they disclose, that they are the keeper of vital secrets, and are therefore above the standard rules of the game in the judicial system. In this regard, allegations of the involvement of political figures in the underworld remain true, as truths beyond facts, on a par with the assumed knowledge of the police of criminal networks that leads to fatal encounters with suspects and "notorious gangsters."

The performance of the Bombay police, as depicted by Justice Srikrishna within a strikingly medicalized and bio-political discourse, inevitably leaves one with the distinct suspicion that the police, in fact, have little reliable information on the underworld. This very suspicion was indicated in an article that was quite sympathetic to the police. The journalist, Lyla Bavadam, wrote: "The high degree of frustration, especially in the crime and narcotics branches, is also attributed to a legal system which puts the burden of proof on the prosecution." She then quotes an officer, who says: "In gang-related cases the burden of proof should be on the accused."[!])[42]

Instead, the police, often with Shiv Sena's support, have consistently produced an essentially moralizing narrative of the underworld (and its political allies) as the cause of all evil; the centers of the narrative are the dons, who provide Mumbai's modern urban landscape with a structure and a plot. The primary effect of this narrative has been what I call a perpetual "state effect": the police emerge as representative of the public interest and the guarantors of public order above petty interests, as an understaffed and neglected force constantly subjected to the politically motivated transfer of officers.[43]

The police force reinforces this depiction of itself as the victim of political games by its rather adept handling of the press. Numerous articles describe the plight of ordinary constables, and the stress and hardship the police face. In one article, police psychiatrist Dr. Katara stated that the main problem in the police force was "stress . . . manifesting itself in alcoholism, frustration and anxiety." Katara admitted that although the constables' level of tension has not changed dramatically from what it was in the past, the stress is greater now because "the cop of today is better educated and a family man . . . [and so] his ability to absorb stress has decreased." Dr. Katara believes that this apparent softening of the police has to do with the lack of recognition of police work, the lack of equipment, and the lack of good housing for the police: "The policeman is thrust with being the upholder of the law. Yet he is living in a dingy chawl."[44] This and similar articles all reach the same conclusion: If the police were given more resources, there would be less crime in Mumbai and the underworld would vanish.

The other side of the police force is rarely told. The enormously profitable system of *hafta* (bribes), which, according to several estimates, provides even a constable with a substantial income, has never been charted or thoroughly investigated. But the mere fact that holders of degrees are among those who aspire to become constables in the police force—a job with no chance of promotion owing to the continued existence of an archaic colonial system—suggests the economic potential such a position offers.[45] There are indications that some criminal networks work hand in glove with members of the police force and that many of the "encounter killings" carried out by the police are, in fact, *suparis* (contract killings), ordered and paid for by criminal networks. In 1996 the Anti-Corruption Bureau of Maharashtra finished its investigation of several departments in the state and concluded that the police department tops the list regarding virtually every type of corrupt practice.[46]

This shows that amid the dominant bio-political rationalities governing the police are cracks and voids that allow large-scale parallel systems of hafta to operate. It also indicates that the logic of sovereign power and the associated obligations surrounding reciprocity and honor attached to communities of blood extend from both Shiv Sena and criminal networks deep into the police force. This coexistence of intersecting modalities of power, and the tentative and improvised nature of both the exercise of multiple forms of sovereignty and of bio-political governance, is probably one of the most crucial features of postcolonial urban governance in India.

In view of the historical trajectory of Shiv Sena and the urban world of Mumbai, it seems clear that the schism between these two modes of authority was intensified during Shiv Sena's tenure in power. The space wherein competing sovereigns fight over resources and territories both within and beyond the formal jurisdiction of the state has indeed expanded. In these battles the ordinary sainik has had little "enjoyment of power," and there has been less governance in the lives of ordinary people in Mumbai. The enjoyment has been entirely on the side of the Thackeray clan and other modern sovereigns in the city.

Politics as Permanent Performance

ON 17 July 2000 the city of Thane, once again, was the scene of a rather astonishing political performance. News had just broken that the Maharashtra government, at the behest of former sainik Chhagan Bhujbal, intended to prosecute Bal Thackeray for his well-known role in precipitating riots in the state. In protest, angry Shiv Sena workers attacked the mayor's office in Thane, throwing stones and breaking windows and furniture. Most curious about the episode was that the mayor himself, Ramesh Vaiti, a Shiv Sena leader representing the organization's majority coalition in the Thane Municipal Corporation, was leading the angry men who were destroying the premises. That morning, as the news broke, Vaiti stepped out of his role as mayor and into his sainik identity in order to attack a public building, which, in administrative terms, was relatively independent of the state authorities against whom the sainiks reacted, and was the very office to which he owed his public standing and influence. This episode reveals an essential quality about Shiv Sena but something even more distinctive about the relationship between politics, state, and society in contemporary India. But, first, let us look into the rest of the story.

Nine days later, on July 25, after warnings were issued to the police that Mumbai and the country would burn if Thackeray were arrested, the arrest came and Thackeray was brought before Magistrate Kamble in Mumbai. Shiv Sena MLAs destroyed seats, furniture, and wiring in the Legislative Assembly in protest against the arrest. Sainiks pelted stones at passing cars and public buses in various parts of the city, but the response to the Sena calls to "let the city burn" was lukewarm, even among local sainiks. Less than an hour later, however, Thackeray was released following Kamble's ruling that the charges against him were too old and that the state had failed to explain why he was being prosecuted more than seven years after his crime, that of encouraging sainiks to burn and kill Muslims throughout the city. The state appealed the ruling, and the cases against Thackeray were sent to a higher court.

What do these events tell us? On the surface, they confirm once again that Thackeray remains above the law, even a year after Shiv Sena was ousted from power in the state government. But Thackeray's case is still pending, and it is clearly uncertain that he will be so easily cleared at higher judicial levels.

It is also apparent that the Maharashtra government is determined to remove the special protection enjoyed by Thackeray and many sainiks since Shiv Sena's reign and since the alleged counterattacks began in 1998 on prominent sainiks by "Muslim gangsters." For years, as many as 206 policemen, 11 vehicles, and an expensive TV surveillance system had been permanently assigned to guard Thackeray and his residence, and another 103 policemen to protect the Thackeray family. In addition, all Sena leaders, MLAs, and numerous shakha pramukhs were given around-the-clock police protection against the alleged threat of gangsters and "antinational elements," the ubiquitous and ill-defined other.

The government had withdrawn this protection before legal charges were made against Thackeray, leaving Sena leaders complaining about threats to their lives and pleading for more guards. Shiv Sena's reliance on state security and its expressed fear of opponents obviously weakened the party's public image, just as it indicated that sainiks no longer could count on the impunity they had enjoyed by the tacit but effective shelter given Shiv Sena by Mumbai's police force.

Did this indicate that the state, at long last, was now trying to exercise its sovereignty through disinterested legality as inscribed in its institutions and thus at least to resemble the Weberian ideal of a state? I think not. These events demonstrated that government agencies in India, just like other dispensers of governance and violence in the country, have become dependent on their ability to perform, that is, to create a public spectacle of action and authority. The classic and essentially bureaucratic notion of the state as a machine that works slowly and steadily regardless of "political interference" is no longer tenable. Like other modern states, India is indeed a complex network of routines and institutions, but it is also a state fragmented and governed by many different forces, compulsions, and rationalities. By no means does the Indian state hold a monopoly of governance or violence. State institutions and procedures, such as taking legal action through a police force, thus constitute only one of several possible responses. But the state's action against Thackeray presupposed both a will and a strategy, legal preparations, withdrawal of police protection from the Sena, political coverage from Delhi, the right timing, and cautious tactics. It was a political spectacle aimed at strengthening the ruling coalition, but it was also a move supported by the police who saw the chance to strengthen their own position vis-à-vis their former protectors. As Deputy Chief Minister Chagan Bhujbal, the moving spirit behind the spectacle, told a journalist: "For the first time in Mumbai's history we ensured that the Sena could not engage in widespread violence. . . . Today we have proved that we are serious about implementing what we say. For nine months people thought this government was a joke. No one is laughing today."[1] This performance suddenly, and clearly, enabled the state to appear in its sublime form—as the sovereign authority and center of society.

THE ANATOMY OF POLITICAL SOCIETY

This unstable character of state power in India was also confirmed by the events in Thane described above. To Thane's Shiv Sena mayor, the administrative apparatus over which he was presiding was only one of several sites of power. When the state suddenly became coherent in its effort to take action against his leader, Vaiti stepped out of his role as mayor and into that of street fighter, publicly attacking the state as well as his own office. This indicates the pertinence of Chatterjee's distinction between the state and civil society, on the one hand, as the realm of governance and negotiation of interest cast in a legal and formal framework, and the "political society," on the other, as the realm of negotiations and struggles between state and population that take place through political parties, movements, and informal networks in a far more chaotic form (Chatterjee 1998, 57–69).

As Mayor Vaiti began to destroy his office, he stepped into a "political society" that, for decades, had been the preferred habitat of organizations like Shiv Sena. Political society is the expansive realm of public protest, public violence, and local mobilizations in which Shiv Sena has thrived and perfected its political mode. It is the realm that has enabled wider sections in Indian society to participate in politics; thus it has deepened democracy and transformed Indian society over the last decades. But political society has also enabled competing forms of sovereignty—political parties, movements, and gangsters—to grow and diversify to the extent that they have encroached on the sovereignty of the state, so clearly exemplified in Mumbai. Society's legitimate resistance to state power, or an opposition based on the ethics of community and culture, has a long and distinguished history in the Indian anticolonial, nationalist tradition from Gandhi on. To denounce *rajkaraan* (politics), to separate the nation and its cultures from the realm of rational statecraft, and to adopt a moral, antipolitical critique of political leaders is possibly the most legitimate and the most common oppositional stance in contemporary India. This stance, which normally marks a moral high ground for criticizing the government and abiding by the law, only becomes unsettling to the sovereignty of state power when it turns into an outright denial of the government's legitimacy. This is, for instance, what has occurred in the campaigns of the Vishwa Hindu Parishad for the construction of a Ram temple in Ayodhya since the late 1980s.[2] In most cases, however, "anti-politics" remains within the classical Lockean idea of the moral right to oppose an illegitimate government in order to retain, or rescue, society, and thus create the "Politick Society . . . the Agreement which every one has with the rest to incorporate, and act as one Body, and so be one distinct Commonwealth" (Locke 1988, 406).

The realm Mayor Vaiti stepped into that day in Thane was, in some ways, however, the direct opposite of Locke's idea of a political society. It was not a realm for creating "one Body" and the common good, not the scene of formal deputations presenting demands and arguing their case according to established procedures. Political society in India is something more unruly and unpredictable, a theater of dispersed—sometimes anarchic, sometimes highly organized—collective performances and protests, ritualized violence in public spaces and equally ritualized destruction of public property. At times this dissent is in opposition to the government and the police force; at other times it is pitched against political opponents or other communities. It is routinely challenging and often disregards questions of law and due process. Political society in contemporary India is not about generating new rules; its primary drive is to contest existing rules in the broadest sense, to defy the law, and, most important, to make a community or cause as visible as possible in order to claim certain benefits, public services, or entitlements for that community or cause.

Protests, the construction of political spectacles in public arenas, and the defiance of law are not unique to India, of course, but are integral to the struggle for democracy and civil liberties worldwide. But in India the public, political spectacle has an enormously rich and varied history, for there it has been informed by the anticolonial legacy of civil disobedience and sustained by an ever more inclusive, yet intensely competitive, democracy. In Maharashtra the regional ethnohistorical imaginary provided a wide repertoire of public performances that the Sena and other political actors have drawn on and further developed. As elsewhere in India, Bombay and Maharashtra have seen a certain "banalization" of public rituals and gestures originating in the nationalist movement, as well as a proliferation of political performances at all levels of public life—from pupils in provincial schools staging a protest in Gandhian style, to farmers blocking roads in remote districts, to local councilors going on hunger strikes in their municipal chambers, and so on.

Two features make India's political society unique in relation to most other societies, however, and both are tied to the scale, duration, and postcolonial character of India's democratic experience. First, negotiations and public manifestations in India are generally conducted on a huge scale and are enormously intense, and India's political and social movements often become exceptionally complex, with capable and strong actors scrambling for visibility, public resources, and recognition of their demands and identity. This has to do not only with the sheer pressure on scarce resources but also with the success of democracy in terms of providing a stage on which demands of many kinds can be formulated and fought over. This has produced a cultural climate conducive to such plural expressions. India's continued poverty, deprivation, illiteracy, and exclusion of large segments of the population from organized society and the economy all translate into an enormous need for the collective representation of demands from all kinds of movements, organizations, and informal and local operators from social workers to dadas.

Second, several parts of India have seen the emergence of movements and parties that, like Shiv Sena, have created complex, permanent networks within and beyond the state's jurisdiction that include forms of loyalty and informal brokerage hardly conforming to procedures of a law-abiding civil society. This intricate combination of formal organizations and informal networks spiraling through government institutions has at times challenged the sovereignty of the state as the final site of adjudication and decision making. The Hindu nationalist movement, the Communist Party in West Bengal, the Dravidian movement in Tamil Nadu, and certainly Shiv Sena come to mind as examples of such centers of power and claims to sovereignty operating both beyond and within the state in postcolonial India.

I contend that Shiv Sena and the transformations of Mumbai may teach us something important about how political society has developed in India. The Sena has expanded the scope of political society in Maharashtra by defying every rule and convention of democracy—such as abiding by laws, respecting adversaries, and pursuing political ends by peaceful means. The Sena has ritualized systematic and excessive violence as a political instrument; it has, without precedent, tried to use state power and public resources to further the interests of its leadership and to deflect the legal process in order to create de facto impunity for its activists. As a result, the emergence and rule of Shiv Sena has undoubtedly weakened the reach, efficacy, and authority of the government bureaucracy and has allowed the police force to become an independent political factor in its own right.

Shiv Sena attempted to remain rooted in political society as a site for permanent protest and negotiation of entitlements while also governing in a manner reminiscent of Thackeray's rhetoric—making no pretense of honoring the rules of civility, disregarding formal procedures, and abusing opponents in every imaginable way. For thirty years Shiv Sena has perfected the possibilities of political society, making it a realm of "pure politics"—the permanent suspension of every rule and legal provision, the constant juggling of possibilities and alliances, a situation of constant flux tending toward entropy. With Shiv Sena in power, "pure politics" entered the heart of the state, forcing government agencies to carry out policies in the realm of competitive and permanent public performances in order to be effective, or merely visible. A government that is not visible, tangible, and able to deliver on its promises—cheap housing, dead criminals, cheap meals, pomp and ceremony—becomes illegitimate. This logic has guided most of Shiv Sena's policies—as is true of competitive populist schemes launched in many other parts of India. Although this notion of politics as permanent performance has far from penetrated all corners of the bureaucracy, it has boiled politics down to its essential core: Politics, like naming, is a performative process that seeks retroactively to fix and stabilize identities, to invent constituencies and audiences, to create state effects by making the state visible, and to narrate and represent "society" through speech and public spectacles.

Two larger issues emerge from these observations. The first concerns how we study and understand "the political" in India and other postcolonial societies. The implication of my argument throughout this book is that performances and spectacles in public spaces—from central squares to street corners in the slums—must be the focus of our attention. This is the generative political moment par excellence, the heart of political society, and the site where historical imaginaries, the state, and notions of community and "society" become visible and effective. We must, in other words, chart and understand the mundane forms of politics and how political identities and notions of rights and citizenship are formed not by seeing them as a reflection of something else or as already being grounded in community, caste, or class; rather, we must study the political as it is formed and given life through acts of representation.

Another task awaiting the future anthropology of politics in India is to chart the tacit rules that govern and specify this zone of public spectacles and "political society" and its relationship to the state and to notions of community. What are the unspoken rules, for instance, that make it plausible for the Legislative Assembly in the Indian state of Madhya Pradesh recently to reject a complaint from an MLA that he had been beaten up by the police while participating in a rally. When entering the public realm, he was told, his status as legislator made no difference; apparently, being beaten up was a risk he had to take when moving about in political society. We must also inquire into the implicit understandings that make it not only expected but somehow entirely acceptable that demonstrators in Indian cities routinely destroy public property—buses, buildings, police chowkis— even injure policemen. This is rarely, if ever, regarded as a punishable offense. Only the killing of innocent people constitutes a transgression of what seems to have become acceptable norms of behavior in political society.

The other issue concerns how current forms of political society affects the distinctions between state, community, and society, features that are so vital to how ordinary Indians, as well as social scientists, make sense of their world. My contention is that however useful Chatterjee's distinction between state/civil society, on the one hand, and political society, on the other, has been, it remains bound by his distinction between a state supposedly governed by rationality and legality, and another realm governed by a conceptual register derived from communities and various local forms of authority. If one takes a closer look at what actually occurs in political society and the way an organization like Shiv Sena links communities with the logic and languages of the state, can one still maintain a clear distinction between state and community? Or is it still possible to distinguish the "state" from "political society"?

To my mind it may be more pertinent to investigate how political society and its imperatives of permanent performance penetrate the bureaucracy and suspend the idea of the state as an entity in itself, as a predictable "machine," thus forcing the state constantly to reinvent itself and present itself anew through a series of spectacles. This process also implies that the notion of the Indian state as capable of providing resources, of guaranteeing entitlements through legislation, of stabilizing community identities through official recognition, and solving conflicts through adjudication is no longer as certain or as stable as it was when confidence in the efficacy of the state's legal framework was stronger. We thus need to rethink what the state means and how it presents itself in everyday life, and explore how governance has become organized around competing languages—bio-political rationalities as well as various forms of sovereignty (legal, personal, etc.)—both within and beyond the state.

OTHER WORLDS OF MUMBAI

This book has told the story of how Bombay became Mumbai because of the success of a particularly violent and virulent interpretation of the rich ethnohistorical imaginary in western India. Shiv Sena has played a central role in this story, and some readers, with good reason, will object that I have paid scant attention to other forces, other worlds, and other ideas in Mumbai. As I indicated in my descriptions of the city's Muslim worlds, Mumbai indeed has an infinite number of other, more benign, and, in a human sense, far more interesting and rich environments than those that have nurtured Shiv Sena: unions, artists, NGOs, self-help groups, religious communities, and so on. A major omission in this book is, in fact, the vigorous Dalit movement in Mumbai and elsewhere in Maharashtra. Not only is the world of the Dalit communities dynamic and intriguing, it has also provided a strong antidote to Shiv Sena and Hindu nationalism for several decades. Neither time nor resources enabled me to do justice to this significant part of Mumbai's popular world.

I found it necessary, however, to relate this story because Shiv Sena's success has caused many deaths and much destruction, ultimately transforming the very notions of politics, public behavior, civility, and legality, which has implications for every citizen in the mega-city. I have also emphasized throughout that Shiv Sena, its violent rhetoric and practices, its ideas of regional history, its intolerance, and so forth, are features considerably less exceptional in Mumbai than they sometimes are made out to be. I have ventured as well to assert that Shiv Sena has pushed beyond legality many of the qualities of India's political society that we salute— its energy, its irreverence, its democratization of public space, its vernacularization of democracy—forcing these admirable qualities into the realm of "pure politics," naked violence, that may jeopardize the small bit of freedom that even Mumbai's poorest slum dweller still enjoys. Chatterjee acknowledges, along with most of us, that the forces set in motion in India's political society have their own immense momentum:

> Rights and rules have to be, seemingly, negotiated afresh. Only those voices are heard that can make the loudest voice and speak on behalf of the largest number. There is violence in the air. Not everything that happens here is desirable or worthy of approval. But, then, how can we be sure that what we desire or approve is what is truly good? Who can decide that except those who go through the dangerously creative process of politics itself? (Chatterjee 2000, 20)

My contention is that as long as India's political society produces and makes ample room for such lethal phenomena as Shiv Sena, stronger ethical stands than Chatterjee seems willing to allow may need to be taken in favor of upholding a rule of law in a more classical sense.

The uncomfortable reality of Mumbai's violent political society, its communal polarization, and its deteriorating living conditions and governance encloses the activities of all those who oppose this reality: the determination of hundreds of NGOs, citizen groups, trade unions, and many others to instill forms of justice based on equal citizenship rather than on the measure of one's "nuisance value," the countering of violence with violence. Shiv Sena may be out of power for now, but the conditions, imaginaries, and public culture that enabled that party to rise and rule are still alive and well in Mumbai.

Notes

Introduction
The Proper Name

1. Appadurai and Breckenridge (1996, 5) define public culture as "a zone of cultural debate" where national, global, and local discourses and representations " . . . encounter, interrogate, and contest one another in new and unexpected ways."

2. The demand for the renaming of Bombay was on the agenda of the Samyukta Maharashtra Samiti, the movement that successfully campaigned in the 1950s for the formation of the state of Maharashtra on the basis of linguistic distinctions. The Bombay Municipal Corporation has used the name frequently since 1986, and many Congress politicians for decades have strongly supported the use of the vernacular name. For an overview of the uses of the name, see *Times of India*, 23 November 1995.

3. Many studies of urban India were undertaken in later years (Kumar 1992; Breckenridge 1996, to name but a few), but the study of contemporary urban life in India is nowhere near the sophistication one finds in the study of urban practices in Latin America, for example, nor does it compare to the density of studies of rural India.

4. Exceptions include Crapanzano 1980 and Grosrichard 1998. For a recent reflection on the usefulness of psychoanalysis in anthropology, see, for example, Moore 1994; de Latour 1994; Ewing 1997; and Moore 1998.

5. See, for example, Zizek 1989; 1992a; 1992b; and 1993. See also Lacan 1977 [1966, in French]; 1978; and 1992.

Chapter 1
Deccan Pastoral: The Making of an
Ethnohistorical Imagination in Western India

1. Veronique Bénéï's (2000) recent research on education in Maharashtrian schools is charting some of this territory.

2. As pointed out by N. K. Wagle (1989, 51–66) and Stewart Gordon (1994) in his recent work on the Maratha Empire, the medieval *bhakti* tradition in the Deccan implied a considerable degree of Hindu-Muslim symbiosis—both at the level of writing and textual interpretation, where Muslim poet-saints like Shah Muni and Shekh Mahammad made important contributions to the *bhakti* traditions, and at the level of religious practice, where syncretic forms of worship of *bhakti* saints and Muslim *pirs* became widespread in rural areas and gradually spread to northern India as well.

3. These regional eulogies have been opposed by historians, who argue that the Maratha expansion never tried to construct an empire but relied heavily on Mughal forms of land distribution, taxation, and administration. In Habib's classical work,

this incapacity of state formation had to do with the logic of entropy and divisions among landowning groups and caste communities. This is "at least one explanation of why the impetus towards empire building in medieval India came so repeatedly from foreign conquerors" (Habib 1963, 169). Even Kadam's otherwise praising account of the Maratha commanders endorses this view. "The principle that in unity lies strength and in wider unity, wider strength, was unknown and not implemented in the policies of the Marathas" (Kadam 1993, 6).

4. For an overview of the conflicts between reformers and orthodox Brahmans, see Tucker 1976; Naregal 1998. For an account of missionary critiques of Hindu practices, see O'Hanlon 1985, 67–86; for a more specific discussion of the controversial "Age of Consent Bill" and the issue of remarriage, see O'Hanlon 1991.

5. In the section entitled "Population" of the *District Gazetteer* from 1885, Chitpavans are mentioned as the first community, and a very detailed and sympathetic account of their daily life and rituals are given in more than fifty pages. The text praises the Chitpavans for their well-known "stinginess, hardness, and craftiness," characterizes them as intelligent and daring, and opines that "no Hindus have shown greater administrative talent or acuteness" (99–158).

6. For a structural analysis of the two different myths of Ganesh that revolve around his ambiguous sexuality as a balancer between the male and female principles in the universe, see Courtright 1988.

7. See Gordon 1993, 13–17. Recent historical research has pointed out how many caste groups emerged out of military and other types of service for rulers in various places in the subcontinent. Hence the flexibility and openness of caste boundaries and the "Kshatriya-ization" of various groups into dominant groups, for example, the incorporation of the tribal Bhils into *Rajput* lineages. See also Dirks 1987.

8. Government of Maharashtra, Department of Cooperation and Rural Development, *Report of the Committee on Democratic Decentralization* (Bombay: Government Central Press, 1961).

9. Carter has argued that the primary cohesive factor among Marathas is, in fact, political power. Marathas constitute a "political class" engaged in endless factional infighting and rivalry at all levels but they are also accepted as specialists in this vocation by most other caste groups (Carter 1975, 147–79). For a quantitative demonstration of the continued dominance of Marathas at all levels in the political institutions in Maharashtra, see Vora 1999.

Chapter 2
Bombay and the Politics of Urban Desire

1. From 1860 to the 1930s Bombay was the third largest cotton market in the world. For an authoritative study of the development of an indigenous bourgeoisie in Bombay, see Bagchi 1973. For a recent overview of the evolution of trade and industry in Bombay in the colonial period, see Markovits 1995.

2. As Chandavarkar has recently shown, the relative size of confessional and linguistic groups in Bombay remained almost stable from 1891 to 1931 in spite of a population growth from 0.7 million to 1.4 million. The proportion of Hindus remained at 65–68 percent, Muslims at 18–20 percent, and Christians at 5–7 per-

cent. The share of Marathi speakers decreased slowly from 51 percent in 1881 to 47 percent in 1931, whereas the share of Gujarati speakers remained at 20.9 percent. The share of Hindi speakers grew from 14.8 to 17.0 percent (Chandavarkar 1994, 31–32).

3. In her introduction to the second volume of Patel and Thorner's useful volumes on modern Bombay, Alice Thorner observes that the city's cultural mix not only provided a vibrant atmosphere of socioeconomic competition but also made available new, uncharted, and liberating territory for cultural expressions and innovations (Patel and Thorner 1995, xiv). See also Conlon's interesting and indulgent celebration of the city's diverse public culture in his essay on "dining out" in Bombay (Conlon 1996, 90–127).

4. See, for example, Lele 1990, 170–71. For a study of the increased exploitation of cheap female labor in small-scale industries in the region, see Deshpande and Deshpande 1992.

5. The SMS won 113 out of a total of 153 State Legislative Assembly seats in the region, and as many as 22 out of 41 Lok Sabha seats (Lele 1990, 168).

6. The interplay between the changing social organization and commercialization of agriculture in western Maharashtra and the relatively limited options available in mills in Bombay in this period is well explored in village studies by H. C. Dandekar (1986) and T. N. Valunjkar (1966).

7. Interview in *Marmik Mehfil*, 25 May 1997. The incident and the subsequent drafting of an oath for Shiv sainiks in which they promise to help their fellow Maharashtrians, to promote initiative and industriousness, and to boycott non-Maharashtrian shops and restaurants is carefully recorded in Vaibhav Purandare's recent hagiographical account of the trajectory of Shiv Sena (Purandare 1999, 27–45).

8. Reported in *Navakaal*, 31 October 1966. The founding and early phases of Shiv Sena has been analyzed in Katzenstein 1981; Gupta 1982; and Joshi 1970. Julia Eckert's recent work represents a more contemporary and comprehensive analysis of Shiv Sena as a movement, an ideology, and a public mood (Eckert 2000).

9. The proportion of inhabitants in Bombay born outside the city decreased from 72.1 percent in 1951 to 64.5 percent in 1961. The proportion of Maharashtrians decreased only by 1 percent in the same decade, and the proportion of South Indians remained stable (Katzenstein 1981, 55–56). Gupta reaches a similar conclusion: "The South Indians . . . are not the largest category of non-Marathi migrants in Greater Bombay [in the 1970s—T.B.H.]. . . . The population of Greater Bombay is increasing though the contribution of migrants shows a downwards trend" (Gupta 1982, 49).

10. Gupta quotes a senior Communist worker as saying, "A generation was brought up by the communists to believe in the *Samyukta Maharashtra Samiti*" (Gupta 1982, 59). One of the most colorful leaders of the Communist Party of India (CPI) in Bombay, Comrade Dange, was one of the most effective ideologues of the SMS.

11. In Purandare's *The Sena Story*, there are repeated references to George Fernandes (now Union Minister of Defense in India) as a "family friend of the Thackeray clan." The author narrates an incident from the early 1980s, when Shiv Sena was in a deep crisis and flirted with the idea of "practical socialism." Thackeray had invited Comrade Dange to address his followers, and he was received with

tumultuous applause. According to Purandare, Thackeray acknowledged and admired Dange's rhetorical skills but could neither trust him nor make an alliance with him (Purandare 1999, 229–32).

12. Heuzé (1992) has dealt with the sense of loss of self-respect, pride, and strength among ordinary sainiks as key motivating factors for their joining the Sena. In the second part of his recent documentary film, *Fathers, Sons, and Holy Wars*, Anand Patwardhan represents Shiv Sena as a symptom of a repressed and distorted masculinity in urban India. See also the analysis of the film by Rustom Bharucha (1995).

13. Interview in Bombay, 24 September 1992.

14. In an interview on 2 February 1993, Pramod Nawalkar, Shiv Sena MLA and, for decades, a member of the Municipal Corporation, repeatedly emphasized, as did so many other Shiv Sena leaders, that Shiv Sena primarily did "social work" (in most cases a metaphor for local patronage) and had no professional politicians.

15. In the early phase of Shiv Sena's existence, the organization especially promoted the Ganpatiutsav as a quintessential Maharashtrian festival. Promoting Ganesh was a way to make Bombay more Maharashtrian in complexion. In her recent analysis of the historical development of the iconographies of *mandap tableaux* (displays, paintings and figures produced for the festival) displayed during the Ganpatiutsav, Raminder Kaur demonstrates convincingly how these tableaux, after having been de-politicized and "culturalized" after Independence, have, since the 1980s, taken an ever more direct political form in their themes as well as in the direct messages displayed. Shiv Sena–sponsored *mandaps* have been leading in this return to the political and nationalist dimensions of the Ganpatiutsav (Kaur 1998, 256–78).

16. Interview with Modhav Joshi, Shiv Sena MLA in Thane City (West) constituency, November 1992.

17. Interview, Thane, 1 February 1993.

18. According to Hemchandra Gupte, a former confidante of Thackeray, his major reason for leaving the party was his growing disgust with the prominence of money and the "goonda'ization" of the party (interview, 5 October 1992).

19. Interview with BKS leader Ganesh Naik, Thane, 17 October 1992.

20. Interview with S. Joshi, former mayor of Bombay and present member of the *Karya Karani* in Shiv Sena headquarters in Dadar, Bombay, 5 October 1992. Joshi estimated the total number of SLS units throughout the state to be 240; they are particularly present in Greater Bombay but are also in Pune, Thane, Aurangabad, Akola, and Vidarbha.

21. Interview, 3 October 1992, with Hemchandra Gupte, physician, formerly Bal Thackeray's family doctor, and Shiv Sena's mayor of Bombay from 1971 to 1972. Dr. Gupte left Shiv Sena in 1976 because of Thackeray's support for Mrs. Gandhi and for the Emergency.

22. B. S. Dhume, former leader of All-India Trade Union Congress, quoted in Purandare 1999, 94–98.

23. For a critical account of the murder of Krishna Desai and Shiv Sena's aggression against the Communist movement, see Vaidiya 1970.

24 Cited in Purandare 1999, 112.

25. Reports in *Navakaal* 18–26 February 1969; Purandare 1999, 122–23.

26. *Navakaal,* 2 February 1969.
27. The incident is described in Purandare 1999, 199–200.
28. Speech at Shivaji Park, 27 October 1982, quoted in Purandare 1999, 204.
29. *Times of India,* 25 February 1979.
30. At the State Assembly elections in 1980 the Muslim League won 0.16 percent of the votes, and no figures were reported for Shiv Sena (Joshi 1995, 16).
31. Gupta's survey of local and middle-level leaders in Shiv Sena in the 1970s shows that they overwhelmingly were young, from the Maratha-Kunbi caste, working-class or lower-middle-class, and not previously involved in political work (Gupta 1982, 108).

Chapter 3
"Say with Pride That We Are Hindus":
Shiv Sena and Communal Populism

1. This is not unique to Bombay, but, as Sudipta Kaviraj has remarked, it is probably the dominant conceptual form in which democracy and notions of rights have been translated and instituted among ordinary Indians (personal communication).
2. *Ma-baap'ism,* as a strategy, is both driven by the fears of the popular world and informed by the utopian Gandhian view of the popular world as a site of a more authentic, pure popular culture. Unselfish work in the service of this people was capable of normatively purifying the rich. This version of paternalism prevails within the RSS and the larger Hindu nationalist movement, for instance (Heuzé 1995, 224–28).
3. Obvious continuities exist between these practices and the organization of *melas* in the colonial period—associations collecting funds and preparing processions for public festivals but also acting as a kind of brotherhood, demanding loyalty and at times even indulging in street fighting (Chandavarkar 1994, 212–15).
4. This is taken from an interesting compilation of material and evidence produced by official commissions of enquiry into communal violence in the 1970s and early 1980s (Ghosh 1985). The author, S. K. Ghosh, is a retired inspector general of police, and the materials are mainly summaries of official reports and comparisons of trends and tendencies therein. The section on the 1970 riots in Maharashtra is based exclusively on the "Report of the Commission of Inquiry into the Communal Disturbances at Bhiwandi, Jalgaon, and Mahad in May 1970" (n.d.), headed by Justice Madon.
5. The use of loudspeakers remains a major bone of contention in the state. Many Hindus feel provoked by what they view as undue assertiveness of the Muslim community, allegedly backed by the government, which suddenly adds a new dimension to the presence of a Muslim community in many localities. For the Hindu nationalist organizations, this alleged "decision" by Antulay provided a perfect example of Congress's "appeasement of Muslims." Despite my rather systematic searches in newspapers and archives, however, I have been unable to locate any particular indication that the government of Maharashtra issued their permission. More likely, this incident is an effect of pure "ideological conjecture" in a situation characterized by increasing anti-Muslim sentiments in the state.

6. Campaign launched by the Vishwa Hindu Parishad to strengthen national and spiritual unity among Hindus. The campaign involved processions from all corners of India converging in the city of Nagpur, the geographical heart of India and site of RSS's headquarters. See Jaffrelot 1996, 360–62.

7. For an overview of communal riots in Maharashtra since Independence, see Mukadam 1995, 110–26. For a discussion of the militant Hindu organization Patit Pawan Sanghatan, which played a key role in the 1982 riots in Pune, see Hansen 1999, 122–26).

8. In Marathi, *landya* means a penis that has shrunken or is too small, an obvious reference to the circumcision of Muslim men and, implicitly, a reversal of the theme of Hindu effeminacy and weakness versus Muslim masculinity and potency, stereotypes the Hindu nationalist discourse inherited from the British imperial typecasting of races based on military skills, and so on. The term *landya* simply conveyed that Muslim men were not so well endowed after all in terms of sexual prowess and potency.

9. Interview with Vasantdada Patil, Bombay, 2 July 1984

10. This is based on reports in *Times of India* and *Indian Express*, 15 May to 6 June 1984; as well as interviews with Shahid Rashid, who covered the events for *Urdu Times*, Bombay; Nikhil Wagle, editor of *Mahanagar* (a Marathi daily in Bombay), 2 October 1992); and Shiv Sena leaders and activists in Thane District. See also Engineer 1991b. The then chief minister of Maharashtra, V. Patil (Congress), was known for his friendly attitude toward Shiv Sena and for his tacit support of the organization in its formative phase. According to Engineer's account, Patil even tried to absolve Shiv Sena of responsibility for the riots; instead, he blamed the Urdu press for spreading false rumors among Muslims, and he refused to hold a judicial inquiry into the events (327–28).

11. Interviews with A. Wankhude, founding member of Shiv Sena, Aurangabad, 1 September 1992; and Subash Patil, former zilla pramukh of Shiv Sena, Aurangabad, 3 September 1992.

12. *Times of India*, 5 July 1984.

13. The Shah Bano case concerned a highly contested verdict in which the Supreme Court granted alimony to a divorced Muslim woman, thereby violating Muslim personal law. After vehement protests, the Rajiv Gandhi government reversed the verdict both to please the conservative Muslim leadership and to reconsolidate the Muslims' waning support of the Congress Party. Not surprisingly, the Hindu nationalist movement used the controversy as proof of the government's undue "pampering" of minorities in the Indian state. Much has been written about this case (see Engineer 1987; Pathak and Rajan 1989; Das 1995; and Chatterjee 1995), but, as Ortner (1995) has pointed out, very few have tried to explore how local circumstances conditioned the highly varied nature and content of Muslim protests at this juncture. I attempt to explore that area in chapter 6 below, in my account of the Muslim community in Bombay during the last two decades.

14. Quoted from T. Setalwad 1995, 238. See also S. Bannerjee 1995, 216–32.

15. "Other Backward Classes" is a residual administrative category designating large but relatively poor caste groups, approximately 52 percent of the population. After the Mandal Commission in 1980 recommended reservations of jobs and

education for these groups, the term became an object of active identification in north India.

16. *Census of India*, vol. 12 (1931): 17.

17. Congress (S) signifies the breakaway party from Congress led by Sharad Pawar between 1978 and 1986.

18. *Indian Express*, 14 January 1988.

19. The following analysis is drawn from translations of fifteen editorials that appeared in *Marmik* and *Samna* and three of Thackeray's major speeches given in the period from 1985 to 1991. The editorials and speeches are in *Hindutva Saar aani Dhaar* (Hindutva: The Essence and the Edge), comp. Shashi Bhalekar, 2nd ed. (Thane: Dimple Publications, 1991) (in Marathi). I also rely on transcriptions of videotaped recordings of a Shiv Sena rally in Narsi, Nanded District, on 4 February 1990, showing speeches of Thackeray and Chagan Bhujbal; as well as transcriptions of a Shiv Sena propaganda video, *Avhan ani Awahan*, used in the State Assembly election campaign in February 1990. Both transcriptions, in English, were used as evidence (exhibit "D" and "I") in Election Petition No. 8 at the High Court, Aurangabad Bench, where a group of Congress members sought to overturn the election of an MLA for Shiv Sena based on illegal and corrupt election practices, including the use of religious propaganda. I also drew information from transcriptions of speeches made by Bal Thackeray and Moreshwar Save, Shiv Sena member of Parliament from Aurangabad, in May 1991 at the sports stadium in Aurangabad, during the Lok Sabha election campaign. These transcriptions were also used in a suit to overturn the election of Moreshwar Save at the High Court of Bombay, Aurangabad Bench. In both cases the elections were successfully overturned and the Shiv Sena legislators in question lost their right to vote, respectively, in Vidhan Sabha and Lok Sabha.

20. Afzulkhan was a leading general in the army of the Mughal emperor Aurangzeb. He fought many battles against Shivaji and, as the myth goes, at one point invited Shivaji to speak of reconciliation and peace. Shivaji, not trusting him, wore steel claws on his fingers. Indeed, Afzulkhan had set a trap for Shivaji, and, as the former embraced his guest as a "sign of friendship," Afzulkhan tried to stab him. Shivaji reacted by ripping open Afzulkhan's body with his steel claws, tearing out his intestines, and miraculously escaping. Thackeray often relates this parable as proof of Maratha bravery and Muslim treason, with Afzulkhan, of course, symbolizing the treacherous enemy.

21. The daily circulation of *Samna* exceeded 100,000 in 1992. Outside Bombay, it competes with the RSS *Tarun Bharat* and a host of local Marathi dailies. In Bombay its chief counterpart remains *Mahanagar*, also a tabloid Marathi daily, which has taken a strong anti–Shiv Sena stand. The journalist and outspoken editor of *Mahanagar*, Nikhil Wagle, has been physically assaulted several times by members of Shiv Sena. In 1993 *Samna* published a Hindi edition, *Dopahar ka Saamna*, which has become a spectacular success in Bombay.

22. For a more complete discussion of this alliance and the problems and apprehensions it has created over the years in BJP, see Hansen 1998, 121–62.

23. The nine points were as follows: (1) changing the name of the country from Bharat to Hindusthan; (2) establishing stable prices on five essential commodities for the next five years; (3) offering so-called remunerative prices to farm-

ers (a position taken over from the popular farmer's movement, Shetkari Sangha-tana); (4) forming an autonomous board to manage all state religious institutions; (5) devising a comprehensive pension scheme applicable to workers in all sectors; (6) implementing Marathi as the official state language; (7) forming a committee to stop the oppression of women; (8) providing improved assistance to unemployed youths; (9) resolving the Maharashtra-Karnataka border issue concerning Belgaum (*Indian Express*, 2 January 1989).

24. *Shiv Sena—Bha-Ja-Pa Vachanama* (Pledge of Shiv Sena—BJP), January 1990.

25. Advertisement in *Sakal*, 24 February 1990.

26. The nomination of Manohar Joshi, a Brahman, as parliamentary leader of the alliance made Sharad Pawar say: "Distribute Sweets! *Peshwa* rule is here again!" *(Sakal*, 13 January 1991).

27. *Kesari*, 18 May 1991.

28. On evaluating the results of Shiv Sena's work, Thackeray emphasized the employment of young Marathi speakers in prestigious jobs: "It would have been difficult for my boys to enter a five-star hotel [without Shiv Sena—T.B.H.]. You will now find young boys in five-star hotels saying *Jai Maharashtra*; then there are Maharashtrian air hostesses and pursers in the Air India and Indian Airlines" (interview with Bal Thackeray, Bombay, 19 November 1992).

29. See *Times of India* 18–20 February 1992. That three city councilors and several MLAs had been murdered in internal fights with "business rivals" in 1991–92 was an indication of Shiv Sena's deep involvement in Bombay's underworld.

30. *Times of India*, 16 May 1992

31. *Sunday*, 2–8 August 1992.

Chapter 4
Thane City: The Making of Political Dadaism

1. Thane Municipal Corporation 1988, 47–48.

2. Interview with Satish Pradhan, 1 February 1993, in Thane.

3. Satish Pradhan was later promoted to be among Shiv Sena's so-called twelve leaders, the *Karya Karani*, and is today a member of Parliament (Rajya Sabha) for Shiv Sena. Prakash Paranjape was the leader of the Shiv Sena councilors in Thane Municipal Corporation and Shiv Sena's mayoral candidate for many years; he was later elected a member of Parliament for Shiv Sena.

4. Interview, 2 February 1993, in Kalyan.

5. *Gazetteer of the Bombay Presidency, Thana District*, vol. 13, part 1, p. 228 (facsimile reproduction, Pune 1984).

6. The official arguments forwarded by Shiv Sena to prove the "Hindu-ness" of the shrine all refer to the unmistakable traces of a variety of Hindu practices in these celebrations. See the report in *Lok Satta*, 14 February 1993.

7. *Navakaal*, 6 May 1991.

8. *Saamna*, 8 May 1991.

9. Interview with Manohar Gadhwe, 10 November 1992, in Thane.

10. In my numerous conversations with Anand Dighe, he repeatedly stressed that his overriding criterion for recruiting sainiks was their loyalty to him and to

Shiv Sena; the next prerequisite was their aggressiveness. Their skills and their ability to work were less important.

11. Interview with Rajan Vichare, 25 September 1992, Thane.

12. Ibid.

13. Ibid.

14. Interview with Mohan Goswami, former Shiv sainik and assistant to Dighe from 1987 to 1990. Goswami, originally from Uttar Pradesh, the large state in north India, left Shiv Sena because he was disgusted with its parochialism, and, as he said, "[its] hostility to north Indian *bhaiyas*, like myself." He admitted that a decisive element in his decision to quit was that he had been denied a ticket for the 1992 municipal elections (interview, 5 February 1993, in Thane).

15. The chain of events leading up to the killing of Khopkar, the arrest of Dighe, and other local political incidents in Thane City has been corroborated with the help of the local Marathi daily *San Mitra*, March–May 1989. These accounts, as well as other information regarding local politics in Thane, were verified with former councilors; with the Thane editor of *Lok Satta*, a major Marathi daily; with Milind Balal, *Times of India* correspondent in Thane; and with numerous local activists and administrators.

16. Interview, 25 October 1992, in Thane.

17. Interview, 28 January 1993, in Thane.

18. The following quotations are derived from my interviews and conversations with families in various Shiv Sena strongholds in Thane City between July 1992 and April 1993.

19. *Times of India*, 21 January 1997. Reports on clashes between sainiks and BJP activists in *Mid-Day*, 18 February 1997, and *Times of India*, 18 February 1997.

20. *Times of India*, 13 January 1997.

21. *Lok Satta*, 5 March 1997.

Chapter 5
Riots, Policing, and Truth Telling in Bombay

1. Interview in *Frontline*, 1 January 1993.

2. *Lokprabha*, 10 January 1993

3. Interview in Mumbai, 16 November 1995.

4. The anatomy of rumors during riots and the psychological causes that account for this suspension of a normal sense of judgment has recently been explored by Sudhir Kakar (1995, 31–66).

5. For a condensed overview of the events before, during, and after the riots, see Sharma 1995.

6. The evidence of women's increasing involvement in the riots was collected by Gopal Guru, Pune University, and scholars at the Women's University in Bombay in February and March 1993.

7. In December 1993 by-elections were held for six municipal seats in Bombay. Shiv Sena won four of these seats, all in areas affected by the riots. At that time, most Bombay residents with whom I spoke were convinced that Shiv Sena, far from being a spent force, was likely to stage a major comeback in Bombay politics.

Shiv Sena's victory in the 1995 State Assembly election, especially in the Bombay region, only confirmed that its performance during the riots had dramatically improved its political fortunes.

8. After the riots, many Shiv Sena leaders at the local levels led a concerted boycott campaign against Muslim shops and businesses, threatening Muslim employees in companies and harassing Muslim children and teachers in schools. In public buses, trains, and the streets, Muslims were shouted at, abused, and harassed. Odd pamphlets and lists were circulated—not necessarily by Shiv Sena—naming shops and businesses to be boycotted, and actually asking Hindu doctors to rape their Muslim female patients so that the women would give birth to Hindu offspring.

9. Interview, 27 January 1993.

10. For an elaboration of this argument, see Hansen and Stepputat 2001.

11. The literature on kingship in precolonial and colonial India is vast. Landmarks in the literature are Dumont 1980; Dirks 1987; and Inden 1990; see also Cohn 1983 and Price 1996.

12. Akhil Gupta's analysis of corruption as a social practice around which ordinary Indians deliberate the nature of the state and its ideal separation from the social is exemplary as a way to grasp the everyday meanings and significance of *sarkar* (Gupta 1995).

13. This draws on my own presence at hearings in November 1996 and from January to March 1997, as well as on written affidavits from a range of police officers and civilians obtained from court officials .

14. *Mid-Day,* 5 April 1997.

15. Interview, 18 February 1993.

16. *Mid-Day,* 12 April 1997.

17. Ibid., 16 April 1997.

18. The legal intricacies of this unprecedented move is outlined by R. Padmanabhan in *Frontline,* 18 April 1997. The High Court in Mumbai sentenced Thackeray to a week of "simple imprisonment" on the grounds of contempt of court. Thackeray was forced to appear in the magistrate's court in the Bombay suburb of Bandra on 17 February, where he was released on bail. Meanwhile, the court was surrounded by thousands of angry Shiv sainiks shouting slogans and demanding the Senapati's immediate release (*Mid-Day,* 18 February 1997).

19. *Times of India,* 4 April 1997.

20. Ibid., 25 May 1997. The commission's terms of reference was expanded to include an investigation of "the circumstances and the immediate cause of the incidents commonly known as the serial bomb-blasts on 12 March 1993, which occurred in the Bombay Police Commissionerate area," and, further, whether these were linked by common causes or "a common design" to the riots investigated by the commission (Srikrishna 1998, 58).

21. For an overview of the proceedings of the TADA court, see "Justice for Whom," in *Humanscape,* December 1995.

22. Independent human rights groups organized the "Indian People's Human Rights Commission," which, shortly after the riots, set up an inquiry headed by two retired judges of the Bombay High Court, and thus was also framed in the

legal language of the state. Their report, *The Peoples Verdict*, was published in August 1993 and concluded that Shiv Sena, as well as a limited and incompetent police force, should bear the main responsibility for the riots.

23. *The Pioneer*, 4 February 1996.

24. Memo from the Commissioner of Police, Bombay, December 1926 (quoted in Chandavarkar 1998, 161).

25. *Bombay Chronicle*, 28 February 1946.

26. *Bombay Sentinel*, 25 February 1946.

27. *Bombay Chronicle* 8 March 1946.

28. Ibid., 7 March 1946.

29. See Dhareshwar and Srivatsan's piece on police practices concerning the arrests of young "rowdies," their subsequent classification as "rowdy sheeters," and so on (Dhareshwar and Srivatsan 1996).

30. For the want of better recruits from the Bombay Presidency, the police recruited many *Pardeshis* (Hindus from north India). As one officer stated, however, "they are proverbially honest and faithful, but their brain power is very limited. . . . They are well-fitted for guards and escorts. For the work of unarmed police such men are entirely unsuitable" (quoted in Chandavarkar 1998, 187).

31. In the predominantly Muslim neighborhoods where I worked, most families come from north India, and the structures of the *biraderi*—the clanlike and durable relations of trust between families mostly of the same caste (but not always)—remain of paramount importance when it comes to helping one another, getting jobs, marrying, recruiting new labor from the villages, borrowing money, and so on. In the urban economy, however, relations and economic networks cut across these structures, and *biraderi* often seems to function as a last resort in times of crises or serious decisions.

32. Interview with Basheer Patel, MLA, Samajwadi Party, in Umerkhadi, 10 December 1996.

33. Visvanathan presents evidence of the activities and scale of Dawood's gang or networks but quotes no sources, apparently because most of these are of a sensitive nature internal to government departments (Visvanathan 1998, 118–47). The problem in this method is that Visvanathan, who is highly critical of the practices of the Indian state, ultimately contributes to a continued mythology of the "truths" owned and controlled by the state. My proposition would be, instead, that the "truth" is that the knowledge that forms the basis of state and police actions is flimsy, fragmented, and generally uncorroborated.

34. *Times of India*, 27 November 1995.

35. Ibid., 11 March 1996.

36. The individual who was this driving force was Sushoba Bharve, an activist and self-professed Gandhian social worker (interview in Worli, 19 February 1997).

37. S. Bharve confirmed this view when she said, "Respectable people are not very interested in working with the police. The tout will always come forward, but we did not want that. So we worked really hard to find good people with constructive views. It was very difficult" (ibid.).

38. Tyagi also initiated slightly more creative events such as regular sports days where police teams would play cricket against the local Muslims or where a team of Hindus would play against a Muslim team, as was done in Agripada, which has long witnessed the almost ritualized clashes between Hindus and Muslims after cricket matches between India and Pakistan. In this neighborhood, where the Hindu side is known as Jammu and the Muslim side as Kashmir, the concept worked quite well. "Now they fight it out, but we are there watching them so it does not go out of hand," one enthusiastic police constable told me.

Chapter 6
In the Muslim Mohalla

1. The Memon community had already strongly established itself in Karachi, and, in the years after Partition, significant numbers of Memons from the Porbhander area in Khatiawar on the Gujarat coast migrated to Karachi. Memons continue to occupy a powerful position in trade, finance, and manufacturing in Karachi.

2. Interview with A. Jabar, Agripada, 2 December 1996.

3. Interview in Mumbai on 6 December 1996 with Samuel Augustine, who acted as negotiator on behalf of the ansaris in their confrontation with the Municipal Corporation in 1956–57.

4. Interview with A.A., Madanpura, 28 November 1996.

5. Interview with A. Jabar, secretary of the Bharatiya Weavers Cooperative, Agripada, and member of CPI, 4 December 1996.

6. Interview, 28 January 1997.

7. Interview, Agripada, 2 February 1997.

8. According to Engineer, nothing religious demands Bohras to be traders but merely a long-standing community ethos developed over centuries (Engineer 1980, 145–47).

9. The return of a massive number of Gulf migrants presented a serious problem for the government of Kerala, which had to reabsorb these men into the state economy (Saith 1992, 101–146). In the following years many Keralites did return to the Gulf, but the labor market there was less stable than previously. See reports in *Frontline*, 27 October 1996. For an overview of the economy of labor migration from India to the Middle East, see Amjad 1989.

10. For a more elaborate analysis of the contradictions and styles of narration of the experience of migrant work, see Hansen 2000b.

11. A biographical sketch of the founder of the Bareilvy interpretation of South Asian Islam, Ahmad Riza Khan, and a discussion of the practical worship of Bareilvis can be found in Sanyal 1995. See also Jamaluddin 1981.

12. Interview, Nagpada, 4 December 1996.

13. See newspaper reports in *Indian Express*, 19, 20 January 1998; and *Asian Age*, 20 January 1998.

14. For a discussion of the Tabligh movement, see Ziiya-ul-Hasan 1981. See also the discussion in Hasan 1996, 196–202; and Ahmed 1991.

15. Dr. Naik's organization is actually a subsidiary of the Islamic Propagation Centre International, established in Durban, South Africa, in 1962 by Ahmed Deedat, an autodidact Muslim preacher who has become famous for engaging leading evangelists in theological debates.

16. See Ahmed 1991; and Hasan 1996, 202–210.

17. *Blitz Weekly*, 20 March 1993. SIMI is also mentioned in the Srikrishna Commission report as one of the organizations that issued "extremely provocative writing" in Urdu on blackboards throughout central Mumbai (Srikrishna 1998, 166–67).

18. In a pamphlet distributed to members of *Jamaat-e-Islami* before the 1996 election, members were told that they could only exercise their franchise if they voted for candidates opposed to gambling, liquor, corruption, prostitution, and so on, as well as for candidates who were "reputed to be gentlemen" and were sympathetic to "the Muslim viewpoint on education, personal law, honor, language, etc."

19. Statistics I obtained from Mumbai Municipal Corporation concerning enrollment rates, drop-out rates, and the number of students showing up for examinations between 1990 and 1995 demonstrate that approximately 120,000 children attended Urdu schools in Mumbai in this period. The number of students in these schools has been steadily growing for decades but began to stagnate and decrease after 1993, whereas the attendance at municipal schools with other languages of instruction has continued to grow during the entire period.

20. "Memorandum" submitted to the Chief Minister of Maharashtra by the "Julaha/Ansari Community Service Center, Bombay," 11 August 1990.

21. *The Observer*, 11 May 1997; *Indian Express*, 7 May 1997; *Times of India*, 25 May 1997; *Observer*, 12 October 1997.

22. A notable exceptions is P. A. Sebastian from the Committee for the Protection of Democratic Rights, who called the two hundred deaths per year of those in custody an indication of "the brutalization of the police force . . . sanctioned by the highest authorities in the government" (*Times of India*, 18 September 1997).

23. *Hindustan Times*, 25 August 1997.

24. *Times of India*, 25 August 1997.

25. *Indian Express*, 5 May 1997.

26. From the portrait of the dons in "Gang Wars and Aftermath," *Caravan*, 2 May 1984, 18–27.

27. See, for example, "Encounter with the Don," *The Daily*, 26 April 1987.

28. See, for instance, the "drama-documentary" novel by Amrita Shah: *The Avengers: The Inside Story of Bombay's Secret Gang Wars, Imprint*, November 1983; see also the report on contract killings in *Bombay*, 7–21 June 1988.

29. *Times of India*, 10 October 1983.

30. "The Dons also Rise," *The Week*, 28 October 1984.

31. The investigation of the incident was reported in *Times of India*, 21 March 1994.

32. "The Warlord," *Illustrated Weekly of India*, 10 July 1988, 38–41.

33. Ibid., 41.

34. *India Today*, 7 December 1998, 14.

Chapter 7
Living the Dream: Governance, Graft, and Goons

1. From the pamphlet *Shiv Sena at a Glance*, November 1995.

2. For an overview of the trajectory of the Shiv Sena–BJP alliance, the 1995 election that brought the alliance to power, and the performance of the government until 1997, see Hansen 1998, 121–62.

3. In Lacanian usage the *objét petit a* stands for the irreducible sign of the Real, that is, the frightening and fascinating dimensions that cannot be symbolized and encompassed within a prevailing social-cultural order, and therefore prevents the closure of identities and cultural horizons.

4. *Shiv Sena at a Glance*, Shivsena Rajyapramukh Parishad, Mumbai 18–19 November 1995.

5. Hansen 1998, 309–13.

6. *Asian Age*, 28 February 1997.

7. See extensive reports on the resignation drama in *The Hindu*, 24 March 1998.

8. Lyla Bavadam, in *Frontline*, 26 February 1999.

9. *Times of India*, 12 February 1997.

10. Ibid., 7 August 1975.

11. Ibid., 31 July 1975.

12. Ibid., 26 July 1975.

13. Ibid., 25 July 1975.

14. One of the stated objectives of the corporation was to privatize as many projects as possible, just as it was stated that the building of expressways would be given top priority (*Indian Express*, 22 May 1996).

15. For an overview of Bombay's developmental problems, see the special report in *Sunday*, 21–27 April 1996.

16. *Observer*, 4 May 1997

17. Thackeray, in *Sunday*, 21–27 April 1996.

18. *Indian Express*, 30 July 1995.

19. The official Marathi pamphlet is entitled "The Slum Rehabilitation Scheme: Houses of Permanent Structure (*pucca*) for 40 lakhs Slumdwellers," Government of Maharashtra, Mumbai 1996. The pamphlet, printed with bright colors and pictures of modern high-rise buildings, has seventeen pages of instructions and directives and a large appendix outlining the detailed rules and stipulations regarding eligibility, procedure, different categories of beneficiaries, financing of accessory facilities such as roads, water and electricity, and so on.

20. *Indian Express*, 19 October 1996.

21. Interview with officials from the Slum Up-Gradation Program, Bombay Municipal Corporation, 23 November 1996.

22. Interview in Mumbai, 29 November 1996.

23. *Times of India*, 21 December 1997.

24. See figures from the Government of Maharashtra and the Mumbai Police in the report in *Frontline*, 28 August 1998.

25. *Indian Express,* 19 October 1995. In these reports, as so many others in the press, the distinction between proper citizens inhabiting society and beggars, slum dwellers, squatters, and other poor and marginalized groups outside society is evident and characteristic of both liberal and Hindu nationalist analyses of social problems in India.

26. The details of government excesses during the Emergency period have, until recently, remained relatively unexplored by academics. One reason may be the ambivalent relationship of the Indian Left to this experiment of a bio-political dictatorship in the name of the secular nation. Emma Tarlo's forthcoming book on Delhi during Emergency rule is a highly welcome step toward understanding this period (Tarlo 2001).

27. *Times of India,* 29 August 1975.

28. In a recent paper Veena Naregal argues, however, that Cable Sena is rather inefficient and not viewed by cable operators as a reliable source of protection or networking (Naregal 1999).

29. Rajadhyaksha and Willemen 1995, 335.

30. Rumor has it that Thackeray, whose vanity is well known, was particularly incensed that the film depicted him, or a character like him, as a rather ugly man with buck teeth.

31. Quotes from an interview with Thackeray, *Indian Express,* 2 September 1995.

32. Interview, *India Today,* 21 December 1998.

33. *Hindustan Times,* 15 May 1998.

34. *The Hindu,* 8 March 1998.

35. *India Today,* 9 August 1999.

36. *Frontline,* 29 January 1999.

37. *India Today,* 30 March 1998. The same article claims that Tiger Memon, allegedly the main figure behind the 1993 bombings, is now a leading figure in what is termed a "Crush India program" (33).

38. See, for example, *Frontline,* 21 January 2000.

39. Extensive reports have appeared on the "Gawli phenomenon" since his release from prison (e.g., *Indian Express,* 6 August 1997; and *Sunday,* 6–11 January 1997).

40. Interview, *Frontline,* 9 April 1999.

41. Mendonca quoted in *Asian Age,* 9 November 1997.

42. *Frontline,* 22 May 1998.

43. There seems to be no dearth of journalists ready to narrate such heroic tales about the police. The headline to an article on the plight of constables during the riots read: "Unarmed They Faced the Berserk Mobs" (*The Daily,* 22 December 1992); and a more recent article on Bombay's police force of almost forty thousand argued that "the understaffed and ill-equipped police force is no match for those in the underworld" (*Frontline,* 22 May 1998).

44. *Times of India,* 3 February 1997.

45. See reports in *Indian Express,* 9 January 1996.

46. Ibid., 25 June 1996.

Conclusion
Politics as Permanent Performance

1. Interview with Deputy Chief Minister Chagan Bhujbal, *Frontline*, 18 August 2000.

2. In July 2000 A. G. Kishore of the Vishwa Hindu Parishad told a reporter: "The construction of a Ram temple is not a matter of adjudication. No Constitution, no laws, no government and no Prime Minister can stop our work" (*Frontline*, 7 July 2000).

Glossary

Ajlaf — Muslims of lower caste descent.

Akhada — wrestling ground

Akhand Bharat — undivided India

Ansar — helper (of the Prophet)

Ashraf — Muslims of noble descent or higher caste

Badli — casual labourer

Badmash — ciminal, rogue

Bahujan samaj — oppressed communities

Bandh — strike/closure of shops and services

Bania — trader

Bhagwa dwaj — saffron flag

Bhaiyas — colloquial term for North Indians

Bhajan — Hindu devotional songs

Bhakti — devotional form of Hindu worship

Bharatiya — Indian/national

Bhatji — colloquial term for priests, brahmins

Bhaubaund — patri-linear group

Biraderi — kinship-group, clan

Burqah — veil

Chauk (chowk) — square, neighborhood

Chowki — police post

Chawls — tenements

Dada — strongman

Dada'ism — strongman style of politics

Dadagiri — strongman power

Dalal — middle-man, broker

Dargah — Muslim shrine

Dassera — Hindu festival

Devak — totem

Dhangar — shepherd community in Maharashtra

Dharmayuddh — holy war

Durbar — court

Ganesh — Hindu god

Ganpatiutsav — festival of Ganesh

Gajkaaran — ringworm

Gata pramukh — deputy leader (of shakha)

Ghanta naad — ringing of temple bells (to celebrate the domolition of Babri Masjid in December 1992)

Ghar — family

Goonda — muscleman

Hadith — commentaries on the Koran

Hafta — lit. "weekly," regular bribe

Haj — pilgrimmage of Mecca

Haraam — unclean, forbidden (within Islam)

Hindu samaj — Hindu community

Hutatma — martyr

Isthana — gathering

Jagirdar — feudatory

Janva — sacred thread

Jati — community, sub caste

Jazbati — to be sentimental

Jhagdalu — one who fights often, bellicose

Jouissance — enjoyment of something disturbing or unknown

Karya Karani — council of leaders (in Shiv Sena)

Khandani — donation

Kula — clan

Lalbhai — literally "red brother," communist

Lal bavta — red flag

Lok Sabha — lower house in the Indian Parliment

Landya — colloquial term for small penis

Lok Sabha — Indian Parliament

Ma-baap'ism — paternalist style of politics

Madrasis — colloquial derogatory term for South Indians

Maha-aarti — public mass prayer promoted by Shiv Sena in December 1992

Maharashtra dharma — spirit of Maharashtra

Mahila Agadhi — women's wing of Shiv Sena

Mandals — committee

Mandap tableaux — stage/exhibition displayed during Ganpatiutsav

Marathi manus — Marathi speaking person

Mard — virile men

Margattha — to be stubborn or staunch

Masjid — mosque

Mathadi — porter

Matka — gambling

Mabaap'ism — paternalist style of politics

Maza — enjoyment

Mela — party, congregation

Mitra mandal — friend's association

Mohalla — neighborhood

Morcha — demonstration

Nafs — biological/physical powers — somethimes referred to as "the lower self"

Nagarpithas — city fathers

Nagarsevaks — city volunteers/workers

Nallah — swamp/low lying area

Namaz — Muslim prayer

Navrati — Gujarati festival celebrating the gods of artisans

Neta — leader (in Shiv Sena)

Nishta — loyalty

Objet petit a — impurity, sign of a larger, if imprecise, threat and anxiety

Panchayati Raj — three-tier structure of local government in India

Patil — village headman in the Decan area

Patilki — Maratha fighting spirit

Pehwan — wrestler

Peshwa — prime minister

Pir — Muslim saint in the Sufi tradition

Qawwali — Muslim devotional song

Rajkaaran — politics

Rajput — warrior caste of north-western India

Rajya Sabha — upper house in the Indian parliament

Roti — Indian bread

Sahanshakti — tolerance

Sahas — courage

Samadhi — Hindu shrine

Samaj — community

Samajwadi — socialist

Sardars — commanders, high offical

Sarkar — government

Savarna jati — caste Hindus

Senapati — army commander

Shakha — local unit (of Shiv Sena as well as RSS)

Shakha pramukh — leader of the shakha

Shetji — colloquial term for landowner, big man

Shibirs — ideological training in Mahila Aghadi, Shiv Sena's women's wing

Shivaji Maharaj — famous 18th century Maratha warrior king

Shivaji Jayanti — festival commemorating the death anniversary of Shivaji

Shivrajya — rule of Shivaji

Shivshakti — power of Shivaji

Sufism — mysticism/popular practices within Islam

Supari — contract killing

Swapaneer nagari — city of dreams

Tabligh — piety, purification of community of beleivers (among Muslims)

Talaq — divorce

Tanzim — organization (of community of beleivers)

Tarbiyah — character building (as used within Students Islamic Movement of India)

Tokshahi — dictatorship

Trishul — trident

Upa-netas — deputy leaders (in Shiv Sena)

Ustad — master

Vada pav — bread with vegetable sauce

Varna — Vedic fourfold social ranking

Vibhag pramukh — area leader (in Shiv Sena)

Videshi — foreign

Vidhan Sabha — State Legislative Assembly

Zamindar — landlord entrusted with tax collection during British rule

Zhunkar bhankar — scheme providing cheap meals for the poor promoted by Shiv Sena

Zilla parishad — district level elected body in the Panchayati Raj structure

Zilla Zamparka Pramukh — advisor for district leaders (in Shiv Sena)

Zopadpattis — slums

Bibliography

Ahmed, Mumtaz. 1991. "Islamic Fundamentalisms in South Asia: The Jamaat-i-Islami and Tablighi Jamaat." In *Fundamentalism and the State*, edited by Scott Appleby and M. Marty, 352–438. Chicago: University of Chicago Press.

Alberoni, Francesco. 1984. *Movement and Institution*. New York: Columbia University Press.

Alter, Joseph. 1994. "Somatic Nationalism: Indian Wrestling and Militant Hinduism. *Modern Asian Studies* 28 (3): 557–88.

Althusser, Louis. 1984. *Essays on Ideology*. London: Verso.

Amjad, R., ed. 1989. *To the Gulf and Back: Studies on the Economic Impact of Asian Labour Migration*. New Delhi: ILO/ARTEP.

Appadurai, Arjun. 1997. *Modernity at Large: Cultural Dimensions of Globalization*. Delhi: Oxford University Press.

———. 2000. "Spectral Housing and Urban Cleansing: Notes on Millenial Mumbai." *Public Culture* 12 (3).

Appadurai, Arjun, and Carol Breckenridge. 1996. "Public Modernity in India." In *Consuming Modernity: Public Culture in a South Asian World*, edited by Carol A. Breckenridge, 1–20. Delhi: Oxford University Press.

Appadurai, A., and J. Holston. 1996. "Cities and Citizenship." *Public Culture* 8 (2): 187–204.

Attwood, Donald W. 1993. *Raising Cane: The Political Economy of Sugar in Western India*. Delhi: Oxford University Press.

Bagchi, Amiya K. 1973. *Private Investment in India, 1900–1939*. Cambridge: Cambridge University Press.

Balibar, Etienne. 1991. "The Nation Form: History and Ideology." In *Race, Nation, Class: Ambiguous Identities*, edited by Etienne Balibar and Immanuel Wallerstein, 86–107. London: Verso.

———. 1998. "Violence, Ideality, and Cruelty." *New Formations* 35 (Autumn): 7–18.

Bannerjee, Sikata. 1995. "Hindu Nationalism and the Construction of Woman: The Shiv Sena Organises Women in Bombay." In *Women and Right-Wing Movements: Indian Experiences*, edited by Tanika Sarkar and Urvashi Butalia, 216–32. London: Zed.

Bayly, Chris A. 1998. *Origins of Nationality in South Asia*. Delhi: Oxford University Press.

Bénéï, Véronique. 1999. "Reappropriating Colonial Documents in Kolhapur (Maharashtra): Variations on a Nationalist Theme." *Modern Asian Studies* 33 (4): 913–50.

———. 2000. "Teaching Nationalism in Maharashtra Schools." In *The Everyday State in India*, edited by Véronique Bénéï and C. J. Fuller, 194–220. Delhi: Social Sciences Press.

Bharucha, Rustom. 1995. "Dismantling Men." *Economic and Political Weekly 30* (July 1): 1610–16.

Billig, Michael. 1995. *Banal Nationalism*. London: Sage.

Bourdieu, Pierre. 1984. *Distinction: A Social Critique of Taste*. London: Routledge and Kegan Paul.

Breckenridge, Carol, ed. 1996. *Consuming Modernity: Public Culture in Contemporary India*. Delhi: Oxford University Press.

Burchell, Graham, Colin Gordon, and Peter Miller, eds. 1991. *The Foucault Effect: Studies in Governmentality*. London: Harvester Wheatsheaf.

Carter, Anthony T. 1975. *Elite Politics in Rural India: Political Stratification and Political Alliances in Western Maharashtra*. Cambridge: Cambridge University Press.

Cashman, Richard. 1970. "The Political Recruitment of the God Ganpati." *The Indian Economic and Social History Review* 7 (3): 347–73.

———. 1975. *The Myth of the Lokamanya: Tilak and Mass Politics in Maharashtra*. Berkeley: University of California Press.

Chandavarkar, Rajnarayan. 1994. *The Origins of Industrial Capitalism in India: Business Strategies and the Working Classes in Bombay, 1900–1940*. Cambridge: Cambridge University Press.

———. 1998. *Imperial Power and Popular Politics: Class, Resistance, and the State in India, 1850–1950*. Cambridge: Cambridge University Press.

Chatterjee, Partha. 1993. *The Nation and Its Fragments*. Princeton, N.J.: Princeton University Press.

———. 1995. "Religious Minorities and the Secular State: Notes on an Indian Impasse." *Public Culture* 8 (Fall): 11–39.

———. 1998. "Beyond the Nation? Or Within?" *Social Text* 16 (3): 57–69.

———. 2000. "Democracy and the Violence of the State: A Political Negotiation of Death." Paper presented at the Cultural Studies Workshop in Bharatpur, February 2000.

Chousalkar, Ashok. 1989. "The Politics of Hindu Communal Organisations in Maharashtra." In *Religion, State, and Politics in India*, edited by Moin Shakir, 73–89. Delhi: Ajanta.

Cohn, Bernard. 1983. "Representing Authority in Victorian India." In *The Invention of Tradition*, edited by Eric Hobsbawm and Terence Ranger, 165–209. Cambridge: Cambridge University Press.

Conlon, Frank. 1996. "Dining Out in Bombay." In *Consuming Modernity*, edited by Carol Breckenridge, 90–127. Delhi: Oxford University Press.

Courtright, Paul B. 1988. "The Ganesh Festival in Maharashtra: Some Observations." In *The Experience of Hinduism: Essays on Religion in Maharashtra*, edited by Ellinor Zelliot and Maxine Berntsen, 76–93. Albany: State University of New York Press.

Crapanzano, Vincent. 1980. *Tuhami: Portrait of a Morrocan*. Chicago: The University of Chicago Press.

Dandekar, Hemlata. 1986. *Men to Bombay, Women at Home*. Ann Arbor: Michigan Papers on South and South East Asia, University of Michigan.

Das, Veena. 1995. *Critical Events*. Delhi: Oxford University Press.

Deluz, Ariane, and Suzette Heald, eds. 1994. *Anthropology and Psychoanalysis: An Encounter through Culture*. London: Routledge.

Deshpande, P. Y. 1960. "Emotional Integration and Power Politics." In *Problems in Maharashtra*, edited by G. Gadgil, 123–34. Bombay: Inland Printers.

Deshpande, S., and L. Deshpande. 1992. "New Economic Policy and Female Employment." *Economic and Political Weekly* 27, no. 41 (October 10): 2248–52.

Deshpande, S. H., ed. 1973. *Economy of Maharashtra*. Bombay: Samaj Prabodhan Sanstha.

Dhareshwar, V., and R. Srivatsan. 1996. "'Rowdy Sheeters': An Essay on Subalternity and Politics." In Subaltern Studies series 9, edited by Shahid Amin and Dipesh Chakrabarty, 201–31. Delhi: Oxford University Press.

Dirks, Nicholas. 1987. *The Hollow Crown: Ethnohistory of an Indian Kingdom*. Cambridge: Cambridge University Press.

Dumont, Louis. 1980. *Homo Hierarchicus*. Chicago: University of Chicago Press.

Eckert, Julia M. 2000. "Participation and the Politics of Violence: Towards the Sociology of an Anti-Democratic Movement." Berlin: Dissertation zur Verlage am Fachbereich Politik und Sozialwissenschaften and der Freien Universität Berlin.

Engineer, Ashgar Ali. 1980. *The Bohras*. Ghaziabad: Vikas.

———. 1984. *Bhiwandi-Bombay Riots: Analysis and Documentation*. Bombay: Institute of Islamic Studies.

———, ed. 1987. *The Shah Bano Controversy*. Bombay: Sangam.

———, ed. 1991a. *Mandal Commission Controversy*. New Delhi. Ajanta.

———, ed. 1991b. *Communal Riots in Post-Independence India*. New Delhi: Sangam.

———. 1996. *The OBC Muslims and Their Problems*. Mumbai: Centre for Study of Society and Secularism.

Epstein, S.J.M. 1988. *The Earthy Soil: Bombay Peasants and the Indian Nationalist Movement, 1919–1947*. Delhi: Oxford University Press.

Ewing, Katherine P. 1997. *Arguing Sainthood. Modernity, Psychoanalysis, and Islam*. Durham, N.C.: Duke University Press.

Faruqi, Ziya-ul-Hasan. 1981. "Orthodoxy and Heterodoxy in India." In *Communal and Pan-Islamic Trends in Colonial India*, edited by Musirul Hasan, 382–99. Delhi: Manohar.

Foucault, Michel. 1984. "Right of Death and Power over Life." In *The Foucault Reader*, edited by Paul Rabinow, 258–72. New York: Pantheon.

———. 1991a. "Politics and the Study of Discourse." In *The Foucault Effect: Studies in Governmentality*, edited by Graham Burchell, Colin Gordon, and Peter Miller, 53–72. London: Harvester Wheatsheaf.

———. 1991b. "Governmentality." In *The Foucault Effect: Studies in Governmentality*, edited by Graham Burchell, Colin Gordon, and Peter Miller, 87–104. London: Harvester Wheatsheaf.

Gadgil, D. R. 1942. *The Industrial Evolution and India in Recent Times*. Bombay: Oxford University Press.

Gadgil, Gangadhar, ed. 1960. *Problems of Maharashtra: Report from a Seminar in May 1960 Regarding the Prospects and Problems of the New Maharashtrian State*. Bombay: Inland Printers.

Gangar, Amrit. 1995. "Films from the City of Dreams." In *Bombay: Mosaic of Modern Culture*, edited by Sujata Patel and Alice Thorner, 210–24. Bombay: Oxford University Press.

Gardner, Katy. 1995. *Global Migrants, Local Lives.* Oxford: Oxford University Press.

Gavaskar, Mahesh. 1995. "Colonialism within Colonialism: Phule's Critique of Brahmin Power." Paper presented at the conference "Cultures of Modernity," Mysore, November 18–23.

Ghosh, S. K. 1985. *Communal Riots in India.* New Delhi: Hashish.

Girard, René. 1977. *Violence and the Sacred,* translated by P. Gregory. Baltimore: The Johns Hopkins University Press.

Gokhale, Jayashree. 1993. *From Concessions to Confrontation: The Politics of an Indian Untouchable Community.* Bombay: Popular Prakashan.

Gordon, Stewart. 1993. *The Marathas, 1600–1818.* New Cambridge History of India series 2. Cambridge: Cambridge University Press.

———. 1994. *Marathas, Marauders, and State Formation in Eighteenth Century India.* Delhi: Oxford University Press.

Grosrichard, A. 1998. *In the Sultan's Court.* London: Verso.

Guneratne, Anthony R. 1997. "Religious Conflict, Popular Culture, and the Troubled Spectators of Recent Indian Film." *Contemporary South Asia* 6 (2): 177–89.

Gupta, Akhil. 1995. "Blurred Boundaries: The Discourse of Corruption, the Culture of Politics and the Imagined State." *American Ethnologist* 22 (2): 375–402.

———. 1998. *Postcolonial Development.* Durham, N.C.: Duke University Press.

Gupta, Dipankar. 1982. *Nativism in a Metropolis.* Delhi: Manohar.

Guru, Gopal. 1995. "Assembly Elections in Maharashtra: Realignment of Forces." *Economic and Political Weekly* 30 (April 8): 733–36.

Habib, Irfan. 1999 [1963]. *The Agrarian System of Mughal India.* 2nd ed. Delhi: Oxford University Press.

Hansen, Thomas B. 1996a. "Recuperating Masculinity: Hindu Nationalism, Violence, and the Exorcism of the Muslim 'Other.'" *Critique of Anthropology* 16 (2): 137–72.

———. 1996b. "The Vernacularisation of Hindutva: BJP and Shiv Sena in Rural Maharashtra." *Contributions to Indian Sociology* 30 (2): 177–214.

———. 1998. "BJP and the Politics of Hindutva in Maharashtra." In *The BJP and Compulsions of Politics in India,* edited by Thomas Blom Hansen and Christophe Jaffrelot, 121–63. Delhi: Oxford University Press.

———. 1999. *The Saffron Wave: Hindu Nationalism and Democracy in Modern India.* Princeton, N.J.: Princeton University Press.

———. 2000a. "Predicaments of Secularism: Muslim Identities in Mumbai." *Journal of the Royal Anthropological Society* 6 (2): 255–72.

———. 2000b. "Bridging the Gulf: Migration, Modernity, and Identity among Muslims in Mumbai." In *Empire, Migration, and Community,* edited by Crispin Bates, 261–85. London: Macmillan.

Hansen, Thomas B., and Finn Stepputat, eds. 2001. *States of Imagination: Ethnographic Explorations of the Postcolonial State.* Durham, N.C.: Duke University Press.

Harris, Nigel. 1978. *Economic Development of Cities and Planning: The Case of Bombay.* London: Oxford University Press.

———. 1995. "Bombay in the Global Economy." In *Bombay: Metaphor for Modern India,* edited by S. Patel and A. Thorner, 47–63. Bombay: Oxford University Press.

Hasan, Musirul. 1985. "'Congress Muslims' and Indian Nationalism: Dilemma and Decline, 1928–34." *South Asia* 15 (1–2): 102–120.

———. 1990. "Adjustment and Accommodation: Indian Muslims after Partition." *Social Scientist* 18, nos. 8–9 (August–September): 48–66.

———. 1996. *Legacy of a Divided Nation.* London: Hurst.

Heuzé, Gerard. 1992. "Shiv Sena: From Unemployment Exchange to National Populism." *Economic and Political Weekly* 27 (October 3): 2189–95; (October 10): 2253–63.

———. 1995. "Cultural Populism: The Appeal of the Shiv Sena." In *Bombay: Metaphor of Modern India,* edited by S. Patel and A. Thorner, 213–47. Bombay: Oxford University Press.

Inden, Ronald. 1990. *Imagining India.* London: Blackwell.

Jaffrelot, Christophe. 1996. *The Hindu Nationalist Movement in Indian Politics.* New York: Columbia University Press.

———. 1998. "The Politics of Processions and Hindu-Muslim Riots." In *Community Conflicts and the State in India,* edited by Atul Kohli and Amrita Basu, 58–92. Delhi: Oxford University Press.

Jamaluddin, Syed. 1981. "Bareilvis and the Khilafat Movement." In *Communal and Pan-Islamic Trends in Colonial India,* edited by Musirul Hasan, 400–413. Delhi: Manohar.

Johnson, Gordon. 1973. *Provincial Politics and Indian Nationalism: Bombay and the Indian National Congress 1880–1915.* Cambridge: Cambridge University Press.

Joshi, Ram. 1970. "The Shiv Sena: A Movement in Search of Legitimacy." *Asian Survey* 10 (11): 967–79.

———. 1995. "Politics in Maharashtra: An Overview." In *Politics in Maharashtra,* edited by Usha Thakkar and Mangesh Kulkarni, 1–16. Bombay: Himalaya.

Kadam, Vasant. 1993. *Maratha Confederacy: A Study in Its Origin and Development.* New Delhi: Munshiram Manoharlal.

Kakar, Sudhir. 1989. *Intimate Relations.* Delhi: Oxford University Press.

———. 1995. *The Colours of Violence.* Delhi: Viking.

Kantorowicz, Ernest. 1957. *The King's Two Bodies.* Princeton, N.J.: Princeton University Press.

Kaviraj, Sudipta. 1997a. "The Modern State in India." In *Dynamics of State Formation—India and Europe Compared,* edited by Martin Doornbos and Sudipta Kaviraj, 225–50. New Delhi: Sage.

———. 1997b. "Filth and the Public Sphere: Concepts and Practices about Space in Calcutta." *Public Culture* 24 (1): 83–114.

———. 1998. "The Culture of Representative Democracy." In *Wages of Freedom: Fifty Years of the Indian Nation-State,* edited by Partha Chatterjee, 147–75. Delhi: Oxford University Press.

Kaviraj, Sudipta. Katzenstein, Mary F. 1981. *Equality and Ethnicity—Shiv Sena Party and Preferential Policies in Bombay.* Ithaca: Cornell University Press.

Katzenstein, Mary F., Uday S. Mehta, and Usha Thakkar. 1997. "The Rebirth of Shiv Sena: The Symbiosis of Discursive and Institutional Power." *Journal of Asian Studies* 56 (2): 371–90.

Kaur, Raminder. 1998. "Performative Politics: Artworks, Festival Praxis, and Nationalism with Special Reference to the Ganpati Utsava in Western India." Ph.D. dissertation. London University, Department of Anthropology, School of Oriental and African Studies.

Khilnani, Sunil. 1997. *The Idea of India.* Harmondsworth: Penguin.

Kojéve, Alexander. 1969. *Introduction to the Reading of Hegel.* New York: Basic Books.

Kosambi, Meera. 1995. "British Bombay and Marathi Mumbai: Some Nineteenth Century Perceptions." In *Bombay: Mosaic of Modern Culture*, edited by Sujata Patel and Alice Thorner, 3–34. Bombay: Oxford University Press.

Koselleck, Reinhard. 1985. *Futures Past: On the Semantics of Historical Time.* Cambridge, Mass.: MIT Press.

Kripke, Saul. 1980. *Naming and Necessity.* Cambridge, Mass.: Harvard University Press.

Krishnaswamy, J. 1966. "A Riot in Bombay, August 11, 1893: A Study of Hindu-Muslim Relations in Western India in the Nineteenth Century." Ph.D. dissertation. University of Chicago, Department of History.

Kulkarni, Mangesh. 1997. "The Illustrated Weekly Case." *The Secularist* 29 (168): 125–34.

Kumar, Nita. 1992. *The Artisans of Banaras: Popular Culture and Identity, 1988–1986.* Princeton, N.J.: Princeton University Press.

Kumar, Ravinder. 1968. *Western India in the Nineteenth Century.* London: Routledge and Kegan Paul.

Lacan, Jacques. 1977 [1966]. *Ecrits: A Selection.* New York: Norton.

———. 1978 [1964]. *The Four Fundamental Concepts of Psychoanalysis.* New York: Norton.

———. 1992 [1986]. *The Ethics of Psychoanalysis.* New York: Norton.

Laclau, Ernesto. 1990. *Reflections on the Revolutions of our Time.* London: Verso.

Lefort, Claude. 1988. *Democracy and Political Theory.* Cambridge: Polity.

Lele, Jayant. 1990. "Caste, Class, and Dominance: Political Mobilization in Maharashtra." In *Dominance and State Power in Modern India*, edited by Francine Frankel and M.S.A. Rao, 115–211. Vol. 2. Delhi: Oxford University Press.

———. 1995. "Saffronization of Shiv Sena: The Political Economy of City, State, and Nation." In *Bombay. Metaphor of Modern India*, edited by Sujata Patel and Alice Thorner, 165–212. Bombay: Oxford University Press.

Locke, John. 1988 [1689]. *Two Treatises of Government.* Cambridge: Cambridge University Press.

Lomova-Oppokova, Marina. 1999. "Marathas: The Role of Kinship Relations in the Social and Political Life of Maharashtra." In *Home, Family and Kinship in Maharashtra*, edited by Irina Glushkova and Rajendra Vora, 185–98. Delhi: Oxford University Press.

Luhrmann, Tanya. M. 1996. *The Good Parsi: The Fate of a Colonial Elite in a Postcolonial Society.* Delhi: Oxford University Press.

Mallison, Françoise. 1995. "Bombay as the Intellectual Capital of the Gujaratis." In *Bombay: Mosaic of Modern Culture,* edited by Sujata Patel and Alice Thorner, 76–87. Bombay: Oxford University Press.

Markovits, Claude. 1995. "Bombay as a Business Centre in the Colonial Period: A Comparison with Calcutta." In *Bombay. Metaphor for Modern India,* edited by S. Patel and A. Thorner, 26–46. Bombay: Oxford University Press.

Masselos, Jim. 1973. *Towards Nationalism.* Bombay: Popular Prakashan.

———. 1976. "Power in the Bombay Mohalla, 1904–15: An Initial Exploration of the World of the Indian Urban Muslim." *South Asia* 4:75–95.

———. 1982. "Change and Custom in the Format of the Bombay Moharram Festival during the Nineteenth and Twentieth Centuries." *South Asia* 12:47–67.

———. 1994. "The Bombay Riots of January 1993: The Politics of Urban Conflagration." *South Asia* 24 (special issue): 79–95.

Mayur, Rashmi, and P. R. Vohra, eds. 1986. *Bombay 2000 A.D.* Bombay: Lions Club.

Mitchell, Timothy. 1999. "Economy and the State Effect." In *State/Culture,* edited by G. Steinmetz, 76–97. Ithaca: Cornell University Press.

Moore, Henrietta L. 1994. "Gendered Persons: Dialogues between Anthropology and Psychoanalysis." In *Anthropology and Psychoanalysis: An Encounter through Culture,* edited by Ariane Deluz and Suzette Heald, 131–48. London: Routledge.

———. 1998. "Anthropology and Initiation." *New Formations* 35 (autumn): 19–27.

Mukadam, Abdul Kadam. 1995. "Communalism in Maharashtra." In *Politics in Maharashtra,* edited by Usha Thakkar and Mangesh Kulkarni, 110–26. Bombay: Himalaya.

Nandy, Ashish. 1980. *At the Edge of Psychology.* Delhi: Oxford University Press.

———. 1983. *The Intimate Enemy.* Delhi: Oxford University Press.

Narain, Iqbal, ed. 1974. *Panchayati Raj Administration in Maharashtra.* Bombay: Popular Prakashan.

Naregal, Veena. 1998. "English in the Colonial University and the Politics of Language: The Emergence of a Public Sphere in Western India, 1830–1880." Ph.D. dissertation. London University, Department of Political Studies. School of Oriental and African Studies.

———. 1999. "Integrating Corporate Interests, Local and Media Networks: Cable Operations in Bombay." Unpublished manuscript.

O'Hanlon, Rosalind. 1985. *Caste, Conflict, and Ideology: Mahatma Jotirao Phule and Low Caste Protest in Nineteenth-century Western India.* Cambridge: Cambridge University Press.

———. 1991. "Issues of Widowhood: Gender and Resistance in Colonial Western India." In *Contesting Power: Resistance and Everyday Social Relations in South Asia,* edited by Douglas Haynes and Gyan Prakash, 62–108. Berkeley: University of California Press.

Omvedt, Gail. 1976. *Cultural Revolt in a Colonial Society: The Non-Brahman Movement in Western India, 1873 to 1930.* Bombay: Scientific Socialist Education Trust.

Ortner, Sherry. 1995. "Resistance and the Problem of Ethnographic Refusal." *Comparative Studies in Society and History* 37 (1): 173–93.

Padgaonkar, Dilip. 1993. "This Is Not Bombay." In *When Bombay Burned*, edited by Dilip Padgaonkar, 1–11. Delhi: UBPSD Press.

Patel, Sujata, and Alice Thorner, eds. 1995. *Bombay: Metaphor for Modern India.* Bombay: Oxford University Press.

Pathak, Zakia, and Rajeshwari Sunder Rajan. 1989. "Shahbano." *Signs* 14 (3): 558–82.

Patterson, Maureen. 1988. "The Shifting Fortunes of the Chitpavan Brahmins: Focus on 1948." In *City, Countryside, and Society in Maharashtra*, edited by D. W. Attwood., Milton Israel, and N. K. Wagle, 35–58. Toronto: University of Toronto, Centre of South Asian Studies.

Phadke, Y. D. 1979. *Politics and Language.* Bombay: Himalaya.

Pradelles de Latour, Charles-Henry. 1994. "Lacanian Ethnopsychoanalysis." In *Anthropology and Psychoanalysis: An Encounter through Culture*, edited by Ariane Deluz and Suzette Heald, 153–62. London: Routledge.

Prasad, Madhava. 1998. *Ideology of the Hindi Film.* New York: Oxford University Press.

Price, Pamela. 1996. *Kingship and Political Practice in Colonial India.* Cambridge: Cambridge University Press.

Purandare, Vaibhav. 1999. *The Sena Story.* Mumbai: Business Publications.

Rajadhyaksha, A., and P. Willemen, eds. 1995. *Encyclopaedia of Indian Cinema.* Delhi: Oxford University Press.

Ranade, M. G. 1961. *The Rise of Maratha Power.* Bombay: Bombay University Press.

Ravindranath, P. K. 1992. *Sharad Pawar: The Making of a Modern Maratha.* New Delhi: UBSPD Publishers' Distributors.

Rosenthal, Donald B. 1977. *The Expansive Elite: District Politics and State Policy-Making in India.* Berkeley: University of California Press.

Rushdie, Salman. 1995. *The Moor's Last Sigh.* London: Jonathan Cape.

Saith, Ashwani. 1992. "Absorbing External Shocks: The Gulf Crisis, International Migration Linkages, and the Indian Economy, 1990 (with special reference to the impact on Kerala)." *Development and Change* 23 (January 1, 1992): 101–46.

Sanyal, Usha. 1995. "Pîr, Shaikh, and Prophet: The Personalisation of Religious Authority in Ahmad Riza Khan's Life." In *Muslim Communities in South Asia*, edited by T. N. Madan. Delhi: Manohar.

Sardesai, G. S. 1946. *New History of the Marathas.* Bombay. Bombay Press.

Sardesai, Rajdeep. 1993. "The Great Betrayal." In *When Bombay Burned*, edited by D. Padgaonkar, 179–210. New Delhi: UBSPD.

———. 1995. "The Shiv Sena's New Avatar: Marathi Chauvinism and Hindu Communalism." In *Politics in Maharashtra*, edited by Usha Thakkar and Mangesh Kulkarni, 127–46. Bombay: Himalaya.

Sarkar, Tanika, and Urvashi Butalia, eds. 1995. *Women and Right-Wing Movements: Indian Experiences.* London: Zed.

Searle-Chatterjee, Mary. 1994. "'Wahabi' Sectarianism among Muslims of Banares." *Contemporary South Asia* 3 (2): 83–93.

Setalwad, Teesta. 1995. "The Woman Shiv Sainik and Her Sister Swayamsevika." In *Women and Right-Wing Movements: Indian Experiences*, edited by Tanika Sarkar and Urvashi Butalia. 233–44. London: Zed.

Sharma, Kalpana. 1995. "Chronicle of a Riot Foretold." In *Bombay: Metaphor for Modern India*, edited by Sujata Patel and Alice Thorner, 268–86. Bombay: Oxford University Press.

Sirsikar, V. M. 1995. *Politics in Maharashtra: An Overview*. Hyderabad: Orient Longman.

Sunthankar, B. R. 1993. *Maharashtra, 1858–1920*. Bombay: Popular Book Depot.

Talib, Mohammad. 1997. "The Tablighis in the Making of Muslim Identity." *Comparative Studies of South Asia, Africa, and the Middle East* 17 (1): 32–51.

Tarlo, Emma. 2001. *Unsettling Memories: Narratives of the "Emergency" in Delhi*. London: Hurst.

Taussig, Michael. 1997. *The Magic of the State*. New York: Routledge.

Tope, T. K. 1960. "Social Problems in Maharashtra." In *Problems of Maharashtra*, edited by G. Gadgil, 116–24. Bombay: Inland Printers.

Tucker, Richard. 1970. "From Dharmashastra to Politics." *The Indian Economic and Social History Review* 7 (3): 325–45.

———. 1972. *Ranade and the Roots of Indian Nationalism*. Bombay: Popular Prakashan.

———. 1976. "Hindu Traditionalism and Nationalist Ideologies in Nineteenth-Century Maharashtra." *Modern Asian Studies* 10 (3): 321–48.

Wagle, Narendra K. 1989. "Hindu-Muslim Interaction in Medieval Maharashtra." In *Hinduism Reconsidered*, edited by Günther D. Sontheimer and Hermann Kulke, 51–66. Delhi: Manohar.

———, ed. 1980. *Images of Maharashtra*. London: Curzon.

Valunjkar, T. N. 1966. *Social Organisation, Migration, and Change in a Village Community*. Pune: Deccan College, Dissertation series.

Van Wersch, H. 1992. *The Bombay Textile Strike, 1982–83*. Delhi: Oxford University Press.

Visvanathan, Shiv. 1998a. "The Early Years." In *Foul Play: Chronicles of Corruption 1947–1997*, edited by Shiv Visvanathan and Harsh Sethi, 12–44. New Delhi: Banyan.

———. 1998b. "Notes on the Bombay Blasts." In *Foul Play: Chronicles of Corruption 1947–1997*, edited by Shiv Visvanathan and Harsh Sethi, 118–28. New Delhi. Banyan.

Visvanathan, Shiv, and Harsh Sethi, eds. 1998. *Foul Play: Chronicles of Corruption, 1947–1997*. New Delhi: Banyan.

Vohra, Prem. 1986. "Bombay's Future." In *Bombay 2000 A.D.*, edited by Rashmi Mayur and Prem Vohra, 240–46. Bombay: Lion's Club.

Vora, Rajendra. 1996. "Shift of Power from Rural to Urban Sector." *Economic and Political Weekly* 31 (January 13): 171–73.

———. 1999. "Dominant Lineages and Political Power in Maharashtra." In *Home, Family, and Kinship in Maharashtra*, edited by Irina Glushkova and Rajendra Vora, 199–219. Delhi: Oxford University Press.

Wolpert, Stanley. 1962. *Tilak and Gokhale*. Berkeley: University of California Press.

Zelliot, Eleanor. 1970. "Learning the Use of Political Means: The Mahars of Maharashtra." In *Caste in Indian Politics*, edited by Rajni Kothari, 29–69. New Delhi: Orient Longman.

———. 1992. *From Untouchable to Dalit: Essays on the Ambedkar Movement.* Delhi: Manohar.

Zelliot, Eleanor, and Maxine Berntsen, eds. 1989. *The Experience of Hinduism: Essays on Religion in Maharashtra.* Albany: State University of New York Press.

Zizek, Slavoj. 1989. *The Sublime Object of Ideology.* London: Verso.

———. 1992a. "Eastern Europe's Republics of Gilead." In *Dimensions of Radical Democracy* edited by Chantal Mouffe, 193–211. London: Verso.

———. 1992b. *For They Know Not What They Do.* London: Verso.

———. 1993. *Tarrying with the Negative.* Durham, N.C.: Duke University Press.

Texts in Marathi

Bedekar, Sudhir, Slabha Brahma, R. P. Nene, and Datta Desai. 1991. *Hindu— Muslim Tanar* (Hindu—Muslim tensions). Pune: Shankar Brahma Samaj Vigynan Granthala.

Dandekar, V. M. 1986. *Maharashtrateel Audyogik Vikendrikaran* (Industrial decentralisation in Maharashtra). Pune: Pune University.

Pandhere, Shantaram. 1993. *Bhagwa Tukobacha, Bamani Kava Sanghaca* (Saffron of Tukoba: Brahminical plot of Sangha). Pune: Sugara Prakashan.

Thackeray, Bal. 1991. *Hindutva Saar aani Dhaar* (Hindutva: The essence and the edge), compiled by Shashi Nalekar. Thane: Dimple.

Pamphlets and Other Documents

The Autumn of the Patriarch: Bal Thackeray's Remote Control Tyranny in Maharashtra. 1996. Mumbai: Committee for the Protection of Democratic Rights.

The People's Verdict: An Inquiry into the December 1992 and January 1993 Riots in Bombay. 1993. Bombay: The Indian People's Human Rights Commission.

Prabhakar Vaidiya. 1970). *Krishna Desai and His Murderers.* Bombay: Eknath Bhagwat.

Shiv Sena at a Glance: Shivsena Rajyapramukh Parishad. 1995. Mumbai, November 18–19.

Shiv Sena Speaks. Bombay, 1967.

Srikrishna, B. N. 1998. *Report of the Srikrishna Commission.* Vols. 1–2. Mumbai, Punwani, and Vrijendra.

Official Documents and Government Publications

Additional Sessions Court at Aurangabad, case nos. 107/1989 and 97/1989.

Additional Sessions Court at Aurangabad, case no. 39/1990.

Census of India, 1931. Vols. 7, 12, 8, 13, 22; Bombay Tables). Bombay: Government Central Press.

Census of India, 1981. Series 12: Maharashtra. Part 13: District Census Handbook (Greater Bombay). Maharashtra, Bombay: Directorate of Census Operations, 1986.

Census of India, 1991. Primary Census Abstract (Final). Maharashtra, Bombay: Census Directorate, 1993.

Development Plan, Thane. Report 1986–2001. 1986. Thane Municipal Corporation, Department of Town Planning, Thane.

Districtwise Selected Indicators, Maharashtra State. 1985. Directorate of Economics and Statistics. Government of Maharashtra, Bombay.

Enthoven, R. E. 1922. *The Tribes and Castes of Bombay Presidency.* Vols. 1–4. Bombay: Government Central Press.

Gazetteer of the Bombay Presidency: Thana District. 1989 [1882]. Vol. 13, part 2. Gazetteers Department, Government of Maharashtra, Bombay.

Gazetteer of Bombay Presidency: Poona District. 1989 [1885]. Vol. 18, part 1. Gazetteers Department, Government of Maharashtra, Bombay.

Gazetteer of India: Aurangabad District. 1977. Gazetteers Department, Government of Maharashtra, Bombay.

Maharashtra High Court: Aurangabad Bench. Election Petition no. 8, 1991.

Poll Statistics: Elections for the Vidhan Sabha, 1978. 1980. Government of Maharashtra, General Administration Department, Bombay.

Poll Statistics: General Elections to the Maharashtra Legislative Assembly, 1980. 1980. Government of Maharashtra, General Administration Department, Bombay.

Poll Statistics: General Elections to Lok Sabha. Maharashtra. 1980. Government of Maharashtra, General Administration Department, Bombay.

Poll Statistics: General Elections to Lok Sabha, 1984. 1986. Vol. 1, parts 1–4. Government of Maharashtra, General Administration Department, Bombay.

Poll Statistics: General Elections to Lok Sabha, 1989. 1993. Government of Maharashtra. General Administration Department, Bombay.

Report of the Committee on Democratic Decentralization. 1961. Department of Cooperation and Rural Development, Government of Maharashtra. Bombay: Government Central Press.

Report of the Fact Finding Committee on Regional Imbalances. 1984. Government of Maharashtra, Planning Department, Bombay.

Report of the Commission of Inquiry into the Communal Disturbances of Bhiwandi, Jalgaon, and Malad in May 1970 (Justice Madan). n.d.

Selected Indicators for Districts in Maharashtra and States in India, 1987–1988. 1990. Directorate of Economics and Statistics, Government of Maharashtra, Bombay.

Selected Indicators for Districts in Maharashtra and States in India, 1988–1989. 1991. Directorate of Economics and Statistics, Government of Maharashtra, Bombay.

Selected Indicators for Districts in Maharashtra and States in India, 1989–1990. 1992. Directorate of Economics and Statistics, Government of Maharashtra, Bombay.

Statistical Abstract of Maharashtra State, 1984–1985, 1985–1986. 1990. Directorate of Economics and Statistics, Government of Maharashtra, Bombay.

The Slum Rehabilitation Scheme: Houses of Permanent Structure (pucca) for 40 lakhs Slumdwellers. 1996. Government of Maharashtra, Mumbai.

Index

Agripada, 135, 157, 160
Ambedkar, B., 33, 34, 84–85
Akhil Bharatiya Sena, 221. *See* Gawli, Arun
Akhil Bharatiya Vidyarthi Parishad, 96
Al-i-Hadith, 176
Ansaris, 176, 183–84
Aurangabad, 86, 91
Azmi, Abu Asim, 224–25

Bareilvy, 173–75
Belgaum, 64–65, 200
Bharatiya Janata Party (BJP), 1, 9, 67, 87,
  94, 96, 113, 128, 177, 197, 205–206;
  government, 194, 196–97, 204–211
Bharatiya Kamgar Sena, 60, 80, 163, 194
Bharatiya Vidyarthi Sena, 96, 203
Bhiwandi, 74, 76–77, 102
Bhujbal, Chhagan, 83, 95–96, 98, 121,
  206, 227–28
Bombay (Mumbai), 1–8, 37–38; battle for,
  42; blasts, 125–26; dreams, 3–6; economy of, 9, 38–39, 40–41; and film, 39–
  40, 213–15; growth of, 47–48; Municipal Corporation, 43, 79, 98, 163, 203,
  205
Brahmans, 199, 203, 204; Chitpavan, 25–
  27, 29–30; and Marathas, 28–29, 96,
  44–45

Chavan, Y. B., 43
Communist Party of India, 49, 62–63, 166
Congress party, 1, 8, 22, 41; and defec-
  tions, 98; hegemony of, 33–36, 126; in
  Maharashtra, 34–36, 67–68, 122–23,
  127. *See also* Maharashtra

Dadas, 180–81; and dadaism, 72–74, 109–
  112, 116. *See also* Shiv Sena
Dalits, 83, 84–85
Dassera, 54
Deccan, 24–28
Deoband, 173–74
Dighe, Anand, 104–109, 112–13, 120. *See
  also* Thane

Emergency, 66–67, 206, 212

Festivals, 29–30, 54, 106–7. *See also* Ganpatiutsav

Ganpatiutsav, 29–30, 33
Gawli, Arun, 22, 185, 192, 221–22

Hafta, 151–52, 225. *See also* police
Hindu Ekta Andolan, 75–76
Hindu nationalism, 9, 89–93, 94–96, 116–
  118
Hutatmas, 42, 64, 84, 121, 124

Ibrahim, Dawood, 22, 125–26, 180, 185,
  189–90, 191–93, 221, 224
ISI (Inter Services Intelligence), 125, 192–
  93
Islam, 76, 172, 179
Islamic Research Foundation, 176–77

Jamaat-e-Islami, 74, 79, 173, 177–79
Joshi, Manohar, 95, 197, 202–203, 214.
  See also Shiv Sena
Joshi, Sudhir, 61

Khaire, Chandrakant, 208–209

Lala, Karim, 188–89

Madanpura, 153, 163–65, 166–67, 170,
  176, 184
Madon Commission 75. *See also* Bhiwandi
Mahars, 34, 83
Mahila Agadhi, 57, 80–81, 214
Maha-aartis, 121, 124
Maharaj, Shahu, 32–33
Maharashtra, 3, 24–28, 33–36, 41, 44–45
  81–82; and dharma, 26, 41–42; forma-
  tion of, 42–45; Legislative Assembly, 35,
  66, 95, 227
Maharashtrians, 34–36, 41–45, 101–103,
  195, 199, 200, 208, 219
Maratha , 24–28, 31–33, 34, 36, 44–45,
  51, 81; empire, 20, 25–27, 91
Maratha-kunbi, 31–33, 34–36, 38, 82, 184
Maratha Mahasangha, 75, 82
Marathi, 1, 3, 7, 23–24, 36, 41–45

Marathi manus, 7, 52
Marmik, 46, 49, 76, 86
Mastaan, Haji, 78, 188, 191; and
  underworld, 78–80
Methodology, 13–16
Mohalla committees, 154–58
Mudaliar, Vardharajan, 189
Mundhe, Gopinath, 185
Muslim community, 148–49; isolation of,
  149–50; and migration, 164–65, 167–
  71; and plebeian politics, 182–83; and
  policing, 147–56
Muslim League, 68, 74, 79, 157, 172, 182,
  184, 191
Muslim Personal Law, 173–75

Nagpada, 68, 78, 155, 157, 160, 166–70,
  176, 179, 182, 184
Naik, Ganesh, 103–104
Naming, 1–4, 36, 232
Nativism, 9, 49–53. See also Shiv Sena
Navrati, 54, 106
Nawalkar, Pramod, 121, 216
Non-Brahman movement, 26–27, 29, 30,
  32, 42
Non-Brahman Party, 32–33

Other Backward Classes (OBC), 71–75,
  97–98; and Mandal Commission 82,
  183–84

Panchayati Raj, 35, 82
Patil, S. K. 149
Patel, Yusuf, 189
Patit Pawan, 76
Pawar, Sharad, 43, 82. See also Congress
  Party
Pehlwan, 166–67, 180–81
Peshwa, 20, 24–26, 27; See also Pune
Phule, Jotirao, 26–27, 32,199. See also
  Non-Brahman movement
Police (in Bombay) 134–39, 147–49,
  185–93; colonial, 147–49, 151; and
  corruption, 150–52; 154, 225. See also
  hafta
Pune, 20, 24–26, 33, 76, 84, 95,
  25–26

Ranade, M. G., 26, 29
Rane, Narendra, 204–205

Rashtriya Swayamsevak Sangh (RSS), 53,
  58, 87, 89, 92–93, 125, 213. See also
  Hindu nationalism
Ratnam, Mani, 189, 214
Riots, 42, 64–65, 74–75, 75–76, 93,
  121–26, 147–49
Rushdie, Salman, 5, 61, 200, 214

Saamna, 49, 86, 91, 94, 203
Samajwadi Party, 172, 175, 181–85
Samyukta Maharashtra Samiti (SMS), 3,
  41–45, 49, 58. See also Marathi
Satyashodhak Samaj, 29. See also
  Non-Brahman movement
Shakeel, Chhota, 222–23
Sheikh, Shabir, 103, 194–95
Shiv Sena, 1, 9, 46–69; and elections,
  94–96; founding of, 46–48; and
  governance, 73–74, 209–211, 213–17;
  ideology of, 46, 49–53, 86–94, 195–97;
  and justice, 50, 55, 219; organization
  of, 56–61; and plebeian politics, 9,
  51–52, 61–66, 70–74; shakhas, 53–57,
  101–102, 114–115; and the state,
  64–65, 66–68, 219, 220; and violence,
  61–65, 74–78, 83–84, 102. See also
  Thackeray
Shivaji, Chhatrapati, 20–22, 25–27, 30, 90;
  and Shivaji Jayanti, 20, 30–31, 53, 75–
  76; and Shiv Sena, 21–22, 53
Shrikrishna Commission, 127, 132–46,
  191; and police, 134–40; report, 143–
  47; and Shiv Sena, 141–43
Shudra, 26–27
Singh, Mulayam, 182. See also Samajwadi
  Party
Sovereignty, 217–19, 225–26, 228–29,
  233; and Thackeray, 219–221. See also
  state
State, 128–30, 216–21; Indian, 130–32,
  145; spectacles, 154–59, 228–32
Sthanik Lokhadikar Samiti, 61. See also
  Shiv Sena
Student's Islamic Movement of India
  (SIMI), 177–79

Tablighi-e-Jamaat, 79, 175–76
TADA, 108; court, 142–43; and Muslims,
  146–47

Ship To:

victor reynoso
1163 ausin way
napa, CA 94558

Ship From:

MILLIE'S BOOKS-AMAZON
8950 PALMER AVE.
RIVER GROVE, IL 60171

Date: 01/30/2008

SKU	Qty	Condition	Title		
4137733U	1	Used	Wages of Violence 9780691088402		

textbooksNow.com

Return Information (cut and attach to the outside of return shipment)

Order #: 058-5955552-7784302

MILLIE'S BOOKS-AMAZON
8950 PALMER AVE.
RIVER GROVE, IL 60171
(Attn: Returns)

DP87180

Order #: 058-5955552-7784302

	Price	Total
	$ 13.99	$ 13.99

Sub Total	$	13.99
Shipping & Handling	$	3.99
Tax	$	0.00
Total	**$**	**17.98**

Order #: 058-5955552-7784302

Refunds: All items must be returned within 30 days of receipt. · Pack your book securely, so it will arrive back to us in its original condition. To avoid delays, please use the return section and label provided with your original packing slip to identify your return. Be sure to include a return reason. · For your protection, we suggest using a traceable, insured shipping service (UPS or Insured Parcel Post). We are not responsible for lost or damaged returns. · Item(s) returned must be received in the original condition as sold and including all additional materials such as CDs, workbooks, etc. · We will initiate a refund of your purchase price including applicable taxes within 5 business days of receipt. Shipping charges will not be refunded unless we have committed an error with your order. · If there is an error with your order or the item is not received in the condition as purchased, please contact us immediately for return assistance.

Reason for Refund/Return:
Condition   Incorrect Item Received   Incorrect Item Ordered   Dropped Class   Purchased Elsewhere   Other

Contact Us: For customer service, email us at customerservice@textbooksNow.com.

Thackeray, Bal, 46, 124; authority of, 57–60; 99–100, 197–200; resignation of, 99–100, 204; and Srikrishna Commission, 201. *See also* Shiv Sena

Thane City, 77, 101–104, 155, 227, 229; Municipal Corporation, 101–102, 110, 227

Tilak, B. G., 29–31

Ulema Council, 172–73, 182

Urdu, 1, 179

Violence, 230–32; politics of 61–66; and sovereignty, 216–22

Wahhabi, 174, 176